Managing Enterprise Projects

Using Microsoft Office Project Server 2003

Gary L. Chefetz
Dale A. Howard

Managing Enterprise Projects
Using Microsoft Office Project Server 2003

Publisher: Soho Corp.
Authors: Gary L. Chefetz, Dale A. Howard
Cover Design: Tony Valenzuela
Cover Photo: Peter Hurley

ISBN 0-9759828-0-X

Library of Congress Control Number: 2004097318

Published and distributed by Soho Corp. dba msProjectExperts, 398 Valley Road, Gillette, NJ 07933 (908) 626-1404 http://www.msprojectexperts.com

EPM Learning

EPM Learning is a complete series of role-based training manuals for professional trainers and corporate training programs. To learn more about the EPM Learning courseware series for Technical Administrators, PMO Administrators, Project Managers, Resource Managers, Executives and Team Members, or to obtain Instructor companion products and materials, contact Soho Corp. by phone (908) 626-1404 or by email info@msprojectexperts.com.

Contents

About the Authors

Gary Chefetz is the founder and President of the Soho Corp. and msProjectExperts, which exist to support businesses and organizations that choose the Microsoft enterprise project management platform. Gary has worked with Microsoft Project since 1995 and has supported Microsoft Project users since the introduction of Project Central in early 2000. Gary continues to receive the prestigious Microsoft Project Most Valuable Professional (MVP) award for his contributions. As a long-time MVP, he works closely with the Microsoft Project product team and support organizations. Gary is dedicated to supporting Microsoft Project Server implementations through his business efforts with clients and through his contributions in the newsgroups. Contact Gary Chefetz online in one of the Microsoft Project newsgroups at msnews.microsoft.com or e-mail him at:

gary_chefetz@msprojectexperts.com

Dale Howard is an enterprise project management trainer/consultant and is Vice President of Educational Services of msProjectExperts. Dale is a Certified Technical Trainer (CTT) who has more than 11 years of experience training and consulting in productivity software. He has worked with Microsoft Project since 1997 and volunteers many hours each week answering user questions in the various Microsoft Project communities. Dale received the prestigious Microsoft Project Most Valuable Professional (MVP) award in 2004 for his expertise with the software and for his contributions to the user communities. Dale is married to Mickey and lives in Denver, Colorado. Contact Dale online in one of the Microsoft Project newsgroups at msnews.microsoft.com or e-mail him at:

dale_howard@msprojectexperts.com

Introduction

Thank your for reading Managing Enterprise Projects Using Microsoft Office Project Server 2003. Herein find a complete learning guide and reference to managing projects using the Microsoft EPM platform. Our goal in writing this training/reference manual is to help you build on your knowledge of the stand-alone tool and bring you up to speed on the new enterprise features and concepts you will need to manage projects using the Microsoft EPM tool set.

We take a systematic approach to the topical ordering in this book beginning with an overview of Project Server. The next three modules teach you how to use Microsoft Project Professional to create an enterprise project, build an enterprise project team, and publish the project. We then dive into the project updating cycle where you learn how team members update progress in Project Web Access and in Outlook, and how you accept and update their progress into the project plan. The following four modules demonstrate how to set up important options in the Home page, along with how to use Risks, Issues, Documents, and Status Reports in Project Web Access. The final four modules teach you how to view information about your enterprise projects and resources across your organization's project portfolio.

Throughout each module, you get a generous amount of Notes, Warnings, and Best Practices. Notes call your attention to important additional information about a subject. Warnings help you to avoid the most common problems experienced by others and Best Practices provide tips for using the tool based on our field experience.

Because you have read this manual, we believe that you will be much more effective using Microsoft Enterprise Project Management tools. If you have questions about the book or are interested in our professional services, please contact us at our office. If you have questions about Microsoft Project or Project Server, contact us through the Microsoft public news groups.

Gary L. Chefetz, Microsoft Project MVP

Dale A. Howard, Microsoft Project MVP

msProjectExperts

Module 01

Introducing Microsoft Project Server

Learning Objectives

After completing this module, you will be able to:

- Understand Project Server's enterprise project management terminology
- Describe the project communications life cycle used in Project Server
- Be familiar with Project Server team collaboration tools
- Understand the concept of publishing with Project Server
- Acquire an overview understanding of OLAP and Project Server analytical tools
- Be familiar with the Enterprise Global file and the Enterprise Resource Pool
- Open and close the Enterprise Resource Pool
- Understand custom and enterprise custom field and outline codes
- Understand how tracking methods impact progress reporting

What Is Microsoft Project Server?

Microsoft Project Server is an enterprise-capable project management automation system. It is designed to support business and industry-specific project management and tracking requirements. Microsoft Project Server is both an out-of-the-box project assignment tracking system and a platform for business-specific configuration and customization.

Project Server is Microsoft's second-generation server-based project management solution. Its predecessor, Project Central, was introduced with Project 2000 and offered workgroup-style collaborative features. With Project Server, Microsoft introduces a more robust architecture that offers enterprise-wide deployment capabilities, lacking in Project Central, and has added a cadre of features to support its enterprise worthiness.

The combination of Microsoft Project 2003 Professional and Project Server provides a powerful enterprise portfolio management system that is rich in features but fraught with complexity and challenges. Our goal is to help you maximize the feature benefits and minimize the frustrations.

Applying Enterprise Project Management Terminology to Microsoft Project Server

In the world of enterprise project management, you hear terms like project, program, and portfolio. How do these terms apply to your organization's project management environment?

According to the Project Management institute (PMI), a *project* is "a temporary endeavor undertaken to create a unique product or service." A project is temporary, meaning that it has a beginning and an end. A project is unique, meaning that it is something that your organization has not done before.

For the purposes of this course, a *program* is "a collection of related projects" and a *portfolio* is "a collection of programs and/or projects within a business unit or across an entire enterprise". Many companies have their own interpretation of these terms, reflecting their approach to project management. Sometimes the sheer size of the organization drives these definitions.

The concept of a portfolio is fairly flexible, depending on the size of the company. A smaller organization may have a single portfolio of projects, whereas a larger business may conceive of an enterprise portfolio made up of numerous departmental or line-of-business portfolios, each containing its own set of programs and projects. However a business conceives these terms, you can model them in Project Server.

Understanding Project Server's Language

Two terms that you must understand in the context of the Project Server environment are "enterprise project" and "enterprise resource." Very specific criteria determine whether a project is an enterprise or non-enterprise project, and whether a resource is an enterprise or local resource.

Enterprise Project

A project is an *enterprise project* when one of the following two conditions is true:

- You create the project using the Microsoft Project Professional client while connected to a Project Server with Enterprise Features enabled
- You import the project to the enterprise using the Import Project to Enterprise wizard in Microsoft Project Professional

No other non-programmatic method of creating an enterprise project is possible because all enterprise projects are stored in the Project Server database.

Enterprise Resource

A resource is an *enterprise resource* when one of the following two conditions is true:

- You create the resource in the Enterprise Resource Pool using the Microsoft Project Professional client while connected to a Project Server with Enterprise Features enabled
- You import the resource into the Enterprise Resource Pool using the Import Resource to Enterprise Wizard in Microsoft Project Professional

If a resource exists in a local project, but does not exist in the Enterprise Resource Pool, then this resource is termed a local resource, meaning that it is local to the project only.

Check In and Check Out

The terms "check in" and "check out" apply to enterprise projects, enterprise resources, and to the Enterprise Global. A user must "check out" any of these before editing, so that others have read-only access to these until they are checked back in.

Using Project Server's Enterprise Resource Management Tools

A centralized enterprise resource pool is key to the advanced resource management functionality in Project Server. The resource pool contains resources and resource attribution that drives functionality like matching people to tasks using skills or based on department or location. The system models these resource attributes in custom Enterprise resource outline codes in Microsoft Project. These might describe practice groups, location, department, or other company specific information that project and resource managers use to intelligently assign resources to task assignments and management can use to drive reporting and analysis. After defining custom outline codes for your organization, the Project Server administrator assigns values for these outline codes to each resource in the Enterprise Resource Pool.

As a project manager, after you complete the task planning process in Microsoft Project Professional, you begin the resource management process by building a team for your project using resources from the Enterprise Resource Pool. Initial resource management activities include assembling the project team and making specific task assignments. Through the use of manual team-building tools such as the Build Team from Enterprise Wizard and the Assign Resources dialog, Project Server allows you to locate resources by both skill and availability, even if you are using a large resource pool. This simplifies the project staffing process not only by leveraging the custom attributes in the pool, but also by providing instant access to availability data enhanced with graphical representations.

In addition to manual staffing tools, Project Server also offers you an automated staffing tool; the Resource Substitution Wizard. This wizard rapidly analyzes the resources in the Enterprise Resource Pool to identify skills and availability for staffing a single project or a group of projects. You can save the resulting staffing results as a recommendation for input into manual team building or directly update the results into the working plan.

Understanding the Project Communications Life Cycle in Project Server

Project Server's core functionality provides a cyclical assignment and update process between project managers and team members. This cycle is the heart of the management system. Work assignments flow from the plan to resources performing the work and resources report progress data back to the plan. This project communication cycle flows through the following steps:

1. The project manager publishes the project plan in the Project Server database, as illustrated in Figure 1-1.

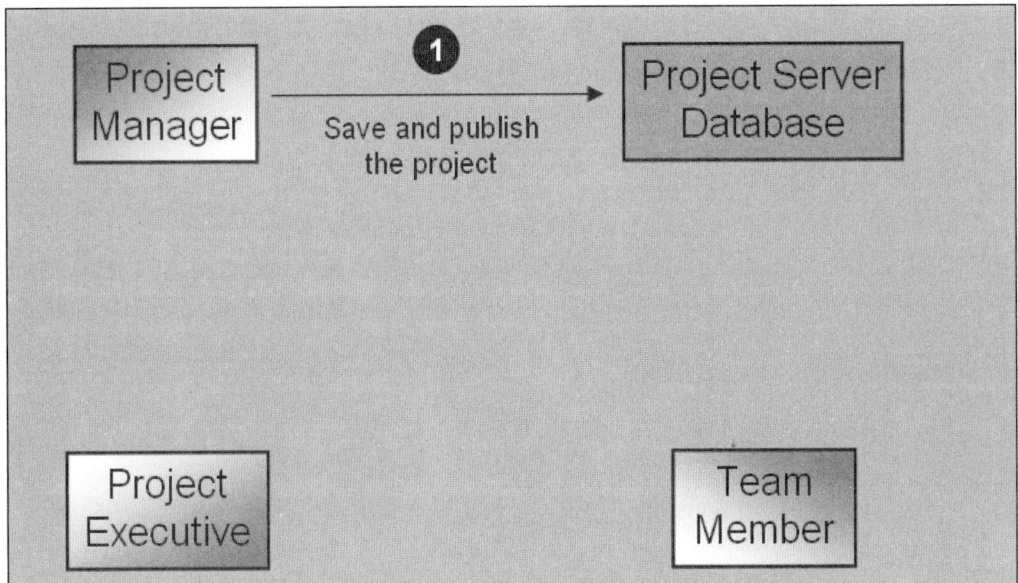

Figure 1-1: Save and publish the project in the Project Server database

2. When the project manager publishes the project in the database, Project Server acts like a messaging service and sends an e-mail message to each resource notifying them of their new task assignments in the project. Using an embedded link in the e-mail message, team members can quickly click to view their task assignments in the project through Project Web Access, as illustrated in Figure 1-2.

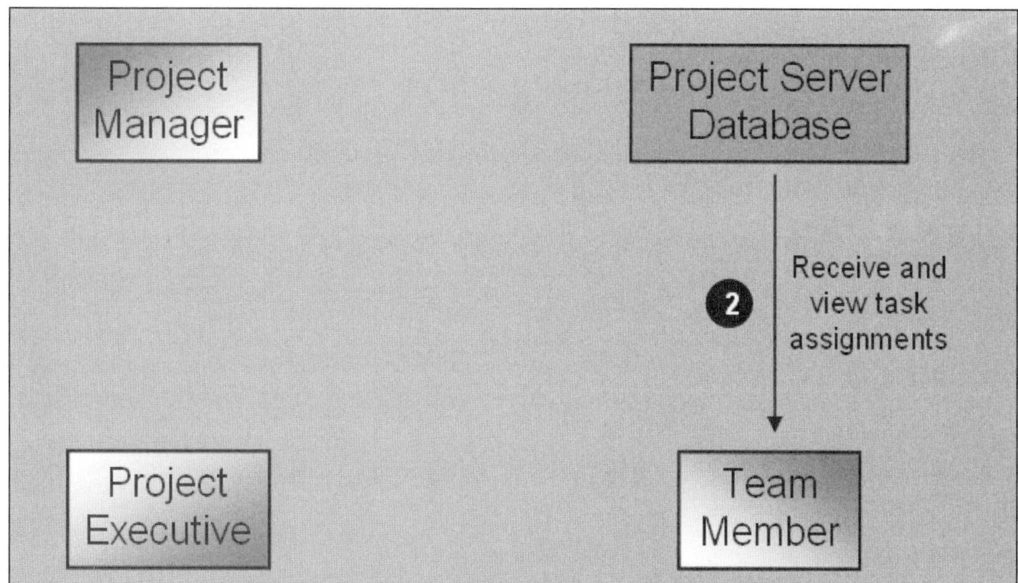

Figure 1-2: Team members receive task assignments in Project Web Access

3. At the end of each reporting period, team members update their actual progress on the project to the Project Server database, as illustrated in Figure 1-3. Actual progress includes completion percentages and/or hours worked on each task, based on the organization's reporting method.

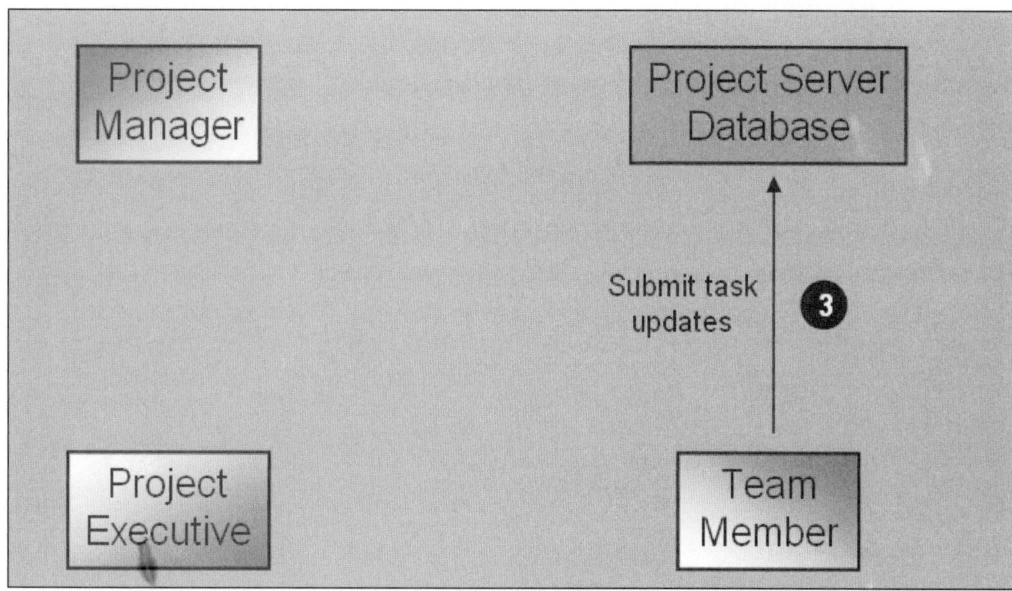

Figure 1-3: Team members submit actual progress for the project

4. The project manager receives and reviews each set of task updates from project team members, as illustrated in Figure 1-4. The project manager can individually accept or reject each task update or process them in total or in batches using automation tools.

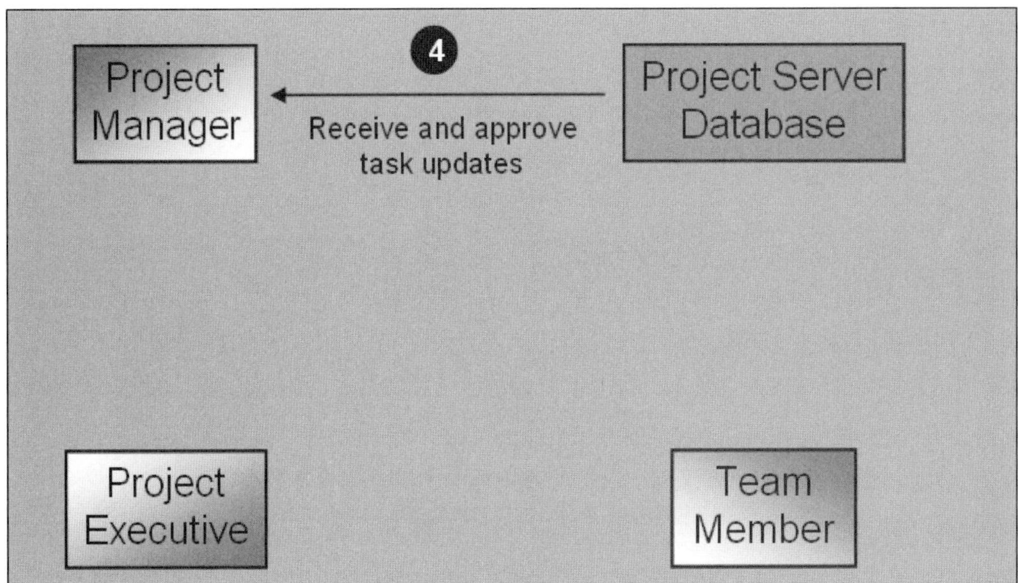

Figure 1-4: Project manager reviews updates from team members

5. After accepting or rejecting each task update, the project manager publishes the latest project schedule changes to the Project Server database, as illustrated in Figure 1-5.

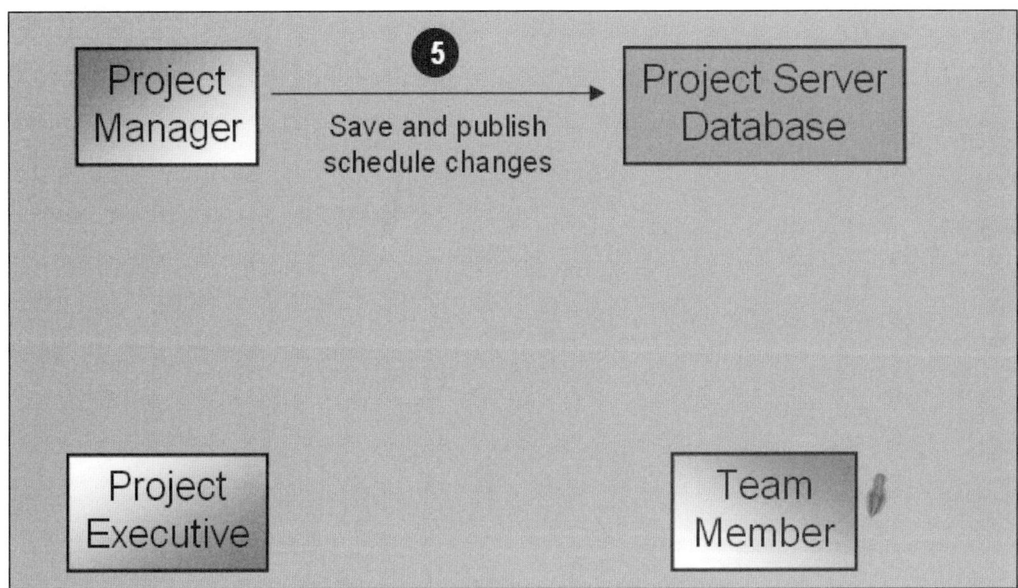

Figure 1-5: Save and publish schedule changes

At any time throughout the life of the project, executives within the organization can view all projects or individual projects in the organization's portfolio, as illustrated in Figure 1-6.

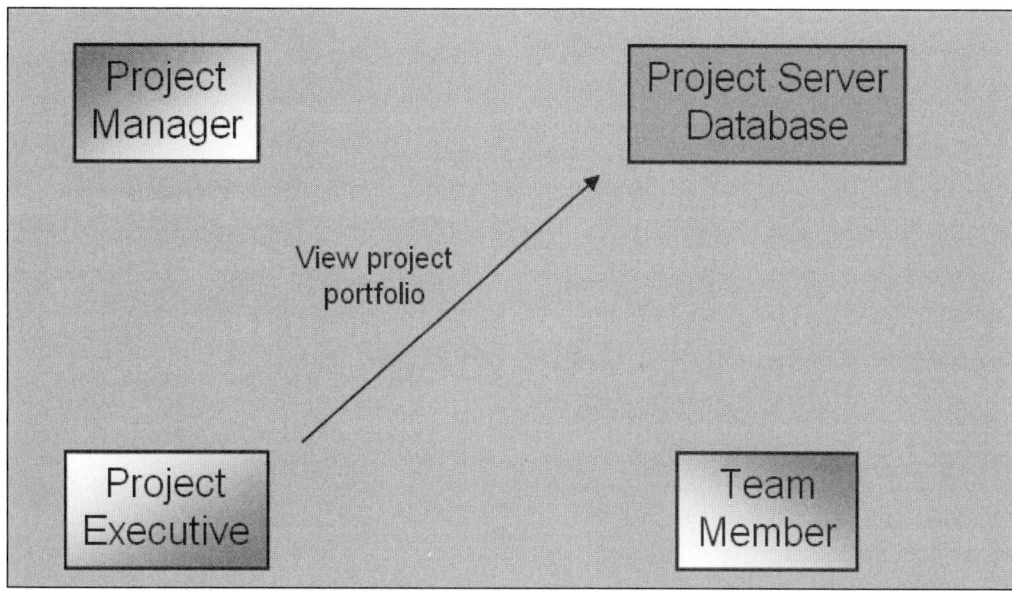

Figure 1-6: Executives view the organization's project portfolio

Additional Collaboration and Management Tools

Beyond the core communication between project managers and project team members, Project Server provides additional features for project team collaboration. Some of these features are native to Project Server, whereas others leverage integration with Windows SharePoint Services (WSS). The features that are native to Project Web access include:

- **Status Reports** – Status Reports allow project managers, resource managers, and executives to establish single or periodic status reports to which team members must respond. Team members may also create their own unrequested reports and submit them at any time.
- **Automated Alerts and Reminders** – Project Server features an automated reminder system that generates e-mail notices for a variety of situations, including reminding team members of upcoming and overdue task work, and status reports that are due. All users have the ability to set their own alerts and reminders, and managers have the added ability to set reminders for their resources.
- **To Do Lists** – Provide an alternative to formal project task tracking allowing all users to manage shared detail not represented in the project plan.

- **Outlook Integration** – Allows users to display Project Web Access components within the Outlook folder and shortcut framework. New functionality in 2003 allows users to push their project tasks to their calendar view in Outlook and report status on their tasks by opening the Outlook appointment.
- **Task Delegation** – Supports a team lead structure where functional leaders participate in the work distribution and management process.
- **Ad hoc Reporting** – Users can quickly print information from data grids in Project Web Access selecting and ordering fields and formatting the results.

Understanding the Windows SharePoint Services Role with Project Server

Each time you save a new project in the Project Server database, the system optionally provisions a new Project workspace on the server running Windows SharePoint Services (WSS). The Project workspace contains the WSS services customized specifically for Project Server, such as document libraries, issues and risks, which a user can access through the Project Web Access interface. When users access the Project workspace directly, they can avail themselves to a collection of other WSS tools that are part of the standard WSS Project workspace template.

- **Document Libraries** are a core WSS service providing document management services such as automatic version control and document check-in and check-out. Users can upload project-related documents of all types to the appropriate project Document libraries. Project specific customizations support linking documents to projects, project tasks, issues, and risks. These documents might include definition documents such as a Project Charter, change control documents, meeting minutes, checklists, etc.
- **Issues and Risk Management** featured in each Project workspace, is available through Project Web Access and through the native Project workspace interface. As the project progresses, users can add project-related issues and risks to the appropriate list and track these through resolution and closure.
- **Lists** including freeform custom list pages as well as specialized preconfigured templates for calendar events, links, picture libraries, contact lists, and announcements give Project managers and team members the tools they need to communicate with each other in a shared web space.
- **Discussions and Surveys** round out the list of standard WSS services. Collaborators can attach discussions to documents or establish discussion lists in the Project workspace.

Understanding Publishing in Project Server

There are four primary groups of tables in the Project Server database, with each group containing a specific type of data. The four groups of Tables are as follows:

- **Project data** – The native data about any project is exposed in the Project Server database in a collection of tables labeled with the prefix "msp_." The system populates the project tables each time the project manager saves a project in the Project Server database.
- **Project Web Access data** – Once a project has been "published" to Project Web Access, the system stores the published data in a collection of tables labeled with the prefix "msp_web."
- **OLAP Cube data** – Each time the system processes the OLAP Cube, it stores the data in a collection of tables labeled with the prefix "msp_cube."
- **View data** – The system stores data used for the processing of business and presentation logic in Project Web Access in a collection of tables labeled with the prefix "msp_view."

In addition to the four main groups of Tables in Project Server, a nominal fifth group contains application settings for Project Server and its connections to its member services.

Warning: Saving a project in the Project Server database is not the same as publishing the project to Project Web Access. When you save a project in the Project Server database by clicking File ➢ Save, the project data remains local to the project tables, and is only partially visible in Project Web Access. When you publish the project by clicking Collaborate ➢ Publish, the system makes the project data completely visible in Project Web Access.

Understanding Analysis Tools

Project Server leverages SQL Server 2000's Analysis Services to provide browser-based access to dimensioned data in OLAP cubes. You can add additional dimensions to the data cubes through the Project interface by adding custom outline codes that group data in a way that is tailored to and meaningful to your business needs.

What Is OLAP?

The OnLine Analytical Processing (OLAP) technology relies upon a multidimensional view of project and resource data. The relational database structure that underpins most transactional applications is two-dimensional. OLAP leverages data cubes based on relational fact sources, which contain preprocessed three-dimensional data typically time-phased and aggregated by business dimension. The advantages of employing OLAP technologies for business analytics include the performance advantages of using preprocessed data and, more important, the transparent enforcement of standardized analytical formulas.

Most portfolio analysis activities rely on custom Portfolio Analyzer views in Project Web Access. If you are familiar with PivotTables and PivotCharts in Excel, you already know how to work with Portfolio Analyzer views.

I created the Portfolio Analyzer view shown in Figure 1-7 by "dragging and dropping" five OLAP cube dimensions into the drop areas of the PivotTable in the view. The system automatically renders the PivotChart in the view based on the PivotTable data. Portfolio Analyzer views offer the full range of Excel charting capabilities in the Web browser, and you can view and manipulate both data and charting on the fly. The primary purpose of analyzer views is to analyze workforce usage, along with availability, project costs, and performance. Users can analyze project data across projects, programs, portfolios, and custom business dimensions which provide powerful insights into business trends and issues. In Figure 1-7, it is plain to see that the workload needs redistribution across the Africa team.

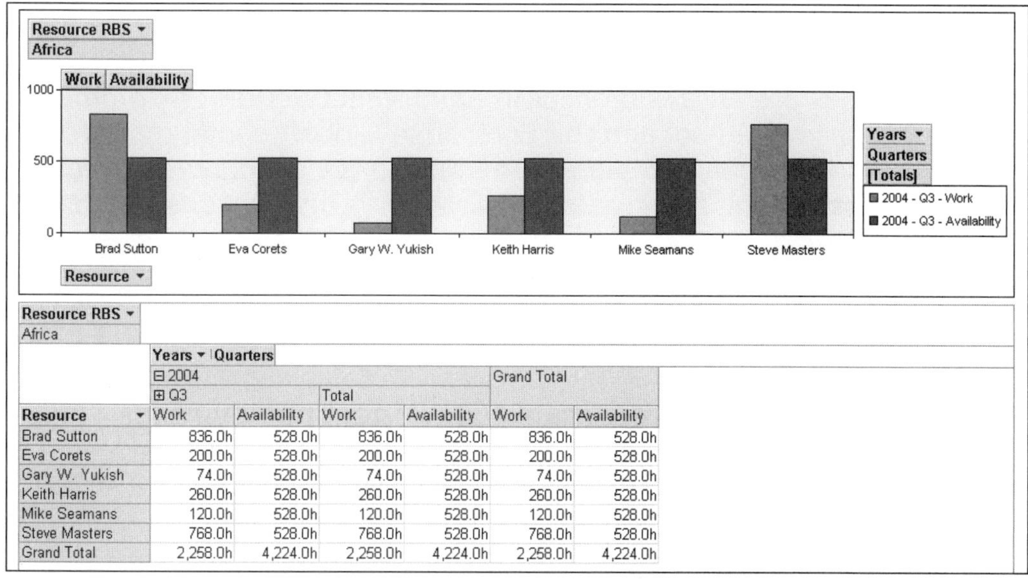

Resource RBS
Africa

Years Quarters

Resource	2004 Q3 Work	2004 Q3 Availability	2004 Total Work	2004 Total Availability	Grand Total Work	Grand Total Availability
Brad Sutton	836.0h	528.0h	836.0h	528.0h	836.0h	528.0h
Eva Corets	200.0h	528.0h	200.0h	528.0h	200.0h	528.0h
Gary W. Yukish	74.0h	528.0h	74.0h	528.0h	74.0h	528.0h
Keith Harris	260.0h	528.0h	260.0h	528.0h	260.0h	528.0h
Mike Seamans	120.0h	528.0h	120.0h	528.0h	120.0h	528.0h
Steve Masters	768.0h	528.0h	768.0h	528.0h	768.0h	528.0h
Grand Total	2,258.0h	4,224.0h	2,258.0h	4,224.0h	2,258.0h	4,224.0h

Figure 1-7: Portfolio Analyzer view displays resource work versus availability

Portfolio Modeling

In addition to the Portfolio Analyzer, Project Server also offers you the Portfolio Modeler tool for portfolio analysis that allows you to perform "what-if" analysis on staffing changes in a single project or across a portfolio of projects. Using this tool can lead you to improving utilization and eliminating resource over allocation. The Portfolio Modeler provides rudimentary what-if analysis but not specific "how-to" feedback. It is the weaker of the two analysis arenas.

Understanding Enterprise Global Concepts

Two global entities are always present in any Project Server environment: the Enterprise Resource Pool and the Enterprise Global (sometimes referred to as the Enterprise Global template). The Enterprise Resource Pool contains all information pertaining to enterprise resources. The Enterprise Global contains all of your company's custom features, such as enterprise Views, Tables, Filters, Groups, Reports, Fields, etc. The system dynamically distributes these custom features to all project managers each time they connect to Project Server through Microsoft Project Professional 2003.

Opening the Enterprise Resource Pool

In some environments, project managers may also function as resource managers. In situations like this, the Project Server administrator must grant Read/Write access to the Enterprise Resource Pool for project managers.

If you are a project manager who also functions as a resource manager, you can add and edit enterprise resources by completing the following steps:

1. Open Project Professional and log in to Project Server
2. Select Tools ➢ Enterprise Options ➢ Open Enterprise Resource Pool

Figure 1-8 shows the Open Enterprise Resources dialog.

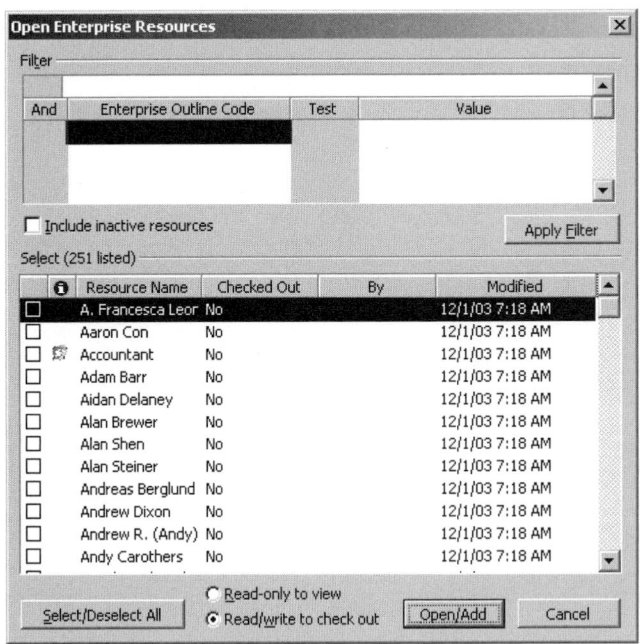

Figure 1-8: Open Enterprise Resources dialog box

3. Select the resources that you want to check out by clicking the individual check box next to the resource name or by using the Select/Deselect all button
4. Click the Open/Add button

The resources open in the Resource Sheet view. The title bar across the top of the Project Professional screen displays "Microsoft Project – Checked-out Enterprise Resources," as shown in Figure 1-9.

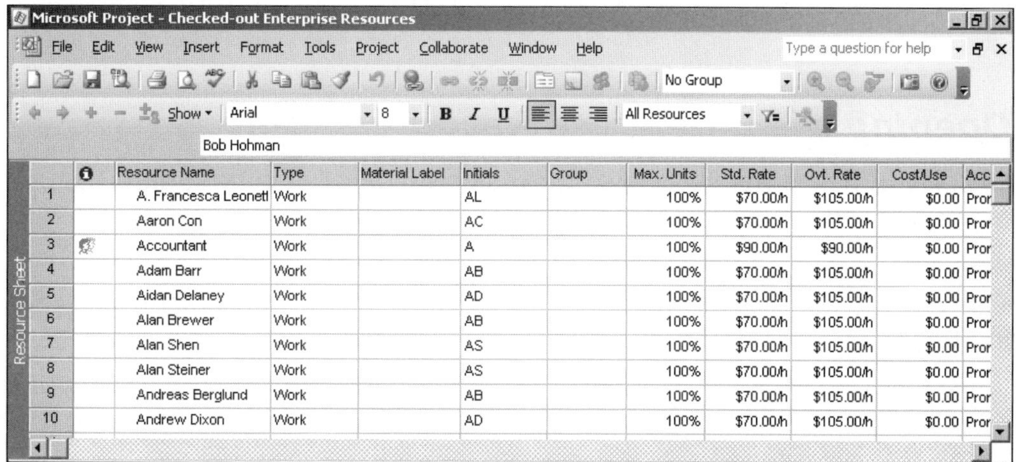

Figure 1-9: Checked out Enterprise Resources Resource Sheet view

5. You can now edit resource information for the checked out resources. You can also add resources at this time; however it's better practice to add new resources by opening the resource pool without selecting any existing resources to check-out
6. Click File ➢ Save to save your changes
7. Click File ➢ Close to close the file and check in your enterprise resources

When opening the resource pool for adding and editing, you can select specific resources to check out, leaving other resources available for others to edit.

Understanding Custom Outline Codes and Custom Fields

Your implementation team must mold the raw functionality provided in Project Server to contour and channel information for your organization's specific requirements. Although the built-in generic information streams provide useful tracking and statistical data, implementers accomplish a more meaningful presentation by seeding the database with custom attributes. These exist in Project Server as custom fields and custom outline codes, which come in two flavors: enterprise and local. Those of you familiar with field customization will find that the process for customizing enterprise fields is the same as it is for local fields in prior versions of Project. The most striking difference is the lack of enterprise Start and Finish fields. These remain available as local fields only.

Administrators manage enterprise fields and outline code definitions centrally. Only administrators or users specifically granted permission can modify these. Project managers can modify local custom fields and outline codes on an individual project basis. Local fields and codes are not available across projects unless you embed them in templates and force everyone to initiate new projects from these templates or you move these from one project to another through the Organizer. Regardless of how you to choose to manage local fields, they are vulnerable to end-user changes. As a project manager, you may or may not participate in managing enterprise fields and outline codes in your organization.

Project Server configuration, to some degree, focuses on enterprise custom fields and outline codes. The most important distinction between a custom enterprise field and a custom enterprise outline code is that Project and Resource enterprise outline codes publish to the OLAP cube as dimensions. Thus, your ability to craft Analyzer output to meet specific requirements is dependent on enterprise outline codes. Consequently, outline codes should follow reporting vectors and you must use them judiciously in the portfolio design.

A new feature of Project Server 2003 is the availability to define up to 10 multi-value enterprise resource outline code fields designed for skills matching. You can use these fields, for instance, to select multiple values for resource language proficiencies. Multi-value outline codes support expanded and more flexible skills matching between Generic resources and human resources in Project Server 2003. Multiple values are not available in enterprise task and enterprise project outline codes.

Traditionally, Microsoft Project offers a complement of fields and outline codes definable at the task/assignment and resource levels. Both remain available as local field sets, and as enterprise fields and outline codes. New with the Project Server generation are Project-level fields and outline codes, which facilitate flexible portfolio designs.

Why Enterprise Fields and Outline Codes Are Important to You

Project stakeholders and management often have difficulty accessing project facts traditionally buried in charter and scope documents. Project Web Access gives you the opportunity to capture and display this information in convenient views that can bring metadata associated with a project to the public eye. Information as mundane as what stage the project is at in the corporate approval process, to stakeholder names and contact information provided in a one-stop source adds value. Of course, you can accomplish the same affect by sharing the project charter document through WSS, but that might be too much clicking and searching for some.

In the Project Center view shown in Figure 1-10, the Project Server administrator added two custom project Text fields, Budget and Schedule, to detail the status of each project in the portfolio. A formula in the field detects the level of budget and schedule variance respectively, and displays a graphic indicator based on the result. Using these indicators, project executives, and stakeholders can quickly ascertain both the budget status and the schedule status of each project in the portfolio.

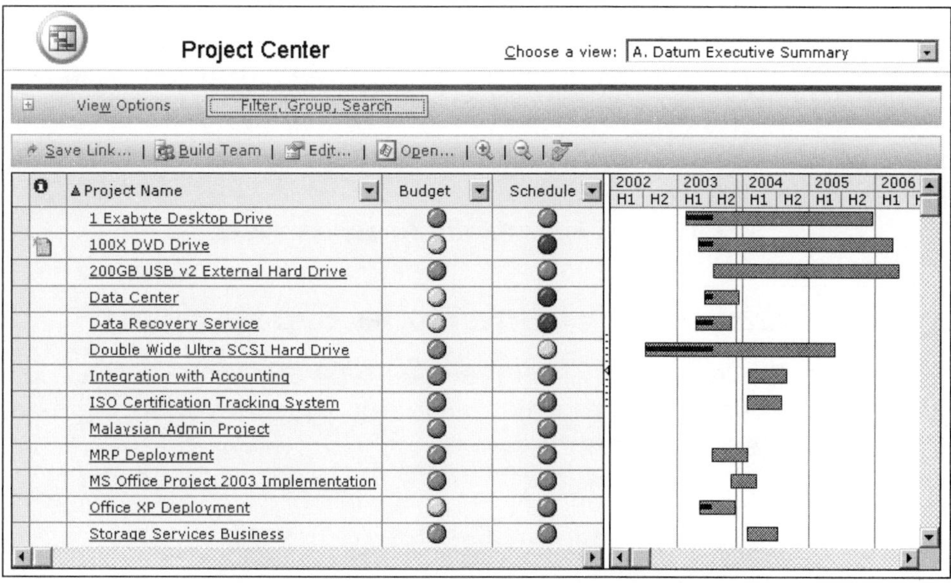

Figure 1-10: Project Center View with stoplight indicators in custom fields

The Portfolio Analyzer view shown in Figure 1-11 demonstrates some of the power of outline codes when using OLAP cube data. Department is an enterprise resource outline code used to filter the resources in the view. Because of this, we can dimension the resource workload for a single department or across multiple departments. By expanding the dimensions we can drill down through the structure of the outline with the system quickly displaying data totals at all these levels.

By way of example, if you wanted to, you could expand the standard time dimension to quarters, months, or days. Without the use of data dimensioning this display would not be possible. The power of Project Server's enterprise resource and enterprise project outline codes is their ability to add your organization's proprietary business dimensions to this very powerful data source.

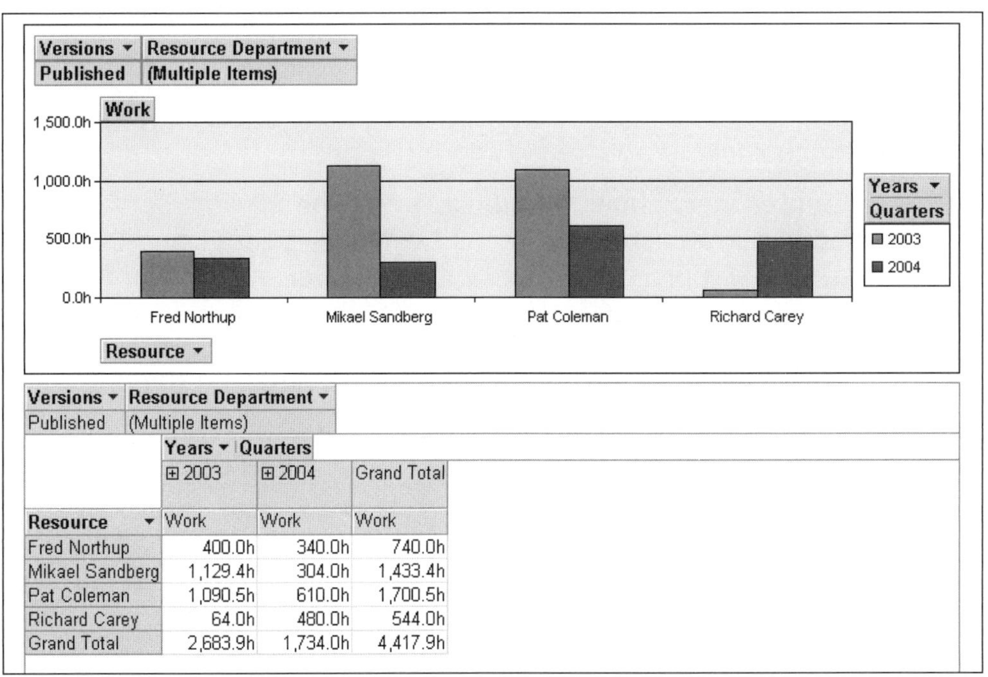

Versions	Resource Department		
Published	(Multiple Items)		
	Years Quarters		
	⊞ 2003	⊞ 2004	Grand Total
Resource	Work	Work	Work
Fred Northup	400.0h	340.0h	740.0h
Mikael Sandberg	1,129.4h	304.0h	1,433.4h
Pat Coleman	1,090.5h	610.0h	1,700.5h
Richard Carey	64.0h	480.0h	544.0h
Grand Total	2,683.9h	1,734.0h	4,417.9h

Figure 1-11: Portfolio Analyzer view

Enterprise Field and Outline Code Types

There are six field types and one outline code type available at the task/assignment, resource, and project levels. At each level are fields of each of the following types and quantities:

- Enterprise **Cost** 1 through 10
- Enterprise **Date** 1 through 30
- Enterprise **Duration** 1 through 10
- Enterprise **Flag** 1 through 20

- Enterprise **Number** 1 through 40
- Enterprise **Text** 1 through 40
- Enterprise **Outline Codes** 1 through 30

Project Server 2003 reserves enterprise resource outline code fields 20-29 for use as multi-value fields and reserves enterprise outline code 30 for the RBS. You can select multiple entries in a multi-value field simply by clicking one or more checkboxes in that field. Figure 1-12 shows the multiple language proficiencies for Aaron Con in the Languages-MV field.

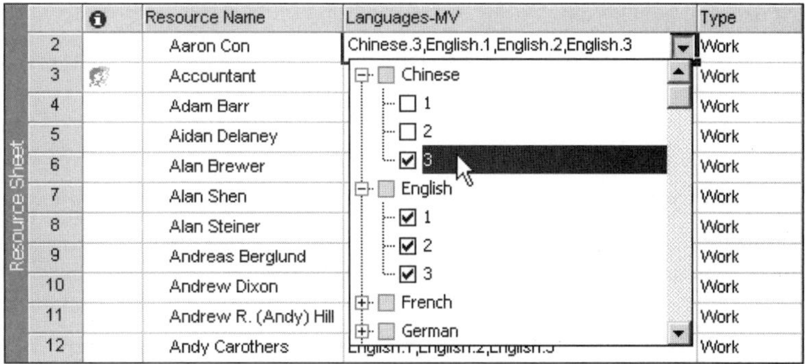

Figure 1-12: Select language proficiency from a multi-value outline code field

Understanding Tracking Method Settings

The tracking method your organization chooses has a significant impact on project team members and their interaction with their timesheets. Not only do some of these options control what data a resource reports, but they also determine the appearance of the timesheet. You must understand the interface impact to decide on tracking method settings. Most importantly, your organization's choice of tracking settings determines the precision at which project data capture occurs.

As part of the Project Server implementation, your organization must make two decisions about tracking method settings:

- Which method of tracking to set as the default
- Whether to "lock down" the default method of tracking, or to allow individual project managers to select their own method of tracking for each project

Once you make these decisions, your Project Server implementer or administrator must set the method of tracking in Project Web Access.

Default Method for Reporting Progress

Project Server offers three default methods for tracking progress. The difference between each tracking method is the information collected and information precision level characteristic of each. These methods are:

- *Percent of work complete*: Resources enter the percent of work complete and work remaining.
- *Actual work done and work remaining*: Resources enter the actual work completed and the work remaining on a task.
- *Hours of work done per day or per week*: Resources enter hours by day or week and work remaining.

"Percent of work complete" is the system default method of tracking progress unless your organization selects another method.

Figure 1-13 shows the upper section of the Tracking settings page in Project Web Access. The Project Server administrator displays this page by selecting Customize Microsoft Project Web Access from the Admin menu.

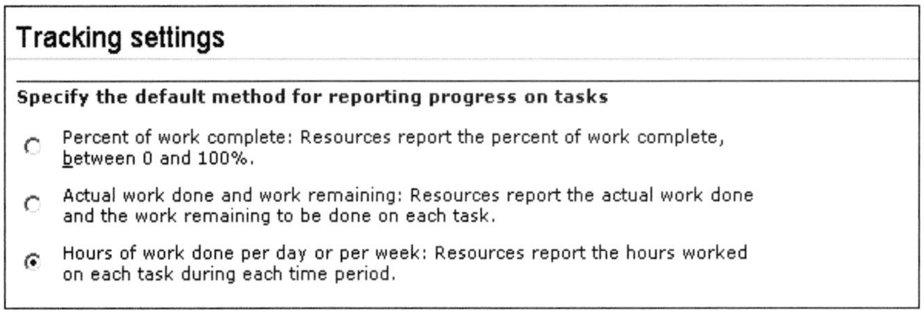

Tracking settings

Specify the default method for reporting progress on tasks

- ○ Percent of work complete: Resources report the percent of work complete, between 0 and 100%.
- ○ Actual work done and work remaining: Resources report the actual work done and the work remaining to be done on each task.
- ◉ Hours of work done per day or per week: Resources report the hours worked on each task during each time period.

Figure 1-13: Tracking settings page in Project Web Access

The Tracking Settings page is accessible only to those in your organization who have Administrator security permissions in Project Web Access.

Figure 1-14 shows the View my tasks page for a team member when "Percent work complete" is the default tracking method. The % Work Complete and Remaining Work columns in the task list are the only columns available for user entry. With this method of tracking progress, the system displays a Gantt chart on the right side of the page. Although you can display a timesheet in place of the Gantt chart by clicking the Timesheet link in the actions pane, you will not be able to enter values in the cells in the timesheet.

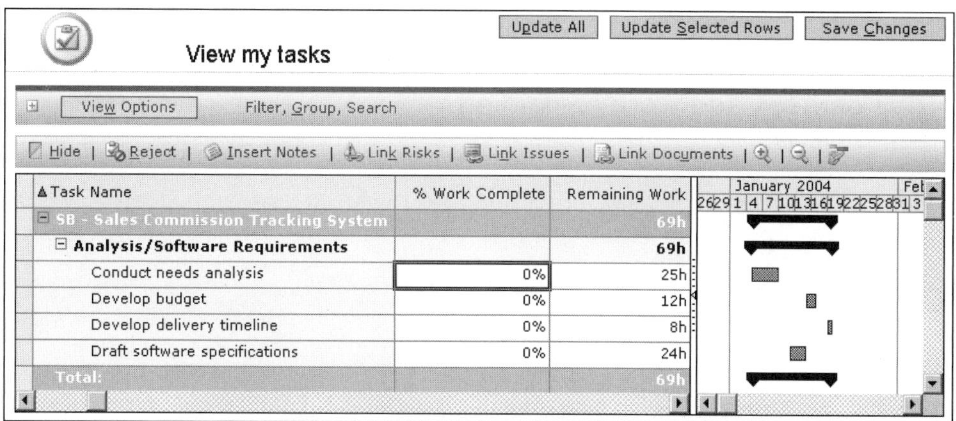

Figure 1-14: View my tasks page using "Percent Work Complete" method

Figure 1-15 shows the View my tasks page for a team member with "Actual work done and work remaining" as the tracking method. The Actual Work and Remaining Work columns in the task sheet are the only columns available for entry of actual data. Again, a Gantt chart rather than a timesheet displays by default on the right side of the page.

Update All | Update Selected Rows | Save Changes

View my tasks

View Options | Filter, Group, Search

Hide | Reject | Insert Notes | Link Risks | Link Issues | Link Documents

Task Name	Actual Work	Remaining Work
SB - Sales Commission Tracking System	0h	69h
Analysis/Software Requirements	0h	69h
Conduct needs analysis	0h	25h
Develop budget	0h	12h
Develop delivery timeline	0h	8h
Draft software specifications	0h	24h
Total:	0h	69h

January 2004

Figure 1-15: View my tasks page using "Actual work done and work remaining" method

Figure 1-16 shows the View my tasks page for a team member with "Hours of work done per day or per week" as the tracking method, along with daily hour entry selected. The Remaining Work column in the task sheet and the Actual Work cells in the timesheet become available for the entry. When selecting this tracking method, a timesheet displays by default on the right side of the page.

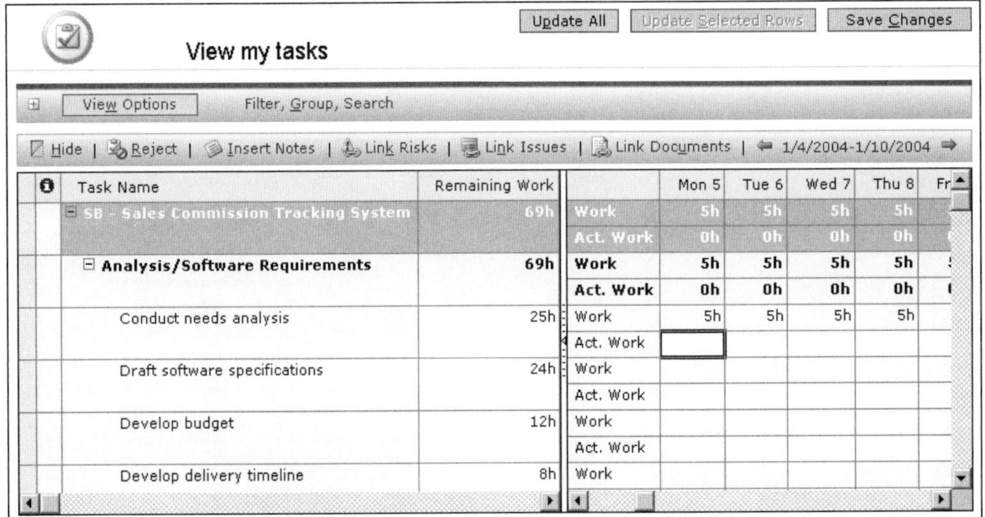

Figure 1-16: View my tasks page with daily timesheet reporting

Lock Down Defaults

As mentioned previously, an organization must decide whether to "lock down" the default method of tracking, or to allow individual project managers to select their own method of tracking for each project. In the Lock down defaults section of Figure 1-17, the method of tracking progress is "locked down" for every project in the organization.

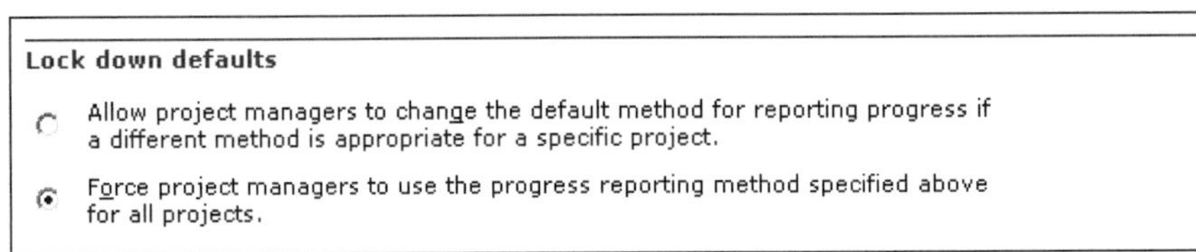

Figure 1-17: Lock down defaults section of Tracking Settings page

Most organizations choose to force project managers to use the default tracking method in an enterprise implementation. The consequence of not locking this down is potential confusion in the minds of resources when their timesheets displaying tasks that use different tracking methods. Moreover, it's difficult to derive reliable performance indices with an assortment of tracking methods.

If your organization does not lock down the default tracking method, a resource must know how to report progress in as many as three or four different ways. Generally, simplicity and uniformity are more desirable. In certain implementations where project teams are static entities, multiple reporting methods may be a viable option.

When your organization does not lock down the default tracking, project managers can change the method of tracking for each of their individual projects by clicking Tools ➢ Customize ➢ Published Fields. Figure 1-18 shows the Customize Published Fields dialog. Select a different method of tracking progress in the Always use a specific method of progress reporting for this project section in the upper left corner of the dialog box.

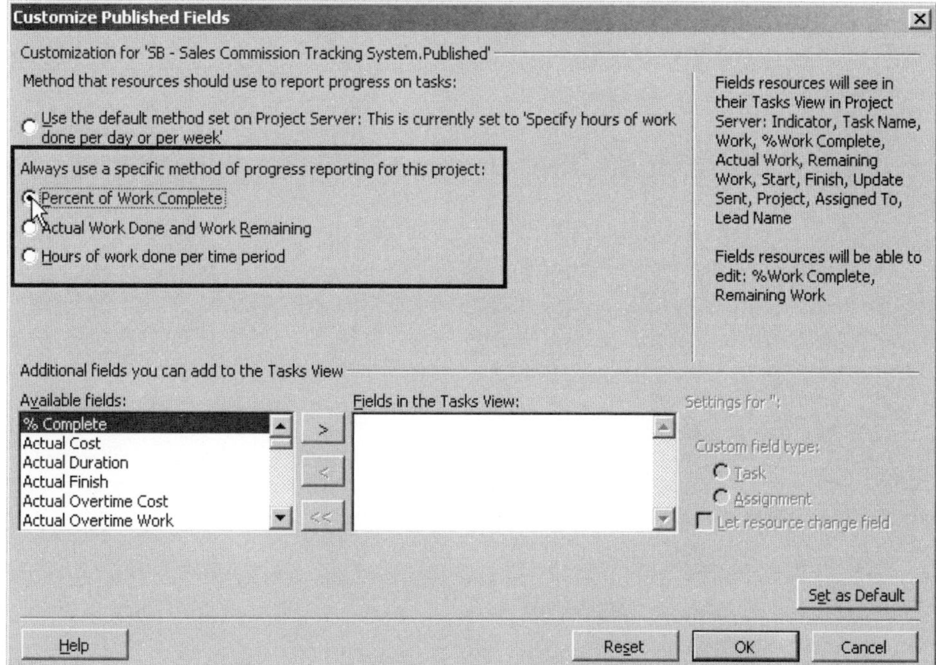

Figure 1-18: Customize Published Fields dialog box

Managed vs. Non-Managed Time Periods

Project Server 2003 allows your organization to set time periods used for tracking progress as either managed or non-managed. You can determine these settings in the Time period settings section of the Tracking Settings page in Project Web Access. Non-managed time periods allow users of both Microsoft Project and Project Web Access to enter actual work values in *any* time period, past, present or future. The Managed time periods feature allows the organization to control the specific time periods in which users may and may not enter actual work values.

Notice in Figures 1-19 and 1-20 that I selected the Non Managed Periods option. The settings for non-managed time periods are based on a weekly or a monthly frequency, and certain options change according to the frequency selected. Figure 1-19 shows the Time period settings section with the Weekly option selected and with the Number of weeks spanned set to 2 weeks. The Project Server administrator can specify between one and four weeks for the number of weeks spanned on each user's timesheet.

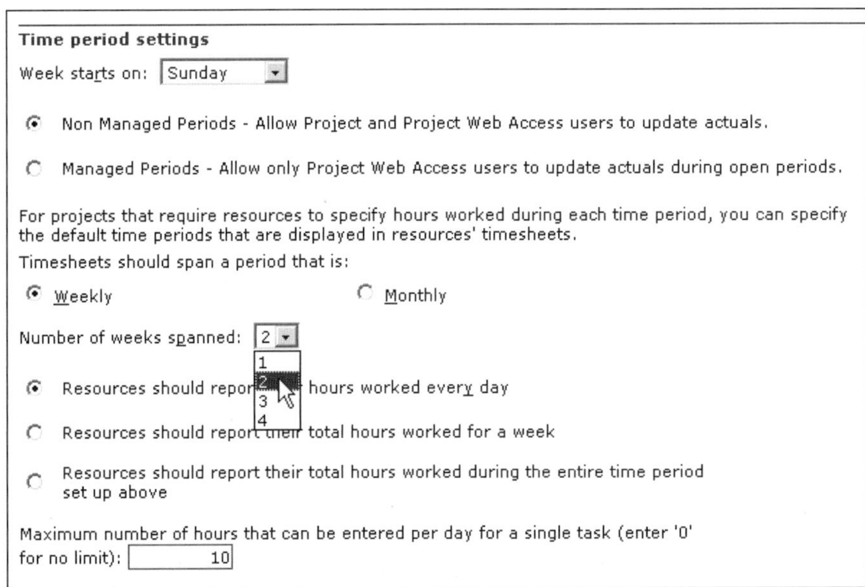

Figure 1-19: Time period settings section with Weekly option selected

In Figure 1-20, the Monthly option is set along with two time periods per month. These two monthly time periods span from the 1st to the 15th and from the 16th to the end of each month. When the Project Server administrator selects a monthly span, a semi-monthly reporting period is enforced by modeling up to three reporting periods and setting the From and To dates using the Period selection drop-down lists.

Time period settings

Week starts on: Sunday

(•) Non Managed Periods - Allow Project and Project Web Access users to update actuals.

( ) Managed Periods - Allow only Project Web Access users to update actuals during open periods.

For projects that require resources to specify hours worked during each time period, you can specify the default time periods that are displayed in resources' timesheets.

Timesheets should span a period that is:

( ) Weekly (•) Monthly

Number of time reporting periods in a month: 2

1
2
3

Period 1: From the 1st to the 15th

Period 2: From the 16th to the end of the month

(•) Resources should report their hours worked every day

( ) Resources should report their total hours worked for a week

( ) Resources should report their total hours worked during the entire time period set up above

Maximum number of hours that can be entered per day for a single task (enter '0' for no limit): 10

Figure 1-20: Time period settings section with Monthly option selected

Remember that by using managed time periods, an organization allows team members to enter actuals only in open time periods, and forbids them from entering actuals in both closed time periods and future time periods. Figure 1-21 shows the Time period settings section with the Managed Periods option selected.

Figure 1-21: Time period settings section with Managed Periods option selected

When selecting the Managed Periods option, you must also specify in which time periods users may enter actual work. You determine these in the Managed Timesheet Periods section of the Tracking Settings page, shown in Figure 1-22.

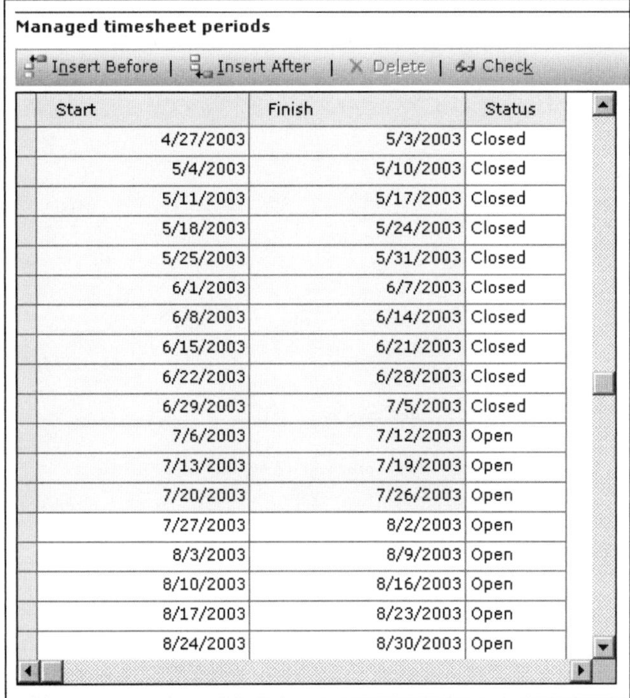

Managed timesheet periods

Insert Before | Insert After | Delete | Check

Start	Finish	Status
4/27/2003	5/3/2003	Closed
5/4/2003	5/10/2003	Closed
5/11/2003	5/17/2003	Closed
5/18/2003	5/24/2003	Closed
5/25/2003	5/31/2003	Closed
6/1/2003	6/7/2003	Closed
6/8/2003	6/14/2003	Closed
6/15/2003	6/21/2003	Closed
6/22/2003	6/28/2003	Closed
6/29/2003	7/5/2003	Closed
7/6/2003	7/12/2003	Open
7/13/2003	7/19/2003	Open
7/20/2003	7/26/2003	Open
7/27/2003	8/2/2003	Open
8/3/2003	8/9/2003	Open
8/10/2003	8/16/2003	Open
8/17/2003	8/23/2003	Open
8/24/2003	8/30/2003	Open

Figure 1-22: Managed timesheet periods section with open and closed periods

Notice in Figure 1-22 that timesheet periods are designated as either Open or Closed. When a timesheet period is Open, team members may enter actuals in any cell during that time period. When a time period is Closed, users are forbidden from entering actuals anywhere in that time period. Closing a time period is how an organization "closes the books" on numbers submitted during a particular time period.

Whether your organization uses managed or non-managed time periods, your organization must also decide how each user's timesheet accepts the input of actuals. Figure 1-23 shows the lower half of the Time period settings section where this is determined in the system.

- (selected) Resources should report their hours worked every day
- Resources should report their total hours worked for a week
- Resources should report their total hours worked during the entire time period set up above

Maximum number of hours that can be entered per day for a single task (enter '0' for no limit): 10

Figure 1-23: Time period settings options for entry of actuals

Selecting the "Resources should report their hours worked every day" option causes the timesheet to provide daily input cells for time entry within the format specified by the span period and number of periods spanned. A weekly timesheet prepared for daily reporting over a one-week time span previously appeared in Figure 1-16.

Selecting the "Resources should report their total hours worked for a week" option opens weekly entry cells on the timesheet for resource hour entries. Figure 1-24 shows a weekly timesheet with a 2-week span with weekly reporting selected.

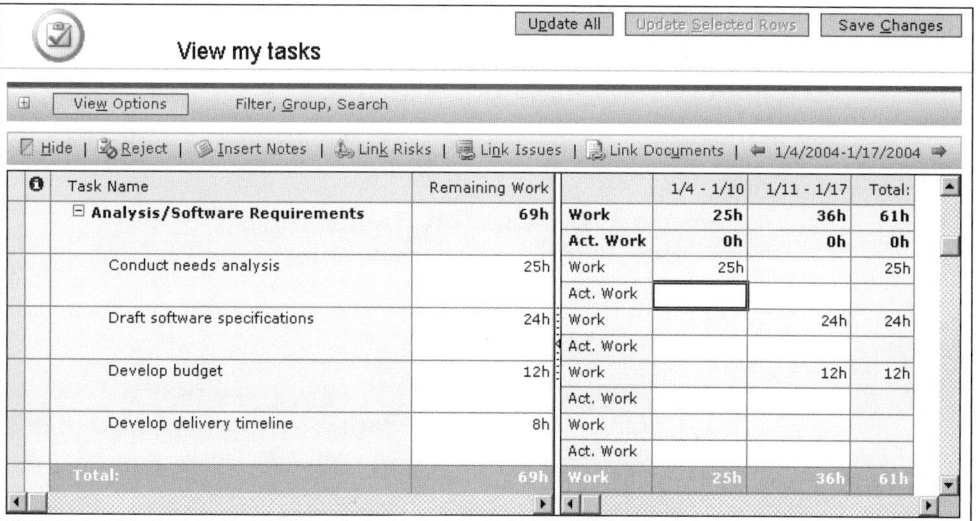

Figure 1-24: View My Tasks page with weekly reporting

Using the "Resources should report their total hours worked during the entire time period set up above" option, the organization causes the input cells to represent the total by time period. This is the setting used to gather totals for nonstandard periods such as semimonthly. Figure 1-25 shows the timesheet with this option selected and configured for semimonthly reporting.

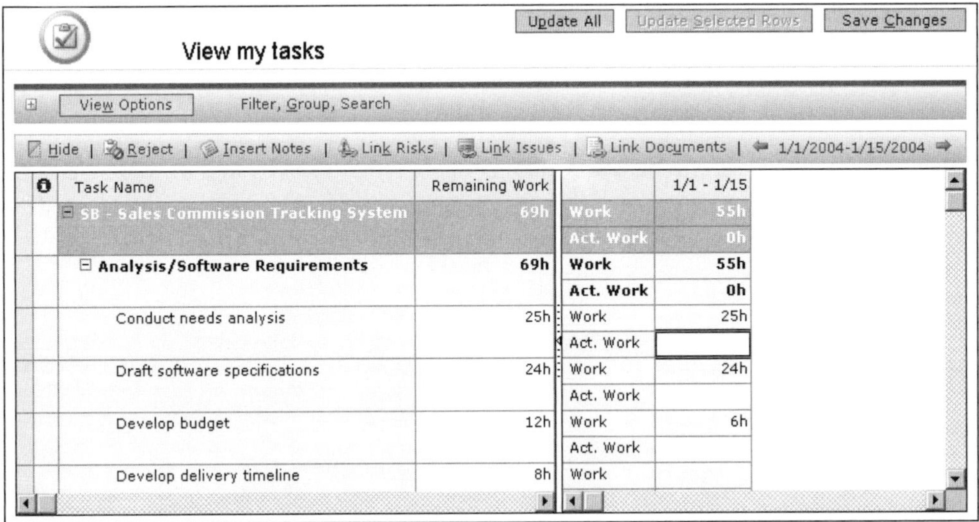

Figure 1-25: View My Tasks page with semimonthly reporting

Warning: Your organization cannot mix daily and weekly reporting methods. If you want your resources to report on a day-by-day basis, select this up front. Once you publish plans using weekly reporting blocks, you cannot easily change this.

In addition to setting the option for how team members report their hours worked each time period, your organization should specify the maximum number of hours a resource may report per day on a task. Doing so limits the daily input to the number specified per task. The system restricts non-daily entries by the aggregate total of the number of working days in the period multiplied by the daily limit. You set this option at the bottom of the Time Period Settings section, shown previously in Figure 1-23.

Define Current Tasks

In Project Server, a "current task" is any task that meets one of the following conditions:

- A task that should have started already but has not started
- A task that has started but is not yet completed
- A task that starts within a specified number of days

In its own section at the bottom of the Tracking Settings page is the option to set the definition of a "current task". This option is set as a specific number of days and the default value is 10 days, as shown in Figure 1-26. The system uses the number you enter here to determine "current tasks" on each team member's task list in their View My Tasks page.

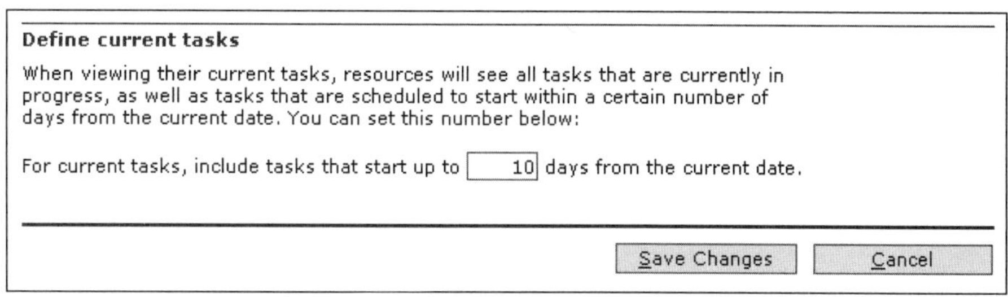

Figure 1-26: Define current tasks section

As you can clearly see, the Tracking Settings you select have a major impact on how actuals are entered by team members. Before you publish any projects, you should carefully consider how your organization measures project progress, and then select the appropriate Tracking Settings values.

Module 02

Creating Enterprise Projects

Learning Objectives

After completing this module, you will be able to:

- Create a new enterprise project from a blank plan and from an enterprise template
- Save enterprise project information and enterprise project plans
- Apply grouping in the Open from Microsoft Office Project Server dialog box
- Work with Offline projects
- Import a project into the enterprise

Creating an Enterprise Project

An Enterprise Project is a project created when one of two conditions is true:

- When created with the Project Professional 2003 client connected to a Project Server with enterprise features enabled
- When imported using the Import Project to Enterprise Wizard that is available on the Tools menu, Enterprise Options menu in the Project Professional 2003 client when connected to a Project Server with enterprise features enabled.

To create a project under condition the first condition, you may begin either with a blank project or with a template. To use a template, click File ➢ New. The New Project side pane displays on the left side of the screen, as shown in Figure 2-1.

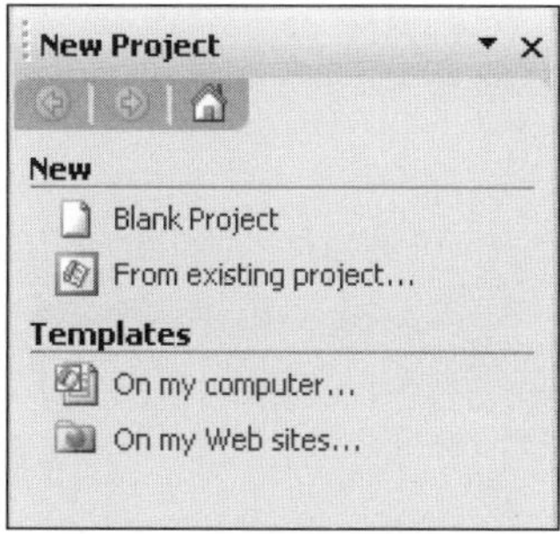

Figure 2-1: New Project sidepane

The New Project side pane allows you the option to create a new project in four ways:

- From a blank project
- From an existing project
- Using local or enterprise templates
- Using templates found on the Web

The On my Web Sites link allows you to browse My Network Places. Selecting the On my computer link opens the Templates dialog shown in Figure 2-2. There are three tabs in the dialog box. The General tab contains your personal templates, while the Project Templates tab contains pre-defined templates that ship with the software. Click the Enterprise Templates tab to find all of your organization's enterprise templates.

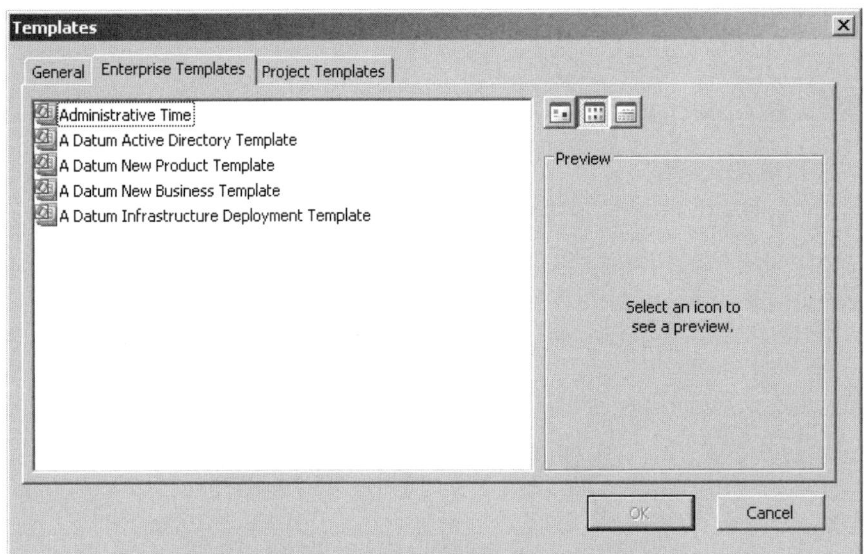

Figure 2-2: Templates dialog box with Enterprise Templates tab selected

To apply the list view of the enterprise templates as shown in Figure 2-2, click the List button in the upper right corner of the Templates dialog box.

Select a template and click the OK button. The first thing you should do with your new project is to name and save it in the Project Server database. Click File ➢ Save to open the Save to Microsoft Project Server dialog shown in Figure 2-3. Name the new project according to the naming convention of your organization and then click the Save button.

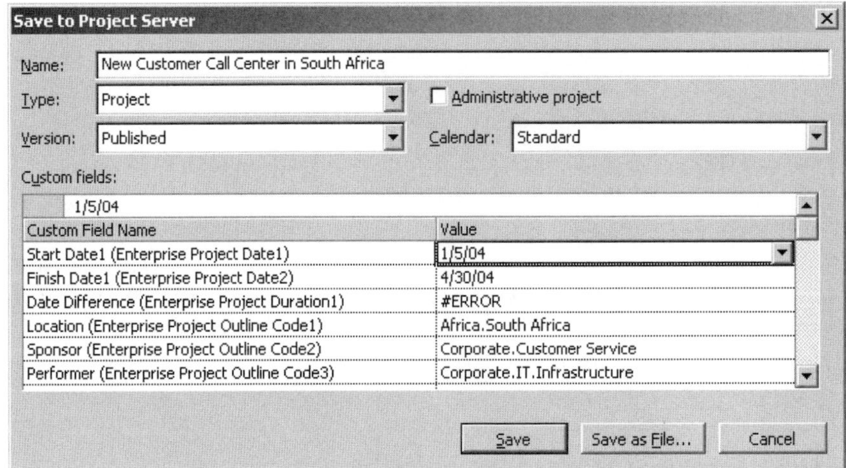

Figure 2-3: Save to Microsoft Project Server dialog box

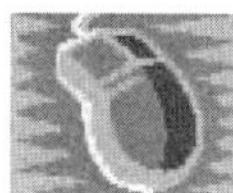

Hands On Exercise

Exercise 2-1

Create a new blank project and save it in the Project Server database.

1. Connect to Project Server if you're not already connected
2. Create a new project from blank project and save it by selecting File ➢ Save
3. Name your new plan student#+test1 (eg: 04test1)
4. Fill in the Enterprise project fields and make your own entry decisions
5. Click Save in the Save to Microsoft Project Server dialog

Exercise 2-2

Create a new project from an enterprise template.

1. Connect to Project Server if you're not already connected
2. From the File menu select New
3. In the New Project side pane, select the On my computer option
4. Click the Enterprise Templates tab and select an enterprise project template for your organization
5. Click the OK button to open it
6. Click the File menu then click Save
7. Name your new plan student#+test2 (eg: 04test2)
8. Fill in the Enterprise project fields and make your own entry decisions
9. Click the Save button

Opening and Closing Project Plans

When you click File ➢ Open, the Open from Microsoft Office Project Server dialog displays as shown in Figure 2-4. In this dialog, you will see only the projects that you have security permissions to see. For each project, the dialog displays the project Name and Version, along with indicators that show if someone has the project checked out and by whom, as well as the last modified date. At the bottom of the dialog, notice that you may open projects read-only or read/write. Clicking the Open from File button opens a traditional file browser. From the file browser window, it is also possible to select other supported file formats and ODBC sources.

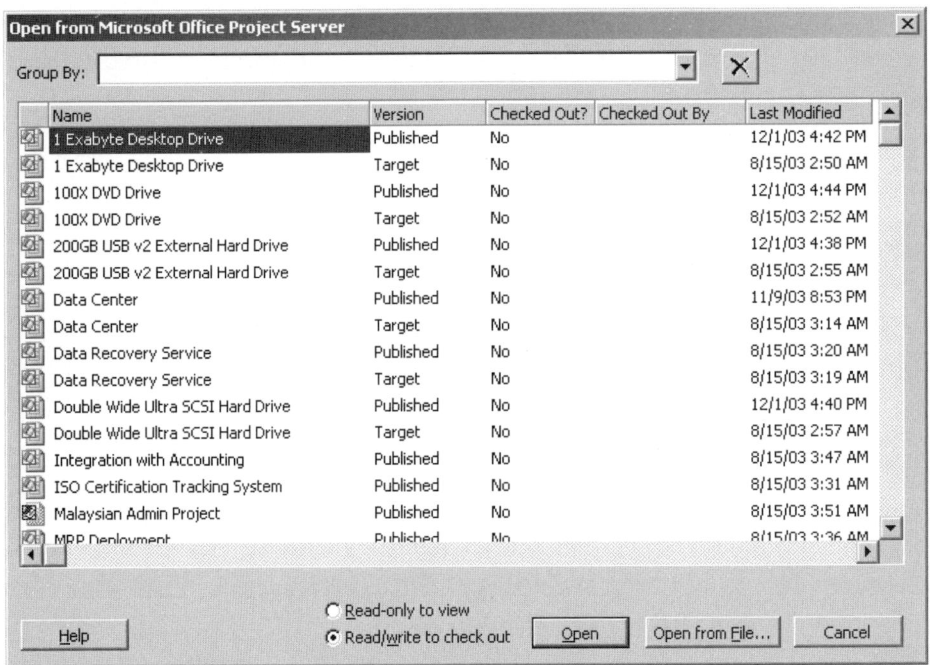

Figure 2-4: Open from Microsoft Office Project Server dialog

The Open from Microsoft Office Project Server dialog contains two new features in Project Server 2003; a Group By pick list and a Delete button. The Group By pick list allows you to group the projects according to one of your organization's custom enterprise project outline code fields. To group your projects, click the Group By pick list and select a custom field. In Figure 2-5, I am selecting the Location field from the Group By pick list.

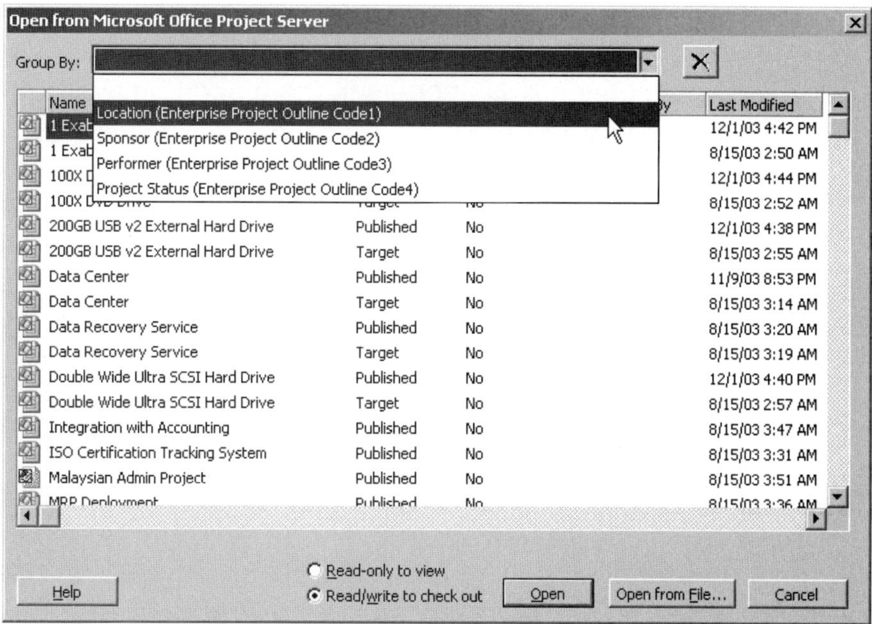

Figure 2-5: Group By pick list in the Open from Microsoft Office Project Server dialog

Once you select an outline code field in the Group By pick list, the system applies grouping to the list of projects according to the values in the selected field. Notice that Location is the field used for grouping in Figure 2-6.

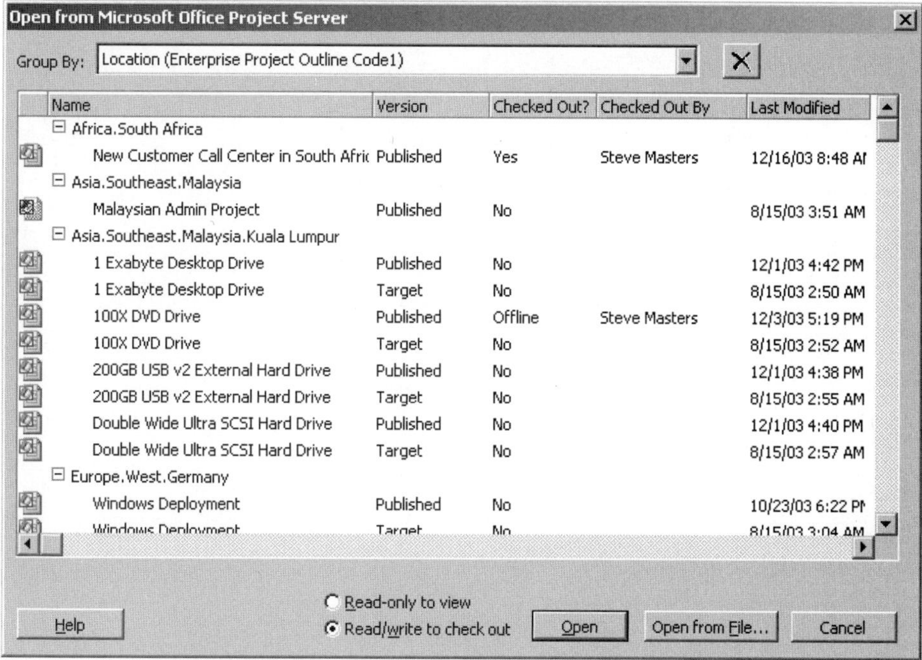

Figure 2-6: Grouping applied in the Open from Microsoft Office Project Server dialog

The Delete button only appears in the Open from Microsoft Office Project Server dialog if the Project Server administrator has given you permission to delete projects.

Warning: If you select a project in the in the Open from Microsoft Office Project Server dialog and then click the Delete button, you will permanently delete the selected project from the Project Server database. There is no Undo command when deleting projects!

Opening a project file marks it as checked out in the system. Referring back to Figure 2-6, any other user attempting to open the project from the server will see that you have it checked out in the Open from Microsoft Office Project Server dialog and the system limits them to the Read-only option.

It is wise to cultivate good habits when opening, saving and closing project files from Project Server. Make it a rule always to use File ➢ Close to close your projects. Remember to save your project before closing it, or the system will prompt you to save it.

Warning: Using the **X** (Close) button in the upper right-hand corner of the project window can lead to your project remaining in a checked out state in the database, even though it appears to close successfully. Close your project plan before closing Microsoft Project Professional.

Hands On Exercise

Exercise 2-3

Open a project from the Project Server database and apply grouping to the project list.

1. Connect to Project Server if you're not already connected
2. From the File menu select Open
3. Look for other plans that are checked out, and note who is working on the plan
4. Click the Group By pick list and select an enterprise project outline code field from the list
5. Open the project you created in Exercise 2-2. The file name with your student #+test2
6. Click File and then click Close to close the file properly

Working with Offline Projects

Microsoft Project Professional and Project Server allow you to work on projects in offline mode in situations where you must travel away from your company's network. If you are a traveling project manager and need to take the project offline for updating, you must first open the plan when connected to your Project Server. To save it as an offline project so that you can update it while you are traveling, select File ➢ Save Offline. The title bar for your project will change to indicate that your project is in offline mode with the addition of [Offline] at the end of the file name, as shown in Figure 2-7. You can see what this looks like to online users by referring back to Figure 2.6.

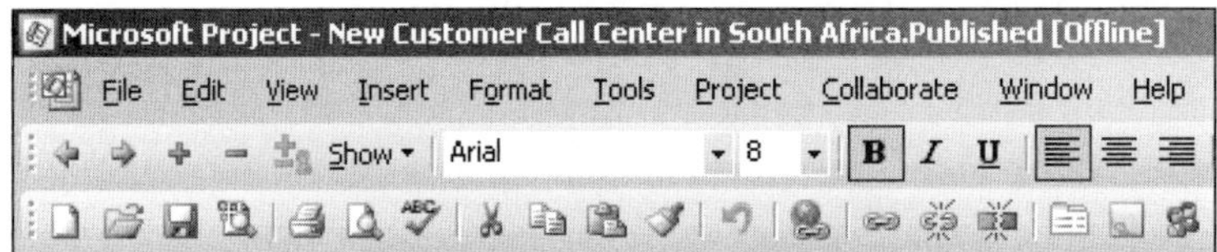

Figure 2-7: Title bar indicates an offline file is open

Saving a project in offline mode is *not* the same as clicking File ➢ Save As, and then saving the file as an .mpp project plan on your hard drive.

While you are traveling, you must log into your local copy of Project Server which varies slightly from the procedure for logging in when connected. You must follow this procedure to work with your offline projects. When you launch Microsoft Project Professional, select your account in the Project Server Accounts dialog, and click the Work Offline button as shown in Figure 2-8. Doing so will log you into Project Server in offline mode and allow you to work with your offline projects.

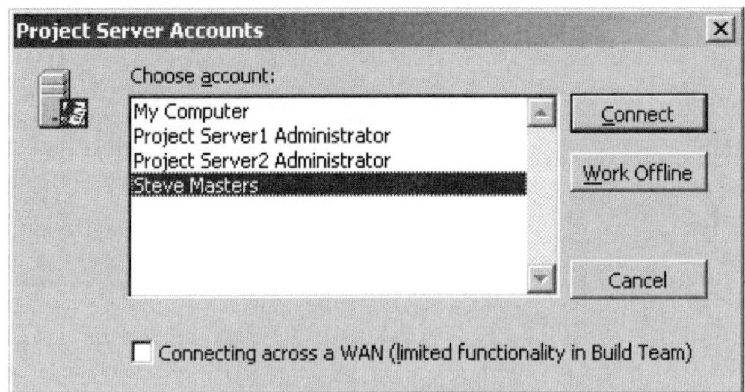

Figure 2-8: Click the Work Offline button to work offline with Project Server

While you are working in offline mode, you can open any offline projects by clicking File ➢ Open. The Open from Microsoft Office Project Server dialog displays only offline projects, as shown in Figure 2-9. Select an offline project and click Open.

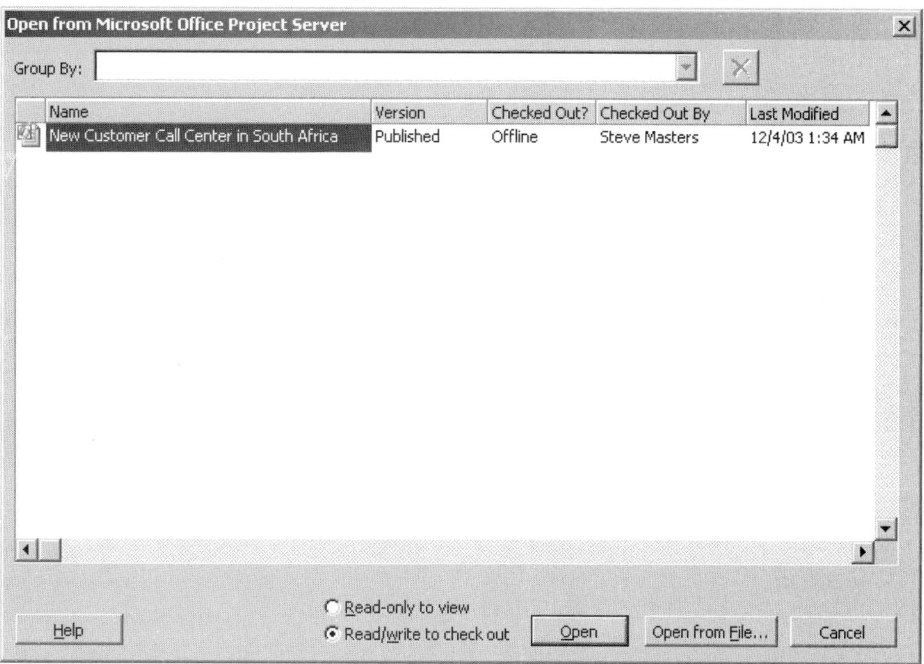

Figure 2-9: Open from Microsoft Office Project Server dialog shows only offline projects

As you update your offline project, you save the project as you normally do by clicking File ➢ Save. While in offline mode, all changes save to a temporary copy of the project on your computer's hard drive.

While working with a project in offline mode, you can perform many activities that you can do while working online, such as adding and editing tasks, setting task dependencies, etc. However, you cannot perform any activity in the project that requires a login connection to the Project Server, such as using the Build Team from Enterprise Wizard.

When you return to your office, log into Project Server normally by selecting your account and clicking Connect in the Project Server Accounts dialog. To open your offline project, simply click File ➢ Open. The Open from Microsoft Office Project Server dialog list all projects to which you have access, including your offline projects, as shown in Figure 2-10. Select your offline project and click Open.

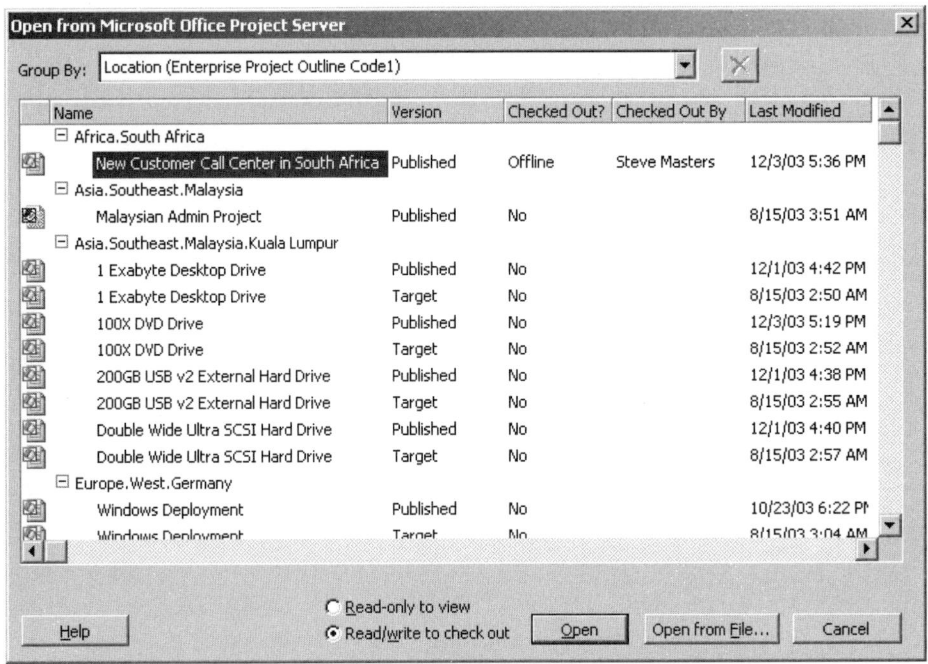

Figure 2-10: Open from Microsoft Office Project Server dialog shows all projects including offline projects

To save the offline project back to the Project Server database as an online project, click File ➤ Save Online. Microsoft Project presents a confirmation dialog box, as shown in Figure 2-11.

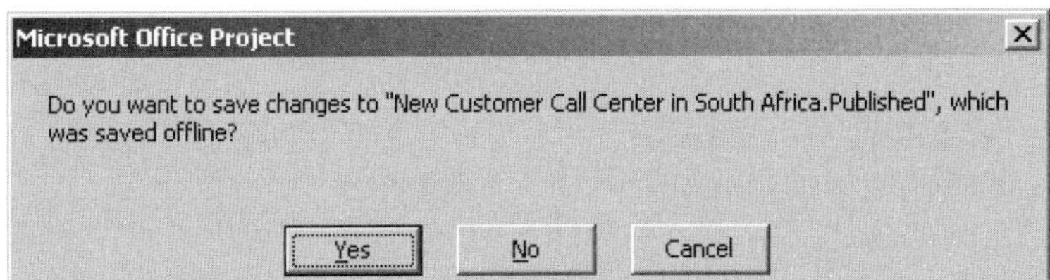

Figure 2-11: Microsoft Office Project confirmation dialog box

Click the Yes button to save the offline project in the database. When you do so, Project Server synchronizes the changes between the offline copy of the project and the online copy of the project in the database.

Hands On Exercise

Exercise 2-4

Save a Project offline and then save it Online.

1. Connect to Project Server if you're not already connected
2. From the File menu select Open
3. Open the project you created in Exercise 2-1 (the file name with your student #+test1)
4. Select Save Offline from the File menu
5. Select Close from the File menu
6. Select Open from the File menu and note that the project displays as an offline project
7. Open the offline project
8. Select Save Online from the File menu to save the plan online
9. When prompted, click the Yes button

Importing Projects

The Import Projects Wizard is a valuable tool that assists you in moving your non-enterprise projects into the enterprise environment. To use this Wizard, you must launch Microsoft Project Professional and be connected to Project Server. Click Tools ➢ Enterprise Options ➢ Import Project to Enterprise to access the Import Projects Wizard. The Welcome page of the Import Projects Wizard displays, as shown in Figure 2-12.

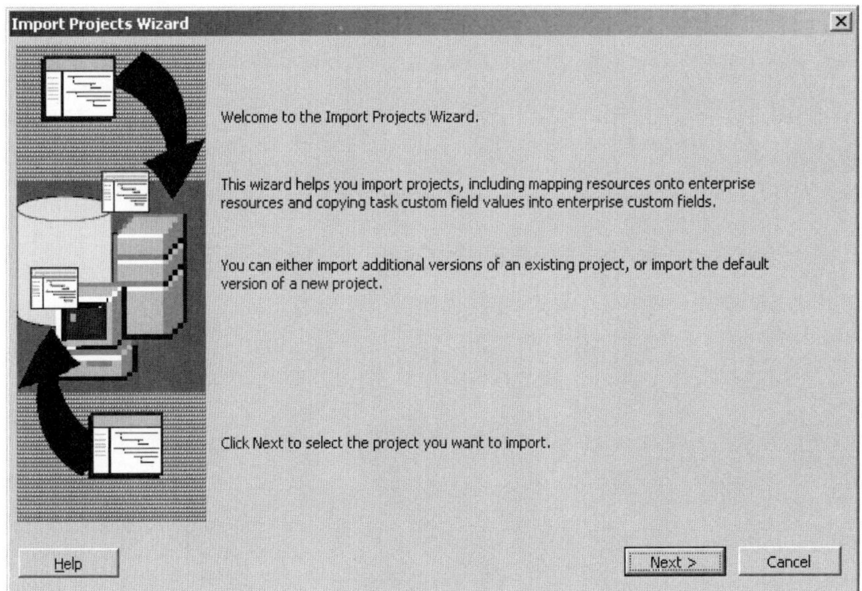

Figure 2-12: Import Projects Wizard Welcome Page

Click the Next button to continue. The system displays the Import Project file browser window shown in Figure 2-13. Navigate to the directory containing the project plan to be imported or click the ODBC button to select an ODBC connection. You can point at projects stored in databases as easily as you can a file. Locate the plan and click Import to activate the import process.

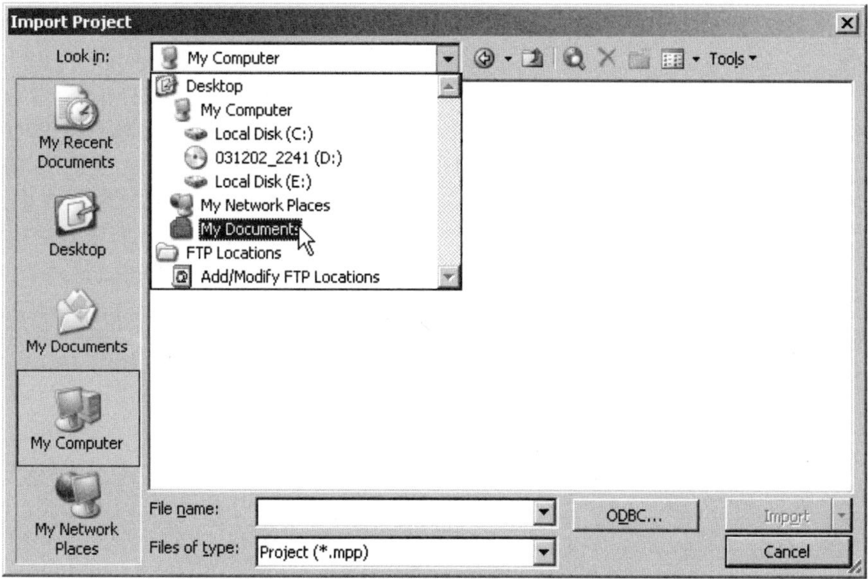

Figure 2-13: Import Project dialog box

Once you have selected your project, the system displays the first dialog shown in Figure 2-14. The dialog provides entry fields to name the project, select a Version, select a Type allowing you to import the project as a regular project or as a template, a Calendar selector for the base calendar and an area in which to provide values for custom Enterprise fields and outline codes. Provide the appropriate values and click the Next button to continue.

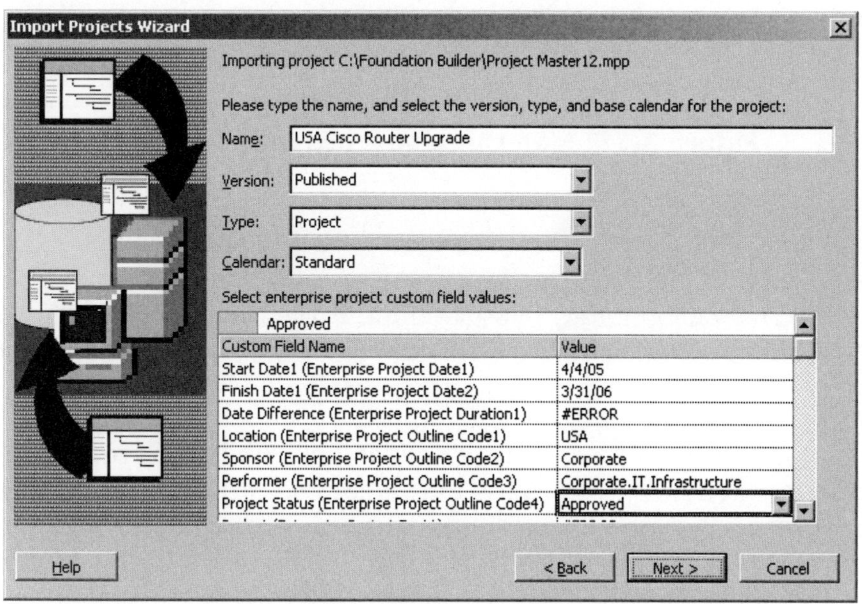

Figure 2-14: Provide custom enterprise information in the enterprise project custom field values

After accepting the project level information, the system displays the Map Project Resources onto Enterprise Resources dialog as shown in Figure 2-15. If the system finds local resources in the source plan whose names match enterprise resources exactly, it automatically maps these for you. For resources that the system does not automatically map, you can either keep the resource as a local resource with a local base calendar or manually map the resource to an enterprise resource. Similarly, if you believe the system has mapped a resource in error, you can make a change here. I am mapping a local resource named Adam L. Barr to an enterprise resource named Adam Barr in the example in Figure 2-15. Once you have mapped your project resources, click the Next button to continue.

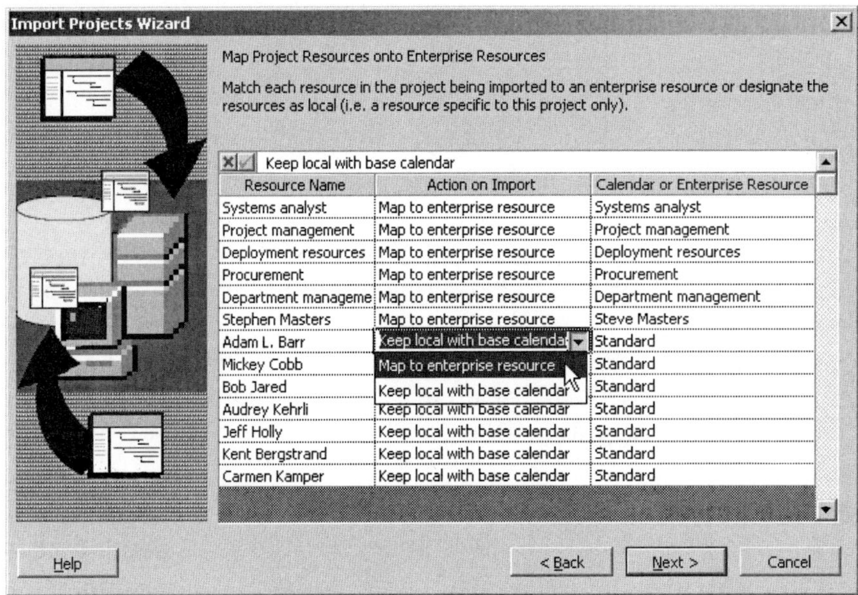

Figure 2-15: Map the resources in the project

Project Server 2002 offered a third option in this dialog to import the local resource into the enterprise resource pool. This action totally bypassed the Project Server security model, and is not present in Project Server 2003 as a result.

The next dialog in the Import Projects Wizard allows you to map values contained in local custom task fields and local custom outline codes in the project to enterprise custom task fields and enterprise custom task outline codes in the Project Server system as shown in Figure 2-16. If any of your enterprise task fields are set to required in the system, they appear here and the system will not let you continue without setting a field mapping to a field that contains a valid value. Remember that when mapping outline codes and custom fields, each field you map must be destined to the same field type. In other words, you must map a local outline code to an Enterprise outline code, text fields to text fields, and so on. Click the Next button to continue.

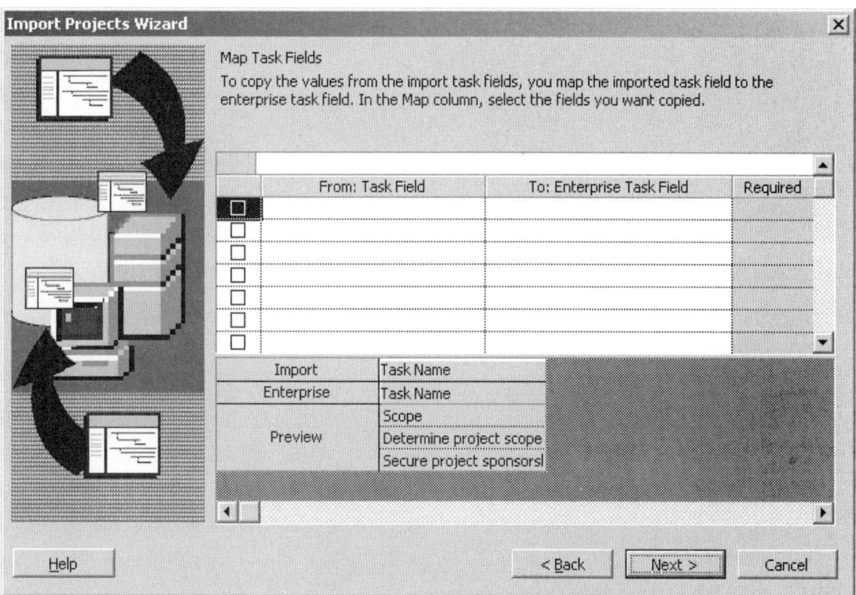

Figure 2-16: Map Task Fields dialog box

The system next examines the tasks for errors. Any errors found will display with a description of the error in the Errors column. In Figure 2-17, I am correcting a local Base Calendar error on three tasks. The system flagged the errors because my enterprise environment does not allow project managers to use local (non-enterprise) base calendars in their projects. Correct each task error as needed and then click the Import button in the tasks summary dialog.

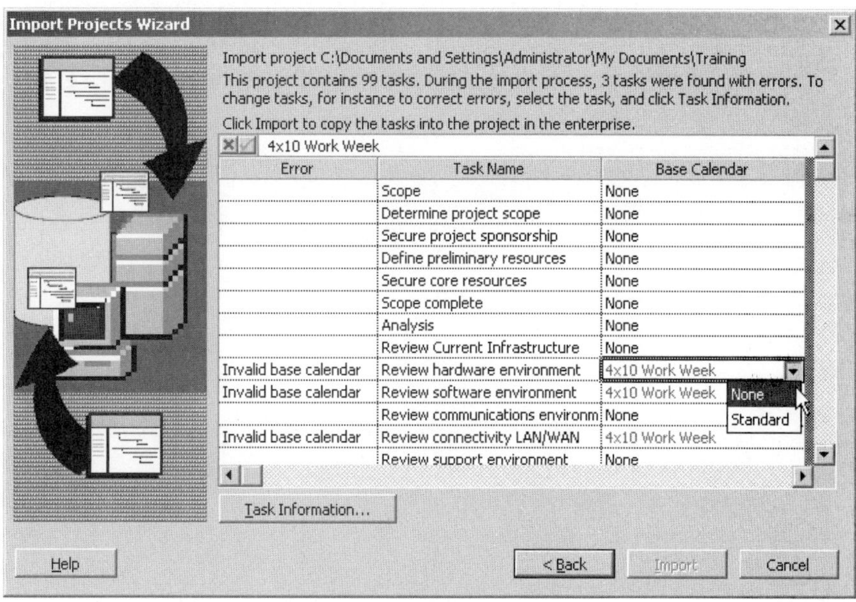

Figure 2-17: Task summary dialog box

To make the process of correcting task errors a little easier, you can also click the Task Information button to open the Task Information dialog for the selected task, as shown in Figure 2-18.

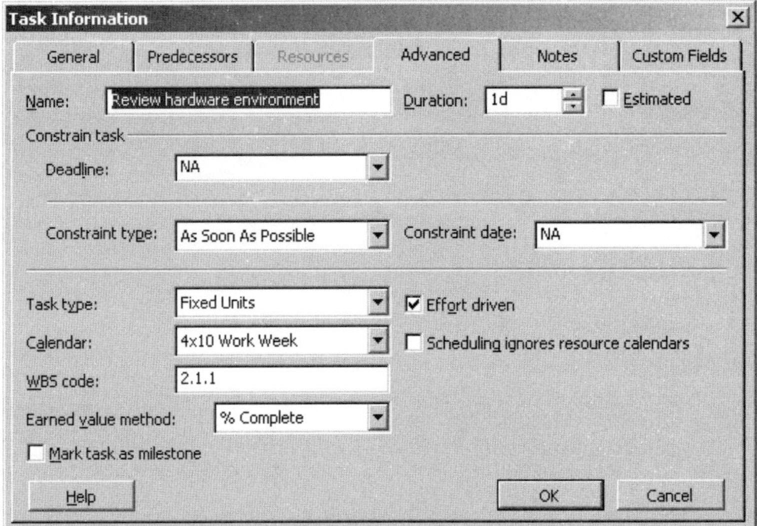

Figure 2-18: Task Information dialog

As the Wizard imports the project, it updates the resources, tasks, and project information as you instructed. When complete, the Import Complete dialog displays as shown in Figure 2-19. The dialog reports the success of the import process and gives you the option to finish or import more projects.

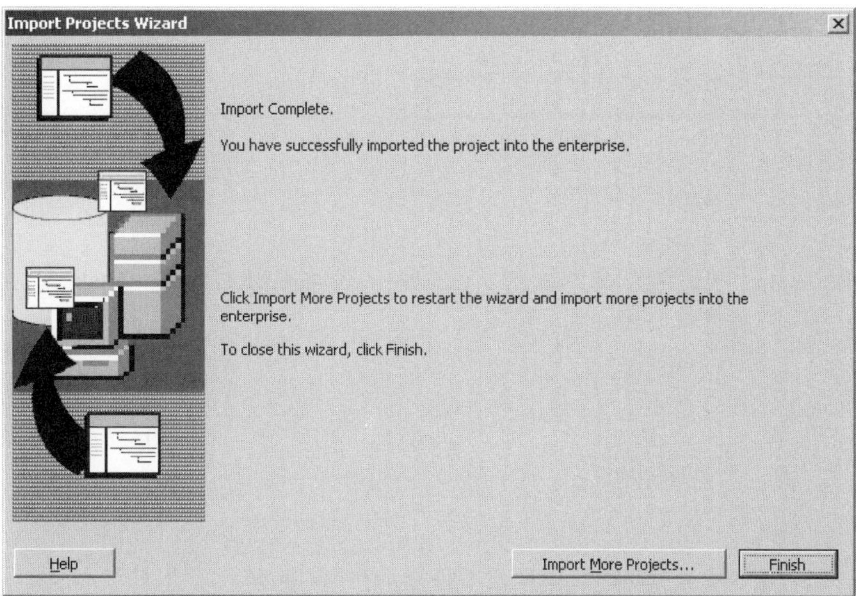

Figure 2-19: Import Complete dialog

Use the Import Project to Enterprise Wizard to import your non-enterprise projects and templates into your Project Server implementation.

Hands On Exercise

Exercise 2-5

Import a project into the Project Server database using the Import Project to Enterprise Wizard.

1. Connect to Project Server if you're not already connected
2. From the Tools menu select Enterprise Options ➢ Import Project to Enterprise
3. Click Next to continue from the Welcome screen
4. Navigate to a folder containing .mpp project files, select a project, and then click the Import button
5. Give your project a new name, enter data into the enterprise fields at your discretion, then click Next to continue
6. Map the local resources to enterprise resources in the enterprise, and map local project fields to enterprise fields if necessary
7. Explore the Task Information dialog from the import wizard and click Next to continue
8. Review the tasks in the project and make calendar changes as necessary, then click Import when you are ready
9. Click Finish when the system completes the import

Module 03

Building Project Teams, Assigning Resources and Leveling Assignments

Learning Objectives

After completing this module, you will be able to:

- Use the Build Team dialog to build a project team from the Enterprise Resource Pool
- Indicate whether project team members are Proposed or Committed to a project
- Assign resources to tasks using two different methods
- Use the Resource Substitution Wizard
- Level resource overallocations

Building a Team

The Build Team dialog in Project 2003 Professional provides you with tools for searching through the enterprise resource pool to find the right resources for your project team. To open the Build Team dialog, click Tools ➢ Build Team from Enterprise. The Build Team dialog displays, as shown in Figure 3-1.

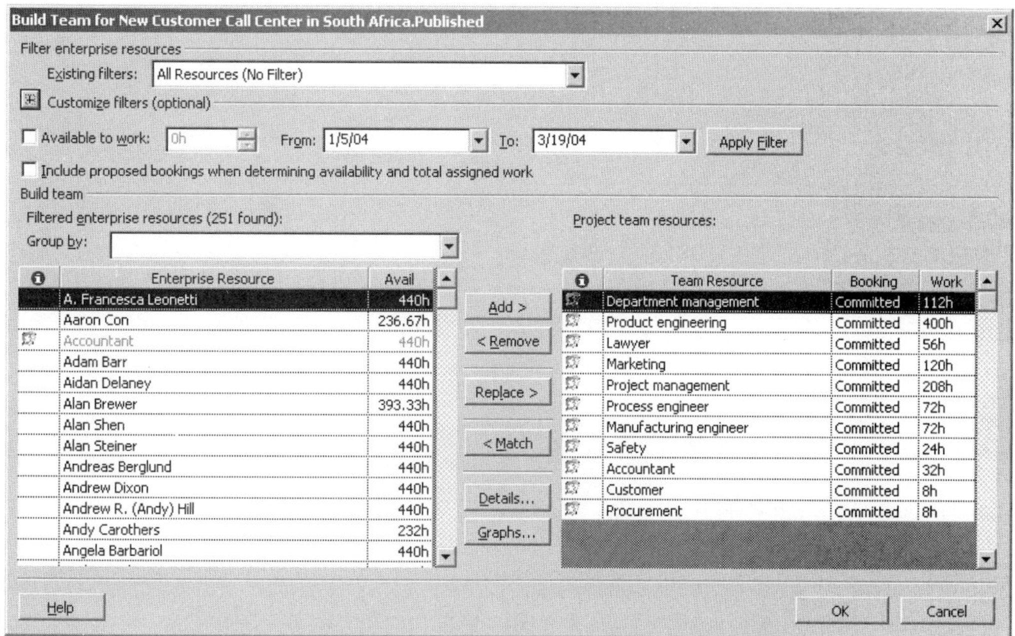

Figure 3-1: Build Team from Enterprise dialog with Customize Filters section collapsed

By default, Microsoft Project shows the Customize filters section collapsed each time you display the dialog. Click the Expand (+) button to the left of the Customize filters section to expand it and show the complete dialog, as displayed in Figure 3-2.

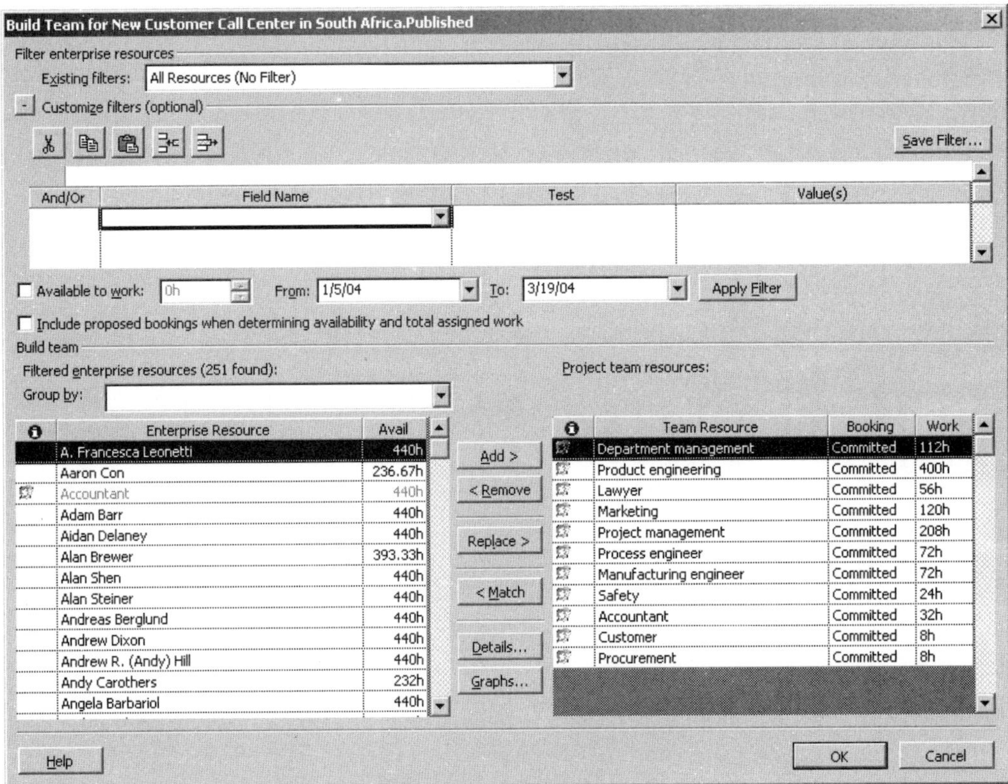

Figure 3-2: Build Team from Enterprise dialog with Customize Filters section expanded

The Build Team dialog searches through your Enterprise Resource Pool, providing you with a quick way to identify resources with the skills, availability, and other criteria needed for the job. The other criteria you can use include anything you have built into resource attribution.

If your Enterprise Resource Pool contains more than 1,000 resources, the system will display a pre-filter dialog to prompt you to filter the enterprise resource list. The system will continue to prompt you to filter the list until the total number of resources displayed is less than 1,000.

The Build Team from Enterprise dialog consists of two sections. The Filter enterprise resources section contains filtering tools to restrict the list of enterprise resources to those that meet your filter criteria. The Build team section consists of two resource lists; the list of resources on the left consists of your current filter list of resources from the Enterprise Resource Pool while the list on the right contains the resources that are members of your project team. Between the two lists are a set of buttons to use for working with the two lists, such as the Add, Remove, Replace, and Match buttons.

Proposed vs. Committed Booking

A new feature in Project Server 2003, the Booking column in the Project team resources list on the right side of the Build Team dialog, allows you to set a booking type for each team member you add to your team. You can book team members as either Proposed or Committed. A proposed booking indicates a tentative commitment for the resource, while a committed booking indicates a firm commitment.

The default Booking type for each project team member is committed. To change the Booking type for any resource, click the pick list in the Booking column for the selected resource and select the desired booking type. In Figure 3-3, I am changing the booking type for Jeff Price from committed to proposed.

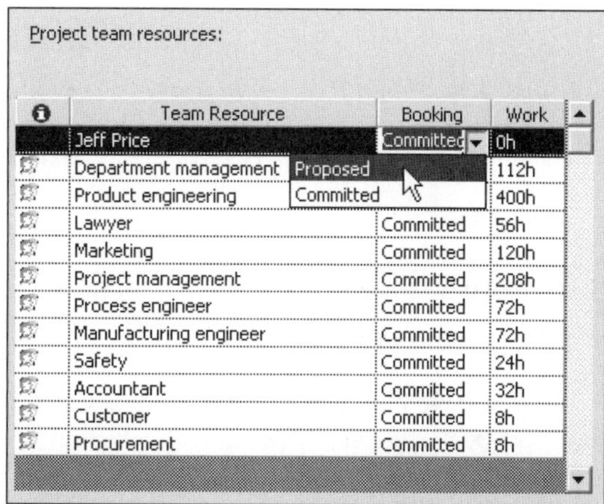

Figure 3-3: Change Booking type to Proposed for a resource

When you book a team member as a proposed resource on a project, the system will handle all task assignments for the proposed resource as proposed assignments. The consequences within Project Server are as follows:

- Published task assignments do not display for any proposed resources on their View My Tasks page
- The projects in which a resource is booked as proposed do not display in the View Resource Availability page, nor do the resource's work hours on proposed task assignments
- Proposed bookings do not affect resource availability. Consequently, these do not appear in the View Resource Availability page.
- The Booking type is a dimension of the OLAP Cube and is available for use in Portfolio Analyzer views

Even though the system does not display task assignments for a Proposed resource on many pages of Project Web Access, the system does display these task assignments in the View resource assignments page of the Resource Center.

When you receive formal approval to begin the execution of your project, remember to change proposed bookings to committed bookings, or substitute committed resources for proposed resources. If you forget to do so, proposed resources in your project will not be able to see their task assignments in the View My Tasks page!

Using Filters in the Build Team Dialog

The Build Team dialog offers three ways to filter resources:

- Use a pre-existing filter
- Create your own custom filter
- Filter for availability within a date range

To use a pre-existing filter, click the Existing filters pick list at the top of the dialog and select a filter. The Existing filters list offers enterprise filters, standard filters, and your personal filters. When you select a filter, the system applies your filter immediately and restricts the enterprise resources list on the left.

Your Project Server administrator can build and save resource filters in the Enterprise Global that are available to all users on the Existing filters list.

To create your own ad hoc custom filter, use the grid in the Customize filters section. The grid consists of four columns: the And/Or, Field Name, Test, and Value(s) columns. In the Field Name column, you can select any resource field available in the system, including both standard and custom fields. In Figure 3-4, I am selecting the Department (Enterprise Resource Outline Code1) field in the Field Name column.

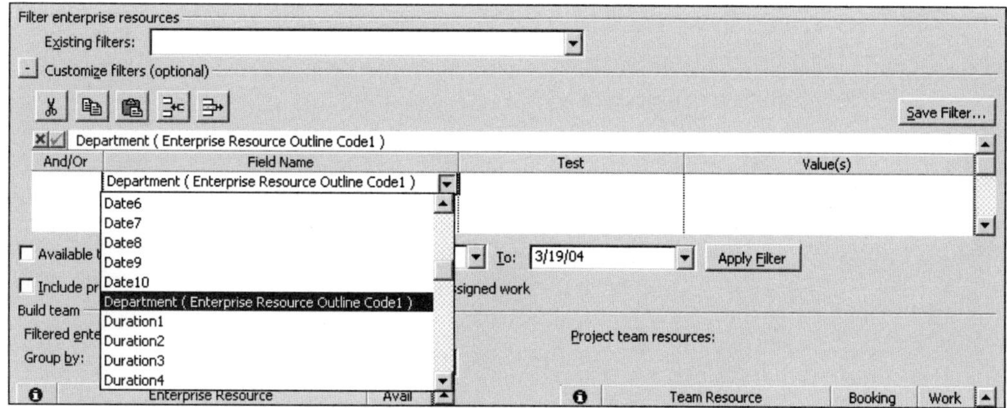

Figure 3-4: Select any resource field in the Field Name column

You must specify the comparison test for your filter criteria in the Test column. The tests available in this column include:

- equals
- does not equal
- is greater than
- is greater than or equal to
- is less than
- is less than or equal to
- is within
- is not within
- contains
- does not contain
- contains exactly

After you specify the Field Name and Test values, you must select or enter a comparison value in the Value(s) column. Unlike its 2002 predecessor, Project Server 2003 displays the list of values found in the resource field selected in the Field Name column. Project Server 2002 expected you to know the possible field values. For example, in Figure 3-5, I am selecting the Accounting value from the list of values found in the Department field.

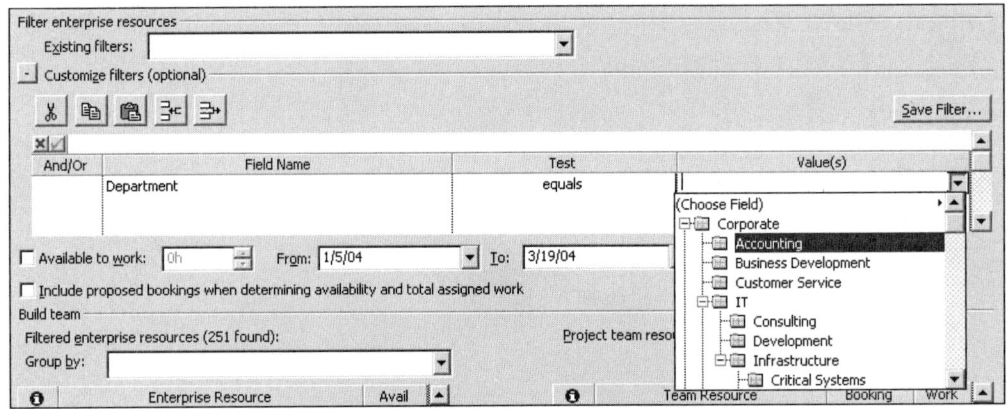

Figure 3-5: Select an entry in the Value(s) column

As you select an item from the list of values in the Value(s) column, you can select an existing field by floating your mouse pointer over the Choose Field option at the top of the pick list. When you do so, a list of available fields will display in place of the list of field values.

The Customize filters grid allows you to specify multiple criteria in your filter by using the And/Or column to add conditions to your custom filter. Figure 3-6, shows a custom filter with conditions placed on both the Department and Language fields to search for members of the Accounting department who are also fluent in French.

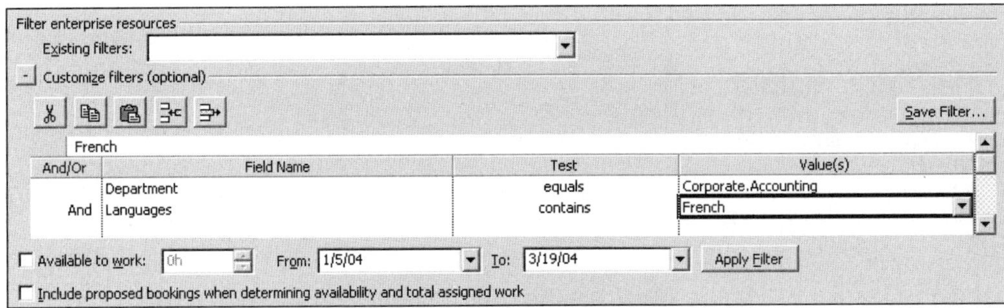

Figure 3-6: Custom filter

When you finish building your custom filter, you must click the Apply Filter button to restrict the enterprise resources list with your filter. Figure 3-7 shows the filter list of enterprise resources that match my filter criteria. Notice that only two members of the Accounting department are also fluent in French.

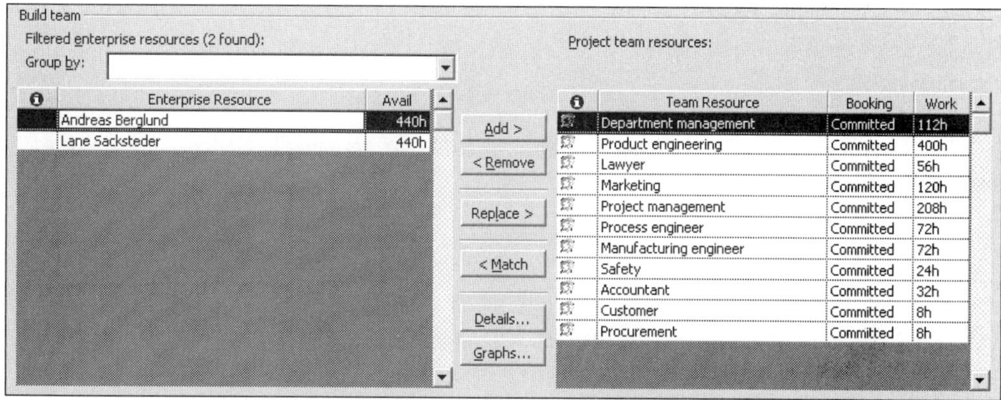

Figure 3-7: Filtered enterprise resources list Accountants who are fluent in French

After you have created and tested your custom filter, you can save it for future use by clicking the Save Filter button. The system displays the Save Filter dialog as shown in Figure 3-8. Give your custom filter an original name and click the OK button to save it.

Figure 3-8: Give your Filter a name and save it

msProjectExperts recommends that you apply a naming convention for your personal custom filters to distinguish them from both the standard filters and the enterprise custom filters. In Figure 3-7, the user has added the initials "SRM" at the beginning of the filter name to indicate that it is a personal custom filter.

Warning: Clicking the Save Filter button in the Build Team dialog box saves the filter in the active project only. To save your custom filter for use in all of your present and future projects, use the Organizer to copy your filter to your Global.mpt file.

In addition to using Existing filters and creating custom filters, you can also restrict the enterprise resources list by testing for availability during a date range. To use availability filtering, complete the following steps:

1. Select the Available to work checkbox to activate availability filtering.
2. Set the availability hours in the Available to work field.
3. Specify a date range by setting dates in the From and To fields.
4. Click the Apply Filter button.

In Figure 3-9, I applied an Existing filter to locate members of the Accounting department who speak French, and then applied an Availability filter to find those who have 32 hours of availability from 1/5/04 to 4/30/04.

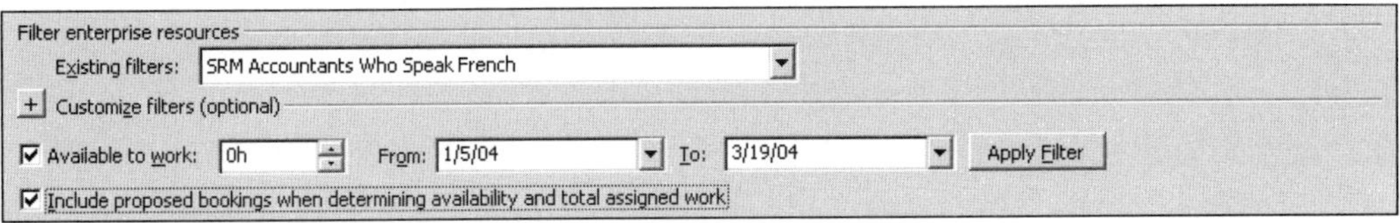

Figure 3-9: Existing filter and Availability filter applied

The system sets the default values in the From and To fields to the current Start and Finish dates for the project.

Finally, you have fourth filtering option in the Build Team dialog that allows you to determine whether the system considers Proposed bookings in the filtering process. To include Proposed bookings, select the Include proposed bookings when determining availability and total assigned work option. To understand how this option works, consider the following example.

Resource A is booked for 40 hours of work as a Proposed resource on a task assignment from October 11-15, 2004 in another manager's project. Resource A matches the filter criteria for the type of resource that you need in your project during the same period. When you build a custom filter and deselect this option, the system will display Resource A as an available resource, whereas if you select the option, the dialog will not display Resource A as an available resource. In Figure 3-9 shown previously, notice that I have selected this option in addition to my Existing and Availability filters.

Using Grouping

The Group by pick list, located just above the Filtered enterprise resources list, gives you yet another way of refining your resource selections by applying grouping to the Filtered enterprise resources list. To group by a value, you can select any resource field available in the system, including both standard and custom fields. When you select a Group by field, the system applies grouping immediately to the resource list, with each group expanded to show all members of the group. As you review your groups of resources, you can collapse or expand each group as you choose. In Figure 3-10, I selected Skills (Enterprise Resource Outline Code20) as the Group by field and then collapsed each of the Executive groups.

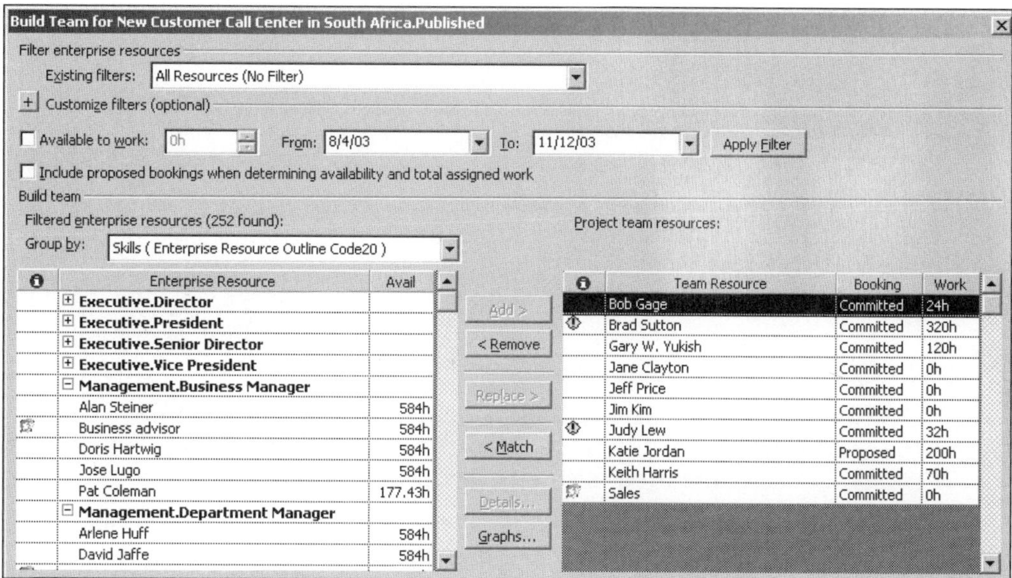

Figure 3-10: Grouping applied to the filtered enterprise resources list

To remove grouping from the Filtered enterprise resources list, select the Group by pick list and select the blank field at the top of the pick list.

Selecting Resources for Your Team

To add resources to your project ream, select one or more resources from the Filtered enterprise resources list on the left, and then click the Add button. To remove resources from your project team, select one or more resources from the Project team resources list on the right, then click the Remove button. When you add a resource to your project team, that particular resource will appear as "grayed out" in the Filtered enterprise resources list. In Figure 3-11, I have just added Aaron Con and Angela Barbariol to the project team and they now appear grayed out on the list of Filtered enterprise resources.

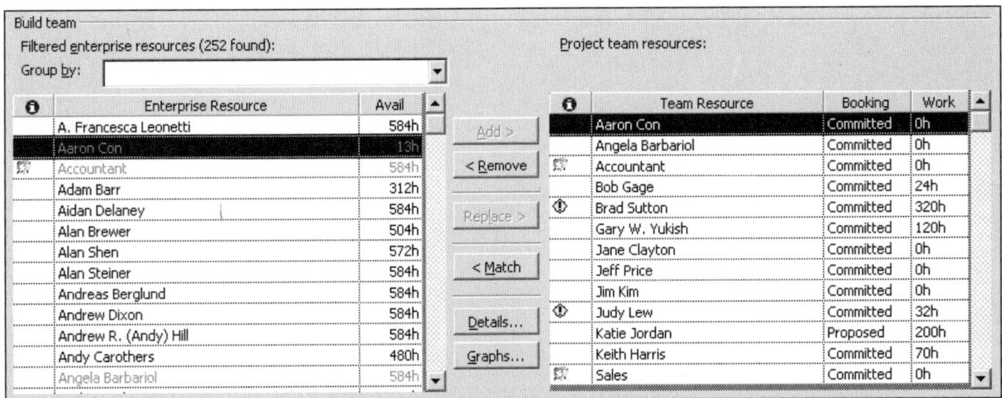

Figure 3-11: Resources appear grayed out on the list of Filtered enterprise resources when they are members of the project team

Notice in Figure 3-11 that the list of Project team resources includes both human resources and a number of Generic resources. The system displays Generic resources with a double-headed icon in the Indicators column of the grid. Notice also that the system displays an overallocation indicator for two resources, Brad Sutton and Judy Lew, who are overallocated either on this project or on one or more projects in the portfolio.

When applicable, the system displays additional indicators in the Build Team from Enterprise dialog, such as overallocation indicators for one or more resources. Float the mouse pointer over the indicator to display more information about the indicator.

To replace resources on the Project team (on the right) resources list with one from the Filtered enterprise resources list (on the left), select a resource in each list, and then click the Replace button. The system replaces the former resource with the new resource on every task assignment in the entire project plan. The system also removes the former resource from the list of Project team resources.

The replace feature in the Build Team dialog is available only when the resource you want to replace has zero actual hours posted to the project. Once a resource has reported hours on a project, you must use the Team Assign dialog to replace that resource.

Use the Match button to match the attributes of a selected Project team resource with those found in the Filtered enterprise resources list. How does the Match button actually work? When you click the Match button, the system applies a customized "contains" filter on the resources in the Filtered enterprise resources list using the attributes of the selected Project team resource that your Project Server administrator has designated for skill matching.

For example, in Figure 3-12, I selected the Manufacturing Engineer generic resource from the list of Project team resources and clicked the Match button, producing the list of Filtered enterprise resources shown in the figure. Notice in the Customize filters section that the system built a custom "contains" filter to match the value found in the Skills-MV field.

In most cases, you will use the Match button to match specific skills between Generic resources and human resources, however the system shows all matches, generic and human allowing you to use this feature to make human-to-human matches as well.

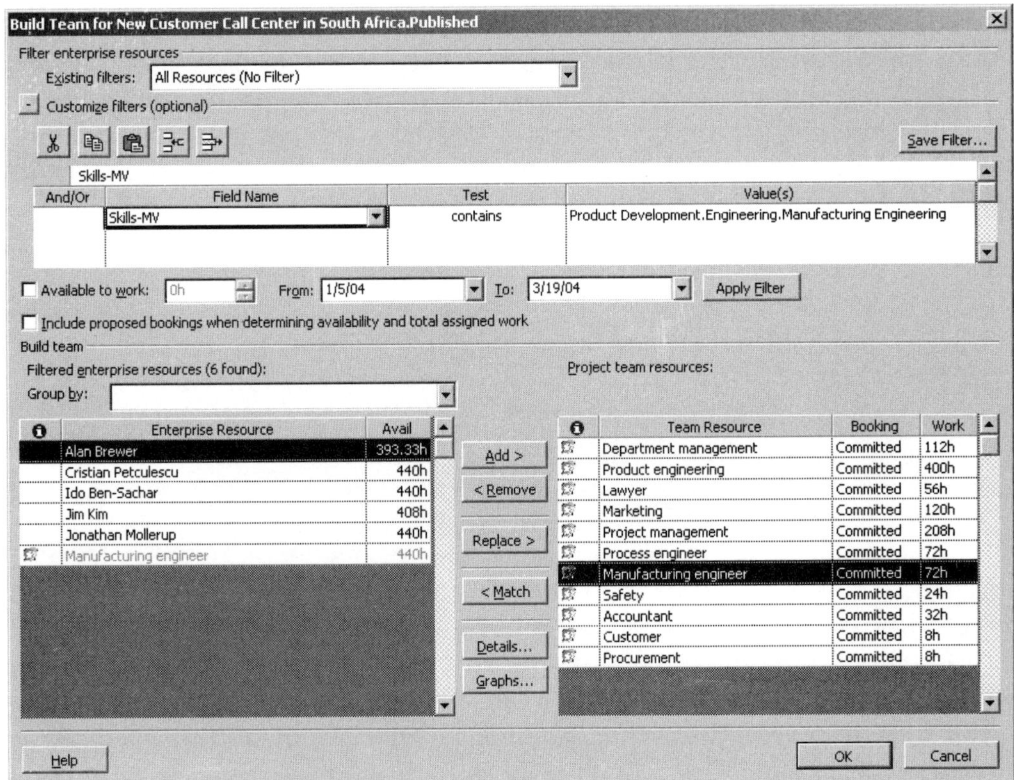

Figure 3-12: Use the Match button to match resource attributes

Viewing Resource Information

Click the Details button to display the Resource Information dialog for the selected resource. Figure 3-13 shows the Resource Information dialog box for Alan Brewer with the Custom Fields tab selected.

You cannot change any of the information found in the Resource Information dialog box unless you have Administrator permissions in the enterprise environment. You must also check out the resource before you can change its standard and custom attributes.

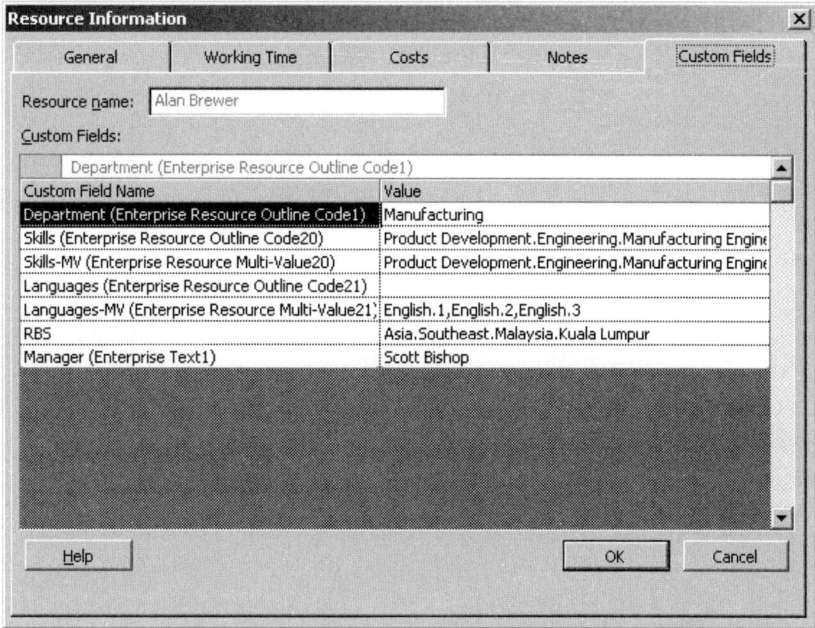

Figure 3-13: Resource Information dialog box

The Build Team dialog also gives you direct access to resource availability information using resource graphs. Select one or more resources and click the Graphs button to open the Graphs dialog shown in Figure 3-14.

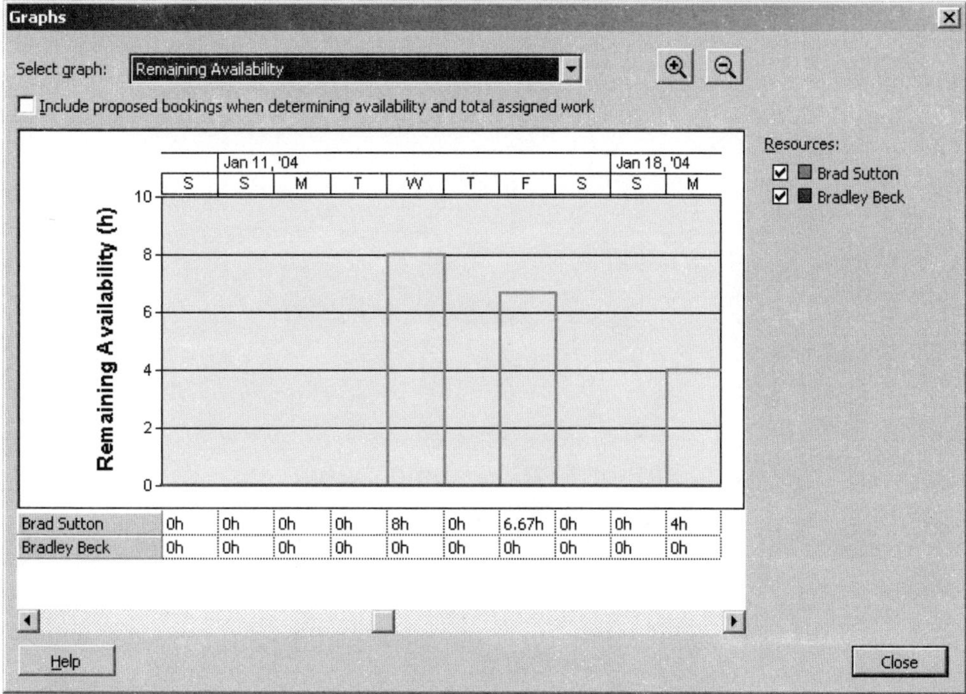

Figure 3-14: Graphs dialog
Remaining Availability graph

Click the Select graph pick list at the top of the dialog and select the type of graph you want to display. Your choices include:

- Remaining Availability
- Work
- Assignment Work

The Remaining Availability graph displays a line chart depicting the Remaining Availability for each selected resource across all projects in the portfolio, as shown previously in Figure 3-14. Below the graph, the system displays a timescaled data grid showing the Remaining Availability values for each resource.

The Work graph displays a line chart depicting the total amount of assigned Work for each selected resource across all projects in the portfolio, as shown in Figure 3-15. Below the graph is a timescaled data grid showing the Work values for each resource and the totals for all resources.

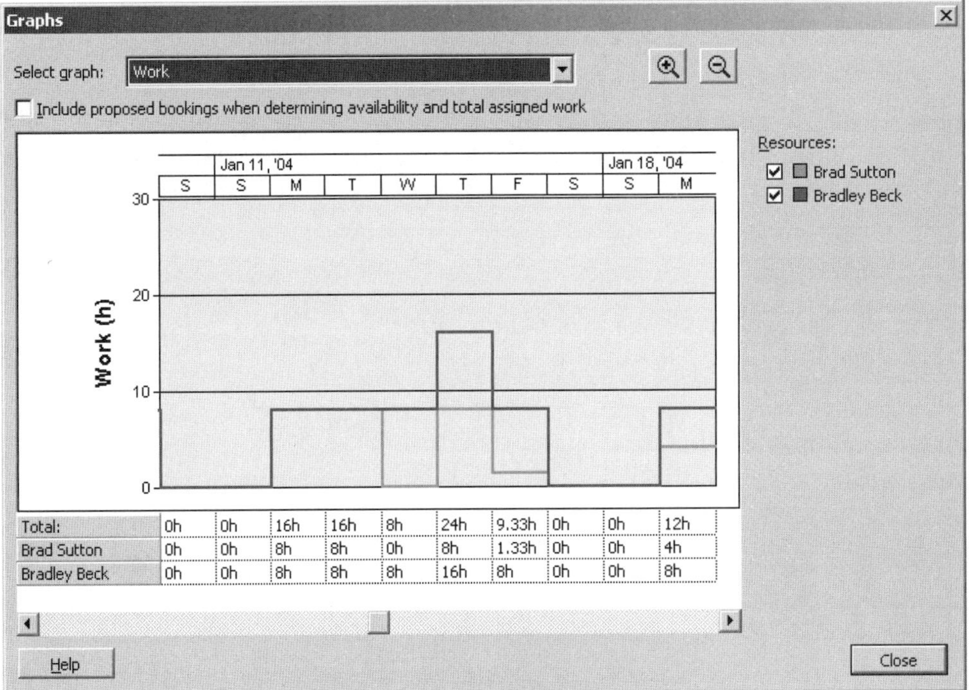

Figure 3-15: Graphs dialog Work graph

The Assignment Work graph displays a combined stacked bar chart and line chart for each selected resource, as shown in Figure 3-16. The stacked bar chart contains one bar segment for the total Work for all selected resources in the Current Project, along with another bar segment for the total Work for all selected resources in all Other Projects. The line chart shows the total Availability for all selected resources. Below the chart appears a time-scaled data grid showing each of the individual values for Current Project, Other Projects, and Availability totaled across all selected resources.

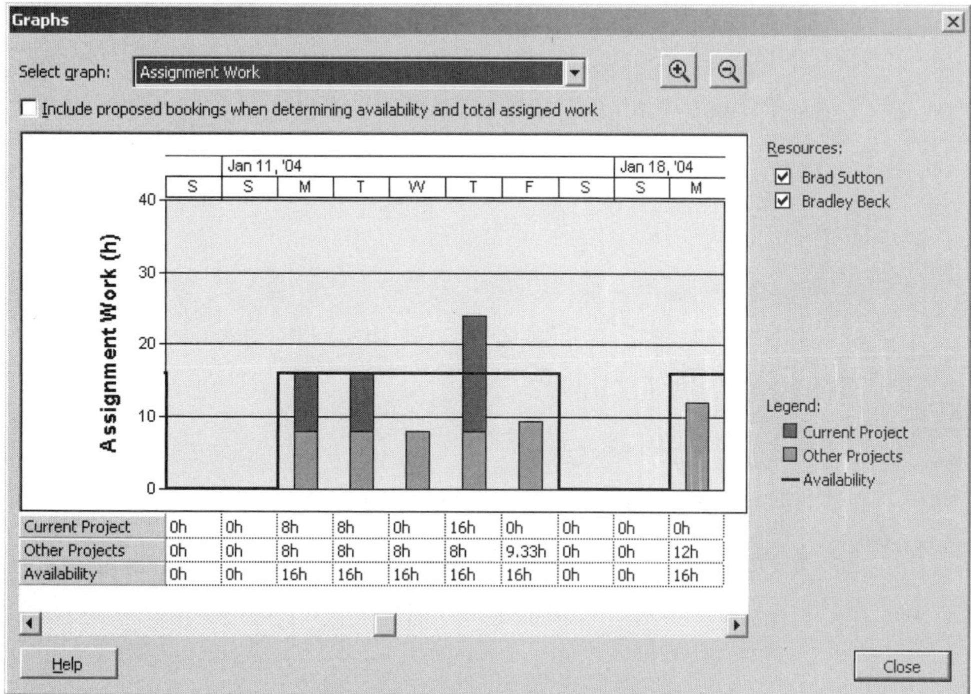

Figure 3-16: Graphs dialog Assignment Work graph

Notice in Figure 3-16 that the selected resources are overallocated on Thursday, January 15, because assignments total 24 work hours when the resources are only available 16 total 16 hours. As the project manager, I may be concerned about this overallocation.

When you select more than one resource, the Graphs dialog, gives you the option to show or hide the graphs for each resource by selecting or deselecting the checkboxes next to each resource name in the Resources list. To determine whether the system includes proposed bookings in each of the three types of graphs, select or deselect the Include proposed bookings checkbox when determining availability and total assigned work option. Use the Zoom In (**+**) and Zoom Out (**–**) to change the timescale displayed in each graph.

Hands On Exercise

Exercise 3-1

Use filtering in Build Team from Enterprise tool.

1. Connect to Project Server if you are not already connected
2. From Project Server, open the project you created in Module 2
3. Click Tools ➤ Build Team from Enterprise
4. Expand the Customize filters section and select an Enterprise Outline code from your business (use a skill code, location code, etc.)
5. Select a Test, then select or type a Value
6. Click the Apply Filter button and note the display changes
7. Set an Available to work filter
8. Explore the Group by options

Exercise 3-2

View resource information in the Build Team from Enterprise tool.

1. Select a resource in the grid on the left and click the Details button to open the Resource Information Dialog
2. Explore the Resource Information dialog
3. Click OK when done

Exercise 3-3

View resource graphs in the Build Team from Enterprise tool.

1. Select a resource in the grid on the left and click the Graphs button
2. Explore the display for one resource and click close when finished
3. Select multiple resources in the grid, then click the Graphs button and explore how the system handles multiple resources in the display
4. Select and deselect the checkboxes for each resource in the dialog to show and hide the resource graph lines

Exercise 3-4

Build a project team in the Build Team from Enterprise tool.

1. Use the Build Team from Enterprise dialog to build a team for your project
2. Add at least one Generic resource to the project team

Exercise 3-5

Use the Build Team from Enterprise tool to match and replace Generic resources with human resources.

1. Select a Generic resource in the right-hand grid and then click the Match button
2. Select a human resource in the left hand grid, then click the Replace button
3. Click OK and review the effect in the plan

Assigning Resources

After you build your team, you will want to assign your team members to specific tasks in your project plan. The system provides you with two methods for assigning resources to tasks. Each of these methods has both advantages and disadvantages. These two methods are:

- Assign Resources dialog
- Task Entry view

Assign Resources Dialog

To open the Assign Resources dialog, select one or more tasks then click the Assign Resources button on the Standard toolbar shown in Figure 3-17.

Figure 3-17: Assign Resources button

You can also activate the Assign Resources dialog by selecting it from the Tools menu. Either choice displays the Assign Resources dialog shown in Figure 3-18.

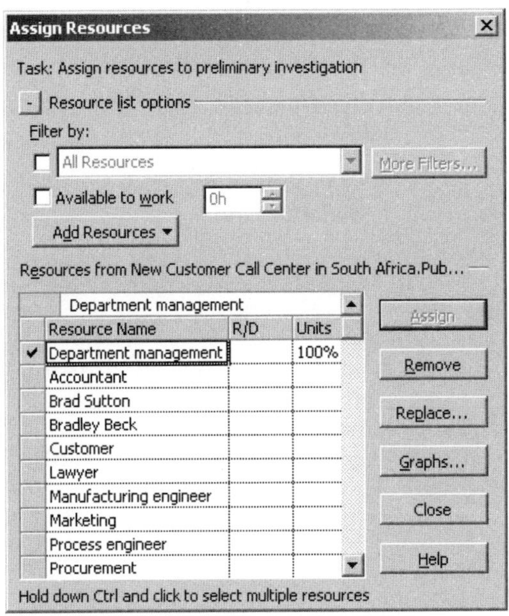

Figure 3-18: Assign Resources dialog box

The advantage of the Assign Resources dialog is that it allows you to control one very important value in the assignment process, which is the Request/Demand (R/D) field. The Resource Substitution Wizard uses the Request/Demand value to determine which resource assignments are eligible for substitution process, and does not alter resource assignments attributed as Demand. I will cover the Resource Substitution Wizard in the next section.

You can select as many tasks as you want when using the Assign Resources dialog. You can also change the selected tasks without closing the dialog box by simply clicking outside the dialog box.

To assign a resource from the Assign Resources dialog box, select one or more tasks, select the desired resource, set the Units value, and then click the Assign button.

You must select a resource and click the Assign button before you can set a Request/Demand value. You cannot select an R/D value for multiple tasks simultaneously, as this value is set for each task individually.

To replace an assigned resource with another resource, select the assigned resource, then click the Replace button. The system displays the Replace Resource dialog, as shown in Figure 3-19. Select the new resource and then click the OK button.

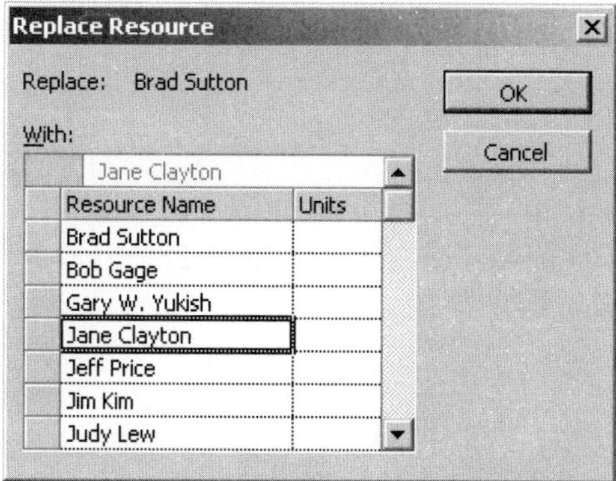

Figure 3-19: Replace Resource dialog

To remove a resource from a task assignment, select the resource and then click the Remove button.

Warning: Be careful when you remove a resource from an Effort Driven task. If you do so, the work assigned to the removed resource will be added to the work assigned to the remaining resources, and will increase the Duration of the task proportionately.

To graph the assignment work and availability for any resources, select one or more resource and then click the Graphs button. The system displays the Graphs dialog, shown previously in Figure 3-14, 3-15, and 3-16.

Task Entry View

Apply the Task Entry view by clicking Window ➢ Split. The Task Entry view is a combination view consisting of the Gantt Chart in the top pane and the Task Form in the bottom pane, as shown in Figure 3-20.

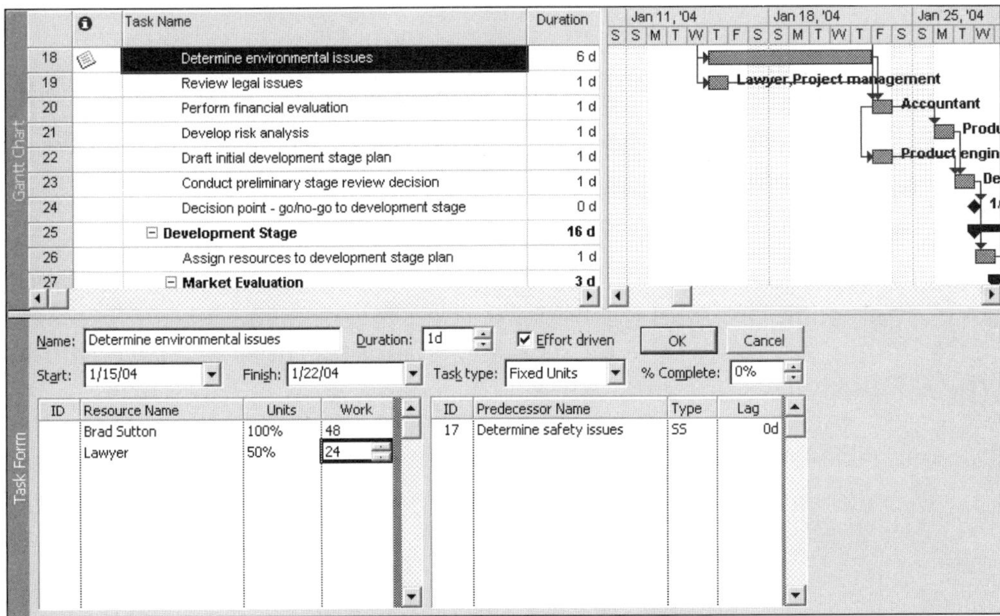

Figure 3-20: Task Entry view

The advantage of the Task Entry view is that it allows you to take complete control over both the task values and the assignment values for each resource. You can easily specify multiple resources along with setting Units, Work, or Duration values. You can also specify whether the resource assignments on the selected task are Effort Driven, and you can even set the Task Type in this view. To assign one or more resources to a task, select the task in the Gantt Chart pane, set the desired values in the Task Form pane, and then click the OK button.

To use the Task Entry view for making initial task assignments, use the following techniques:

1. In the upper pane, select the task for which you want to make task assignments
2. In the lower pane, select one or more resources
3. In the lower pane, set a Units and/or Work value for each resource
4. Click the OK button

Be sure to select only one task in the upper pane as the Task Entry view allows you to make assignments for only one task at a time.

To change the Task Type for any task, complete the following steps:

1. In the upper pane, select the task whose Task Type you wish to change
2. In the lower pane, click the Task Type pick list and select either Fixed Units, Fixed Work, or Fixed Duration
3. Click the OK button

The Task Type value you select determines whether the Units, Work, or Duration value is fixed or "locked" in the assignment process.

To set whether a task is effort driven or non-effort driven, select or deselect the Effort Driven checkbox. You normally use effort driven scheduling to shorten the Duration of a task by adding additional resources to the task. Effort driven scheduling keeps the total Remaining Work constant on the task while you add or remove resources.

To assign additional resources to a task using effort driven scheduling, select one or more additional resources, set a Units value for each resource, and then click the OK button. Do not specify a Work value for each additional resource, as the Work value will be calculated by the system.

msProjectExperts recommends that your organization establish a standard methodology for assigning resources to tasks in all of your organization's projects. Consistent use of a resource assignment methodology by all project managers will provide consistent resource usage information in the Project Server database.

Hands On Exercise

Exercise 3-6

Assign resources to a task using the Assign Resources tool.

1. Using the same project plan from the previous exercise, click the Assign Resources button on the Standard toolbar
2. Select a task in the Gantt chart and notice that the resource selection changes in the Assign Resources dialog
3. Click the Replace button, select an actual resource in the Replace Resource dialog, then click OK
4. Set the R/D value to Demand
5. Adjust the Units value and note the changes in the plan
6. Click the Graphs button and explore the display for one resource
7. Explore filtering in the dialog

Exercise 3-7

Assign resources to a task using the Task Entry view.

1. Select a task and then click Window ➢ Split to apply the Task Entry view
2. Select a resource, and set the Units value to 50% and the Work value to 40 hours
3. Click the OK button and note how the Duration value is calculated for the task
4. Confirm that the Effort Driven option is selected for this task
5. Add a second resource to the task at 50% Units but do not set a Work value for the resource
6. Click the OK button and note how the Duration value is shorted significantly
7. Change the Task Type for the task and click OK
8. Click Window ➢ Remove Split to close the lower pane and return to the Gantt Chart view

Using the Resource Substitution Wizard

The Resource Substitution Wizard is an automation tool that can substitute resources in one project plan or across many plans. The Wizard makes resource substitutions based on skill code, availability, and other user-defined criteria. Because you can apply the Wizard's output directly to plans or save it as a file, it is equally powerful as a modeling tool and as a staffing tool.

The algorithm used by the Wizard will substitute resources based on the following criteria:

- **Skill Set**: The Wizard's primary purpose is to substitute human resources for Generic resources based on a skill set. In order to work correctly, there must be at least one Enterprise Resource Outline Code defined with the "Use this code for matching generic resources" check box selected. In addition, each of your resources must have a value set for this field.
- **Availability**: The Wizard substitutes resources based on availability. To get the best results from the Wizard, you may want to try leveling the plan first before running the Wizard.
- **Request/Demand**: The Wizard substitutes resources based on the R/D value specified for each resource assignment. The Wizard will substitute resources on assignments that are marked as Request, based on the most available matching resource. The Wizard respects all resource assignments marked as Demand and will not substitute resources on these assignments.
- **Priority**: The Wizard weights assignments by the Priority number of each project identified by the user at Wizard run time. The wizard gives Projects with a higher Priority number first consideration when matching resources.
- **Pool Selection**: The Wizard confines its resource selection to the restriction you set at run time. You may select specific resources, the entire pool, or only resources defined in the selected projects.
- **RBS level**: The Wizard applies the RBS condition you specify at run time to the resource selection, if applicable. This feature relies on the value assigned to each resource in the RBS field (Enterprise Resource Outline Code30).
- **Resource Freeze Horizon**: The Wizard will not make resource substitutions on assignments that occur earlier than a specified Resource Freeze Horizon date.

Running the Wizard

Open the project or projects in which you want to run the Resource Substitution Wizard and then click Tools ➢ Substitute Resources.

If you have the Resource Management toolbar displayed, you can click the Resource Substitution Wizard button on the toolbar.

The system displays the Resource Substitution Wizard welcome screen shown in Figure 3-21.

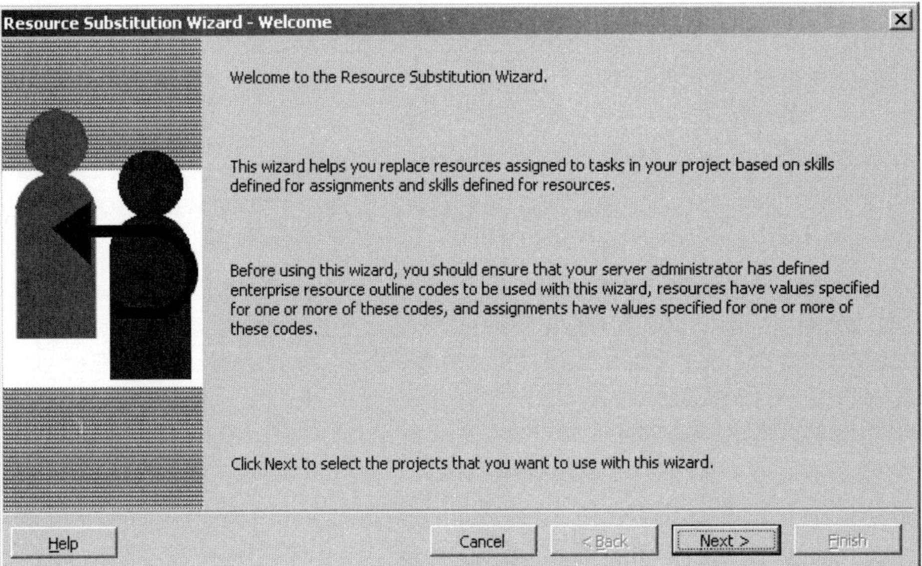

Figure 3-21: Resource Substitution Wizard Welcome page

Click the Next button to continue. The system displays Step 1 of the Wizard, the Choose Projects page, as shown in Figure 3-22.

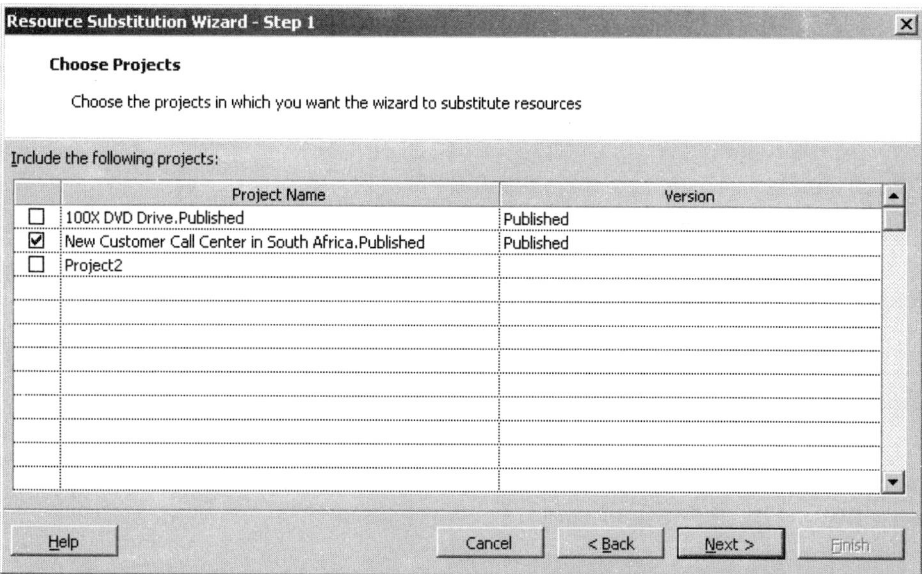

Figure 3-22: Resource Substitution Wizard Choose Projects page

When you run the Resource Substitution Wizard, the system assumes that you want to make resource substitutions on all open projects, including any blank projects you may have open. Deselect any projects in which you do not want resource substitutions performed and then click the Next button. The system displays the Step 2 of the Wizard, the Choose Resources page, as shown in Figure 3-23.

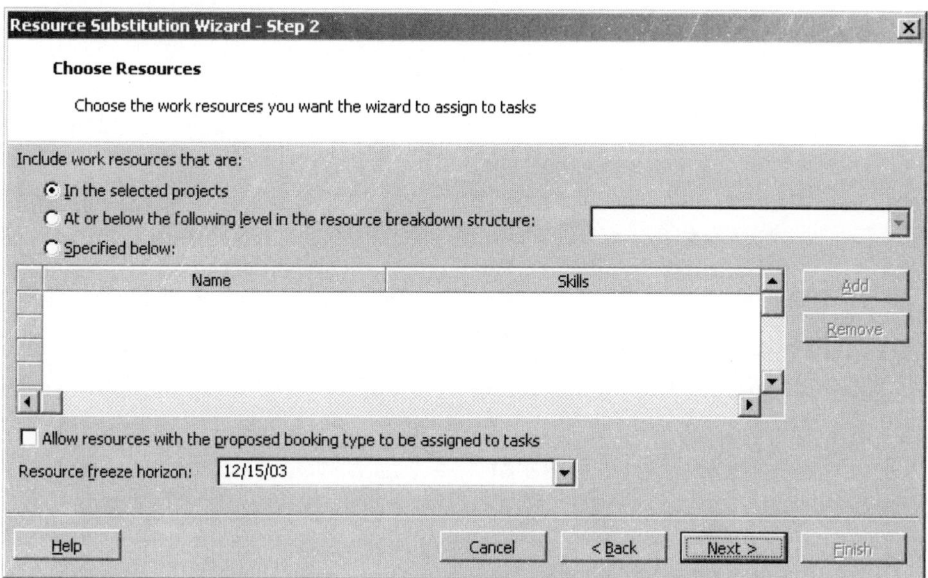

Figure 3-23: Resource Substitution Wizard Choose Resources page

In the Choose Resources page, you must select the resources for the Wizard to consider in the substitution process. There are three resource substitution options:

- **In the selected projects** indicates that one or more of the projects you have selected has a team already built. When you choose this option, the system will use only resources specified in the selected plans.
- **At or below the following level in the Resource Breakdown Structure** allows you to select a branch of your RBS structure. The pick list contains the value list for your RBS. The Wizard will consider all resources at or below that branch of the RBS. For example, in Figure 3-24, I have selected the Africa branch of my RBS structure, which will cause the Wizard to consider resources from Egypt, Jordan, and South Africa in the substitution process.

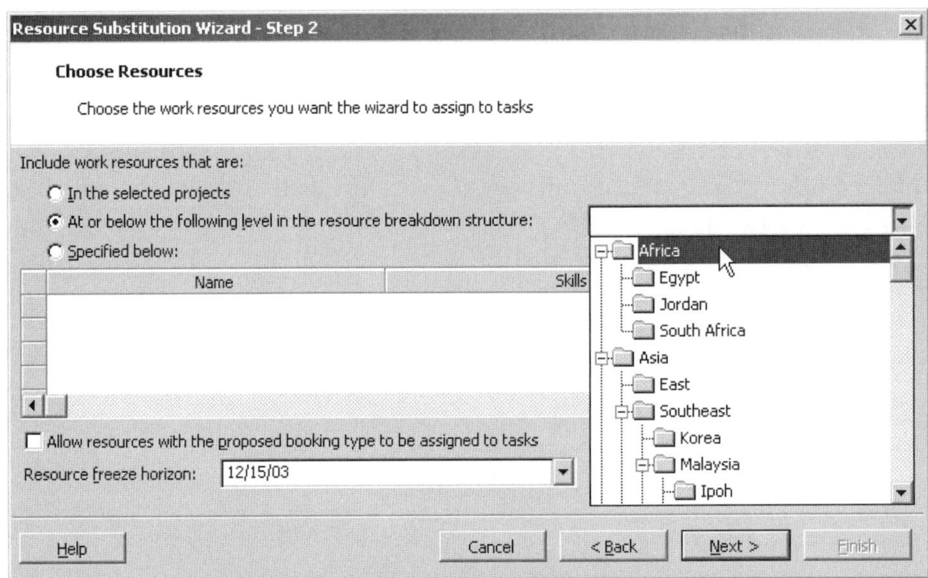

Figure 3-24: Resource Substitution Wizard Select a branch of the RBS structure

- **Specified below** allows you to select resources from the Enterprise Resource Pool by clicking the Add button. The system opens the Build Team dialog with the Replace and Match buttons disabled.

In addition to the options available at the top of the page, there are two more at the bottom of the page. The first option forces the Wizard to consider resources with the Proposed booking type during the substitution process. The second option allows you to specify a Resource Freeze Horizon date before which the Wizard will not substitute resources. Specify your desired settings and then click the Next button to continue. The system displays Step 3 of the Wizard, the Choose Related Projects page, shown in Figure 3-25.

The date of the Resource Freeze Horizon defaults to the current date.

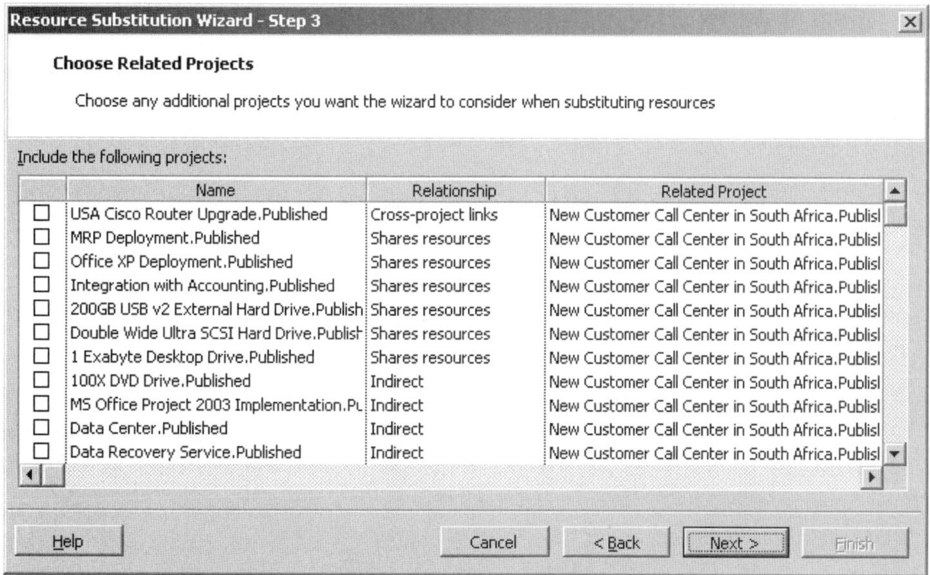

Figure 3-25: Resource Substitution Wizard Choose Related Projects page

Step 3 of the Resource Substitution Wizard displays a list of projects that either have a direct or indirect relationship with one or more of your selected projects. The system determines related projects in two ways: either through cross-project dependencies or by the sharing of common resources. The system defines the type of relationship in the Relationship column. The system defines projects are related through resources as either a direct relationship or an indirect relationship.

A direct relationship exists between two or more projects when they share one or more of the same resources. Because of this direct relationship, resource substitutions made in one project can directly affect any project whose relationship is direct (Shared Resources).

An Indirect relationship exists between your selected projects and other projects when the other projects share one or more resources with a project that has a Direct relationship with one of your selected projects... In other words, the relationship is "second cousin" in nature. To understand the Indirect relationship between projects, consider the example shown in Table 3-1.

Project A	Project B	Project C
Steve Garcia	Steve Garcia	Debbie Kruse
Marcia Bickel	Marcia Bickel	Evie Pruitt
Vic Merchant	Sue Burnett	Sue Burnett
George Stewart	David Erickson	David Erickson

Table 3-1: Project C has an Indirect relationship to Project A

In Table 3-1, Project A has a *direct* (Shares Resources) relationship to Project B through the two common resources, Steve Garcia and Marcia Bickel. Project B has a *direct* (Shares Resources) relationship to Project C through two other shared resources, Sue Burnett and David Erickson. Since Project A is directly related to Project B, and Project B is directly related to Project C, then Project C is *Indirectly* related to Project A. You can visualize this relationship in Figure 3-26.

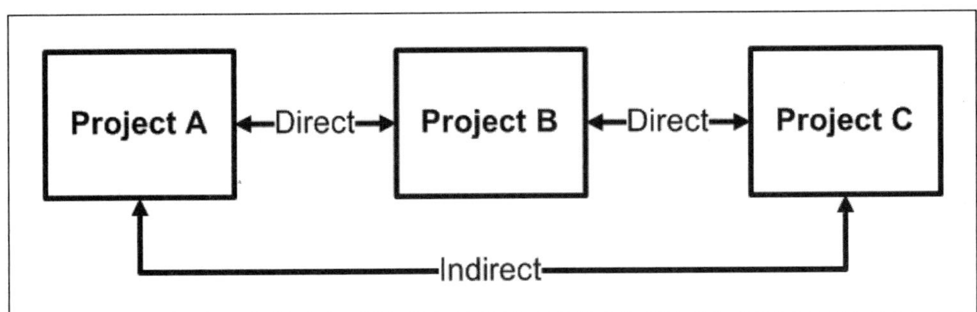

Figure 3-26: Project A has an Indirect relationship with Project C

You may be wondering why is it necessary for the Resource Substitution Wizard to determine whether a project has any kind of relationship with your selected projects. This is done to alert you that your resource substitutions could have a "ripple affect" on the related projects.

With this information in mind, select any related projects in which you want the Wizard to perform resource substitutions and then click the Next button to continue. The system displays Step 4 of the Wizard, the Choose Scheduling Options page, as shown in Figure 3-27.

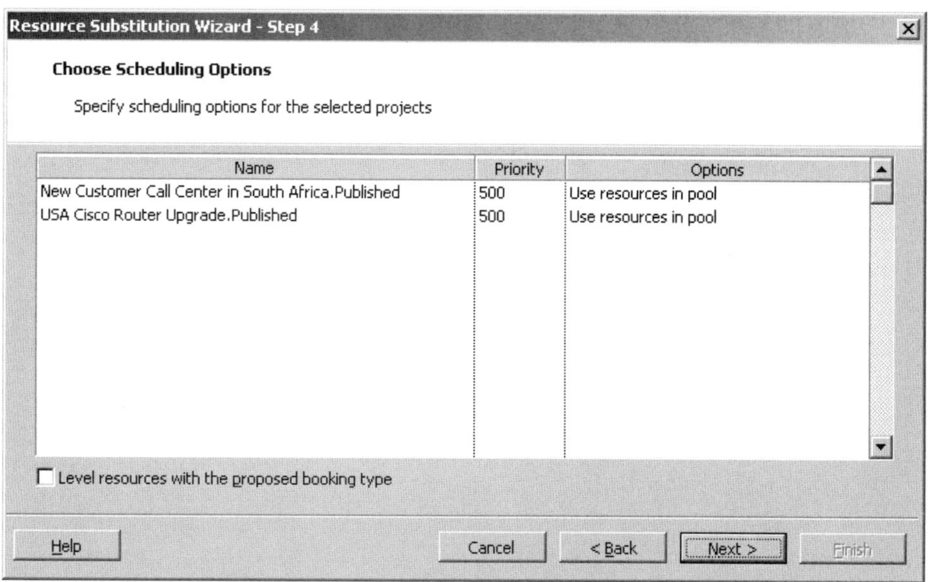

Figure 3-27: Resource Substitution Wizard Choose Scheduling Options page

Step 4 of the Resource Substitution Wizard allows you to set the relative priority for each selected project by increasing or decreasing the Priority number of each project in relationship to the others. You can set the Priority number of each selected project from 0 (lowest priority) to 1000 (highest priority). The wizard uses the priority value for each project to determine which project has first rights to an available resource with the highest priority projects taking precedence.

You may set an Options value for each project to determine whether to substitute resources from the Enterprise Resource Pool or from the selected project only. In addition, you may also choose to use to level Proposed resources that may become overallocated during the substitution process. To do so, select the Level resources with the proposed booking type checkbox and click Next to continue. The system displays Step 5 of the Wizard, the Substitute Resources page, as shown in Figure 3-28.

Select the Use resources in project option if you want to optimize the use of resources in your project team for one or more projects. Select the Use resources in pool option if you want to staff your project with the most available resources for one or more projects.

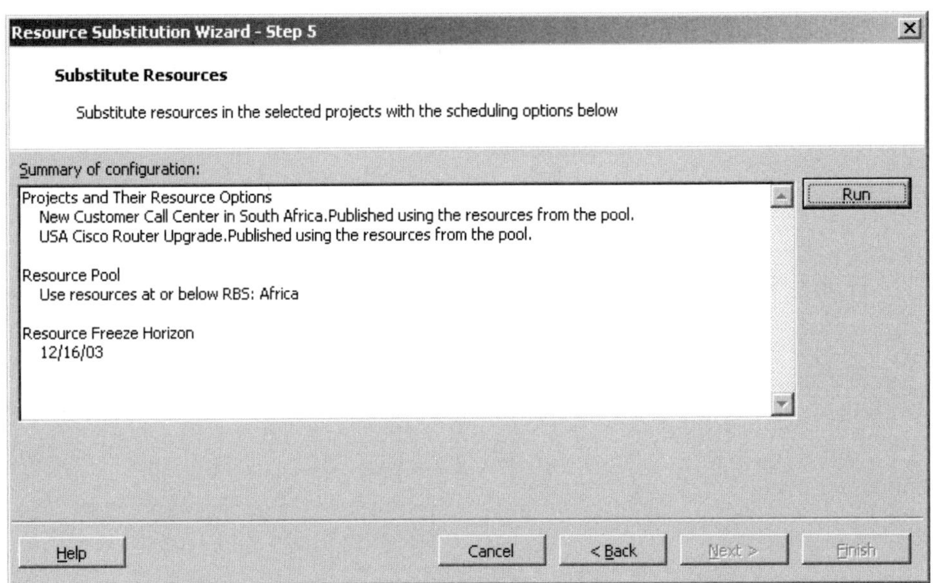

Figure 3-28: Resource Substitution Wizard Substitute Resources page

The page displays a textual summary of the substitution options you have chosen during the previous four steps. If you notice a mistake here, you can either cancel the run or step back through the dialogs to make changes. When you are satisfied with your selections click the Run button to activate the Wizard and make the resource substitutions. After you click the Run button, click the Next button. The system displays Step 6 of the Wizard, the Review Results page, shown in Figure 3-29.

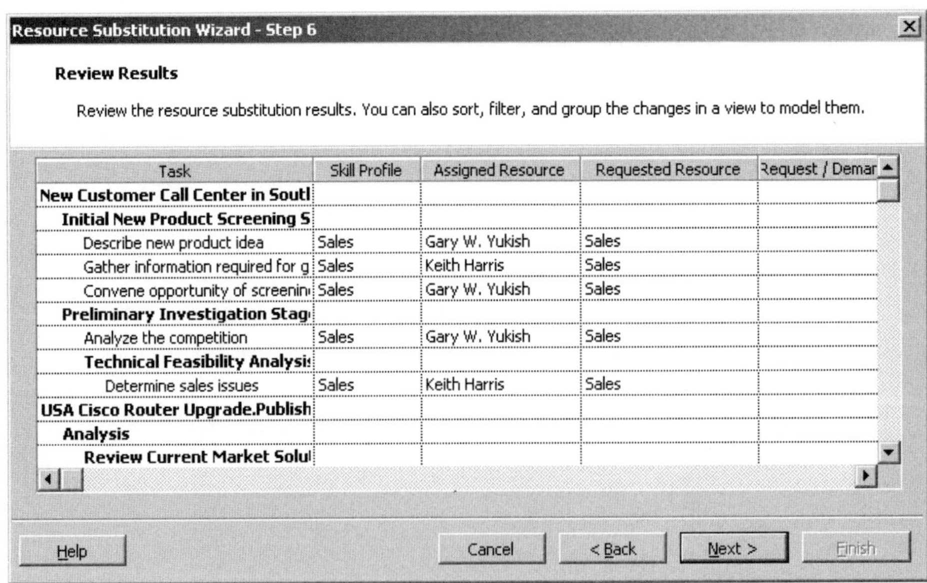

Figure 3-29: Resource Substitution Wizard Review Results page

The system displays the results of the resource substitution process for each task. The display contains the task name, the skill set acted upon, the name of the new resource assigned by the Wizard, the original resource, and the Request/Demand status of the original assignment. Review the results of the resource substitution process and click the Next button when you are satisfied with the results.

msProjectExperts recommends that you thoroughly review the results of the substitution process. Before moving on to Page 7, confirm that the resource substitutions are acceptable to your resource planning needs. If the results of the resource substitution process are not acceptable, click the Cancel button and then make modifications to your projects and/or to the resource assignments in the projects.

The system displays Step 7 of the Wizard, the Choose Update Options page, shown in Figure 3-30.

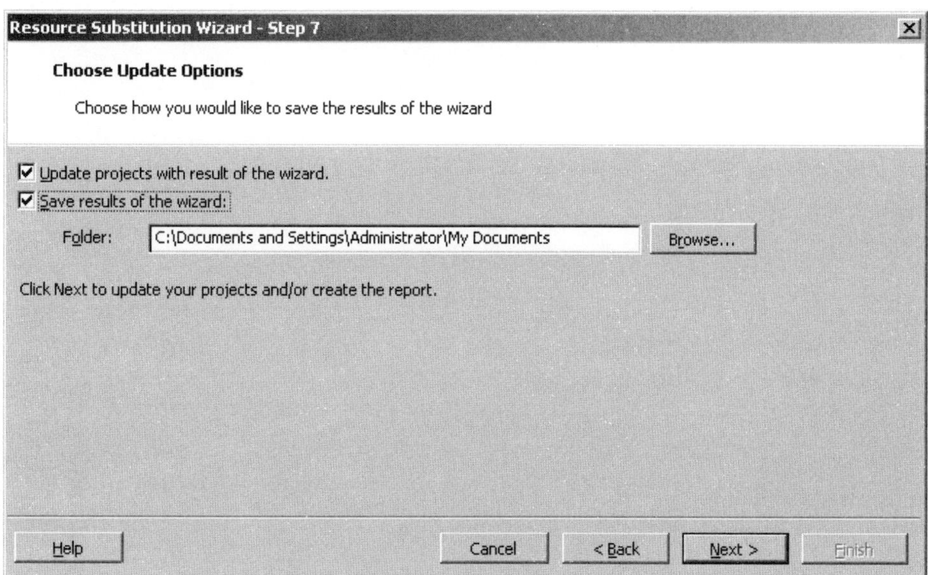

Figure 3-30: Resource Substitution Wizard Review Results page

The Step 7 page allows you to select the destination of the substitution results. To cancel the process and abandon the substitutions, click the Cancel button. To update the selected projects with the chosen resources, select the Update projects with result of the wizard option. To save the results of the substitution process for later review, select the Save results of the wizard option allowing you to save the results as a standard project file to your hard drive or a network version in a network share. Click the Next button to continue. The system displays Step 8 of the Wizard, the Choose Update Options page, as shown in Figure 3-31.

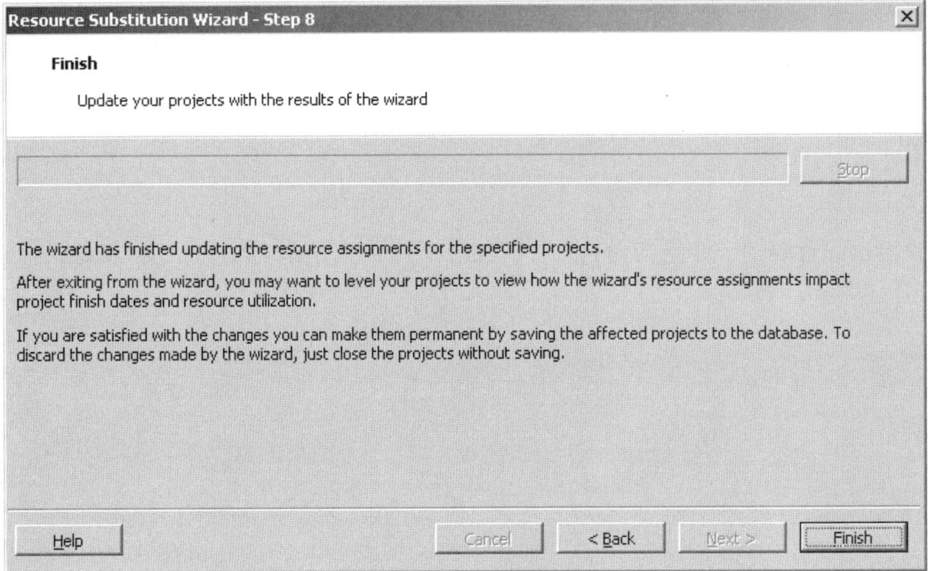

Figure 3-31: Resource Substitution Wizard Finish page

The Finish page is the final step of the Resource Substitution Wizard, where the system makes several suggestions before you proceed. The Wizard suggests leveling the plan to resolve any remaining resource overallocations. The Wizard also informs you that you can still abandon the resource substitution changes to any project simply by not saving the project plan to the database. Click the Finish button to complete the process.

msProjectExperts recommends that you use extreme caution when using the Resource Substitution Wizard. This tool is not a "magic pill" that can solve all of your resource allocation issues, nor will it prevent resource overallocations from occurring in your projects.

msProjectExperts recommends that you use the Resource Substitution Wizard is to do “trial resource loading” on a group of future planned projects for analysis of resource allocation issues. For the most part, you should use the two manual methods for making resource assignments to tasks, which are the Task Entry View and the Assign Resources dialog box.

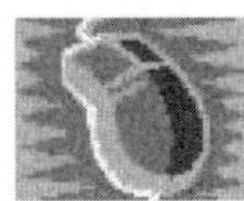

Hands On Exercise

Exercise 3-8

Run the Resource Substitution wizard.

1. Using the same plan you used in Exercise 3-6, make sure that you have selected at least one actual resource for each generic resource in your plan. You may add up to two actual resources matching the generic resource specified in the plan.
2. From the Tools menu, select Substitute resources, click Next in the welcome screen
3. Select only the project you're working on in the Choose Projects screen
4. Include resources from the selected projects and do not select any related projects
5. Continue clicking the Next button, then click the Run button to run the Wizard
6. View your results
7. Select the Update projects with result of the wizard option and then click Finish

Leveling Overallocated Resources

During the process of assigning resources to tasks, resources may become overallocated. Methodologies for leveling overallocated resources are integral for the effective use of the resource functionality in Project Professional 2003.

Overallocation Defined

A resource overallocation occurs when you assign a resource to perform more work than the resource can accomplish in the working time available. For example, if you assign a resource to perform 32 hours of work in a single 8-hour working day, then that resource is overallocated. Microsoft Project Professional determines which resources are overallocated based on the work values for assigned tasks, the maximum number of units available for the resource, and the calendar used by the resource.

Resource Leveling Defined

Resource leveling is the process of resolving resource overallocations. You have two choices for leveling overallocated resources:

- Manual leveling
- Automatic leveling

Manual leveling includes any approach that you, the project manager, use to resolve the overallocation. Manual methods include approaches such as adding resources to an effort-driven task to shorten the duration of the task, increasing the availability of overallocated resources, or substituting an available resource for the overallocated resource. The number of manual leveling methods available to you is limited only by your own imagination and creativity.

Automatic leveling refers to the use of the built-in leveling routines in Microsoft Project Professional. When the Microsoft Project levels a resource overallocation, the software delays tasks or splits tasks according to single or multiple leveling factors. Keep in mind that automatic leveling cannot and will not change the resources assigned to a task or the assignment Units for each resource on the task.

Basic Leveling Techniques

If you want to tackle automatic leveling using Microsoft Project's built-in leveling capabilities, you should first display the Resource Management toolbar by clicking View ➢ Toolbars ➢ Resource Management. This toolbar contains links to the Resource Allocation view, the Task Entry view, as well as the ability to launch the Resource Substitution Wizard, find overallocations, and add users from the pool.

While you are engaged in resource leveling, a couple of Views will be useful to you. The Leveling Gantt view displays the pre-leveling and post-leveling view of each task in your project. To apply this view, click View ➢ More Views ➢ Leveling Gantt. The Resource Allocation view also allows you to level one overallocated resource at a time. To apply this view, click View ➢ More Views ➢ Resource Overallocation.

Microsoft Project Professional supports two types of leveling scenarios. You can level a plan only within its available slack or you can completely level the plan. If you choose to level a plan within its available slack, the system will level all overallocations to the best of its ability, but will not change the finish date of your project. You can use this approach to determine the head count your project will require in order to meet the date. If you level the project completely, the system will attempt to level every resource overallocation, which often results is a finish date later than originally scheduled.

If you want to know the earliest realistic date that you project can finish, then level the project completely. If you absolutely must finish the project by a certain date, then you should level only within available slack, and then use other methods of manual leveling to finish the leveling process.

To use the automatic leveling capabilities of Microsoft Project Professional, click Tools ➢ Level Resources. The Resource Leveling dialog displays as shown in Figure 3-32.

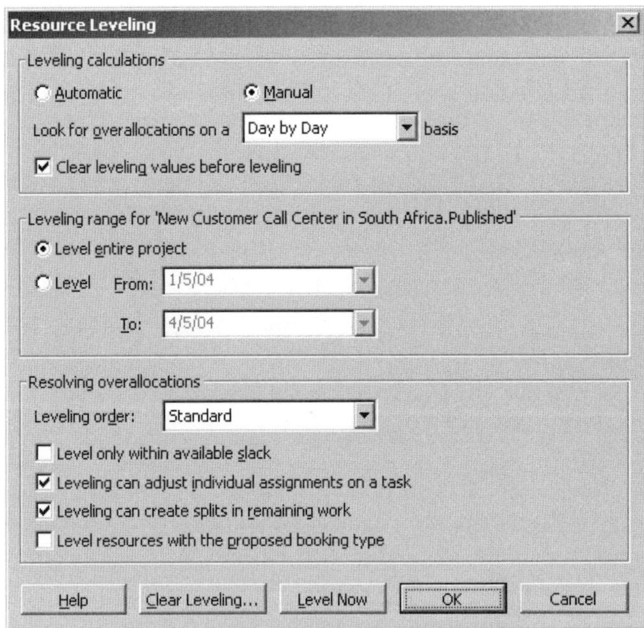

Figure 3-32: Resource Leveling dialog box

The Resource Leveling dialog offers you three sets of leveling options:

- Leveling calculations
- Leveling range
- Resolving Overallocations

The first *Leveling calculation* option allows you set the calculations to either Automatic or Manual. To maintain as much control of the leveling process as possible, you should set the Leveling calculations option to Manual so that the system will level only when you click the Level Now button. If you select the Clear leveling values before leveling option, the system will remove any leveling previously applied before leveling your project. If you deselect this option, the system will level on top of previous values. You can also specify the time sensitivity used in leveling by setting the Look for overallocations on a basis option of minutes, hours, days, weeks, or months.

msProjectExperts recommends that you never select Automatic leveling in the Resource Leveling dialog box. When applied, Automatic Leveling will not only level the active project, but will also level all other open projects in need of leveling, and do so without asking your permission!

The *Leveling range* option allows you to select tasks for leveling based on a date range or you may simply select the entire project.

The *Resolving overallocations* section offers several important options. The Leveling Order option affects how the system determines which tasks to delay or split when resolving resource allocations. You should select either the Standard or Priority, Standard order for leveling. Select the Level only within available slack option to force the system to honor the finish date set of your project. Select the Leveling can adjust individual assignments on a task option to allow the system to make changes to one resource assigned to a task independently from another resource assigned to the same task. Select the Leveling can create splits in remaining work option to allow the system to split tasks to resolve overallocations. Select the Level resources with the proposed booking type option to include Proposed resources in the leveling process.

The Standard leveling order uses five factors to determine which tasks to delay or split. These factors are predecessors, amount of total slack, start date, priority number, and constraints. The Priority, Standard leveling order uses the same five factors, but it gives precedence to the task Priority number.

By default, Microsoft Project Professional *does not* level overallocated resources with the Proposed booking type. Because all resource overallocations are a risk to your project finish date, msProjectExperts recommends that you include resources with the Proposed booking type in the leveling process.

After selecting your leveling options, click the Level Now button. If you have a resource View currently applied, the system displays the Level Now dialog, as is shown in Figure 3-33. You may select the Entire Pool option to level all overallocated resources or you can choose the Selected resources option to level only those resources that you have selected. Click OK when you are ready and the system performs the leveling according to your specifications.

Figure 3-33: Level Now dialog box

For best results with resource leveling, use the following methodology when leveling overallocated resources:

1. Level in any resource view, such as the Resource Usage view
2. Level only one overallocated resource at a time
3. Clear the results of resource leveling in any task view, such as the Leveling Gantt view

Assigning Leveling Priorities to Tasks

You can set the task priority used by the leveling system by opening the Task Information dialog, shown in Figure 3-34. The Priority field is accessible from the General tab, as shown in the figure. You can set priorities to any value between 0 and 1000, where 1000 indicates to the system not to level and all other priorities are relative to one another. To work with priorities across many tasks, consider inserting the column into a task view such as the Gantt Chart view.

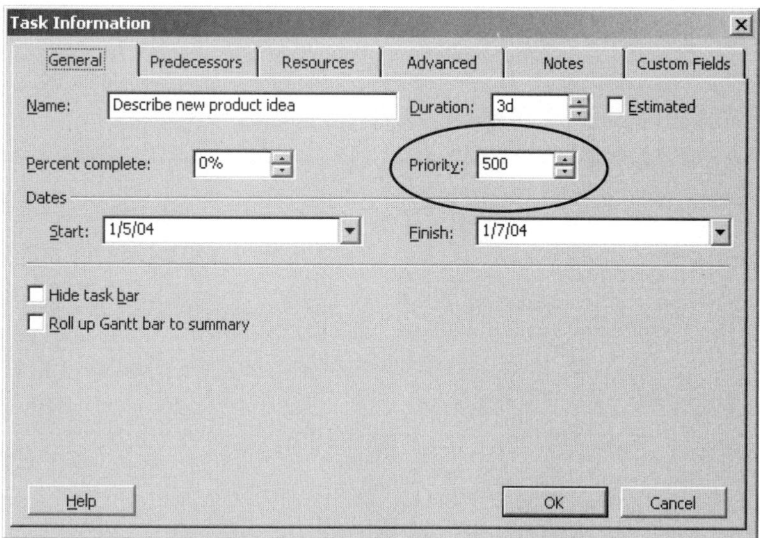

Figure 3-34: Task Information dialog box – Set task priority

For simplicity's sake, this course offers only a brief presentation on resource leveling. Resolving resource overallocations is a complex topic, however, and requires advanced skills in using Microsoft Project 2003. msProjectExperts presents a complete treatment of the subject in the Advanced Microsoft Project 2003 course.

Hands On Exercise

Exercise 3-9

Level overallocated resources.

1. Set leveling priorities for tasks
2. Select Tools ➢ Level Resources
3. Set your leveling options
4. Click Level Now
5. Select Tools ➢ Level Resources and click Clear Leveling
6. Select the Entire project option when prompted
7. Save and close your project plan

Module 04

Publishing and Republishing Work Assignments

Learning Objectives

After completing this module, you will be able to:

- Control default publishing behavior
- Publish work assignments to resources
- Take over assignments for another Project Manager
- Republish assignment information
- Understand the project Spooler
- Request progress
- Add a Published field to the timesheet

Understanding Project Server Publishing

When you publish both the project and the task assignments, following are the default behaviors of Microsoft Project Server:

- The project is visible in both Project Center views and detailed Project views in Project Web Access
- Information in both custom Project and Task fields populates the Project Center views and detailed Project views
- Information about the project is processed in the OLAP cube and is available for viewing in Portfolio Analyzer view
- Resource availability information shown in the Resource Center view includes resource information from the new project
- The new project displays on the list of available projects in the Risks, Issues, and Documents pages
- Resources can see their task assignments for the project on their timesheet in the View My Tasks page
- Resource assignments for the project are visible in the View resource assignments page

The act of publishing assignments controls who will receive task updates from resources working on the project. Project Server designates the project manager who initially publishes the assignments as the Manager of those assignments. The assignment manager receives task updates from team members assigned to the selected tasks.

Although only one project manager may open and revise a project plan at one time, more than one manager can be involved in managing and updating the plan. In some organizations, for instance, multiple resource managers are responsible for assigning work and updating progress in a single plan. To accommodate this, each manager must open the project and publish the assignments for resources they manage. Remember that when you publish an assignment, the updates for that task will flow back to you.

Controlling Default Publishing Behavior

You can control Microsoft Project's default publishing behavior on a project-by-project basis by making changes on the Collaborate tab of the Options dialog. Click Tools menu ➤ Options, and then select the Options tab in the Options dialog shown in Figure 4-1. The Collaborate page of the Options dialog contains the default values for the following Collaboration options:

- The system uses information from the Microsoft Project Server Accounts dialog box to set the values for the *Collaborate using*, *Project Server URL*, and *Identification for Project Server* fields. The information displayed here is set by the session; therefore, the only value you can change is the *E-mail address* field.

To display the Microsoft Project Server Accounts dialog, click Tools ➤ Enterprise Options ➤ Microsoft Office Project Server Accounts.

- *When you select the Allow resources to delegate tasks using Microsoft project Server* option, you give permission to your project team members to delegate their tasks to other resources, providing that your Project Server administrator has enabled task delegation in your environment. If your administrator has disabled task delegation, then this setting will have no effect on the local plan.
- The next option in the dialog, *Publish New and Changed Assignments updates resources' assignments when,* allows you to determine what the system recognizes as a change to an assignment when you use the Publish new and changed assignments feature from the Collaborate menu. Selecting the Start, Finish, % Complete or outline changes option causes the system to mark the task for an update only when one of these factors change. Selecting the Any task information option causes the system to mark a task for updating when any information on the task changes.

This is an important setting, and being aware of it can spare you much grief when trying to understand system behavior. For example, if you select the first of the two options, the system will not update a task simply because you changed the name of the task in the project plan.

- The *On every save, publish the following information to Microsoft Project Server* options allow you to automate publishing with a project save. You have the choice to select one or both New and Changed assignment and/or Project Summary with or without full project plan information.

msProjectExperts recommends that you do not activate the automatic publish on save option and that you retain control of publishing manually to avoid unintended consequences. Imagine that you have decided to spend a day or two making significant changes to your plan and on the first day you decide to save your plan before breaking for lunch. If you forget to turn this option off, the system will push out your half-baked changes to the team.

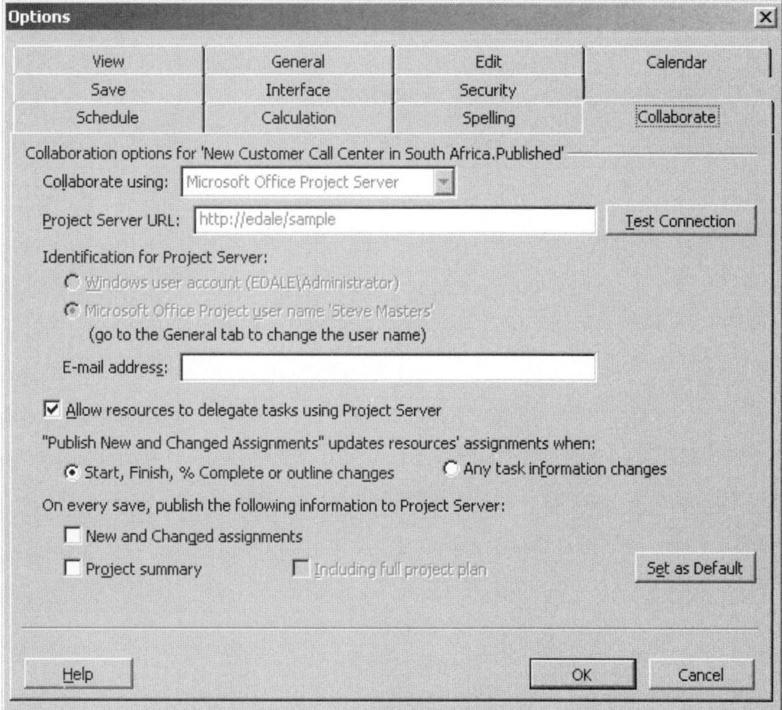

Figure 4-1: Options dialog box Collaborate page

Publishing: Best Practices

As with opening and saving project plans, it is important to develop good publishing habits with Microsoft Project Professional. Some of these good habits include:

- Do not publish resource assignments until you are ready to inform project team members of their task work in the plan.
- When you are ready to publish, it is best to have only one project open.
- When you have been updating a plan, do not publish the plan until after you have saved your changes to the server.
- Do not open a project from the server, save it as an .mpp file, and then attempt to publish the .mpp plan. The system will prevent you from publishing the .mpp project, since it is a non-enterprise project.

Saving a project plan to Project Server takes longer than saving an mpp file. Saving and Publishing take much longer than saving alone. Therefore, you should never activate both auto-save and automatic publishing, as the interruptions to your workflow will quickly become unbearable.

Publishing Assignments and Project Information

You access publishing functions by clicking Collaborate ➢ Publish, as shown in Figure 4-2. You have three publishing choices plus a republish selection. The distinction between the three publishing options is as follows:

- **All Information**: Automatically selects all information eligible to be publishing including new and changed assignments as well as the plan and plan details.
- **New and Changed Assignments**: Selects all new and not previously published assignments as well as assignments that have changed according to the criteria you selected on the Collaborate page of the Options dialog.
- **Project Plan**: Publishes only project information and not assignments to Project Server.
- **Republish Assignments**: Allows the manager to choose assignments for republishing whether or not they have changed according to the system criteria.

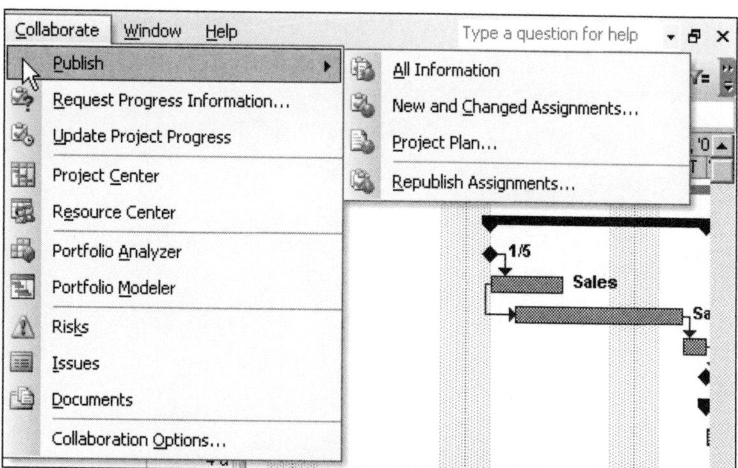

Figure 4-2: Publish menu choices

When you click Collaborate ➢ Publish ➢ All Information, Microsoft Project publishes all available project information and assignments. Before publishing, the system will present the alert shown in Figure 4-3. You may either click OK to continue or Cancel to stop the action. If you click OK, the publishing operation will continue without further user interface activity.

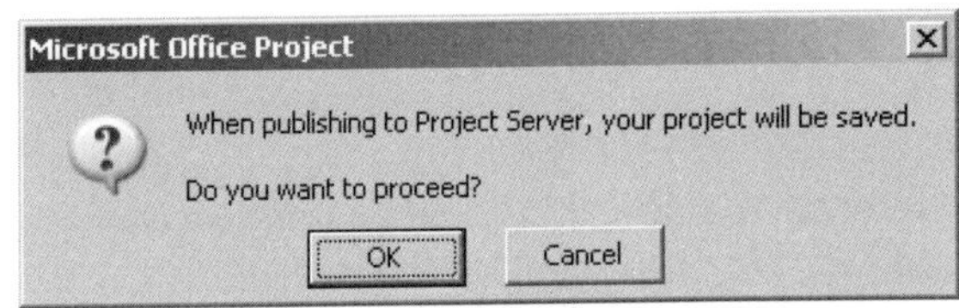

Figure 4-3: Microsoft Project alert

When you click Collaborate ➤ Publish ➤ New and Changed Assignments, the system first displays the same alert box shown in Figure 4-3 and when you click OK, it then opens the Publish New and Changed Assignments dialog shown in Figure 4-4. The system first selects all eligible task assignments and lists them in the dialog. You may refine the selection by choosing either Entire project, Current view, or Selected items from the Publish new and changed assignments for pick list at the top. Selecting the Current view option limits the selection to only what is currently visible in the project view, including any filters you may have applied to the view. Choosing the Selected items option assumes that you have selected one or more tasks in the plan for which to publish assignments. The system groups the assignments by resource. You can change this by selecting the Task radio button below the task list display.

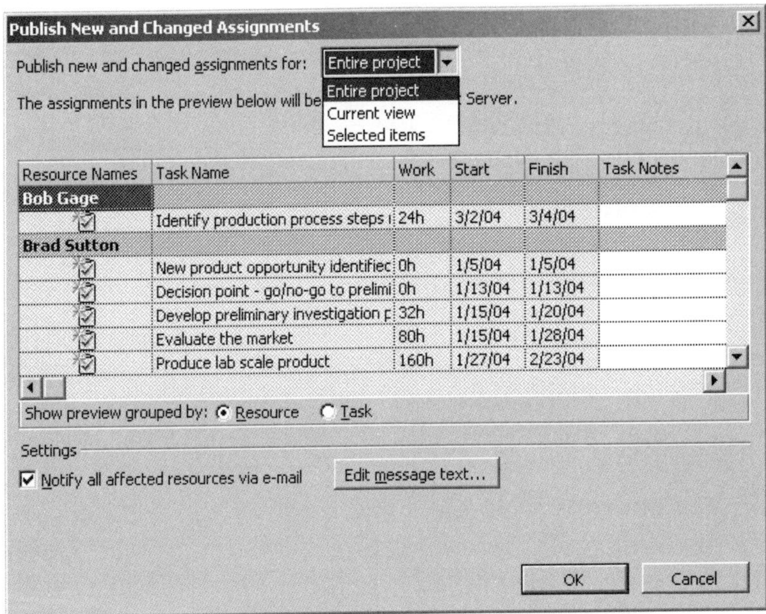

Figure 4-4: Publish New and Changed Assignments dialog box

Publishing assignments generates e-mail notifications to the resources who are receiving the assignments if your system has the notification engine enabled. These notification e-mails contain a link back to Project Web Access. You can personalize the message sent by clicking the Edit message text button to open the Edit message text dialog shown in Figure 4-5. Replace the existing message or add a personalization to it, and then click the OK button.

To stop an e-mail notification from generating, deselect the Notify all affected resources via e-mail option in the Settings section of the dialog.

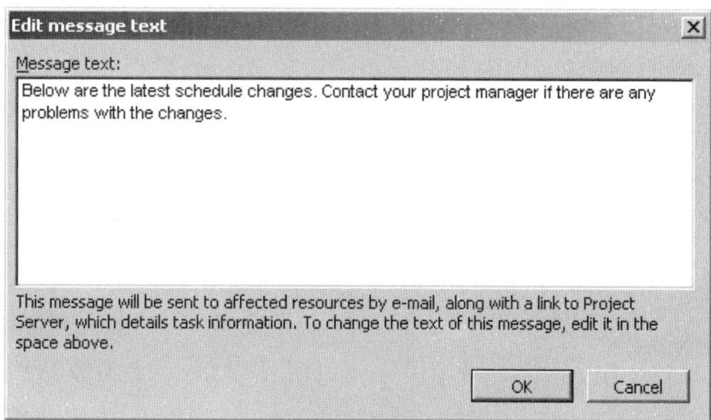

Figure 4-5: Personalize your e-mail message

When you click Collaborate ➢ Publish ➢ Project Plan, the system opens the Publish Project Plan dialog shown in Figure 4-6. Here you can select to publish either the Summary (Project Summary Task) or the entire plan along with the Summary.

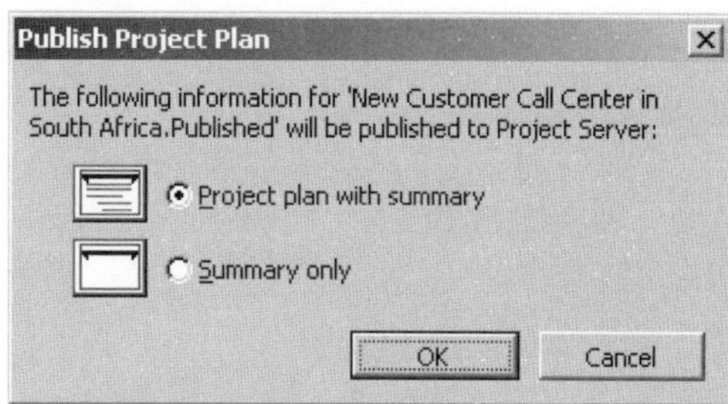

Figure 4-6: Publish Project Plan dialog box

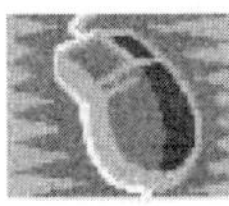

Hands On Exercise

Exercise 4-1

Publish your plan to the Microsoft Project Server.

1. Connect to Project Server if you're not already connected
2. Open your plan student#+test2 (eg: 04test2)
3. Before publishing, make sure that you assign some tasks to some of your special classroom resources.
4. Select Collaborate ➢ Publish ➢ All Information
5. Click OK when prompted
6. Save and close your plan

Republishing Assignments

When you click Collaborate ➢ Publish ➢ Republish Assignments, the system opens essentially the same dialog as the one used for Publishing Assignments. Shown in Figure 4-7, there are several important differences in this dialog besides the title change to Republish Assignments. Notice that there are two different options in the Settings section at the bottom of the dialog.

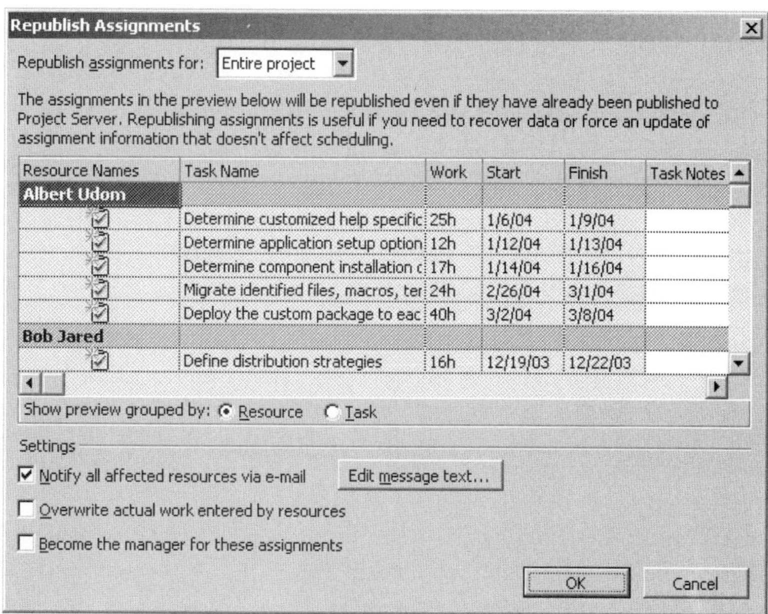

Figure 4-7: Republish Assignments dialog box

You can use the Republish Assignments dialog to resend assignments when resources accidentally hide them, or when a change occurs that does not trigger an update as set in your options. You also use the Republish Assignments dialog to take over management of assignments from another project manager. To take over another project manager's assignments, complete the following steps:

1. Open the other manager's project
2. Select the tasks for which you will become the project manager
3. Click Collaborate ➢ Publish ➢ Republish Assignments
4. Select the Become the manager for these assignments option and click OK.

Completing the preceding steps redirects the task updates from project team members to you instead of the original manager. If this is a temporary takeover, when the original project manager returns to work, that person must complete the exact same steps to return the flow of task updates back to them.

If you de-select the e-mail notification check box, the updates for the tasks will flow to you without the resource being aware of the change.

You can also use the Republish Assignments dialog to "push" task progress from the project plan back to a resource's timesheet in Project Web Access after you have made manual updates to progress within Microsoft Project Professional. For example, if a resource is out sick on reporting day, you as the project manager may need to update their task progress despite not having timesheet input from the resource.

After entering actual progress in the Microsoft Project plan, you will use the Republish Assignments feature to "synch up" the new actual work values with the user's timesheet. To do so, select the Overwrite actual work entered by resources option in the Republish Assignments dialog and click OK.

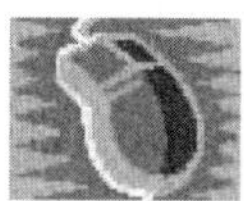

Hands On Exercise

Exercise 4-2

Take ownership of another manager's tasks by republishing the assignments.

1. Open the project plan belonging to the student next to you
2. Select a couple current tasks
3. Select Collaborate ➢ Publish ➢ Republish Assignments
4. Notice the "Overwrite actual work entered by resources" option
5. Select the "Become the manager for these assignments" option
6. Click OK
7. Save and close the plan

Understanding the Microsoft Project Spooler

The Project Spooler works with you behind the scenes as a silent and barely visible partner until something goes wrong. The Project Spooler starts when you launch Project Professional and stays active but idle until it is required. The spooler icon appears in the tray area on the right end of your Windows Taskbar. In Figure 4-8, the spooler icon is the one on the left.

Figure 4-8: Spooler icon at left end of system tray

The spooler functions much like the print spooler on your computer. It queues publishing jobs in the background so you can continue to work uninterrupted when the server cannot immediately respond to your publishing action.

If an error occurs during publishing, the Spooler icon displays a flashing red exclamation point next to the computer graphic, shown in Figure 4-9, and the system displays an alert dialog box shown in Figure 4-10.

Figure 4-9: Spooler icon shows an error

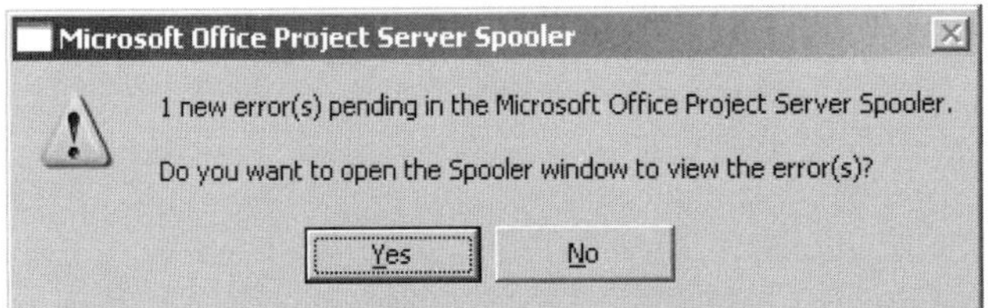

Figure 4-10: Microsoft Project Server Spooler error dialog box

If you click the Yes button in the Spooler dialog or double-click the Spooler icon in the system tray, the system displays the Spooler window shown in Figure 4-11. You can investigate the specific error once the Spooler window is open, however, only two actions are available for solving the Spooler error from the Actions menu: Retry or Undo. Clicking the Retry option will repeat the publishing action, while clicking the Undo button will "roll back" the publishing action.

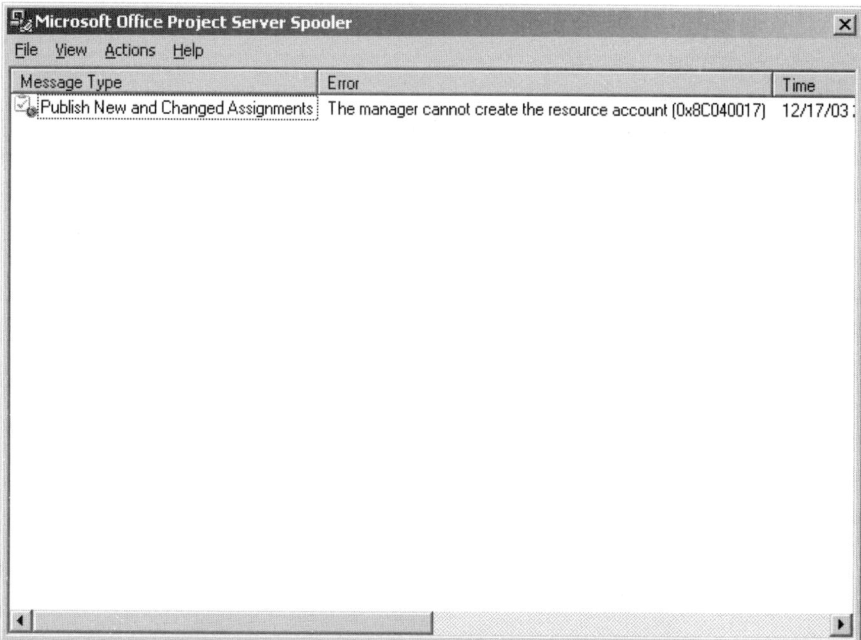

Figure 4-11: View the error detail in the Spooler window

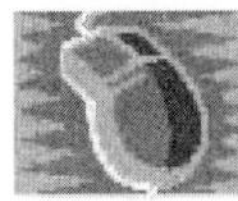

Hands On Exercise

Exercise 4-3

Examine the Microsoft Project Server Spooler for publishing errors.

1. Locate the Spooler icon on the task bar
2. Double click the Spooler icon to open the spooler

Requesting Task Progress Outside the Normal Flow

In the normal flow of project communication, Resources report progress against tasks through their timesheet based on the periodic reporting requirements established by the business. Occasionally you may want to remind a resource that progress is due or to send you a progress report that is out of the ordinary reporting cycle. To accomplish this, click Collaborate ➢ Request Progress Information to open the Request Progress Information dialog shown in Figure 4-12. You will typically do this for specific tasks, so select the tasks first, and the dialog will automatically choose the Selected items option in the Request progress information for field.

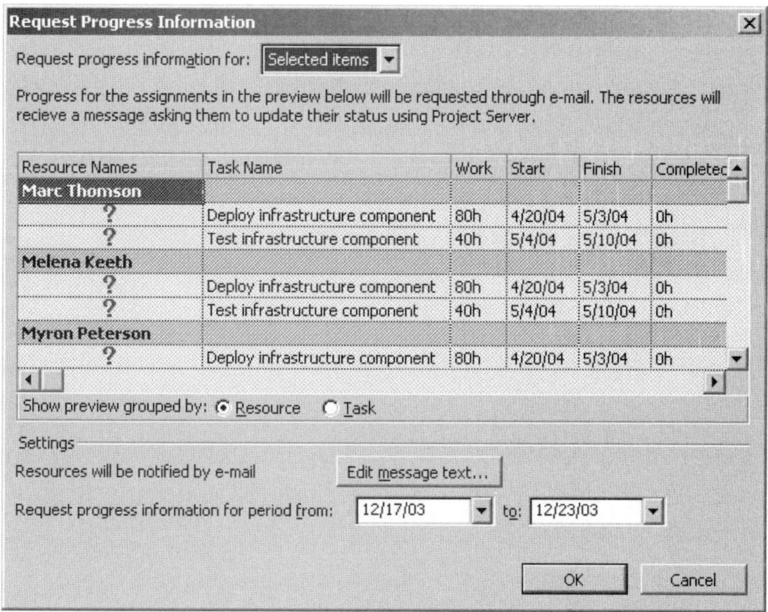

Figure 4-12: Request Progress Information dialog box

The system notifies the affected resources of this request through e-mail. It also marks the task in your plan with the icon shown in Figure 4-13. This icon appears in the indicators field in your project plan. The icon also appears in the users' timesheet indicating that a progress request is pending for the task.

Figure 4-13: Request Progress Information task indicator

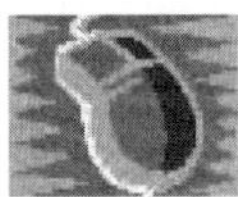

Hands On Exercise

Exercise 4-4

Request progress information from your team members.

1. Open the test2 project plan
2. Select two tasks that have one of the special classroom resources assigned
3. Select Collaborate ➢ Request Progress Information
4. Click OK to send the request
5. Save the project plan

Determining Timesheet (Published) Fields

The default fields displayed in task list portion of each user's timesheet in Project Web Access are the same for each tracking method; however, the fields available for data entry vary. The default fields are:

- Indicator
- Task Name
- Work
- % Work Complete
- Actual Work
- Remaining Work
- Start
- Finish
- Update Sent
- Project
- Assigned to
- Lead Name

You can supplement the default columns by adding additional fields to the list of published fields. Additional fields can include standard fields, custom fields, and enterprise custom fields. You can add these simply to provide additional information to your team member or as additional reporting fields.

To supplement the list of fields available for a project in each team member's timesheet, complete the following steps:

1. Open the project in which you want the additional fields to appear
2. Click Tools ➢ Customize ➢ Published Fields to open the Customize Published Fields dialog shown in Figure 4-14
3. From the Available fields list on the left, select one or more additional fields, and then click the Copy button (**>**)
4. Select each field in the Fields in the Tasks View list. If you want to allow the user to report information through the field, select the Let resource change field option
5. Click the OK button

You will need to republish any previously published assignments in your project to push the change to your resources' time sheets by clicking Collaborate ➢ Publish ➢ Republish Assignments.

In Figure 4-14, notice that I have added the Actual Start and Actual Finish fields to the list of Published fields, and that I have set each field so that the resources can edit the field.

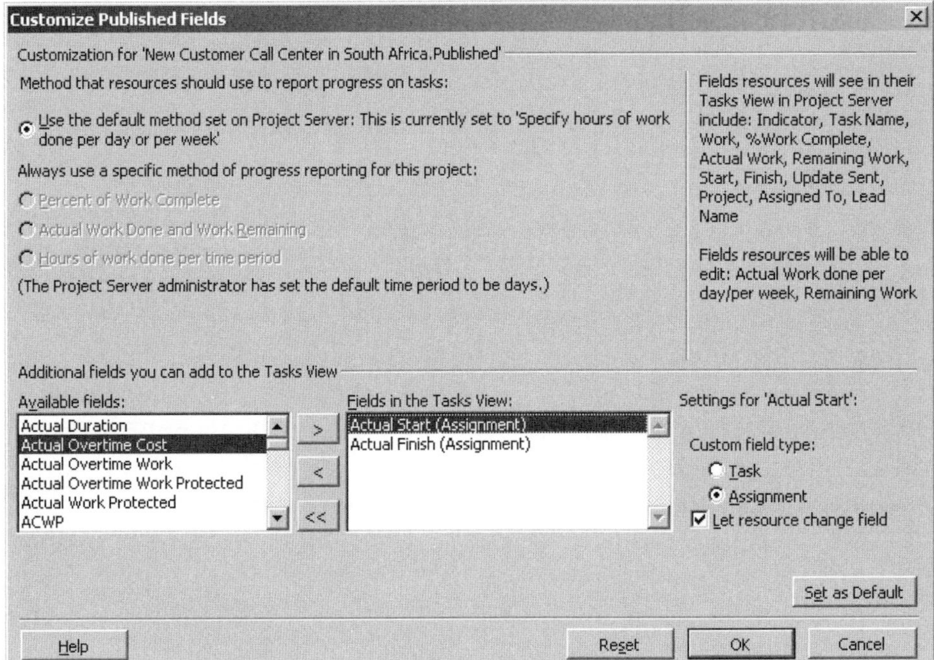

Figure 4-14: Customize Published Fields dialog box

You can add additional Published fields on a project-by-project basis. If your organization wishes to add a standardized list of custom fields for every project, your Project Server administrator should add the additional fields to each of your organization's enterprise project templates.

Once you have added additional columns to your team members' timesheets for a given project, your Project Server administrator must add the fields to the Timesheet view for all users. The Project Server administrator can also determine the order of each field in the Timesheet view.

The system displays the additional Published fields in the task list portion of each team member's View My Tasks page, as shown in Figure 4-15. Notice in the figure that I am entering an Actual Start date for a task.

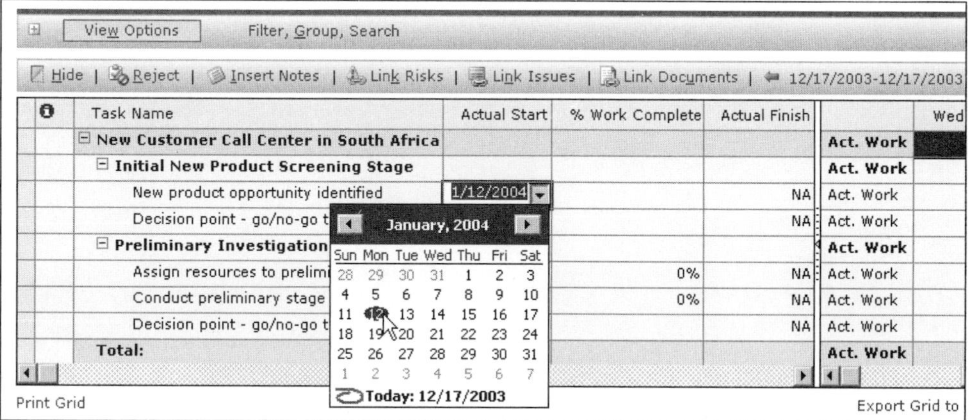

Figure 4-15: Additional Published fields added to the View My Tasks page

When determining the fields that you want pushed to the timesheet, keep in mind that Enterprise Task Fields do not carry discreet values at the assignment level. These are not suitable for capturing values entered by the resources.

Module 05

Project Web Access Overview

Learning Objectives

After completing this module, you will be able to:

- Understand the basic features of the Microsoft Project Web Access user interface
- Select additional options in the Actions pane of a Project Web Access page
- Use Customization Tabs and the Action Bar on a Project Web Access page
- Use the Action Bar on a Project
- Manipulate the data grid on a Project Web Access page
- Print or export the data grid on a Project Web Access page

Using the Project Web Access User Interface

You access information in the Microsoft Project Server through the Microsoft Project Web Access pages in the Internet Explorer. When you enter a valid URL for your company's Project Web Access site in the address bar of the Internet Explorer, the system automatically logs you into the site when you are using Windows Authentication. The Project Web Access Home page displays by default each time you access the site. Figure 5-1 shows a typical Project Manager's home page.

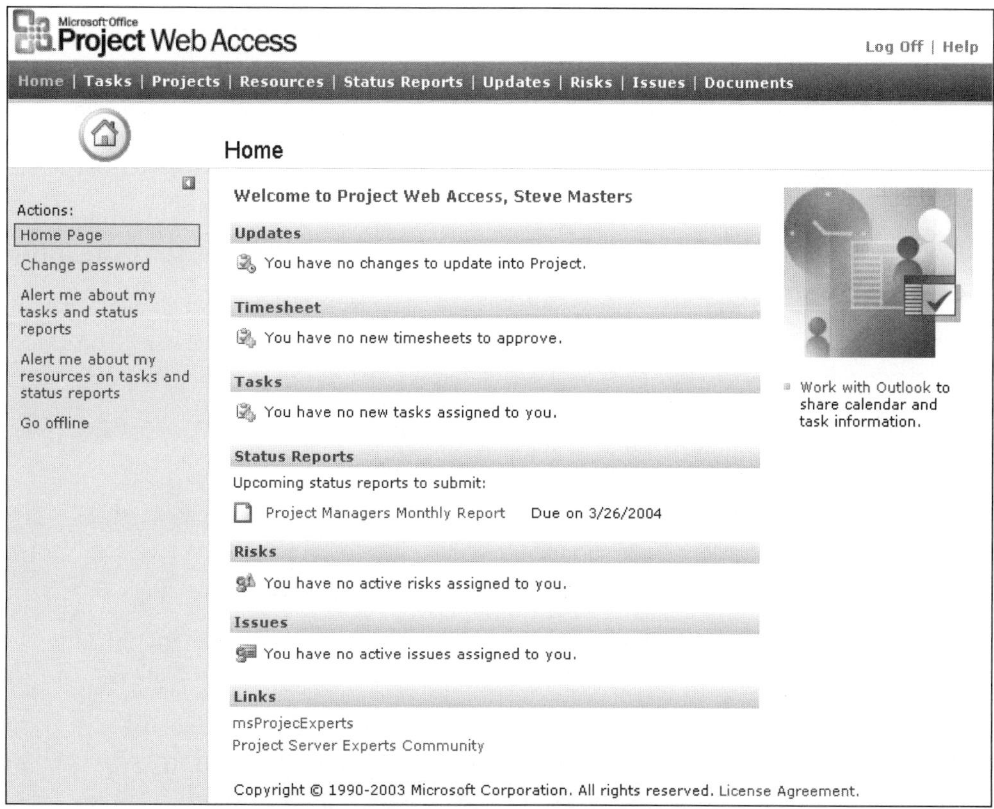

Figure 5-1: Microsoft Project Web Access Home page for a project manager

The central area of the Home page contains links for the relevant sections of Project Web Access, based on your security permissions. In Figure 5-3, there are sections for Updates, Timesheet, Tasks, Status Reports, Risks, Issues, and Links. The Home page for every user contains the Tasks, Status Reports, Issues, and Risks sections. The Updates section appears only on the Home page of project managers. The Timesheet section appears only on the Home page for those users who have timesheet approval authority. The Links section contains hyperlinks for two Internet sites that contain helpful information for project managers.

Menu Bar

The Project Web Access user interface offers a blue and white menu bar at the top of each page. This menu bar lists your viewable selections, based on your role in the project management environment. Figure 5-2 shows the Project Web Access menu bar for a project manager.

Figure 5-2: Project Web Access menu bar

The menu options available on the Project Web Access menu bar include:

- **Home**: The default page which is displayed each time you log into Project Web Access.
- **Tasks**: Displays the View My Tasks page used by all team members to enter and submit actual work values.
- **Projects**: Displays the Project Center page where you can access project views and project analysis features.
- **Resources**: Displays the Resource Center page where you can view resource information and resource analysis features.
- **Status Reports**: Displays the Status Reports Overview page. Managers can use this page to create Status Report requests, while team members will use this page to enter and submit Status Reports.
- **Updates**: Displays the Updates page. Project Managers use the Updates page to receive, review, and update actual progress.
- **Risks**: Displays the Risks page where all interested parties can create risks, track risks, and develop contingency plans in case those risks occur.
- **Documents**: Displays the Documents page where all interested parties can upload documents either to a specific project or to a public document library.
- **Issues**: Displays the Issues page where all interested parties can create and track issues relating to a specific project.
- **Admin**: Displays the Administration Overview page. Administrators use the administration menu to control and manage the Project Server environment.
- **Log Off**: Logs off the current user.
- **Help**: Displays a context-sensitive Help window in a sidepane on the right side of Project Web Access pages.

Actions Pane

Most of the pages in Project Web Access include an actions pane or "sidepane" on the left side of the page. The links in each respective actions pane offer additional actions that you can take. Figure 5-3 shows the actions pane for the Home page, while Figure 5-4 shows the actions pane for View My Tasks page. Figures 5-5 and 5-6 show the actions pane for the Project Center and Resource Center pages respectively.

Keep in mind while viewing the figures that these are samples and that you may see the same menus in your system with slight variations. The selections may vary according to the way your Project Server administrator configures your system and change over time as you use the application. For instance, a link selection appears on some of these as soon as you use the custom link feature for the first time.

Figure 5-3: Home page actions pane

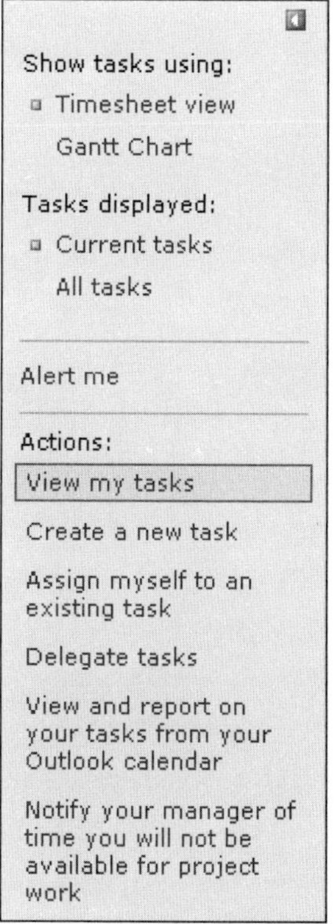

Figure 5-4: View My Tasks actions pane

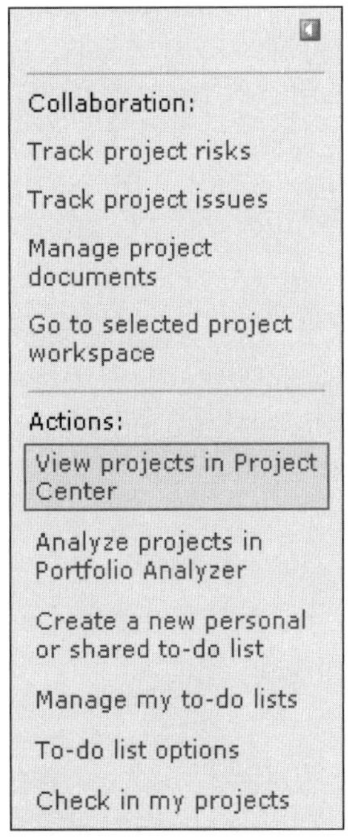

Figure 5-5: Project Center actions pane

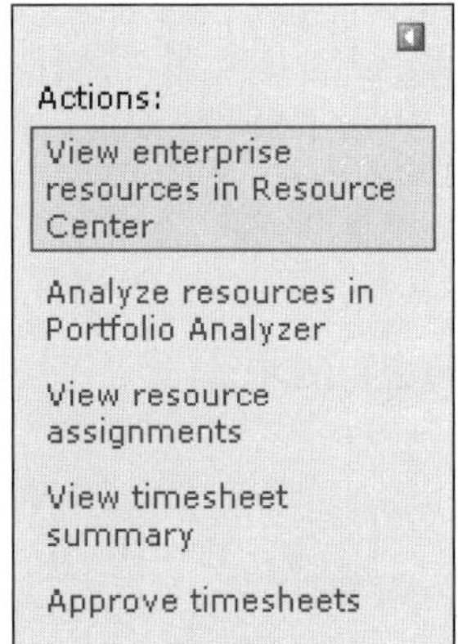

Figure 5-6: Resource Center actions pane

The Home page also contains an additional link on the right side of the page which you can use for setting up Project Web Access to work in conjunction with Outlook. Figure 5-7 shows the Outlook link on the right side of the Home page

Figure 5-7: Home page option for using Outlook

Customization Tabs

Many pages in Project Web Access contain customization tabs at the top of the page, similar to the worksheet tabs found at the bottom of Excel workbooks. When you select each tab, it displays additional options for customizing the information presentation on the current page in Project Web Access.

For example, the View My Tasks page offers the View Options tab, the Filter, Group, Search tab, and the Delegation tab, as shown in Figure 5-8. Notice that all three tabs are collapsed.

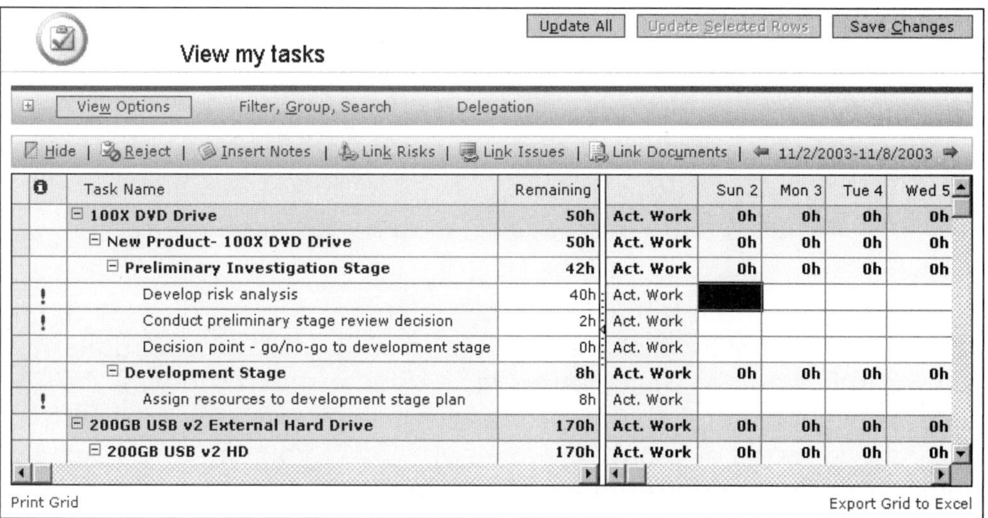

Figure 5-8: View My Tasks page with customization tabs collapsed

You can expand any customization tab to reveal all of its options simply by clicking on it. Once expanded you collapse it by clicking the page tab a second time. Figure 5-9 shows the expanded View Options tab for the View My Tasks page.

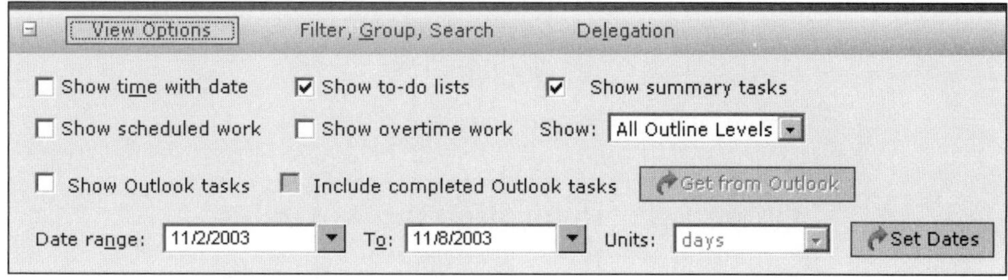

Figure 5-9: View Options tab expanded

The View Options tab offers you the option of viewing additional information on the current page. Two important View options on the View My Tasks page are the Show scheduled work and the Show overtime work options. These options allow you to view scheduled work, actual work, and overtime work in your timesheet.

Figure 5-10 shows the expanded Filter, Group, Search tab. As its name implies, this tab offers you the option of filtering, grouping, or searching the data shown on the current page.

Figure 5-10: Filter, Group, Search tab expanded

The Filter, Group, Search tab allows you to use an existing filter or to create your own custom filter by clicking the Custom Filter button. In addition, you can apply autofiltering to the columns in the page, much the way the autofilter works in Excel. You can also apply grouping to the data on the page, using two levels of grouping. In Figure 5-12, you can apply two levels of grouping to the data on the View My Tasks Page. Finally, you can search through the information on the current page by entering the search text in the Search For text box and then selecting the search fields.

Team members use the Delegation tab for the formal delegation of a task to a colleague. Figure 5-11 shows the Delegation tab on the View My Tasks page.

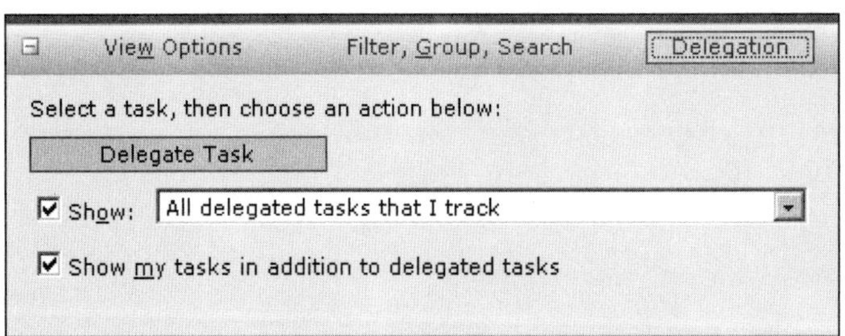

Figure 5-11: Delegation tab expanded

In addition to the Delegate Task button, which allows you to delegate a task to another team member, options are included to show delegated tasks and regular tasks.

Action Bar

Several pages in Project Web Access contain a data grid or "spreadsheet" in the center of the page, including the View My Tasks page, the Project Center and Resource Center pages, and the Updates page. There is an action bar or "toolbar" at the top of the grid on each of these pages. Each action bar offers you additional actions which are to the currently displayed grid. Figures 5-12 through 5-15 show the Action bars for each of these pages.

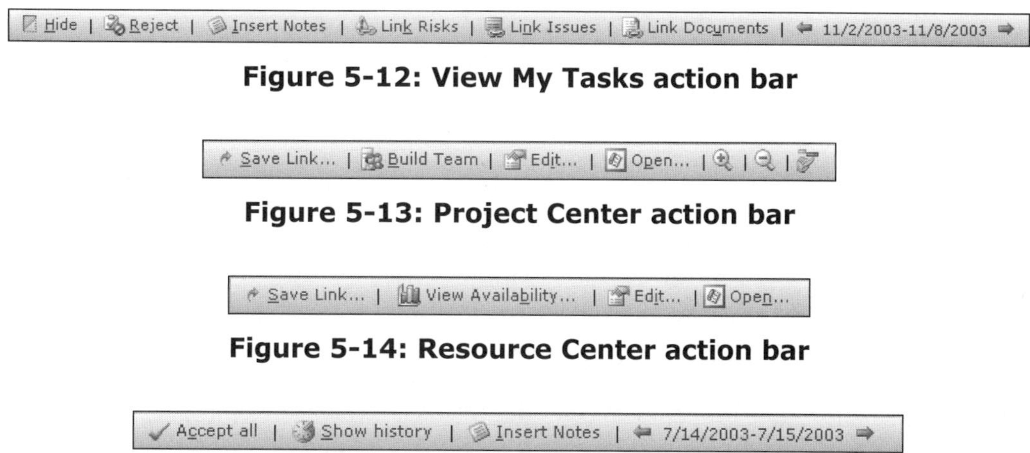

Figure 5-12: View My Tasks action bar

Figure 5-13: Project Center action bar

Figure 5-14: Resource Center action bar

Figure 5-15: Updates action bar

To use the action bar on any of these pages, simply select an item in the data grid and click the desired action button. For example, to link a document to a task on the View My Tasks page, select the desired task in the data grid and then click the Link Documents button on the action bar.

Manipulating the Data Grid

As was mentioned previously, a number of pages in Project Web Access contain a data grid or "spreadsheet" in which to display task, resource, and assignment data. For example, refer to the task grid on the View My Tasks page, as was shown previously in Figure 5-8.

Some grids have a vertical split bar separating the grid into two sections, while other pages contain a single grid only. For example, in Figure 5-8, notice that the system divides the grid on the View My Tasks page into two sections: the task sheet to the left of the split bar, and the timesheet on the right. To work the data in the grid most effectively, it is important to know how to do the following actions:

- **Move the Split Bar**: You move the split bar in the grid, by floating your mouse pointer anywhere over the split bar itself. When the mouse pointer changes from a single arrow to a double-headed arrow, click and hold the split bar to "grab" it, and drag it to the new position on the screen. In Figure 5-16, I am dragging the split bar to the left of the Work Status column.

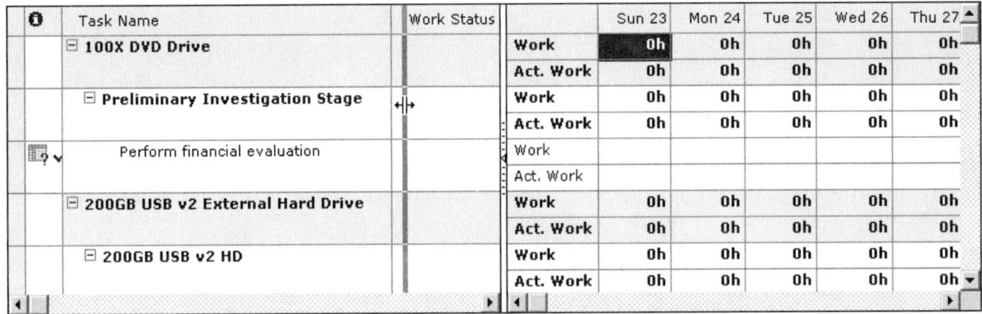

Figure 5-16: Dragging the split bar to the left of the Work Status column

- **Sort the Grid Data**: To sort the data in the grid, click the light blue column header at the top of the column. The first time you click the column header, the system automatically sorts data in the grid in ascending order based on the values in the selected column. To sort a column in descending order, click the column header a second time. I have applied a descending sort to the Work column in Figure 5-17.

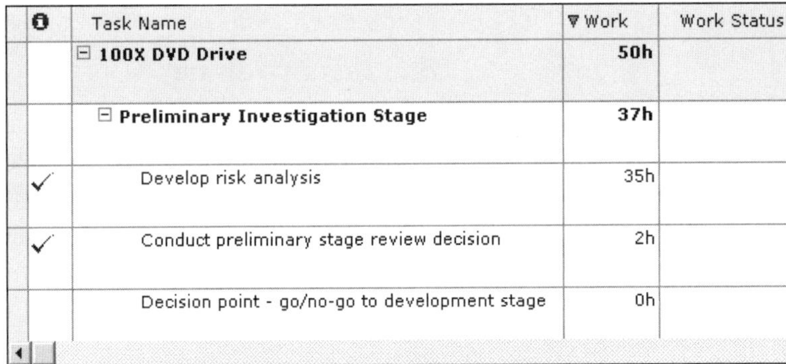

Figure 5-17: Descending sort applied to the Work column

- **Change Column Widths**: To change the width of any column in the grid, position the mouse pointer over the right edge of the column header of the column whose width you wish to change. The mouse pointer will change from a single arrow to a double-headed arrow. Then click and hold the right edge of the column header, and drag the edge of the column to the proper width. Figure 5-18 shows that I am changing the column width of the Work column.

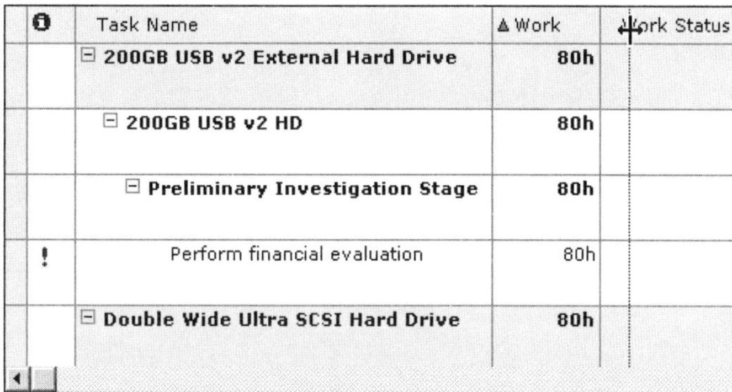

Figure 5-18: Widen the Work column

To widen any column in the grid to "best fit" the data in the column, double-click the gridline on the right edge of the column.

- **Move Columns**: To move any column in the grid, click and hold the light blue column header of the column you wish to move, then drag the column and drop it in its new position in the grid. The system displays a thick black vertical line in the grid at each point at which you can place the column. For example, I am dragging the Remaining Work column to a new position between the Task Name and Work columns in Figure 5-19.

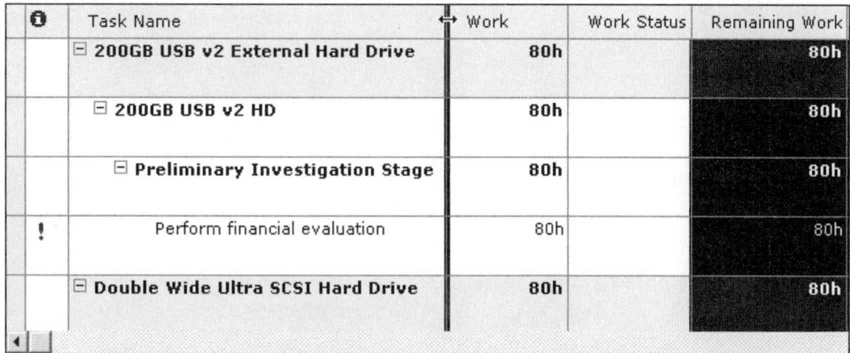

Figure 5-19: Remaining Work column dragged between the Task Name and Work columns

The system automatically save any changes you make to the layout of a grid (such as column order, column width, etc.) on your local computer. These will reappear the next time you visit the page. The changes that you make will not impact the layout of the grid on anyone else's local computer.

Printing the Data Grid

Click the Print Grid link in the lower left corner of the grid page to print the data contained in the respective data grid. The Print Grid page opens in its own window, shown in Figure 5-20, allowing you to make the following selections before printing:

- Select the specific grid columns that you want to print
- Exclude any grid columns you do not wish to print.
- Arrange the grid columns in the order you wish them to be printed
- Format the data in each of the grid columns

Each time you select Print Grid, the system displays the Arrange Columns pane by default, with all of the columns in the page pre-selected for printing. The Print Grid page contains three sections: a top pane for print settings, a toolbar, and a bottom pane for print preview.

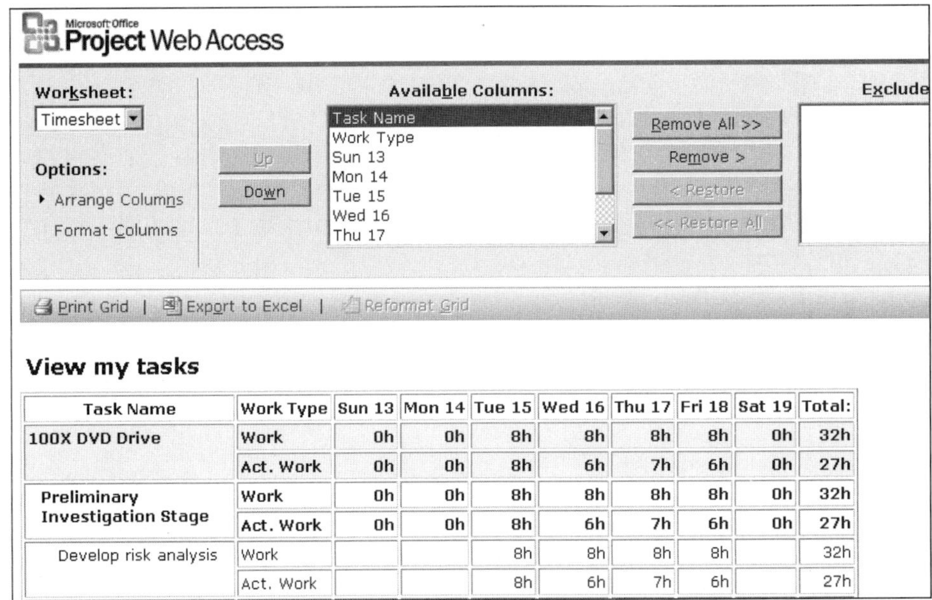

Figure 5-20: Print Grid page for View My Tasks page

The top pane in the Print Grid page contains the options for arranging and formatting the columns. On the left side of the top pane is an actions pane, offering links to display either the Arrange Columns or Format Columns panes.

In addition, the actions pane may also contain additional controls, such as the Worksheet pick list shown in Figure 5-21. In the Print Grid page for the View My Tasks page, the Worksheet pick list offers the option of printing either the Timesheet or the Task Sheet (Grid Data) portion of the grid.

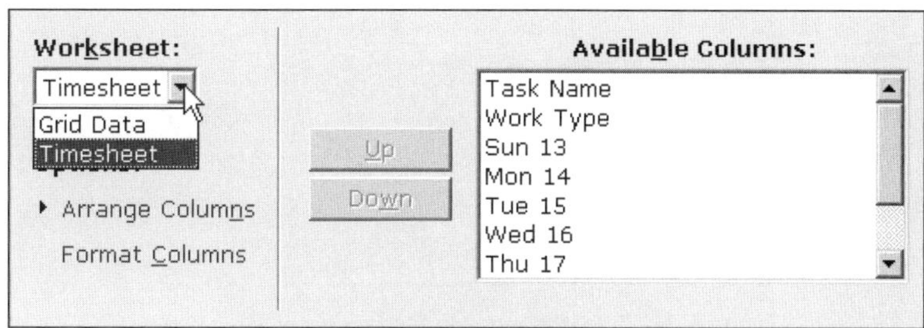

Figure 5-21: Worksheet print options

Because the system includes all columns for printing by default on the Print Grid page, you need only exclude those columns which you do not wish to print. To exclude a column, select any column in the Available Columns list, then click the Remove button. In Figure 5-22 shows the columns for Sun 13 and Sat 19 excluded from printing. To change the order of columns to be printed, select the column(s) whose order you wish to change and click either the Up or Down button.

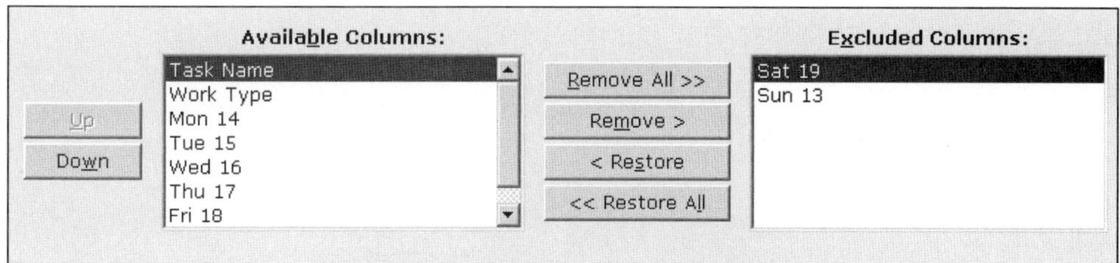

Figure 5-22: Two columns excluded from printing

When you exclude columns from printing, or change the order of columns, you must also click the Reformat Grid button on the Print Grid toolbar to display the latest changes in the print preview pane. What you see in the print preview pane is what will print when you click the Print Grid button.

To format your print columns in the data grid, click the Format Columns link in the actions pane of the Print Grid page. The Format Columns options display in the top pane of the Print Grid page, as is shown in Figure 5-23. Options for formatting the columns in the data grid include setting column widths, data alignment, and text wrapping.

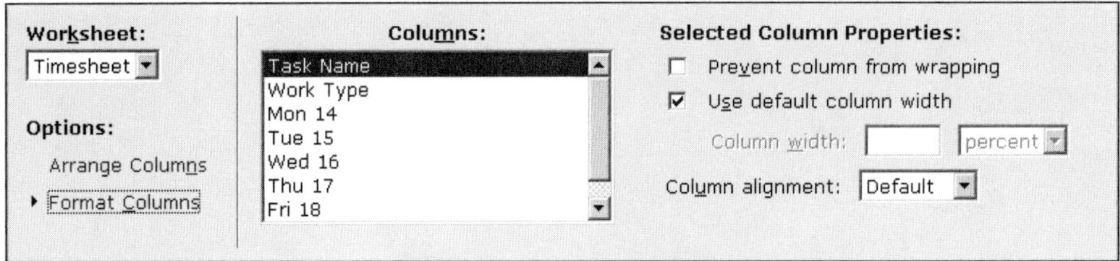

Figure 5-23: Format Columns section of the Print Grid page

When you change the formatting of any columns in the grid, you must also click the Reformat Grid button on the Print Grid toolbar to display the latest formatting changes in the print preview pane.

Once you specify your exclusions and set the formatting of the columns in the data grid, you can print the grid by clicking the Print Grid button on the toolbar. This displays the Print dialog box, shown in Figure 5-24, allowing you to finalize your print settings before printing.

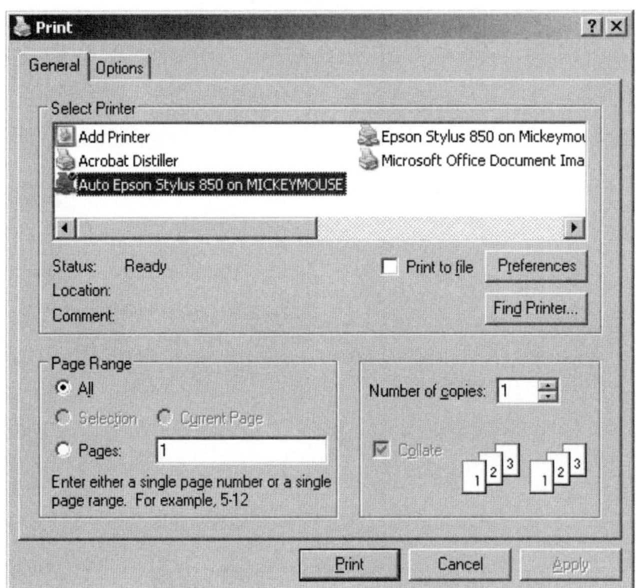

Figure 5-24: Print dialog box on Print Grid page

Exporting the Data Grid to Excel

In addition to printing the data grid, you can also export the data grid to an Excel workbook. You can accomplish this in two ways:

- Click the Export to Excel button on the toolbar while in the Print Grid page
- Click the Export to Excel link in the lower right corner of the data grid page

Using either method of exporting to Excel, you will see a warning dialog box about interacting with an ActiveX control shown in Figure 5-27. Click the Yes button to allow the interaction with the ActiveX control.

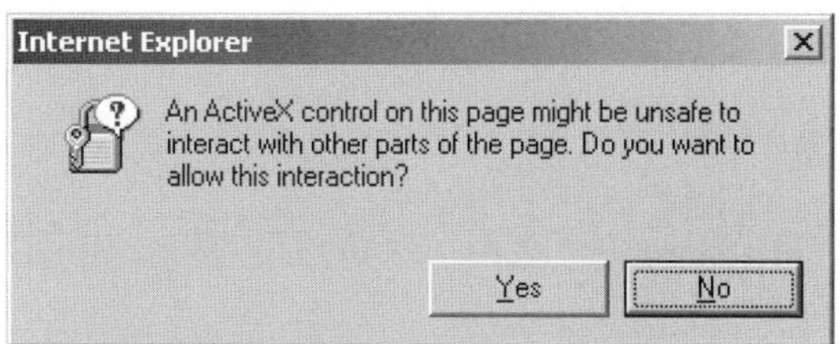

Figure 5-25: ActiveX Control warning dialog box

If you click the No button in the ActiveX warning dialog box, you can choose to export your data to the clipboard instead. From the clipboard, you can save the data as an XML file, which you can open as an XML spreadsheet in Excel.

When you export the grid data to Excel, it is transferred as an XML workbook file containing one or more worksheets as appropriate to the selected data grid. The workbook in Figure 5-26 consists of two worksheets containing information exported from the View My Tasks page. These worksheets contain Timesheet information and the Task Sheet (Grid Data) respectively. The system automatically groups and outlines data in each worksheet for ease of use.

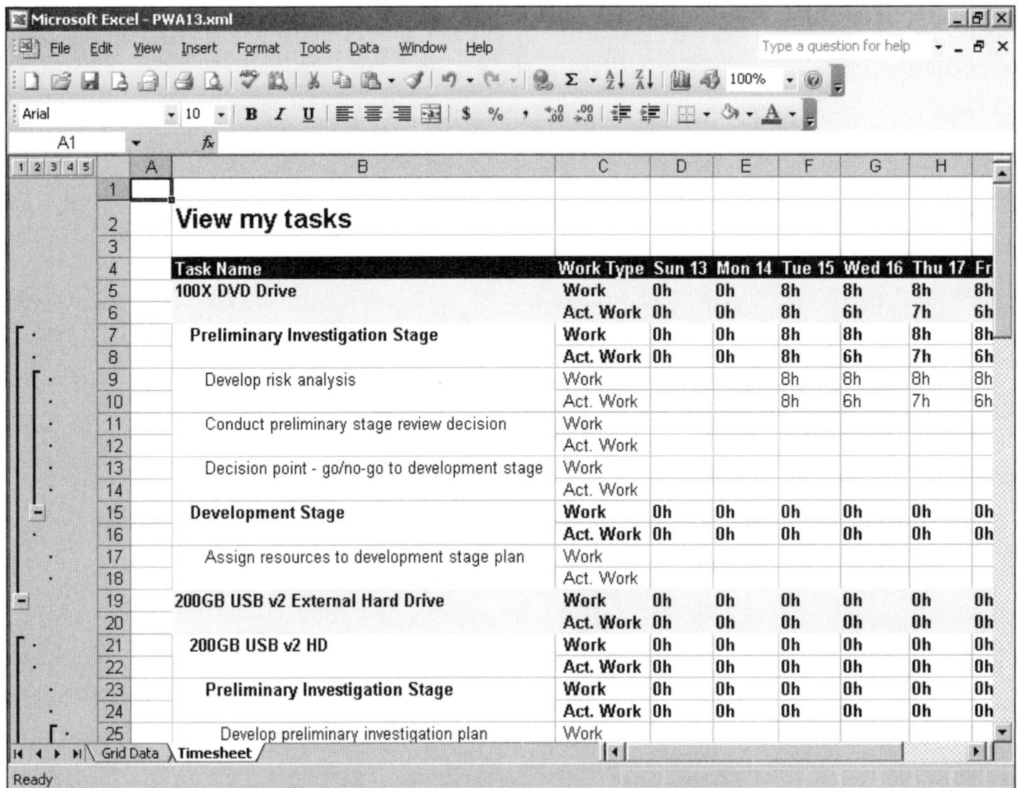

Figure 5-26: Data grid exported to Excel as an XML spreadsheet file

Warning: When you export data in the grid to Excel from the Print Grid page, the exporting process ignores any column exclusions you have set for printing.

Module 06

Tracking Progress through Project Web Access

Learning Objectives

After completing this module, you will be able to:

- Report progress on tasks
- Understand timesheet indicators
- Be familiar with manipulating View options
- Filter, group, and search in the timesheet
- Change displays between timesheet and personal Gantt chart
- Insert a Note on a task
- Propose a new task to your manager
- Reject a task
- Hide a task
- Delegate a task and take a lead role in managing a task
- Link risks, issues, and documents to tasks
- Notify your manager of nonworking time

Working with Tasks in Project Web Access

When you log onto Project Web Access, your personal Home page alerts you to any new task assignments you've received. In figure 6-1, you can see that Keith Harris has four new tasks assigned to him. These four new tasks are the result of a project manager, or managers, publishing New and Changed Assignments in a project.

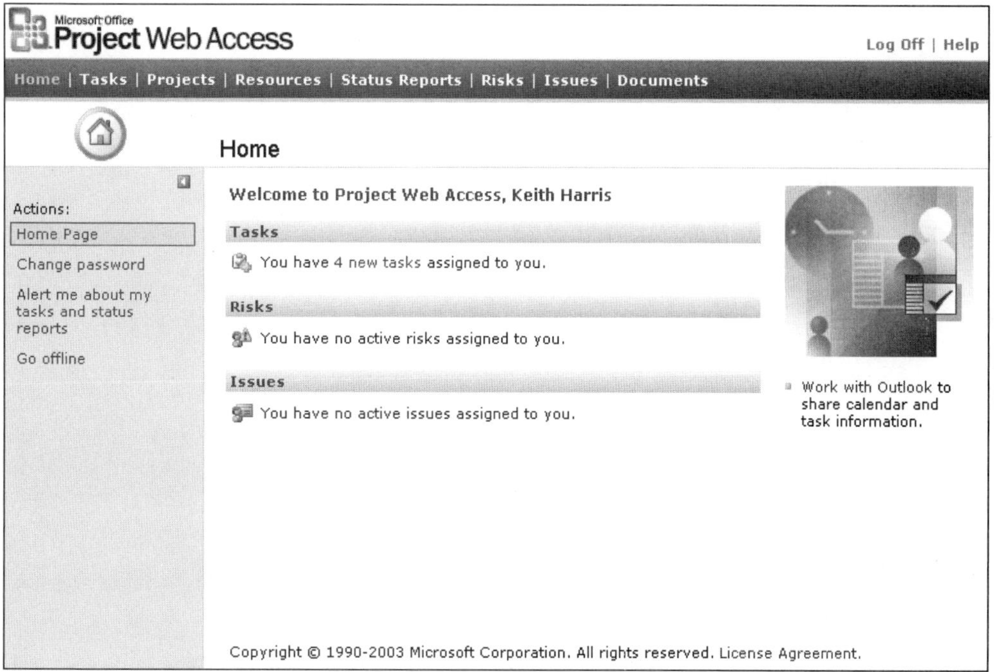

Figure 6-1: Project Web Access Home page

To view your task assignments in the View my tasks page, use one of the following methods:

- Click the Tasks menu at the top of the page
- Click the Tasks link in the information center of the page
- Click the __ new tasks link in the Tasks section of the page

When you select any of these, the system displays the View my tasks page, as shown in Figure 6-2. In the figure, notice the Actions pane on the left side of the page. The options in the top half allow you to choose between a Timesheet view and a Gantt chart view. The lower section lists all of the task-related activities available to you in the View my tasks page. As a resource on a project, here is where you access most of the functions that comprise the core daily work management routine. The functions in the toolbar and the options in the customization tabs augment the activities in the Actions pane. At the heart of this display is the time entry grid itself, which is where resources enter their time and periodically send updates to managers.

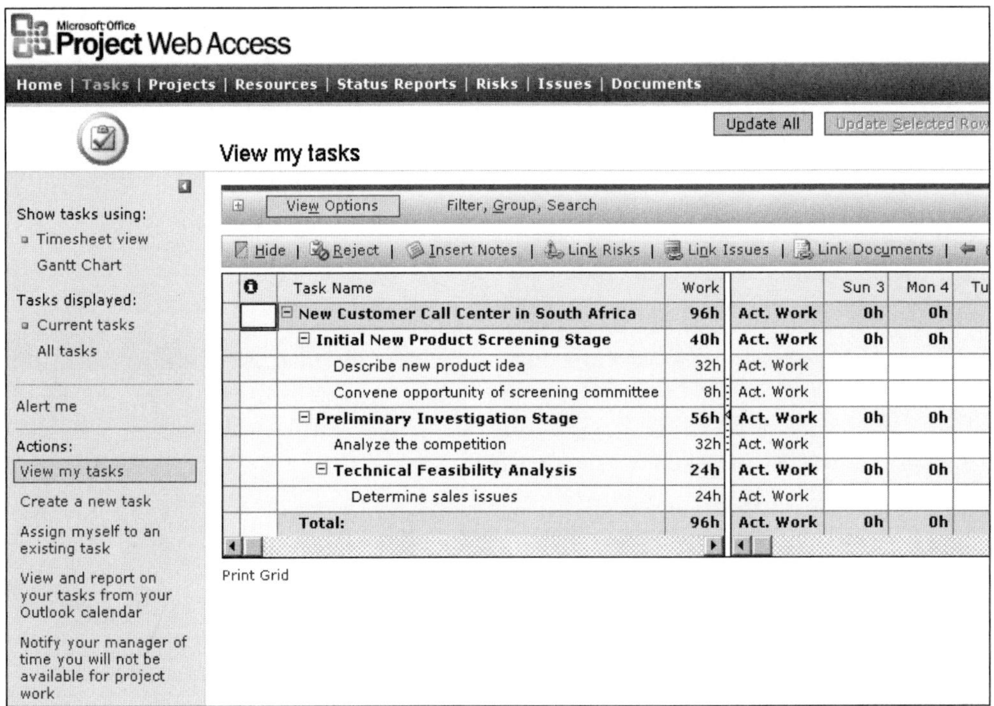

Figure 6-2: View my tasks page
Timesheet view

You access core work management functionality from the View my tasks page, including the following:

- Reporting progress on project tasks according to the tracking method selected for the organization or for the individual project
- Rejecting tasks assigned to you by a manager
- Delegating tasks to other resources
- Creating new tasks for approval by a manager
- Assigning existing tasks to yourself
- Inserting Notes on tasks to communicate additional information to the project manager
- Linking documents, issues, and risks to tasks
- Managing project task assignments in Outlook
- Sending work day changes to managers who need to react to scheduling changes
- Viewing and interacting with assignment information, receiving updates and progress information requests from managers

All of these functional areas support the sharing of project information. Progress reporting, task rejections, and task delegations generate immediate communication events between a resource and the manager of the affected task or tasks. Project Server directs all of these change events to the project managers who act as a gatekeeper for all plan-changing transactions. Inserting Notes, documents, and issues adds a more passive informational flow to the collaborative process.

Understanding the Timesheet

All users of Project Web Access within your organization should be well versed in using the Timesheet view, because everyone in your organization could potentially become a project team member with task assignments. At the very least, make sure that anyone who will have assignment work in the system knows how to use the timesheet.

Timesheet indicators

The Indicators that appear in the column on the left side of the task list alert you to task status, notes, issues, and document links, as well as other timely task information. Table 6-1 shows the indicators that you will commonly see in this column.

To understand the meaning of any indicator, simply float your mouse pointer over the indicator to display a tool tip with an explanation of the indicator.

Indicator	Description
	Task is a new from manager or newly delegated task
!	Task is overdue
	Task has update pending
	Task was updated by the manager
	Task was rejected by the manager
✓	Task is complete
?	Progress information is requested by the manager
	Task delegation requested
	Task delegation approved
	Task delegation approved with actuals to be submitted to the delegator
	Task has Notes
	Task has linked Risks
	Task has linked Issues
	Task has linked Documents
	Task is new but not sent to manager
	Task is new but not yet approved
	Task is new and self-assigned by resource
	Task is a new self-assignment by a resource, but not yet approved
✕	Task has been cancelled by the manager

Table 6-1: Indicator descriptions

Understanding the Timesheet Toolbar

The toolbar shown in Figure 6-3 provides access to a number of functions, including the following:

- **Hide** removes tasks from your timesheet
- **Reject** sends a task rejection for a selected task
- **Insert Notes** allows you to add Notes to tasks
- **Link Risks** allows you to create and link risks to tasks
- **Link Issues** enables you to create and link issues to tasks
- **Link Documents** enables users to link documents to tasks
- **Date Range** selector allows you to set the date range for the display

Figure 6-3: Timesheet toolbar

Activities Available from the Actions Pane

The activities available in the Actions pane on the View my tasks page are as follows:

- **View my tasks** refreshes the current view selected, whether it is the Timesheet or Gantt Chart view
- **Create a New Task** opens the Create new task Wizard
- **Assign myself to an existing Task** opens the Assign myself to an existing task Wizard
- **View and report on your tasks from your Outlook Calendar** allows you to transfer nonworking time from your Outlook calendar
- **Notify Your Manager of time you will not be available for project work** allows you to submit nonworking time such as vacation and sick leave to your manager

View Options

Select the View Options tab at the top of the timesheet display to control the data set displayed in the grid based on standard criteria, by date range, and by type. Expanding the tab reveals the options shown in Figure 6-4. The options that you control on this tab are as follows:

- **Show time with date** determines whether to display both dates and times, or dates only, in the grid
- **Show to-do lists** determines whether to display to-do list tasks in the timesheet
- **Show summary tasks** determines whether to display summary tasks for each task assignment
- **Show scheduled work** determines whether to display scheduled work values in the timesheet portion of the data grid
- **Show overtime work** determines whether to display the actual overtime work field in the timesheet portion of the data grid
- **Show** allows you to expand or collapse the Outline Level of the tasks displayed in the grid
- **Show Outlook Tasks** and **Include completed Outlook Tasks** allows you to display your Outlook tasks in your Project Web Access timesheet and to selectively include completed tasks
- **Date Range** selector fields allow you to change the date range of the display

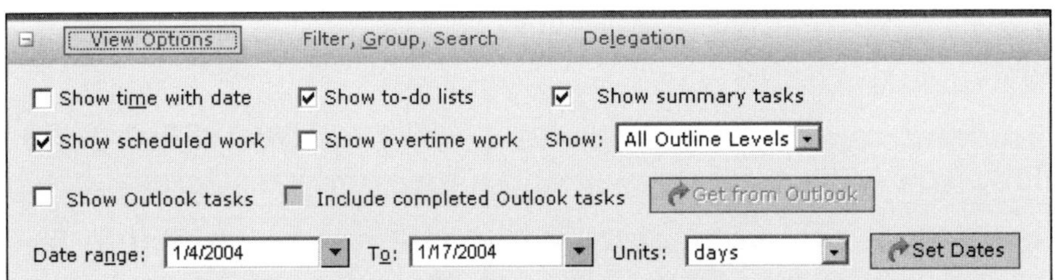

Figure 6-4: Expanded View Options tab

Selecting both the Show scheduled work and Show overtime work options causes the display to change as shown in Figure 6-5.

	Task Name		3/14	3/15	3/16	3/17	3/18	3/19
	Analysis	**Work**	**0h**	**6h**	**8h**	**4h**	**6h**	**7h**
		Act. Work	**0h**	**6h**	**8h**	**4h**	**6h**	**7h**
		Act. Ovt. Work	**0h**	**0h**	**0h**	**0h**	**0h**	**0h**
✓	Review network environment	Work		6h	8h	4h	6h	7h
		Act. Work		6h	8h	4h	6h	7h
		Act. Ovt. Work						
	Identify improvements to network environment	Work						
		Act. Work						
		Act. Ovt. Work						
	Design	**Work**	**0h**	**0h**	**0h**	**0h**	**0h**	**0h**
		Act. Work	**0h**	**0h**	**0h**	**0h**	**0h**	**0h**
		Act. Ovt. Work	**0h**	**0h**	**0h**	**0h**	**0h**	**0h**

Figure 6-5: View includes both Scheduled Work and Actual Overtime Work

You should only use the Show overtime work option if your organization tracks overtime work.

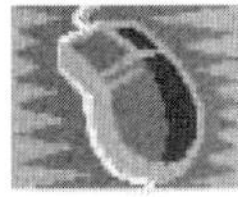

Hands On Exercise

Exercise 6-1

Explore the View Options tab on the View my tasks page of Project Web Access.

1. Logon through Web Access using the credentials provided by your instructor
2. Display the View my tasks page
3. Select and expand the View Options tab
4. Experiment with check boxes and date range options

Filtering, Grouping and Searching the Timesheet View

Besides all the view options you can control, you can apply filtering and grouping to your timesheet view and you can search through tasks on your timesheet to quickly locate specific assignments. Expanding the Filter, Group, Search tab reveals the options shown in Figure 6-6.

Figure 6-6: Timesheet view with Filter, Group, Search tab expanded

Project Web Access offers you a number of predefined filters on the Filter pick list, including:

- All tasks (the default filter)
- Overdue tasks
- Newly assigned tasks
- Completed tasks
- Incomplete tasks
- New tasks added by me
- New assignments added by me
- Tasks deleted by manager
- Tasks changed by a manager
- Tasks pending manager's approval

Click the Custom Filter button to create a new filter on the fly. Combine up to three filter tests on fields in the data grid to restrict the data shown in the view. In Figure 6-7, I am selecting the Project Manager field for a filter that will display tasks from only a certain project manager.

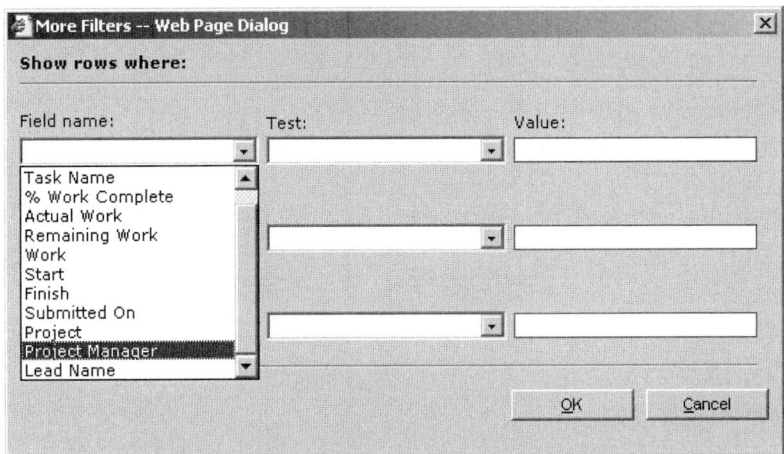

Figure 6-7: Custom filters dialog box

The default display grouping in the timesheet is by Project and the system presents all tasks first by project and then by summary task. You can specify your own grouping requirements. The system allows you to select two levels of grouping using the following fields in the Group by and Then by pick lists:

- Task Name
- % Work Complete
- Actual work
- Remaining Work
- Work
- Start
- Finish
- Submitted On
- Project
- Project Manager
- Lead Name

If you publish additional fields using the Tools ➢ Customize ➢ Published Fields command, and your Project Server administrator includes these fields in the Timesheet view, then these additional fields will also appear on the Group by and Then by pick lists.

The system provides you with a textual search feature in the timesheet. You can enter a sequence of characters consisting of partial words or whole words and search for the characters in the timesheet. Click the Find Next button to activate the search. The system highlights each matching task one instance at a time. You must continue to click the Find Next button to locate each additional match.

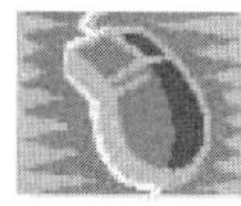

Hands On Exercise

Exercise 6-2

Explore the Filter, Group, Search tab on the View my tasks page of Project Web Access.

1. Make sure you have displayed the View my tasks page
2. Select the Filter, Group, Search tab
3. Select several different filters from the list and apply them, then observe the results
4. Click the Custom Filter button and use the More Filters dialog to build a custom filter
5. Experiment with the Group By selections
6. Use the Search feature to find a task

Displaying the Gantt Chart View

The Gantt Chart selection in the View my tasks interface allows you to select a traditional Gantt style presentation of your tasks. Shown in Figure 6-8, most of the toolbar and option tabs functionality available in the Timesheet view is available in the Gantt chart version as well. The difference is mainly that you cannot track progress with this view when you are tracking hours by period.

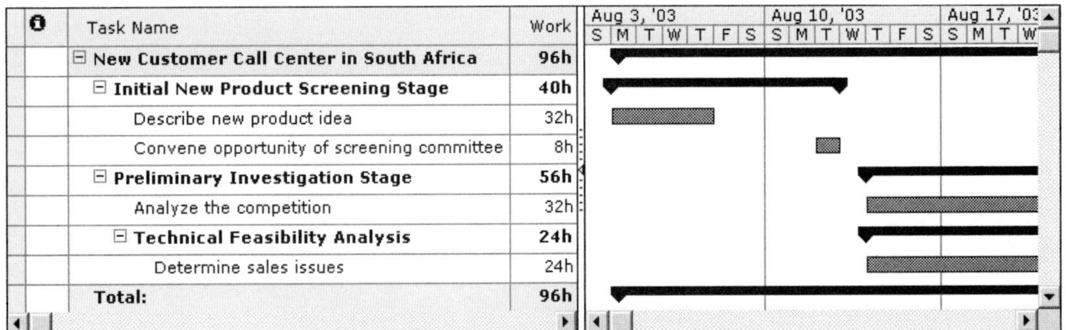

Figure 6-8: Gantt Chart view
View my tasks page

If your organization uses either the Percent of Work Complete or the Actual Work Done and Work Remaining method of reporting progress, you can use the Gantt Chart view to update your managers. If your organization uses the Hours of Work Done Per Day or Per Week method of tracking progress, then you will not be able to use the Gantt Chart view to track progress and must use the Timesheet view instead.

Current Tasks vs. All Tasks

In addition to the choices of displaying your View my tasks page with either a Gantt Chart or a Timesheet, you have the option to display Current Tasks or All Tasks in your timesheet. This option is sometimes a source of frustration for users who do not understand how Project Web Access defines a "current" task. A "current" task is any task that:

- Should have started before today
- Has started already but is not yet completed
- Starts within the next 10 days (or within the time period specified by your Project Server administrator as a current task)

If you select the Current Tasks option, but do not see a particular task that you know should appear on your timesheet, it may not be a "current" task. Click the All Tasks option to see every task on your timesheet.

Reporting Progress in the Timesheet

Your organization uses progress reporting to capture the current state of your assignment work on each task. Your project manager uses the task progress you report to determine the current state of the project. For every organization, accurately tracking project progress is vital to the success of any project.

You report task progress in the View my tasks page of Project Web Access. Depending on your organization's default method of tracking progress, you enter progress in one of three ways:

- If your organization uses the Percent of Work Complete method, enter progress in the % Work Complete and Remaining Work columns.
- If your organization uses the Actual Work Done and Work Remaining method, enter progress in the Actual Work and Remaining Work columns.
- If your organization uses the Hours of Work Done per Day or per Week method, enter progress in the Actual Work cells in the timesheet for the day or week during which you performed the work, and enter your remaining work in the Remaining Work column.

Setting Up the Timesheet to Enter Actuals

To use the Hours of Work Done per Day or per Week method for tracking progress most effectively, I suggest that you first customize the setup of the View my tasks page. To do this, complete the following steps:

1. Click the View Options tab to expand the View options list
2. Select the Show scheduled work option
3. Select the Show summary tasks option, if it is not already displayed

Displaying summary tasks in the timesheet can help you to distinguish between two tasks that have the same name in the same project.

4. Click the View Options tab again to collapse the tab section
5. Drag and drop the Remaining Work field (column) from its present location to a new location to the right of the Task Name column
6. Adjust the column widths of any column, if necessary
7. Scroll the timesheet to the first day of the reporting period

In Figure 6-9, I have set up my View my tasks page according to the steps detailed above.

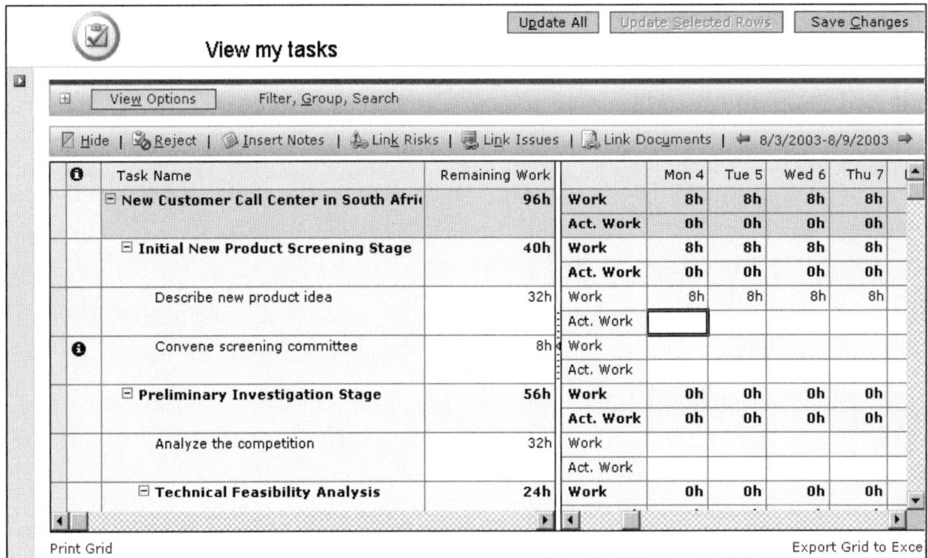

6-9: View my tasks page prepared for progress reporting

Entering and Submitting Progress

After you have setup the View my tasks page for easy entry, you can begin the formal process of entering and submitting progress. Helpful habits to follow include:

- Enter Actual Work values in the Timesheet on a *daily basis* for each task on which you have worked
- Adjust the Remaining Work value at the end of the week if you believe you have more work or less work than the Timesheet has calculated for the task
- If you change the Remaining Work value for any task, document the reason for making the change by clicking the Insert Notes button and adding a note
- If you need to add any type of project documentation, such as a Word or Excel file, click the Link Documents button and upload the document to the Documents library for the project
- If you need to add any type of formal Issue documentation to the task, click the Link Issues button and add the issue to the Issue list for the project
- If you have discovered any previously unknown risks to either the task or to the project as a whole, click the Link Risks button and document the risk

- Save your changes at the end of each day by clicking the Save Changes button (doing so will save the actuals without sending them to the project manager)
- Submit your progress to the manager at the end of the week or as otherwise required by your organization by clicking either the Update Selected Rows or the Update All buttons at the top of the Tasks page

As a best practice, msProjectExperts recommends that you enter actuals on a *daily* basis and update them to your manager on a *weekly* basis.

When you enter progress in the timesheet, the system formats the numbers in red as you enter them. The numbers will remain formatted in red until the manager has updated your progress into the project plan, saved the project plan, and then republished the project plan. You also see indicators in the Indicators column to remind you of the status of your progress.

In Figure 6-10, I entered progress on the task Describe new product idea. I entered 8 hours of work each day from Monday through Wednesday, and entered 6 hours of work on Thursday.

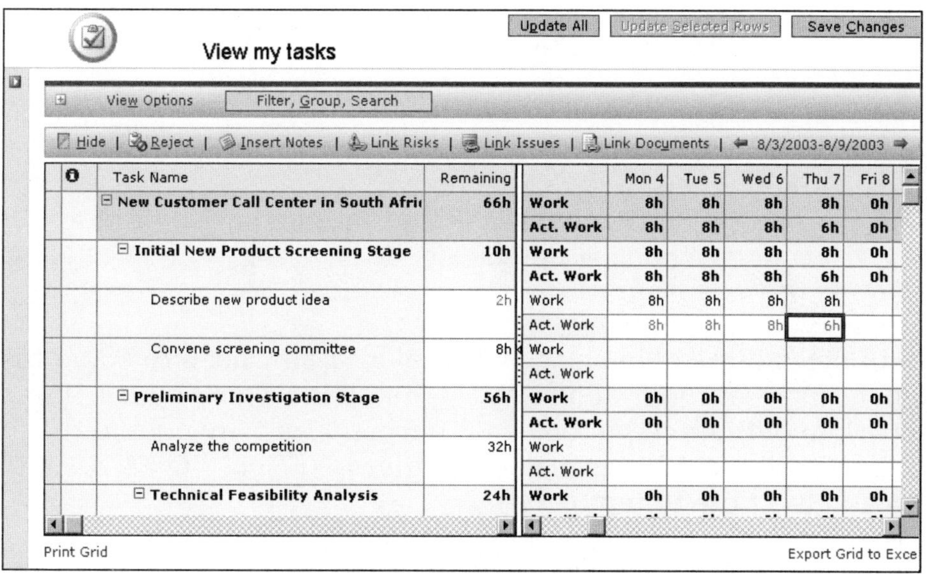

Figure 6-10: Task progress entered in the timesheet

In the previous figure, the system calculates that I have 2 hours of Remaining Work on this task. However, I finished early so I no longer need the two hours of Remaining Work. To show that I finished early, I enter a zero (0) in the Remaining Work column, as shown in Figure 6-11. Notice that the Indicators column shows a completed task symbol for the task.

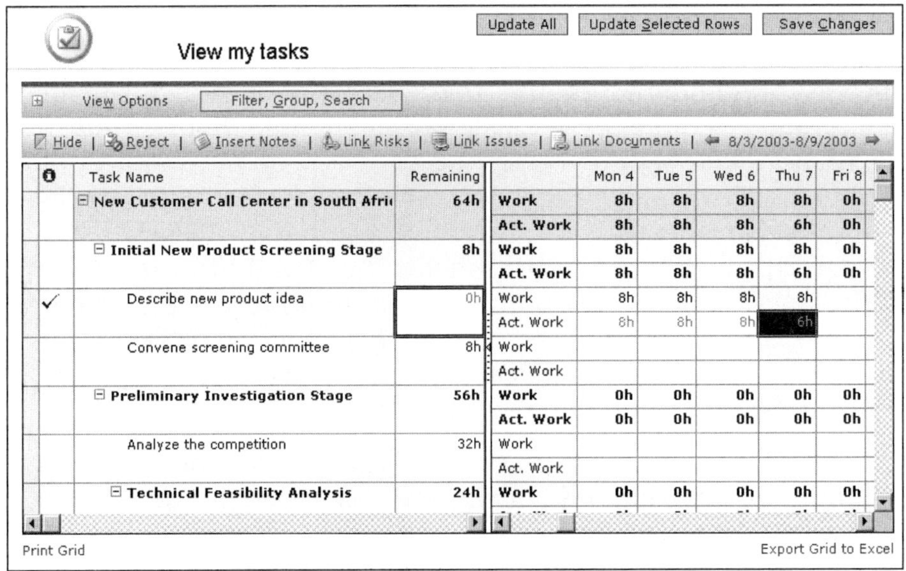

Figure 6-11: Adjust Remaining Work to 0 hours to shown an early finish

The Remaining Work field displays in the timesheet regardless of tracking method. Remaining work is an important input for any task that finishes with more or less work than originally predicted.

Because I adjusted the Remaining Work value, I also need to add a task Note to document the reason for adjusting the number. To add a task Note, click the Insert Note button on the toolbar. I have entered my note in the Project Web Access Assignment Notes dialog, as shown in Figure 6-12. Click the OK button to add the Note to the task.

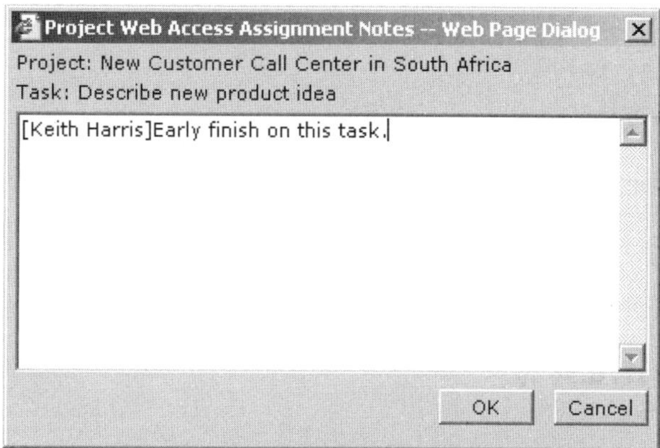

Figure 6-12: Enter a task Note

To submit task progress to your manager, click the Update All button. You can also perform this action selectively by first selecting one or more task rows in the grid for which you have entered progress and then click the Update Selected Rows button. When you use either method, the system submits the task progress to your manager and a Microsoft Project Web Access dialog notifies you that your update succeeded, as displayed in Figure 6-13.

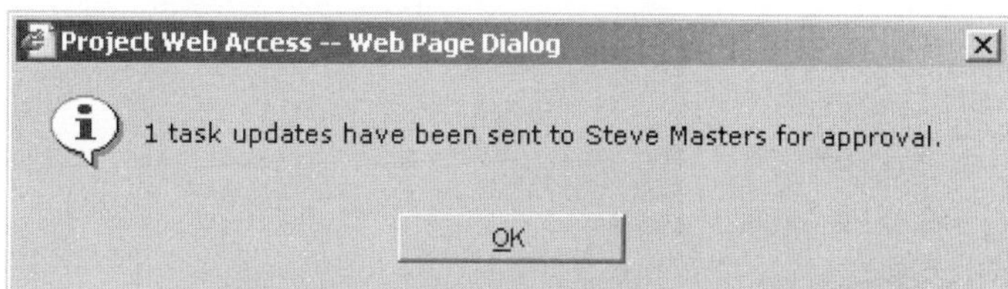

Figure 6-13: Updates sent to the manager

If you are not ready to update progress to your manager, click the Save Changes button to save your entries. The system will store your entries until you are ready to send them. The system confirms your save as shown in Figure 6-14.

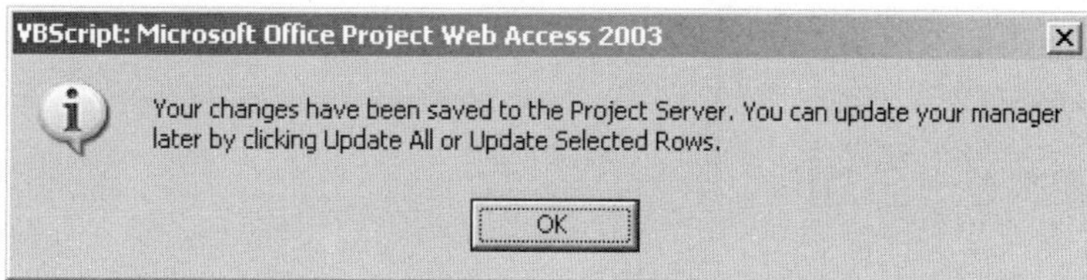

Figure 6-14: Time entries saved

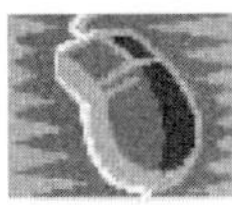

Hands On Exercise

Exercise 6-3

Enter progress in the Timesheet and update the manager.

1. Make sure you have displayed the View my tasks page
2. Select the Timesheet display, if it is not currently displayed
3. Make time entries into your current tasks
4. Click the Save Changes button to save the hour entries without updating the manager
5. Click the Update All button to send the updates to the manager
6. Click OK button when prompted

Using Other Task Activities

Along with reporting progress, other important task-related activities in the View my tasks page include:

- Rejecting tasks
- Delegating tasks
- Creating new tasks
- Assigning yourself to tasks

We will address each of these topics separately in the remainder of this module.

Rejecting a Task

Rejecting a task or tasks through the timesheet is very simple. Highlight the task rows that you want to reject and click the Reject button in the toolbar. The system first displays a warning and confirmation alert as shown in Figure 6-15.

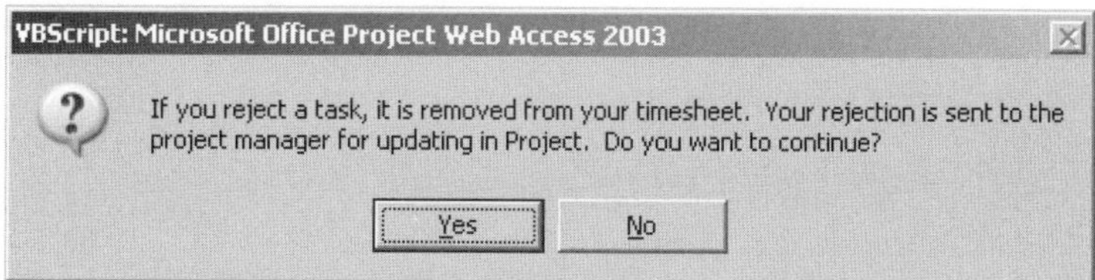

Figure 6-15: Task rejection warning

If you click the Yes button, the system then removes any rejected tasks from your timesheet and sends a notification to the project managers for the affected tasks as shown in Figure 6-16.

Figure 6-16: Task rejections notification

Once you click the Yes button, you have "passed the point of no return" and the system removes the task from your timesheet. Your manager may choose to reject your task rejection, thereby republishing the task and making it reappear on your timesheet. If your manager approves your task rejection, it will no longer appear on your timesheet.

Hands On Exercise

Exercise 6-4

Reject a task assignment from the project manager.

1. Make sure you have displayed the View my tasks page
2. Select the Timesheet display, if it is not currently displayed
3. Select a task without actual reported hours in the timesheet
4. Click the Reject button in the toolbar
5. Click Yes when the warning dialog displays
6. Click OK button when prompted

Delegating a Task

Before you can delegate a task, you must expand the Delegation tab by clicking on it, or by clicking the Delegate tasks link from the Actions pane. The Delegation tab contains the necessary functions to delegate tasks, along with the view options relating to delegated tasks, as shown in Figure 6-17.

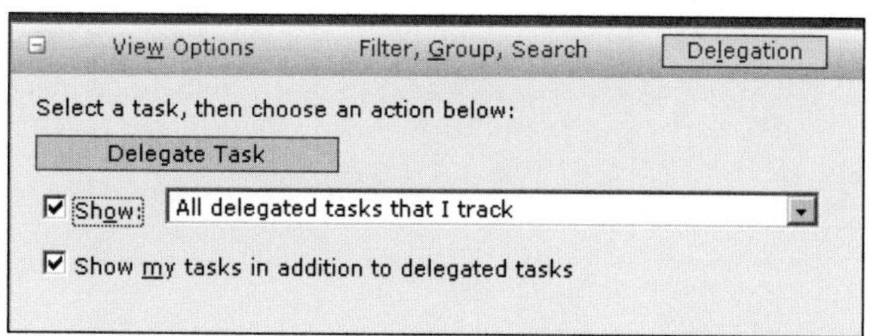

Figure 6-17: Delegation tab expanded

The Show delegated tasks selector on the Delegation tab allows you to select from three choices:

- All delegated tasks that I track
- All delegated tasks that I am the Lead for
- All delegated tasks that I track but am not the Lead for

Additionally, you may choose to show or not show your regular tasks along with the tasks that you have delegated. You may selectively display delegated tasks only. To delegate a task, select the task that you want to delegate, and then click the Delegate Task button. The system opens the Task Delegation page shown in Figure 6-18.

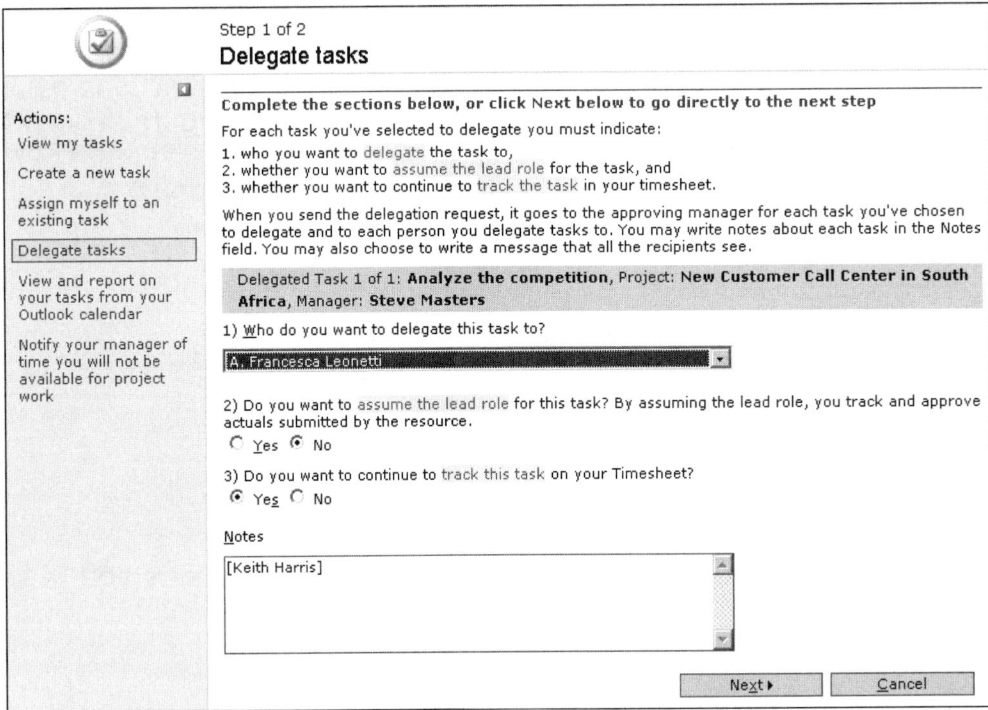

Figure 6-18: Task delegation - Step 1

On the Step 1 page, you must select the person to whom to delegate the task, choose whether to assume the lead role for the delegation, and select whether to track the task in your timesheet. You should also enter a task Note to document the reason for the delegation.

If you assume the Lead Role for the task delegation, the person to whom you delegate the task will update task progress to you. You must review and approve their task progress, and update it to your manager. In a sense, you become an intermediary in the process of updating and approving task progress. You must have security permission in the Project Server system to assume a lead role.

Once you have made your selections, click the Next button at the bottom of the page to continue to the Step 2 page shown in Figure 6-19. You may also click the Cancel button to abandon the delegation process. On the Step 2 page, the system displays a summary of the actions you are about to process. This page is your last opportunity to make changes to your task delegation or cancel the action entirely. Click the Send button to send the delegation proposal to the other resource and to the manager responsible.

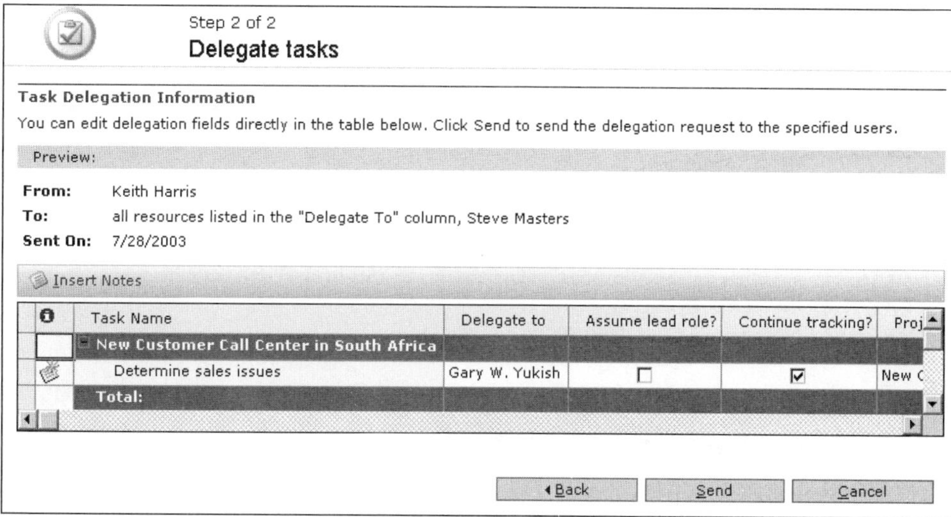

Figure 6-19: Task delegation step 2

After you click Send, the system confirms your successful delegation request as shown in Figure 6-20.

Figure 6-20: Delegation confirmation

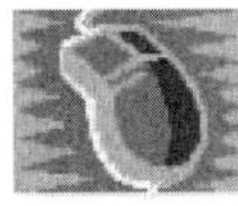

Hands On Exercise

Exercise 6-5

Delegate a task assignment to another team member.

1. Make sure you have displayed the View my tasks page
2. Select the Timesheet display, if it is not currently displayed
3. Select the Delegation tab
4. Select a task in the timesheet and click the Delegate Task button
5. Select a person to whom to delegate the task
6. Leave the next two options at their defaults
7. Add a note to the delegated task
8. Click the Send button when the preview screen displays
9. Click OK button when prompted

Creating a New Task

Team members can create and propose new tasks to their project managers through Microsoft Project Web Access. Whereas the system sends task delegation requests to the project manager the moment you create them, creating new tasks is an explicit two-step process:

1. Create the new task
2. Update the new task to the project manager for approval

To create the new task, click the Create a new task link in the Actions pane. The system opens the Create a New Task page as shown in Figure 6-21.

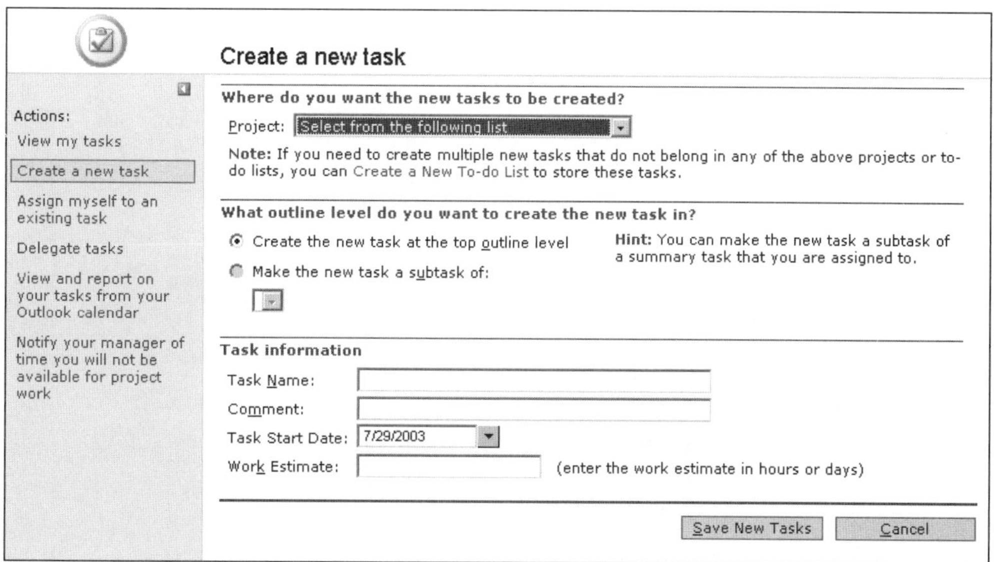

Figure 6-21: Create a new task page

The Project pick list at the top of the page allows you to select an existing project or To-Do list. In the second section of the page, select the outline level for the new task in the selected project. By default, create the task at the top outline level is selected.

If you select a To-Do list from the Project pick list, the system will display the entry page for the selected To-Do list.

In the Task information section of the page, provide a task name and make sure that you add a comment unless you are certain the project manager will know what you're doing. Select a proposed start date and enter a work estimate in hours or days. Indicate which value you are using by typing an "h" or a "d" character after the number you enter. Click the Save New Tasks button to save your new tasks requests to your timesheet.

Once you have created and saved the new task, Project Web Access redisplays your View my tasks page. The new task is now visible in the timesheet and contains indictors that let you know its status. In Figure 6-22, you can see the new task I created, along with the screentip that indicates that I need to send the new task to the project manager for approval and updating into the project plan.

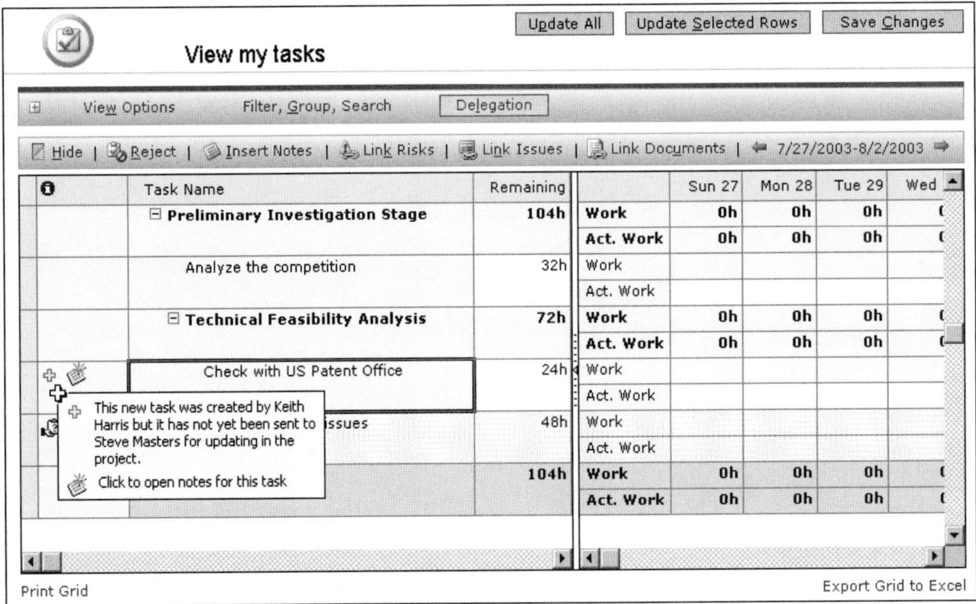

Figure 6-22: New task created on the View my tasks page

Once you create your new task, your second step is to update the new task to the project manager for approval. To send the new task to the project manager, select the task in the task list, and then click the Update Selected Rows button. Alternately, you can simply click Update All which to send your new task and any other pending updates to your project manager(s).

The system allows you to enter actual progress on the new task before you submit it to your project manager. If you do so, the system will submit the new task request to your project manager along with your actual progress.

Using Task Creation for Collaborative Planning

You can leverage the New Task creation feature during the planning phase of your projects to allow team leaders and team members to create some of the tasks in the work plan. In order to allow these users to create tasks that fall below summary tasks in the plan, you must assign the user responsible for creating the tasks to the summary task to begin with. This means that you must at least dummy up this structure in your plan.

In other words, you'll need to create the summary task by both creating it as a task with an appropriate name and by adding at least one subtask to it in order to apply the indentation that, in itself, defines a task as being a summary task. Then you must assign the resource responsible for detailing the tasks below the summary task to the summary task itself.

Assigning resources to summary tasks is not generally a good idea as it causes work demand to be overstated. The system will add the work rollup from the summary task to the resource, as well as the work from each of the individual subtasks. This is not a problem before you enter the phase of a project when you start tracking and for as long as you can live with overstatement of work for the resources doing the planning. Remove the resources from the summary tasks as soon as possible.

Assigning Yourself to an Existing Task

A new feature of Project Server 2003 allows you to assign yourself to an existing task through the View my tasks Page. To do so, click the Assign myself to an existing task link in the Actions pane. The system displays the Assign myself to an existing task page, shown in Figure 6-23. The Projects pick list at the top of the page lists all of the projects in which you are assigned project work. The center section of the page lists all of the tasks to which you can assign yourself.

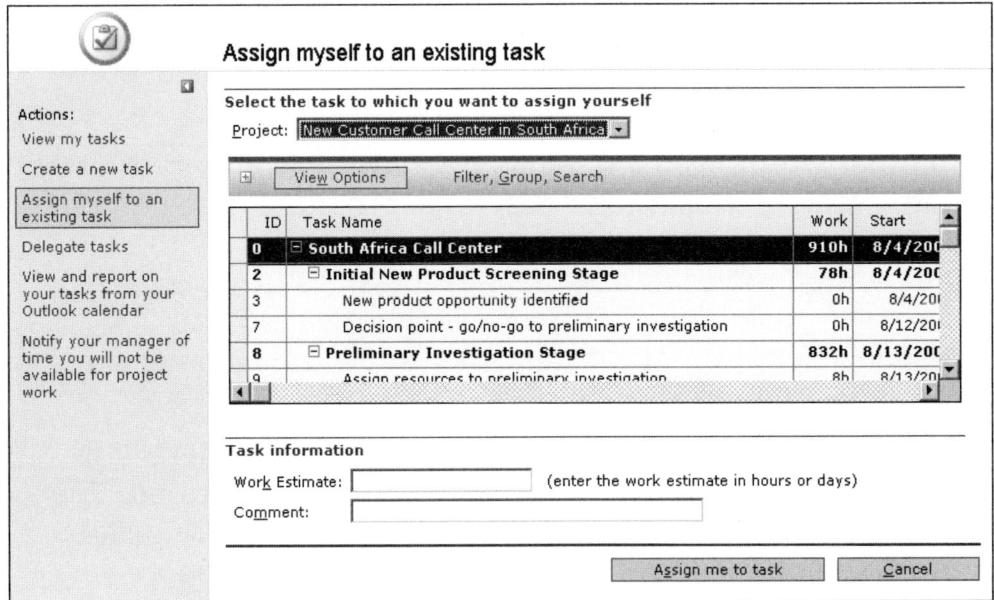

Figure 6-23: Assign myself to an existing task page

To assign yourself to an existing task, select a project from the Project pick list and then select a task from the list of tasks displayed. Enter a Work Estimate of your work on the selected task and an optional Comment, then click the Assign me to task button. The system displays the confirmation message shown in Figure 6-24. Click the OK button to continue. The system redisplays your timesheet, including with the new task assignment. You must click either the Update All or Update Selected Rows button to send the updated task assignment to your manager.

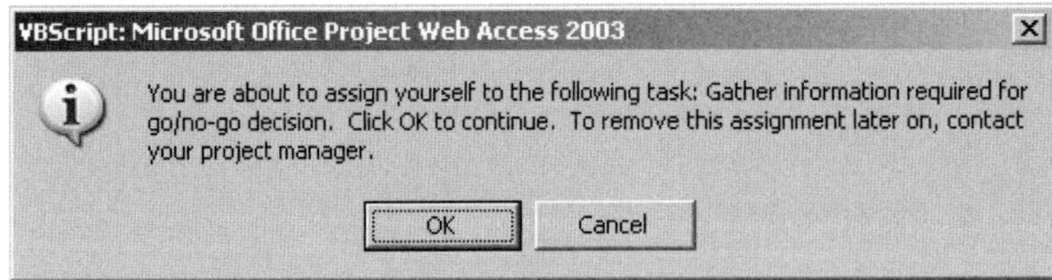

Figure 6-24: Assign myself to an existing task confirmation message

Hands On Exercise

Exercise 6-6

Create and submit a new task to your project manager.

1. Make sure you have displayed the View my tasks page
2. Select the Timesheet display, if it is not currently displayed
3. Click Create a new task in the Actions pane
4. Select a project
5. Enter the task information
6. Click Save New Tasks when complete
7. Hover the mouse pointer over Indicator icon for the new task
8. Click the Update All button

Exercise 6-7

Assign yourself to an existing task.

1. Make sure you have displayed the View my tasks page
2. Select the Timesheet display, if it is not currently displayed
3. Click the Assign myself to an existing task link in the Actions pane
4. Select a project and then select a task
5. Enter a Work Estimate value and a Comment
6. Click the Assign me to task button
7. Click the OK button to confirm the action

Hiding Tasks

Use the Hide task button to remove completed and cancelled tasks from your timesheet. Completed and cancelled tasks will display on your timesheet indefinitely unless you manually hide them from view. Once hidden, tasks do not redisplay unless your manager republishes them. To hide a task, select it in the task list and then click the Hide button. The alert box, shown in Figure 6-25, allows you to confirm your action or cancel it. Click the Yes button to continue.

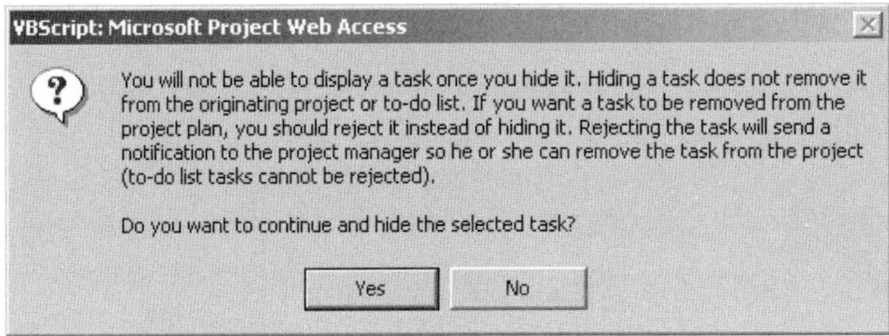

Figure 6-25: Hide task dialog

Hands On Exercise

Exercise 6-8

Hide a task on your timesheet.

1. Make sure you have displayed the View my tasks page
2. Select the Timesheet display, if it is not currently displayed
3. Select a task in the timesheet
4. Click the Hide button on the toolbar
5. Click the Yes button to continue

Inserting Task Notes

To insert a Note for a task, select the task on the View my tasks page and then click on the Insert Notes button on the toolbar. The system opens the Project Web Access Assignment Notes dialog shown in Figure 6-26.

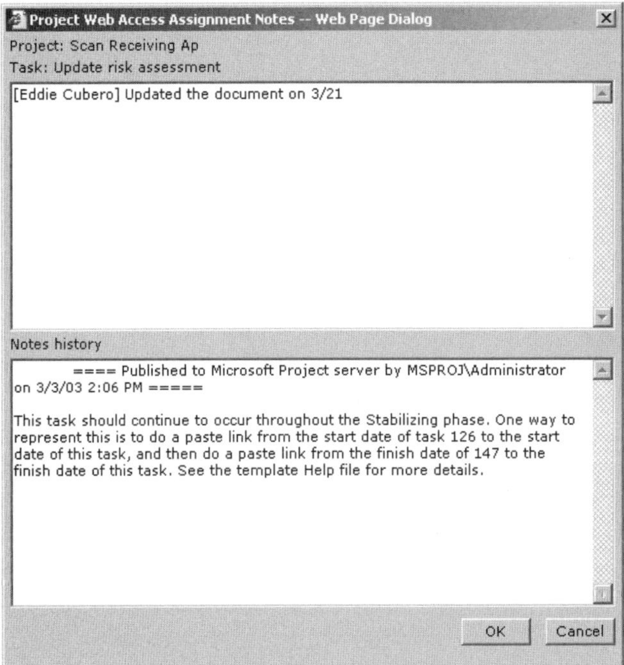

Figure 6-26: Insert a task Note dialog box

The dialog contains a current note area at the top and a history of notes previously added to the task in the bottom half. You may make changes in either text area; however, you should make your new entry in the upper text box. The system annotates the note in the upper text area with your name to indicate that you are the one adding the note. Saving the new note automatically adds a timestamp to the record, as well. Click the OK button to add the note. Your new note now appears when you reopen the notes dialog for the task.

Notes entered through the timesheet are visible to you and the corresponding manager for only the selected task. These notes are not visible to other team members, and cannot be seen in other views in the system other than the View my tasks and Updates views.

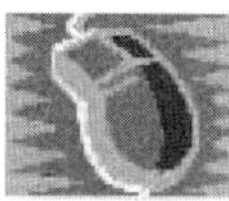

Hands On Exercise

Exercise 6-9

Add a Note to a task.

1. Make sure you have displayed the View my tasks page
2. Select the Timesheet display, if it is not currently displayed
3. Select a task and click the Insert Notes button
4. Add appropriate text for the Note and click the OK button when finished

Linking Documents to Tasks

Link project-related documents to tasks by selecting a task and then clicking on the Link Documents button on the toolbar. The system displays the document list for the selected task, as shown in Figure 6-27. The document list shows all of the documents linked to the task, if any exist. To add an existing document to the document list, click the Upload Document button on the toolbar.

Figure 6-27: Document list for a task

In addition to adding documents at the task level, you can also add documents at the project level by clicking the Documents menu at the top of the Project Web Access page.

Linking Issues to Tasks

An issue is any type of problem or concern which you might have during the life of the project, and which you want to communicate to those who have an interest in the project. Examples of project issues could include a shortage of the necessary resources to complete the project on time, or an unanticipated hardware upgrade that you need to move forward with project work.

Similar to handling document linking, you link issues to tasks by selecting a task and then clicking on the Link Issues button on the toolbar. The system displays the issues list for the selected task, as shown in Figure 6-28. The issues list shows all of the issues linked to the task, if any exist. To add a new issue to the issues list, click the New Issue button on the toolbar. To link the task to existing issues, click the Link Project Issues button.

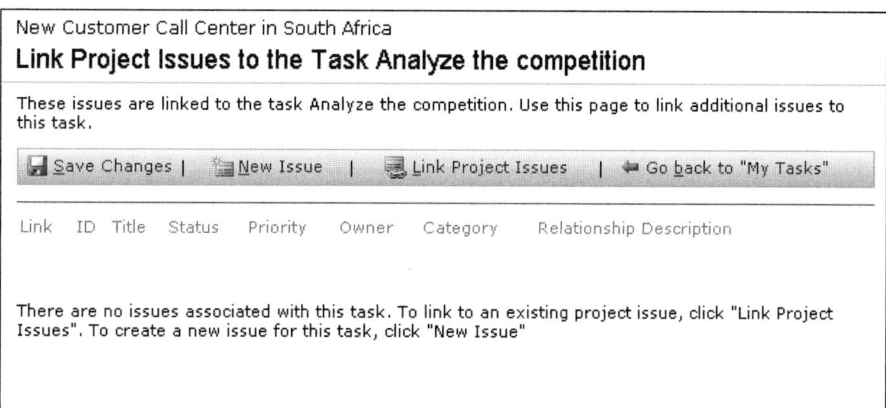

Figure 6-28: Issues list for tasks

In addition to adding issues at the task level, you can also add issues at the project level by clicking the Issues menu at the top of the Project Web Access page.

Linking Risks to Tasks

The Project Management Institute defines a risk as "an uncertain event or condition that, if it occurs, has a positive or negative effect on a project objective." Risks have both causes and consequences. If a risk occurs, the consequence can be either negative or positive. As a part of your organization's risk management methodologies, you may need to log and document known risks to your project work.

As with documents and issues, you can also link risks to tasks by selecting a task and then clicking on the Link Risks button on the toolbar. The system displays the risks list for the selected task, as shown in Figure 6-29. The risks list shows all of the risks linked to the task, if any exist. To add a new risk to the risks list, click the New Risk button on the toolbar. To link the task to existing risks, click the Link Project Risks button.

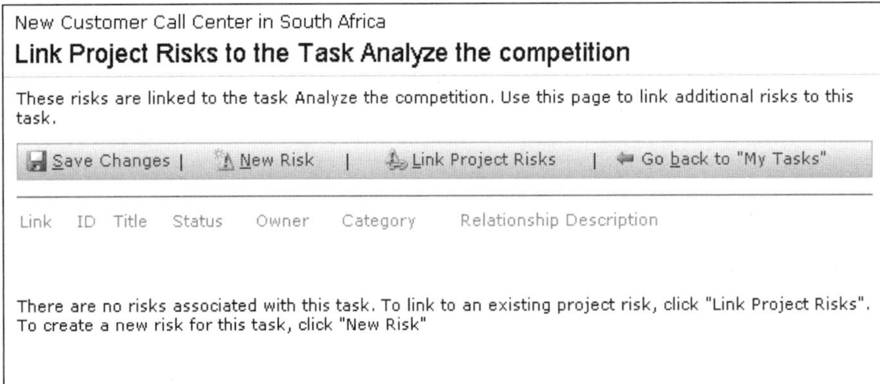

Figure 6-29: Issues list for tasks

In addition to adding risks at the task level, you can also add risks at the project level by clicking the Risks menu at the top of the Project Web Access page.

Managing Project Tasks in Outlook

The View and report on your tasks from your Outlook calendar link in the View my tasks page allows you to import and manage project tasks in Outlook. I will discuss this topic in Module 7, along with other features of using Project Web Access in Outlook.

Notifying Managers of Working Day Changes

Within Project Web Access, you can notify your manager of changes in your working schedule using the Notify your manager of time you will not be available for project work option. Before you can use this option, however, your manager must assign you to at least one task in an Administrative project. Organizations use Administrative projects to track non-project time for employees in the organization.

To notify your manager of a change in work schedule, click the Notify your manager of time you will not be available for project work link in the Actions pane. If a manager has not already assigned you to at least one task in an Administrative project, the system displays the warning page shown in Figure 6-30.

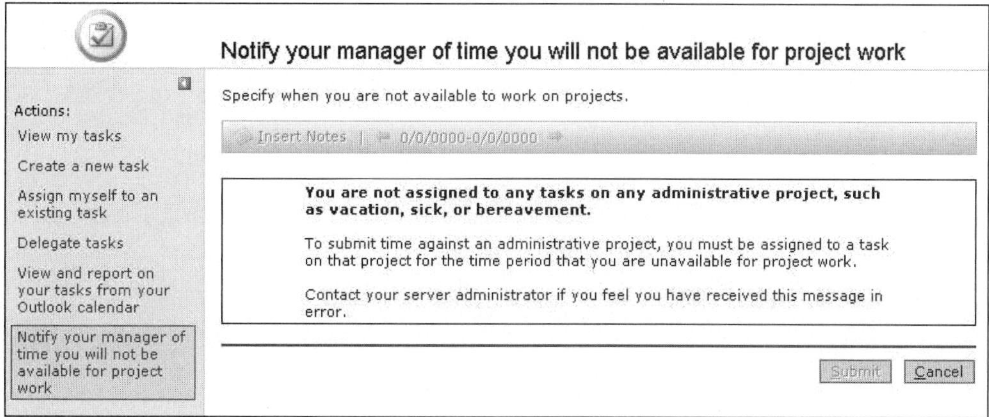

Figure 6-30: Warning page

If a manager has already assigned you to one or more tasks in an Administrative project, the system displays the Notify your manager page shown in Figure 6-31.

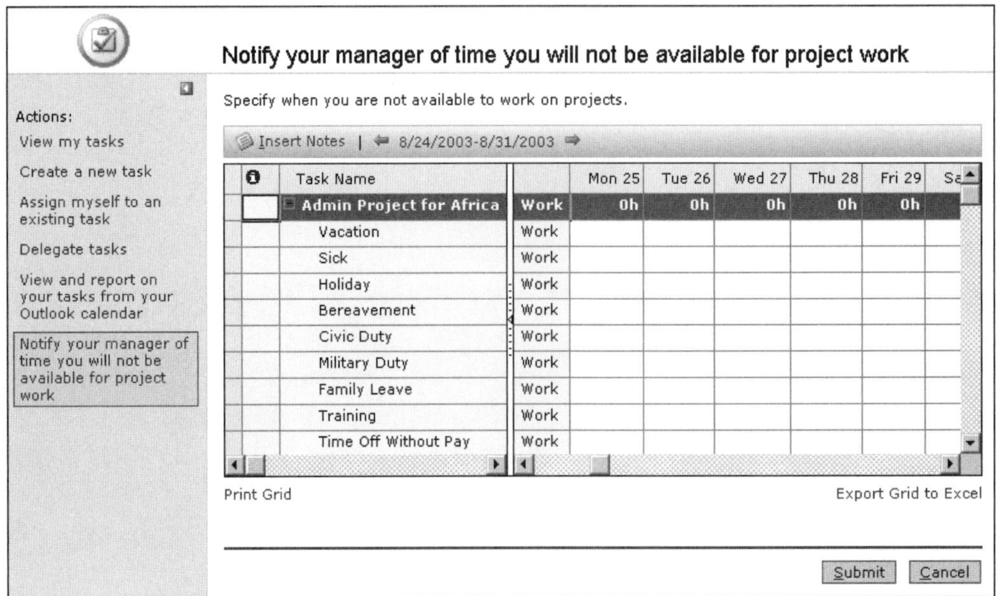

Figure 6-31: Notify your manager of time you will not be available for project work page

Scroll to the desired date in the date grid and select the type of time that causes you to be unavailable for project work. Enter your nonworking time in the date grid and add an optional note by clicking the Insert Note button. When you have finished, click the Submit button. The system displays a confirmation message indicating a successful update of your nonworking time, as shown in Figure 6-32.

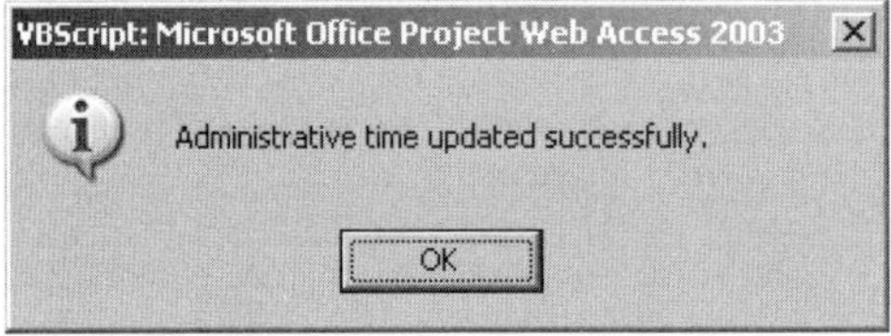

Figure 6-32: Confirmation message

Click the OK button to continue. Your manager will receive your nonworking time update in the same manner as that person would receive your normal task progress updates.

Module 07

Working with Outlook

Learning Objectives

After completing this module, you will be able to:

- Manage your Project Web Access tasks in your Outlook Calendar
- Display Project Web Access pages in Outlook

Managing Project Tasks in Outlook

Shown in Figure 7-1, the Work with Outlook link on the Home page offers you the option to work with Project Web Access in Outlook.

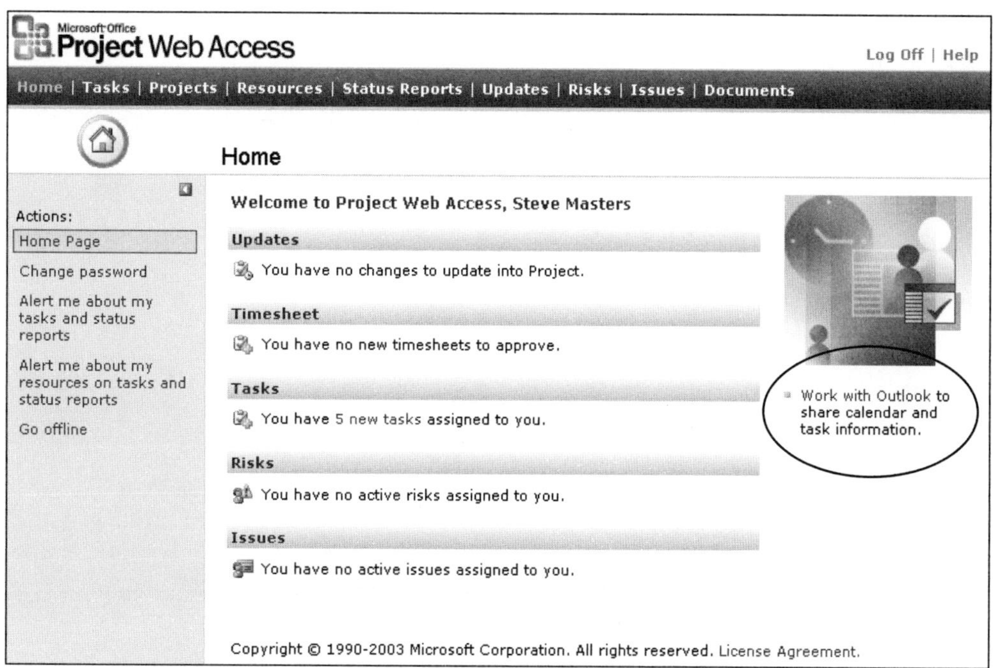

Figure 7-1: Project Web Access home page for a project manager

Shown in Figure 7-2, the View and report on your tasks from your Outlook calendar link also offers you the same option of working with Project Web Access in Outlook.

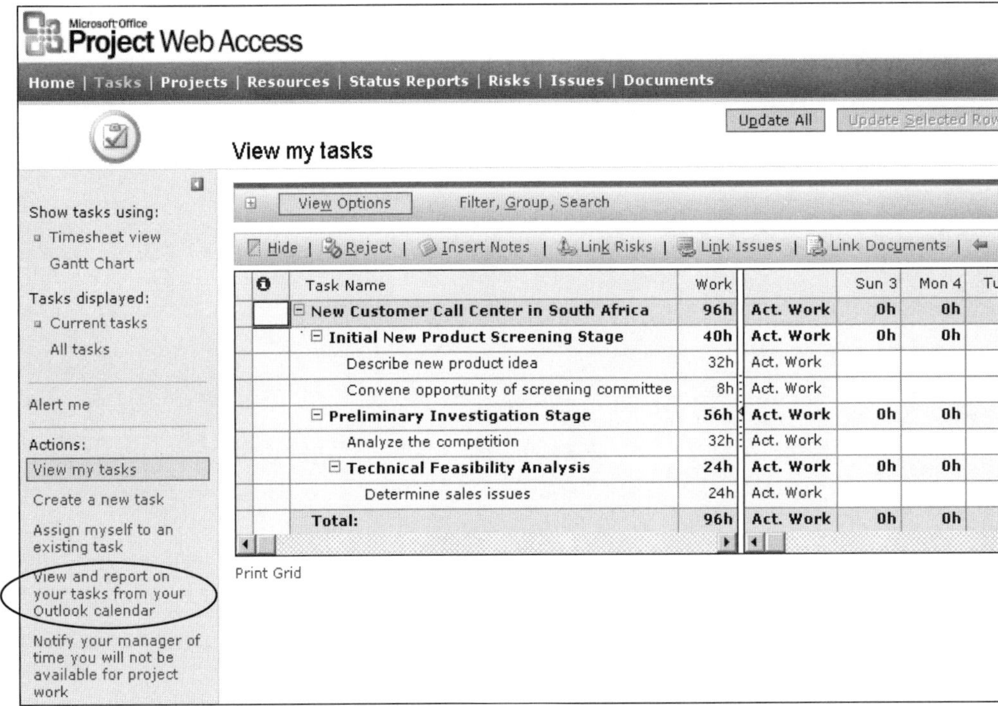

Figure 7-2: View my tasks page Timesheet view

When you click the links shown in either Figure 7-1 or 7-2, the system displays the Work with Outlook page shown in Figure 7-3. This page prompts you to download and install the Outlook add-in.

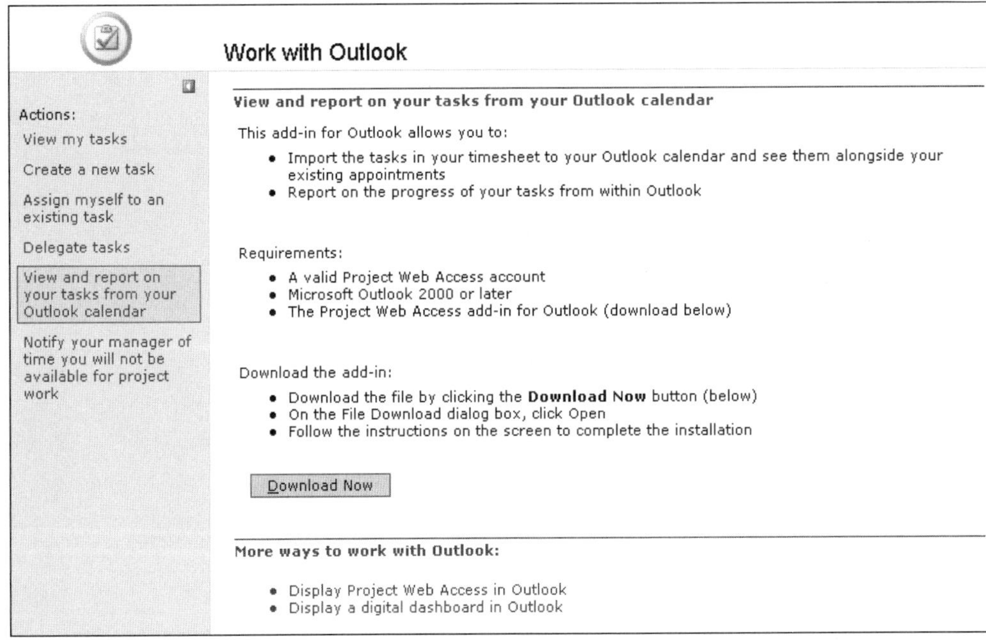

Figure 7-3: Work with Outlook page

Click the Download Now button to begin the process of downloading and installing the add-in. The system displays the dialog shown in Figure 7-4 warning you about a potentially unsafe ActiveX control.

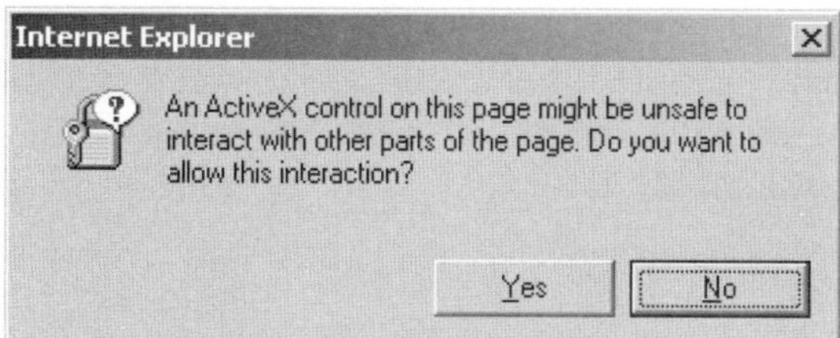

Figure 7-4: ActiveX warning dialog

The appearance of the ActiveX warning dialog is dependent on the security settings in your Internet Explorer browser

Click the Yes button to continue. The system displays the File Download dialog shown in Figure 7-5, and asks whether to save or to open the downloaded ActiveX control.

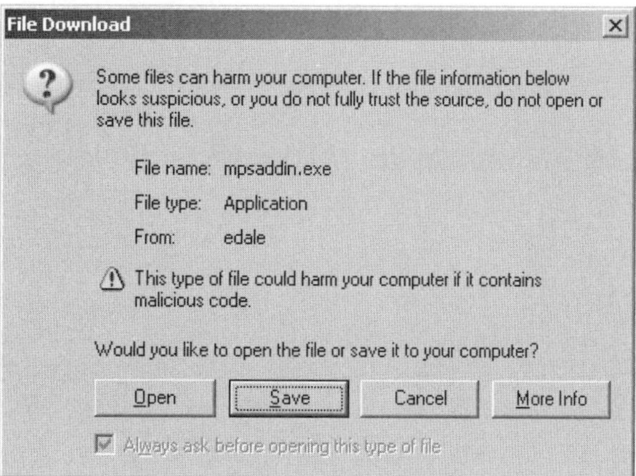

Figure 7-5: File Download dialog

Click the Open button to download and install the ActiveX control. The system displays the Microsoft Office Project Add-In for Outlook dialog shown in Figure 7-6.

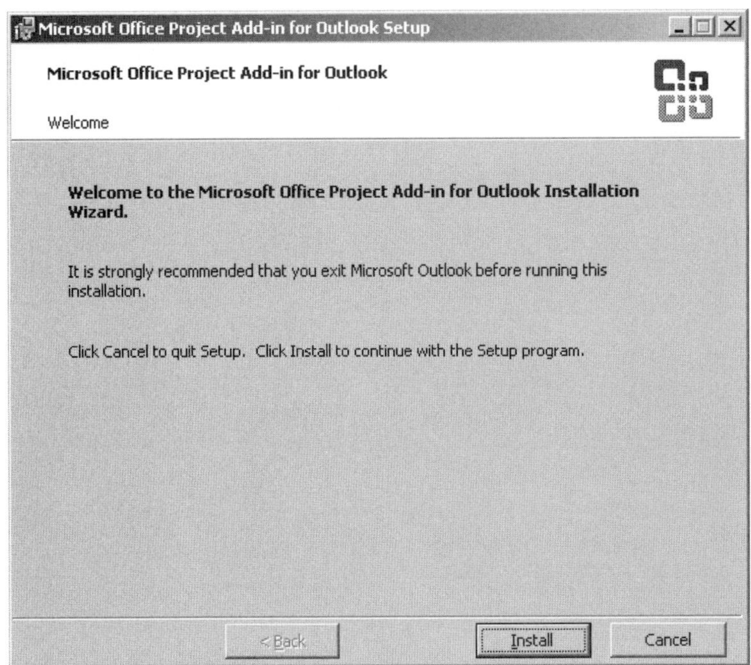

Figure 7-6: Microsoft Office Project Add-In for Outlook dialog

Click the Install button to complete the installation of the add-in. The system displays the confirmation message shown in Figure 7-7. Click the OK button to continue.

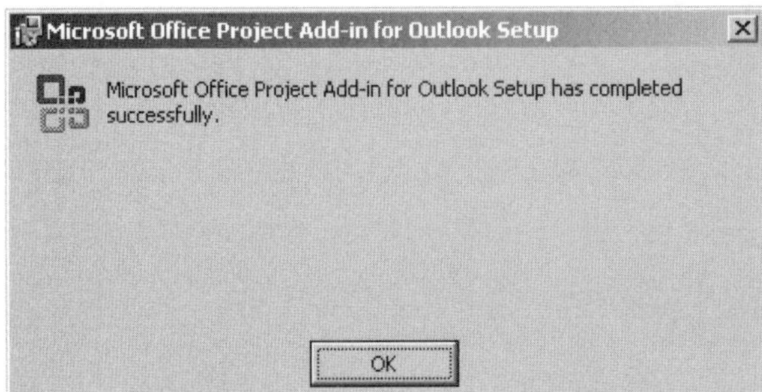

Figure 7-7: Outlook add-in successfully installed

When you have completed the previous steps, you can launch your Outlook program. The first time you launch Outlook after installing the Outlook add-in in Project Web Access, the system automatically opens a Help window in Outlook with more information about how to work with project tasks in Outlook, as shown in Figure 7-8.

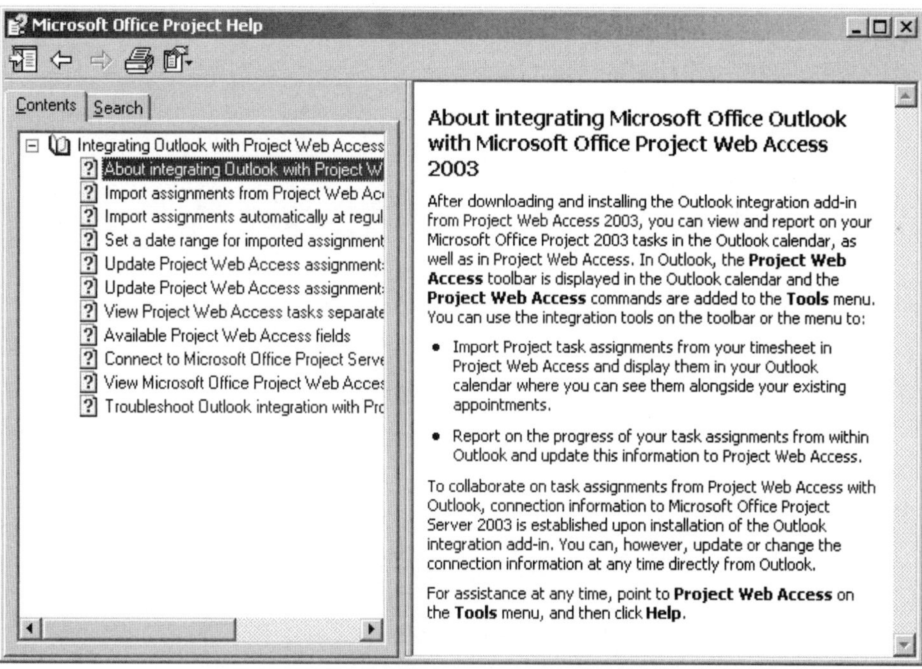

Figure 7-8: Microsoft Office Project Help window in Outlook

When you close the Help window, your Outlook interface will offer two new features: a Project Web Access toolbar and a Project Web Access option on the Tools menu. The system displays these two new features in Figure 7-9 and Figure 7-10.

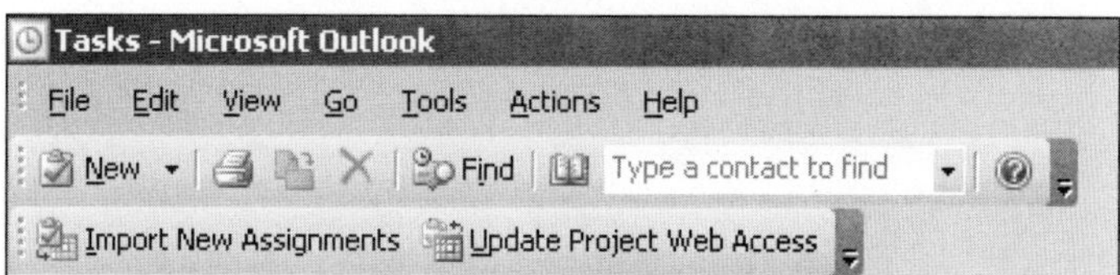

Figure 7-9: Project Web Access toolbar below the Tasks toolbar

If the Project Web Access toolbar is not visible in Outlook, click View ➢ Toolbars and select Project Web Access.

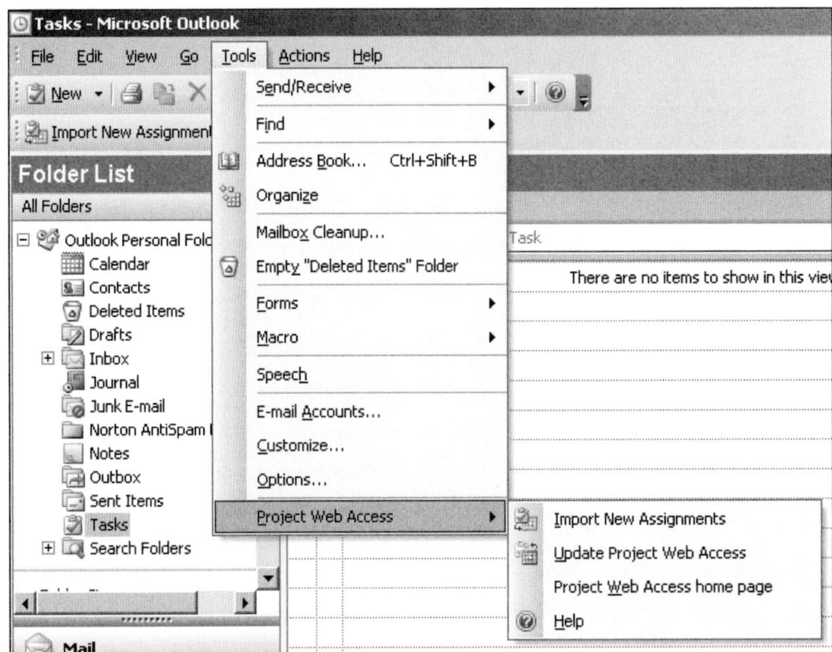

Figure 7-10: Project Web Access option on the Tools menu in Outlook

To work with project tasks in Outlook, you must click the Import New Assignments button. The system displays the Import Assignments from Project Web Access dialog, as shown in Figure 7-11.

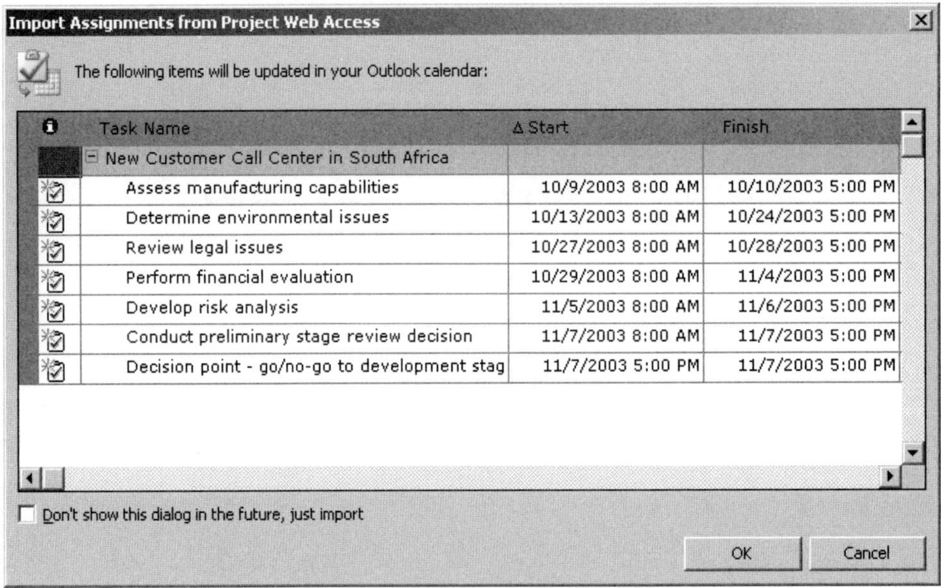

Figure 7-11: Import Assignments from Project Web Access dialog

The dialog is for informational purposes only, and requires no decision on your part except that you click the OK button to confirm the import of assignments into Outlook. If you wish, you may select the Don't show this dialog in the future, just import option to automatically import tasks into Outlook.

The system displays tasks from Project Web Access as appointments on your Outlook calendar. For example, in Figure 7-12 you can see my Project Web Access tasks during the month of October.

Contrary to what you might assume, Outlook does not display Project Web Access tasks on the Tasks page. Project tasks display only as appointments on the Calendar page of Outlook.

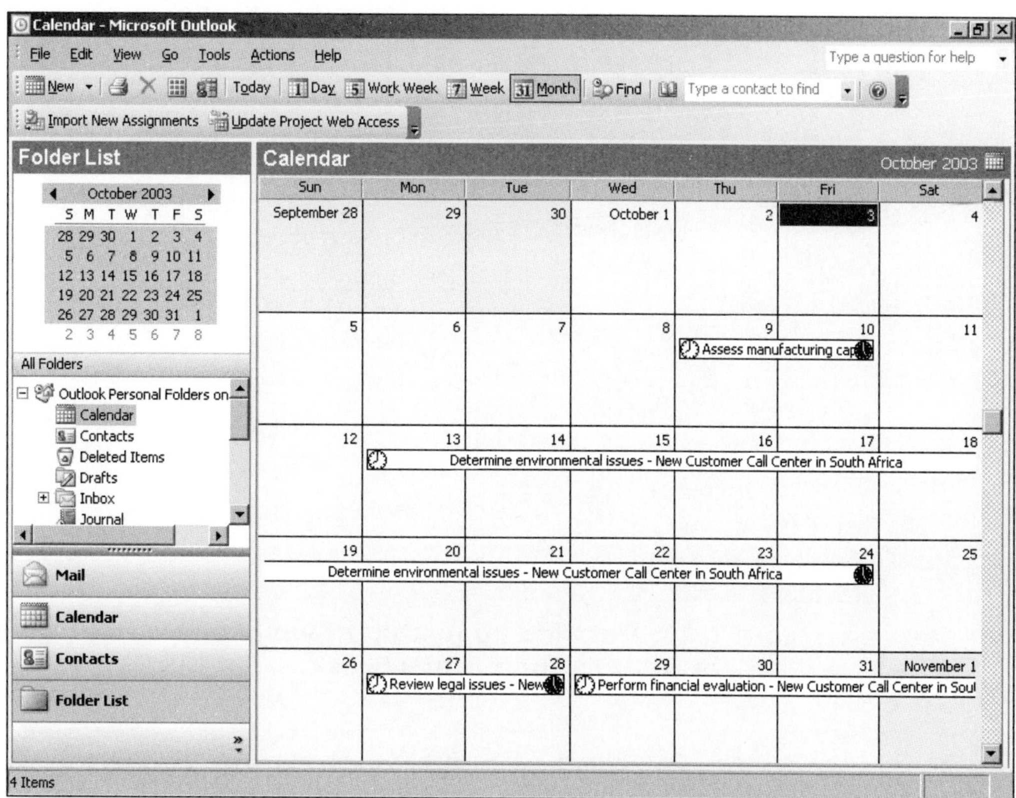

Figure 7-12: Project Web Access tasks as Outlook appointments

To enter progress on any of your project tasks in Outlook, apply the Calendar view and then double-click the project task. Outlook presents the detailed appointment window for the project task. In this window, select the Project Web Access tab to access your timesheet, as shown in Figure 7-13.

To enter progress on a project task in Outlook, use the same method that you would use in Project Web Access:

- Enter Actual Work on the date during which you performed the work
- Adjust the Remaining Work estimate, if necessary
- Insert a task Note if you adjusted the Remaining Work estimate
- To save your changes and not update your project manager, click the Save Changes button
- To update your progress to the project manager, click the Update Project Manager button

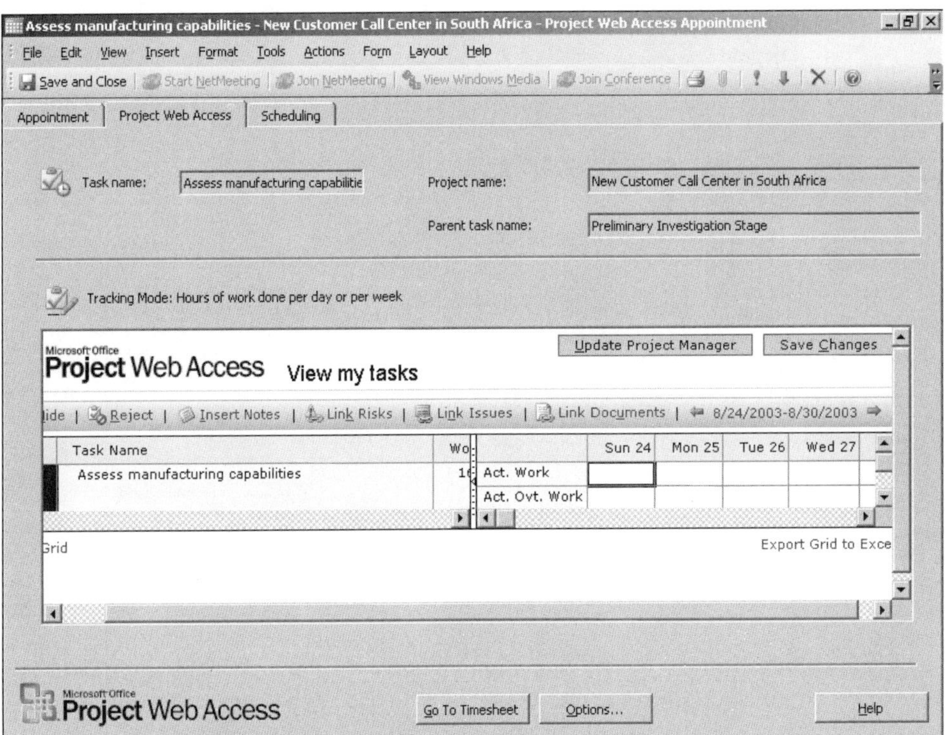

Figure 7-13: Detailed appointment window in Outlook for a project task

Click the Go To Timesheet button to launch your Internet Explorer and navigate to your View my tasks page in Project Web Access.

When you have finished entering progress for your project task in Outlook, click the Save and Close button in the detailed appointment window. If you have saved your project task progress on your timesheet in Outlook, but have not yet updated your project manager, you can update the progress to your manager by clicking the Update Project Web Access button on the Project Web Access toolbar.

Automatically Import Project Tasks into Outlook

If you want to import Project Web Access tasks automatically into your Outlook calendar, you must be using Windows User Account authentication in Project Server. If this is the case, you can set up the process to occur automatically in Outlook by clicking Tools ➤ Options and then selecting the Project Web Access tab, as shown in Figure 7-14. Specify the automatic options that you wish to use in the Options dialog box and then click OK when you are finished.

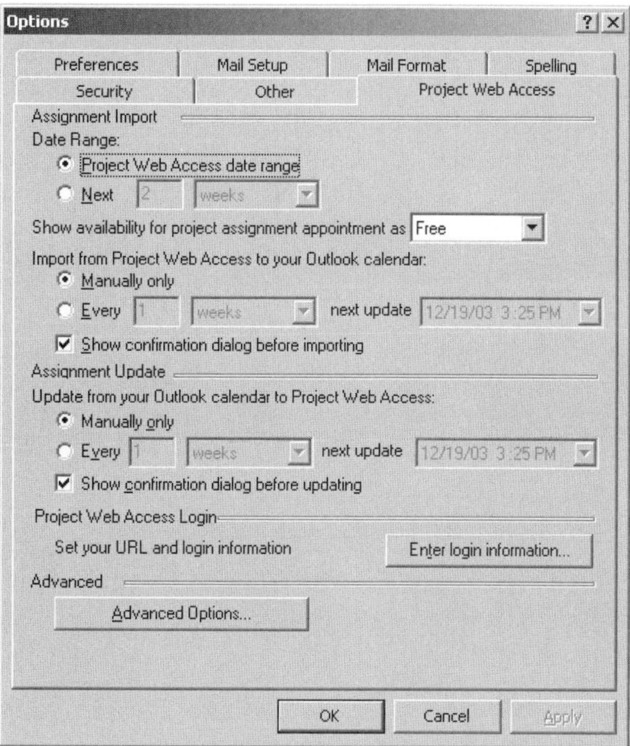

Figure 7-14: Project Web Access options in Outlook Options dialog

Click the Advanced button to determine whether Outlook automatically sends your task updates to your project manager or accepts them only on your timesheet for manual updating to your project manager. You may also choose whether Outlook creates reminders for your Project Web Access tasks in Outlook.

Displaying Project Web Access in Outlook

At the bottom of the Work with Outlook page, there are two additional links in the More ways to work with Outlook section, as shown in Figure 7-15. These links offer you the following options:

- **Display Project Web Access in Outlook** allows you to place a shortcut to a Project Web Access page in Outlook or to display a Project Web Access page as the Home page of a new or existing Outlook folder.
- **Display a digital dashboard in Outlook** allows you to select a link for an existing digital dashboard link and create a shortcut to it in Outlook or display it as the homepage of a new or existing Outlook folder.

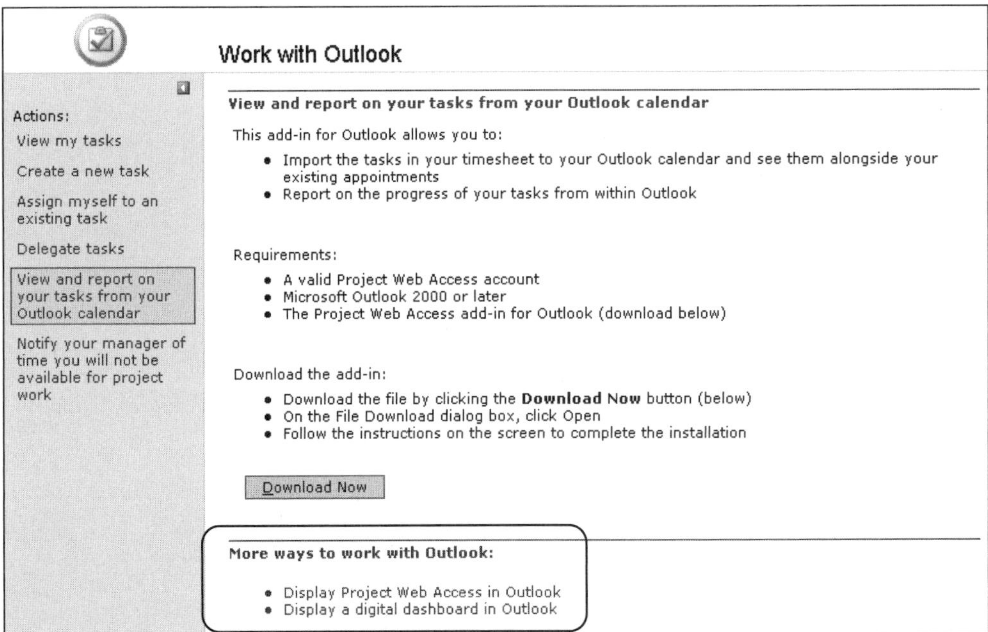

Figure 7-15: Work with Outlook page

When you click the Display Project Web Access in Outlook link, the system displays the familiar ActiveX warning dialog shown previously in Figure 7-4. Click the Yes button to continue. The system displays the Web Page Dialog shown in Figure 7-16. This dialog allows you to determine which specific Project Web Access pages the system will display in Outlook and to determine how Outlook displays the pages.

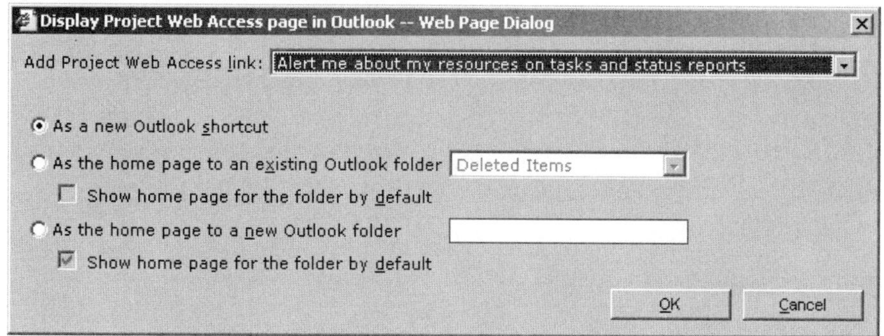

Figure 7-16: Display Project Web Access page in Outlook

Click the Add Project Web Access link pick list and select the page you want to display in Outlook. The pick list contains a user-sensitive list of options based on your permissions within Project Server. For example, the system lists the following pages for a user with Project Manager permissions:

- Alert me about my resources on tasks and status reports
- Alert me about my tasks and status reports
- Analyze projects in Portfolio Analyzer
- Analyze resources in Portfolio Analyzer
- Approve timesheets
- Assign myself to an existing task
- Change password
- Check in my projects
- Create a new personal or shared to-do list
- Create a new task
- Delegate Tasks
- Go offline
- Home Page
- Manage my to-do lists
- Miscellaneous reports
- Notify your manager of time you will not be available for project work
- Request a status report
- Set rules for automatically accepting changes
- Status Reports archive
- Status Reports overview
- Submit a status report

- To-Do list options
- View and report on your tasks from your Outlook calendar
- View and submit issues on all projects
- View and submit issues
- View and submit risks on all projects
- View and submit risks
- View and upload documents on all projects
- View and upload documents
- View and upload public documents
- View enterprise resources in Resource Center
- View history of past task changes
- View issue summary for all projects
- View issue summary for my projects
- View my tasks
- View projects in Project Center
- View resource assignments
- View risk summary for all projects
- View risk summary for my projects
- View status report responses from your team members
- View task changes submitted by resources
- View timesheet summary

As you might surmise, a user with Administrator permissions will see more options on the Add Project Web Access link pick list, while users with Resource Manager, Executive, or Team Member permissions will see fewer options.

In Figure 7-17, notice that I want to display the View my tasks page in Outlook.

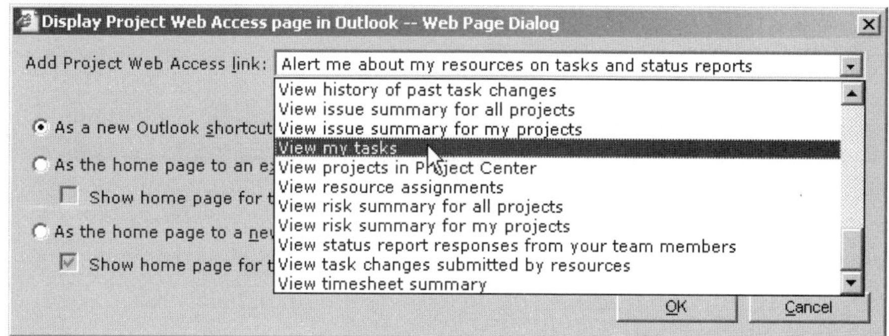

Figure 7-17: Select the View my tasks page to display in Outlook

Once you have selected the Project Web Access page to display in Outlook, you must also select the option for how you want the page displayed in Outlook and then click the OK button. Select the As the home page of a new Outlook folder option to create a new folder in Outlook. Choose the As the home page of an existing folder option if you have already created a folder. If you select either of these two options, Outlook displays your selected Project Web Access page as shown in Figure 7-18.

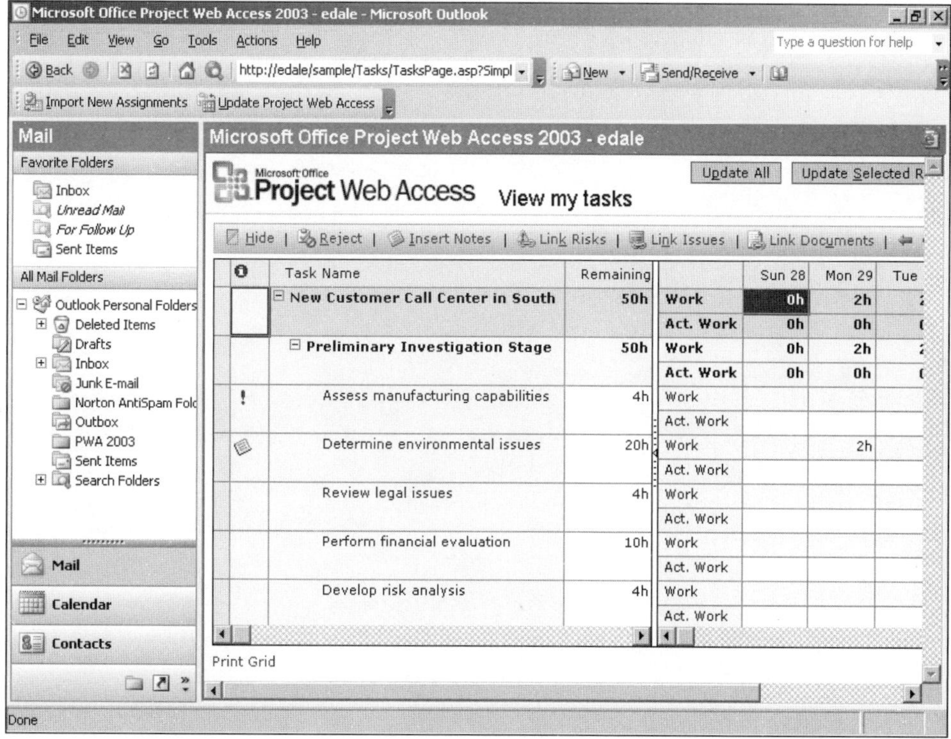

Figure 7-18: Project Web Access page in Outlook

Hands On Exercise

Exercise 7-1

Display Project Web Access in Outlook.

1. Navigate to the Home page in Project Web Access
2. Click the Work with Outlook link on the right side of your Home page
3. In the Display Project Web Access in Outlook dialog, select a Project Web Access page from the pick list
4. Select how the information will be accessed in Outlook
5. Click OK when finished
6. Open Outlook and display the results

Module 08

Updating Progress through Project Web Access

Learning Objectives

After completing this module, you will be able to:

- Set view options on the Updates page in Project Web Access
- Filter, group and search on the Updates page in Project Web Access
- Accept or reject an update from a resource
- Set and run rules for automatically accepting updates from resources
- Approve or reject a timesheet for a resource
- View unsubmitted timesheets for resources

Applying Updates in Project Web Access

The reporting cycle completes through the Project Web Access Updates page where you accept or reject the updates project team members send to you. Notice that when you logon to Project Server, the Home page displays the number of new updates you have pending in the Update section of the page. In Figure 8-1, Steve Masters has six task changes indicated in the Updates section of his Home page.

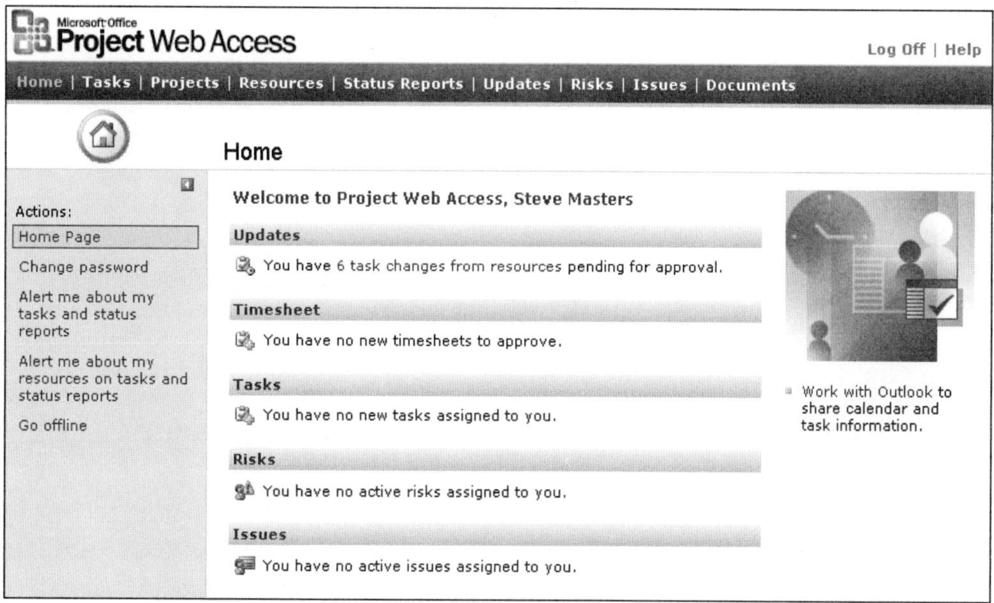

Figure 8-1: Home page with 6 task changes in Updates section of page

Click the Updates link or the Updates menu option on the main navigation menu to display the Updates page shown in Figure 8-2. The Updates page is very similar to the View my tasks display. For example, both pages allow you to apply either a Timesheet or Gantt Chart format to the view. In addition, the View Options and Filter, Group, Search sections are nearly identical in both pages. In the case of the Updates page, however, an Apply Rules tab replaces the Delegation tab seen in the View my tasks page. The similarity is not surprising in that both pages deal with precisely the same information. Of course, the Updates page presents the information from the project manager's point of view.

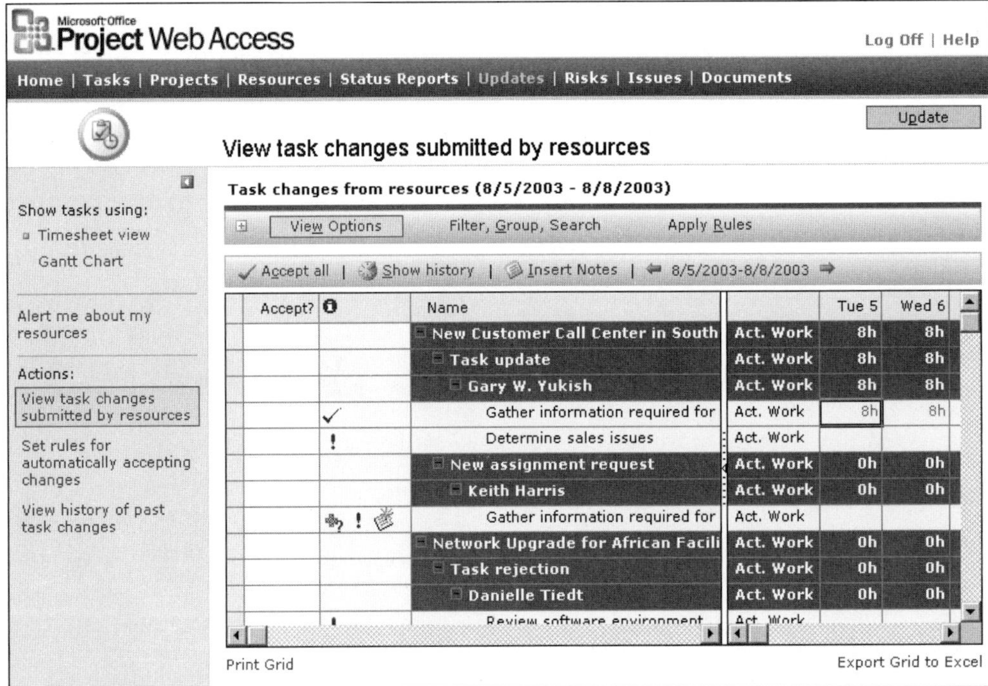

Figure 8-2: View task changes submitted by resources

The Actions pane on the left side of the Updates page allows you to apply either a Timesheet view or a Gantt chart view to personalize your updates page. Click the Alert me about my resources link to set up e-mail alerts about the assignment work of your resources. This is accomplished on the on the Alert me about my resources on task updates page, which I will discuss in the Module 9 on using the features of the Home page.

A selection for setting up rules for automatic update processing complements the Apply Rules selection on the activities menu. Use the selection from the Actions pane to create rules, and then use the Apply Rules tab to apply your rules to the updates received. Finally, the Actions pane also contains a link for viewing a history of past task changes.

Setting View Options

Expanding the View Options tab reveals the view options for the Updates page. As in the View my tasks page, you can display time with dates, show scheduled and overtime work, select the outline level of task updates shown in the view, and navigate to a specific date range. A new feature in Project Server 2003 is the Show timesheet status option. Select this option to determine which team members' timesheets are approved by their resource manager. When this option is selected, the system will place an asterisk symbol next to unapproved work in the Actual Work field. When you float the mouse pointer over an Actual Work value, the system will display a tooltip, as shown in Figure 8-3.

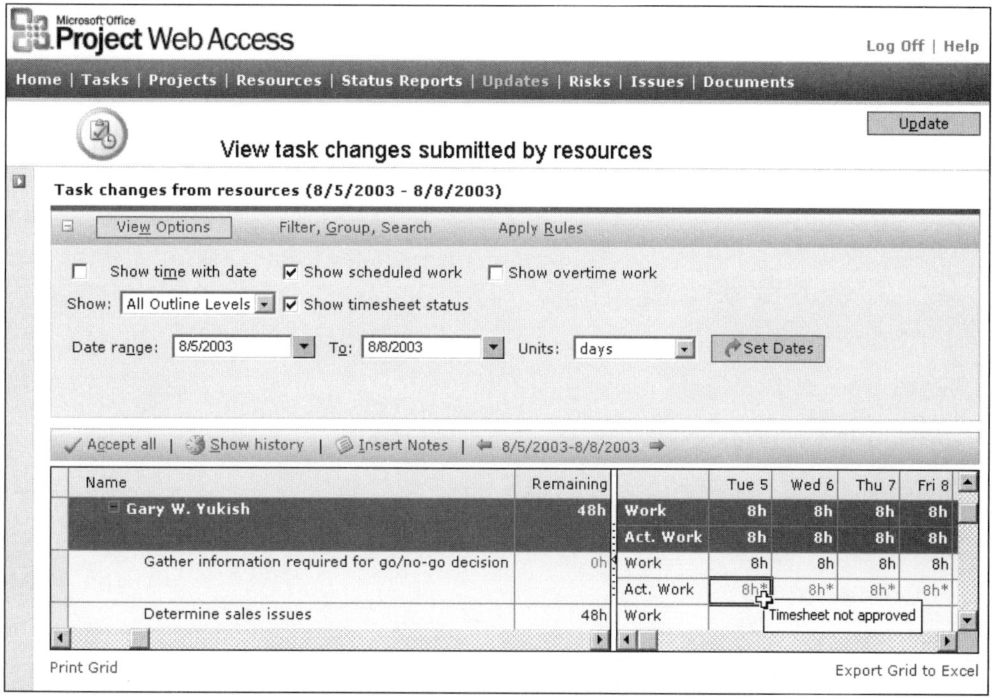

Figure 8-3: Updates page with Show timesheet status option selected

Setting Filter, Group, Search Options

Expanding the Filter, Group, Search tab reveals the options shown in Figure 8-4. Default filters include:

- All task changes
- All task updates
- All new tasks
- All task delegation requests
- All resource declined tasks
- All new assignment requests
- All declined task delegation requests
- All completed tasks
- All incomplete tasks
- All overdue tasks
- All tasks pending for approval
- All tasks updated into Project

Because you can create your own custom filters the same way in the Updates page as in the View my tasks page, we will not cover the process again in this module. In addition to filtering, you can also apply up to three levels of grouping using the following criteria:

- Accept?
- From
- Project
- Task change type
- Sent date
- Work
- Remaining work
- Start
- Finish
- % Complete

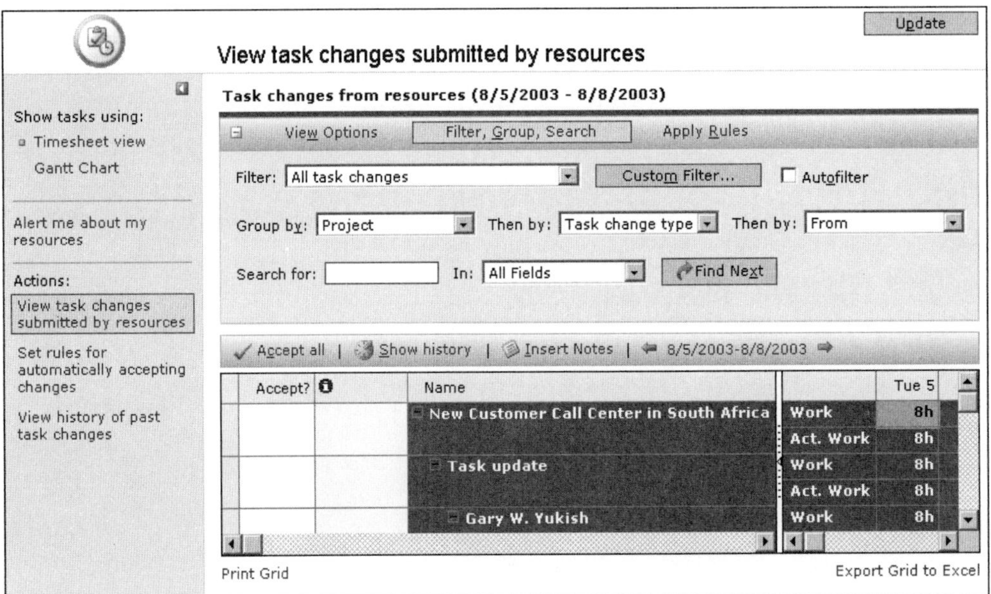

Figure 8-4: Filter, Group, Search options

The default Grouping format applied to the Updates page is by Project, then by Task Change Type, and then by the resource's name (found in the From field).

Accepting and Rejecting Updates

What type of updates will you receive from your team members in the Updates page? Updates can include any of the following:

- Task updates about the current status of task work
- Rejected tasks
- New assignment requests in which a member has assigned himself/herself to an existing task
- New task requests
- Task delegation requests

It is your responsibility as the project manager to either accept or reject any updates submitted by your team members. Accepting a task update automatically transfers the updated task information into the appropriate project plan. If you reject any updates from your team members, the team member will need to take the appropriate action in response to your rejection. This process guarantees that you as the project manager will always serve as the "gatekeeper" between your project team members and the actual project plan.

Before you can process any updates from your project team, you must set an Accept or Reject value in the Accept column. In Figure 8-5, I have accepted the first task update and am accepting the second update as well. You can also use the Accept all button in the tool bar to set all updates in the view to Accept.

When you reject an update, the system will notify the affected resource with an e-mail message. You might reject a task update when a resource accidentally "fat fingers" an actual work value, forgets to update remaining work, or fails to annotate a new task request.

Before you process updates, pay special attention to any task update that includes a Note icon in the Indicators column. A note attached to a task update usually means that your team members are trying to give you additional information about their task updates.

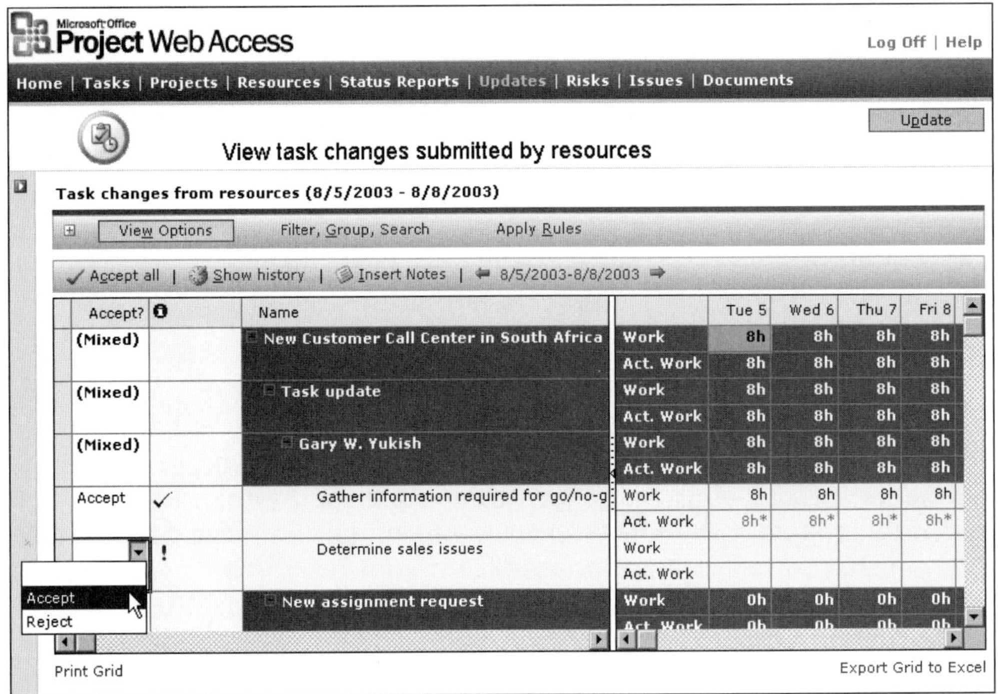

Figure 8-5: Updates page
Accept and reject updates

Click the Update button to accept and reject according to your selections. You may see a logon screen flash briefly as the system goes to work. In processing the updates, the system launches Microsoft Project Professional if it is not already open, and opens any project plans affected by the updates. The system also makes changes to each of the open project plans according to the type of update. Once the system has processed all updates in each project, it displays the confirmation dialog shown in Figure 8-6.

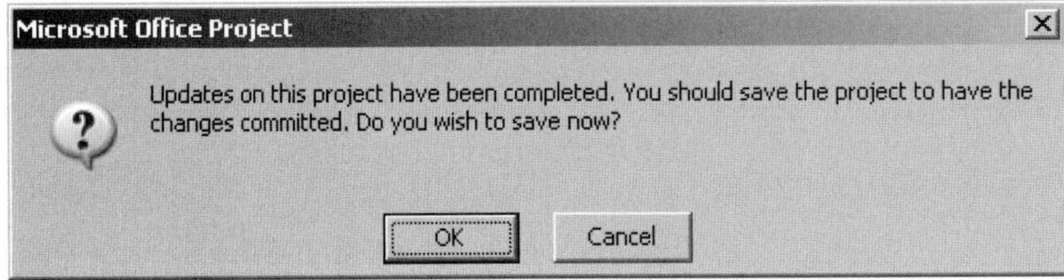

Figure 8-6: Update confirmation dialog

If you want to save the changes to your projects, click the OK button to continue. If you want to review the task changes before saving the project, click the Cancel button.

msProjectExperts recommends that you routinely click the Cancel button after processing the updates. Doing so will allow you to determine which tasks have been updated, which tasks have been affected by the task updates, and how the task updates impact the current state of your project plan. After you have reviewed the results of the update process, remember to save and publish your project using the Collaborate ➤ Publish ➤ All Information command.

When the system completes the updates, it displays the confirmation dialog shown in Figure 8-7. Click the OK button to continue.

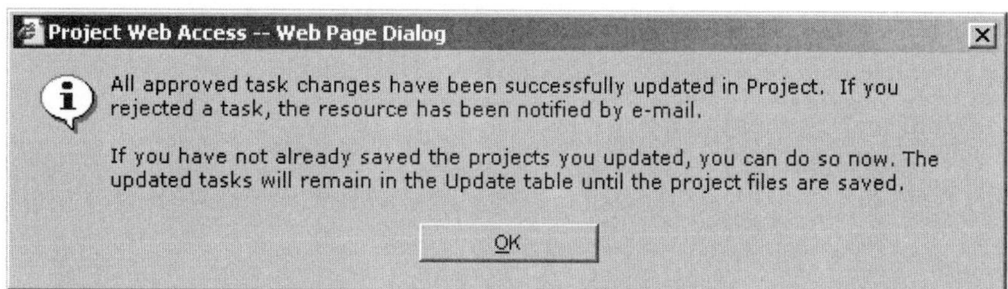

Figure 8-7: Task changes updated

Click the OK button in confirmation dialog and the system redisplays the Updates page. Shown in Figure 8-8, the system indicates that it no longer has information to display. As soon as the next resource sends an update, the view populates.

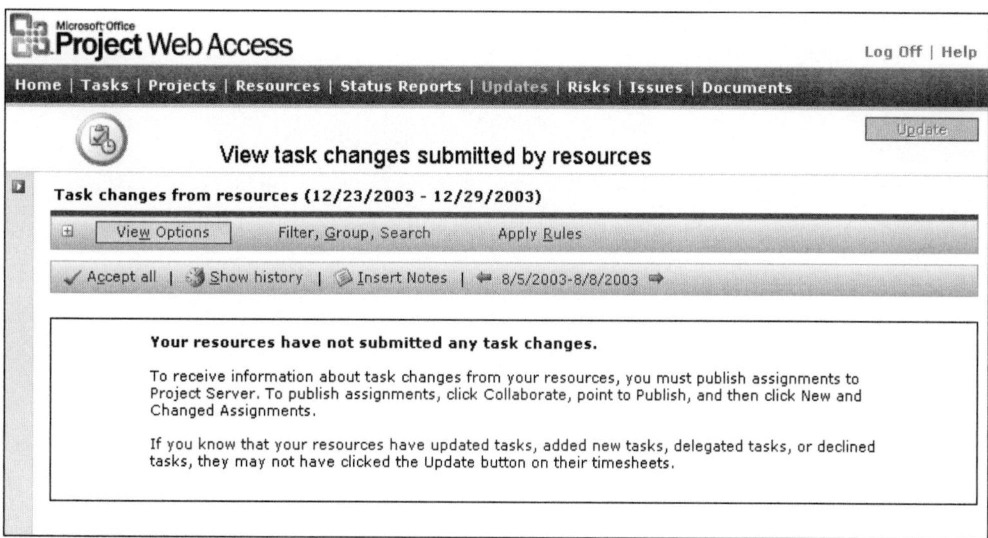

Figure 8-8: No task changes in the queue

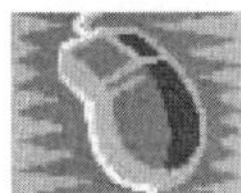

Hands On Exercise

Exercise 8-1

Accept and reject task updates from resources.

1. Select Updates from the main menu in Project Web Access
2. Set Accept on a task line in the left most column
3. Set Reject on a task line in the left most column
4. Note the Accept all button on the toolbar
5. Click the Update button
6. Click the Cancel button to review your task updates
7. Save your project
8. Click OK when prompted

View History of past task changes

Click the View history of past task changes link in the Actions pane or select the Show history button from the tool bar to open the View history of past task changes view shown in Figure 8-9. Use the View Options and Filter, Group, Search functions as you have learned elsewhere in this chapter to refine the data selection shown in the view as well as the presentation.

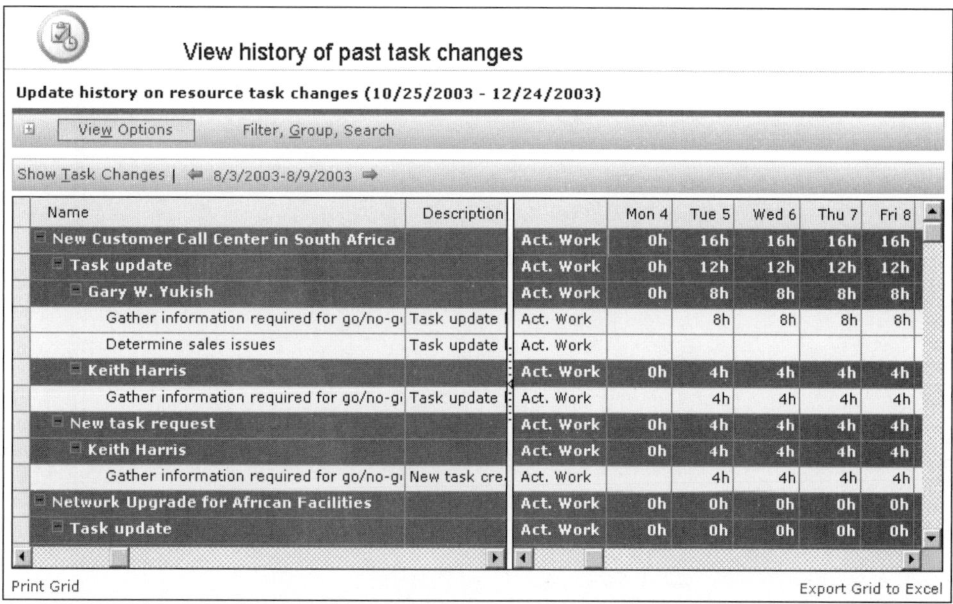

Figure 8-9: View history of past task changes

Hands On Exercise

Exercise 8-2

View the history of past task changes in Project Web Access.

1. From the View task changes submitted by resources screen, click the Show history button on the toolbar
2. When the system displays the screen note that task changes you processed in Exercise 8-1 appear in the grid

Setting Rules for Accepting Task Updates

The Set Rules feature allows you to create logical rules for quickly updating tasks in your projects. When you apply a rule, the system processes only those task changes that meet the criteria defined in the rule. To create a new rule, click the Set rules for automatically accepting changes link in the actions pane. The system applies the Set rules for automatically accepting changes page, as shown in Figure 8-10.

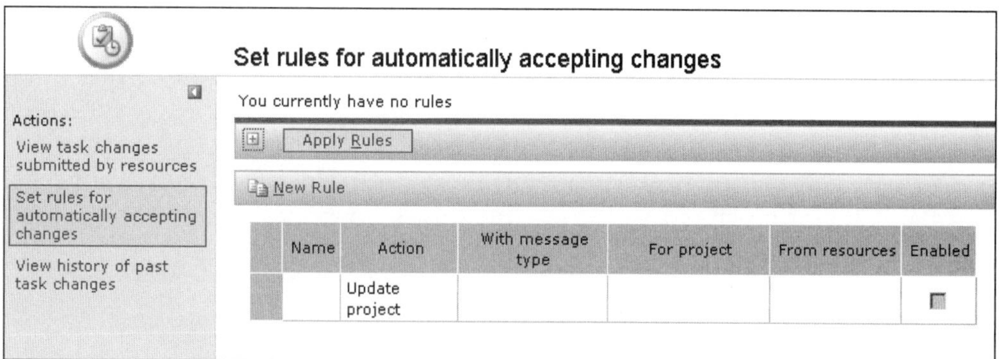

Figure 8-10: Set rules for automatically accepting changes page

Click the New Rule button to open the Step 1 page as shown in Figure 8-11.

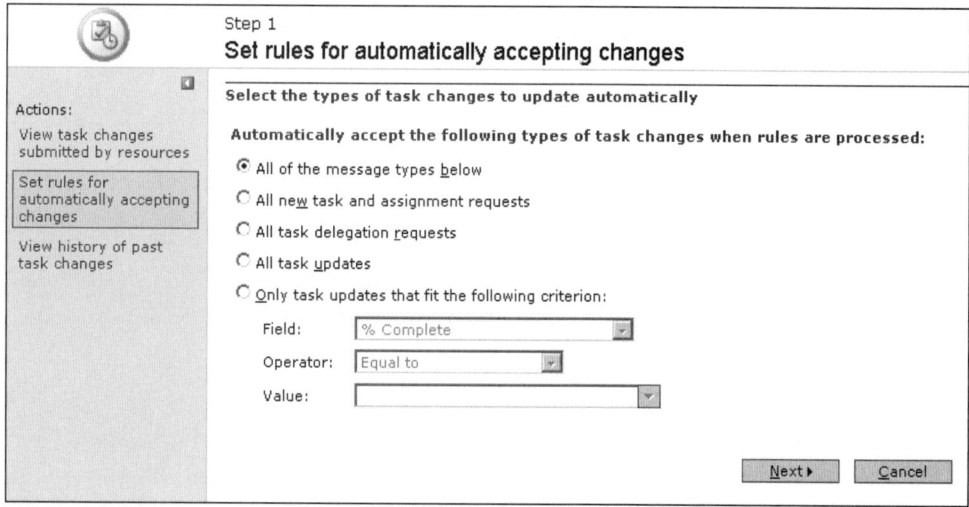

Figure 8-11: Set rules - Step 1

The first step is to select the types of task changes to update automatically. Select one of the following options:

- All of the message types below
- All new task and assignment requests
- All task delegation requests
- All task updates
- Only task updates that fit the following criterion

Select the first option to update all message types, including new task requests, new assignment requests, task delegation requests, and task updates. Select one of the next three options to pinpoint the specific type of message to update automatically. You can create a rule for each message type separately if you wish. Select the last option to create the most specific selection criteria for your new rule, and then set field-based selection tests. In Figure 8-12, notice that I am creating a rule to only update task updates for tasks that are less than 100% complete.

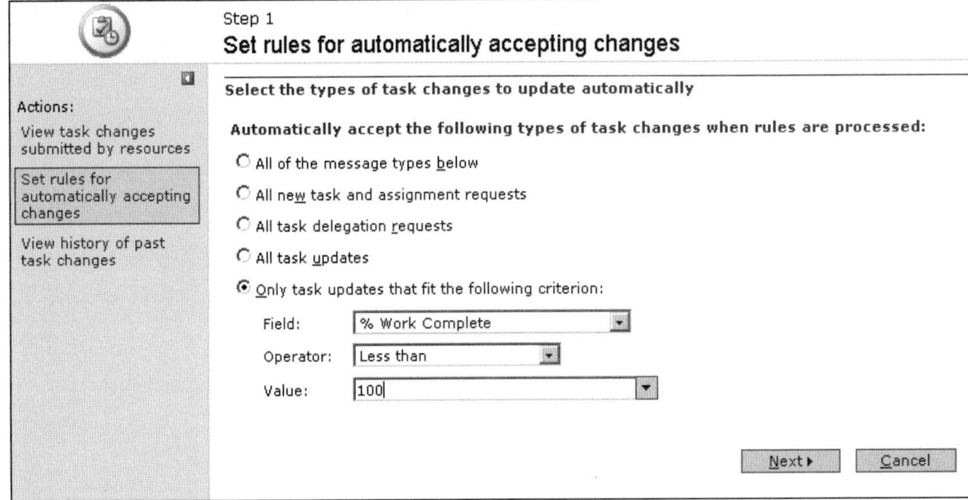

Figure 8-12: Step 1 page
Update tasks less than 100% complete

Click the Next button to display the Step 2 page. Select the projects to which the new rule will apply. Choose the All current and future projects option to update any of your projects automatically. Choose the Only the projects specified below option to select specific projects for updating. Select the projects you wish to update from the Available projects list, and then click the Add button. You can also include any future projects you will create by selecting the Including all future projects option as well. Notice in Figure 8-13 that I have selected two specific projects for automatic updating.

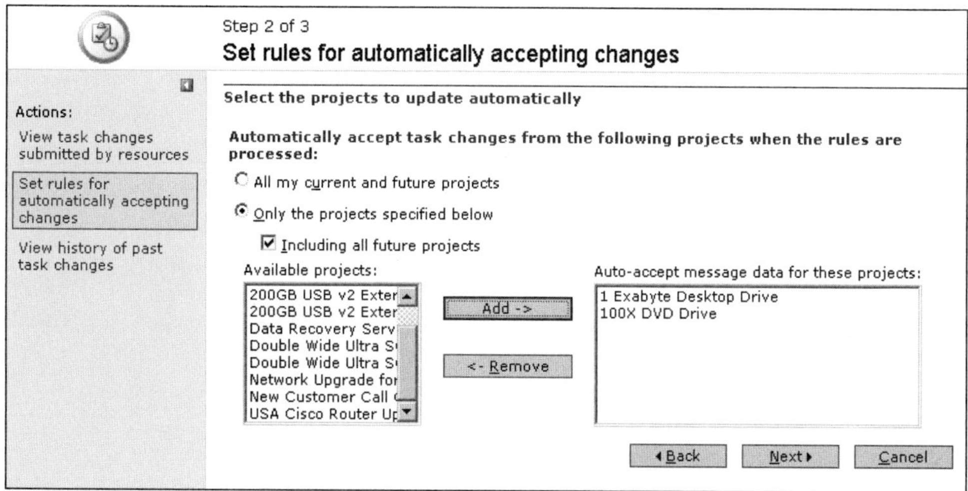

Figure 8-13: Set rules - Step 2
Select projects to which the new rule applies

Click the Next to continue to the Step 3 page, as shown in Figure 8-14.

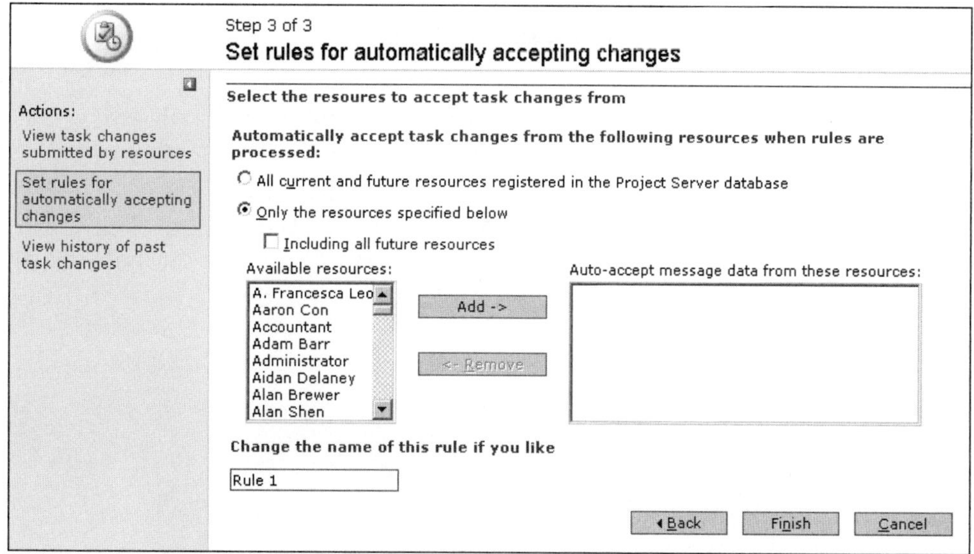

Figure 8-14: Set rules - Step 3
Select resources to which the new rule applies

The last step in the new rule creation process is to select the resources to which the rule applies. As you can see, a rule can be very specific or very broad in its application. You can even create a rule to update a task based on meeting specific criteria that applies to only one resource in only one project. Give your new rule a name and select the desired resources. Click the Finish button to complete the rule creation process.

When you click the Finish button, the Set rules page redisplays showing your new rule indicating an enabled state as shown in Figure 8-15. Note at the top of the Set rules page that once you have created your first rule, the system reports how many rules you have created. The Set rules toolbar offers options to modify, copy, or delete a rule, providing that you have selected a rule in the grid. Use the Copy Rule feature to create new rules based on rules you have previously created. Deselect the Enabled option for a rule to disable the rule without removing it from the system, which allows you to re-enable it later.

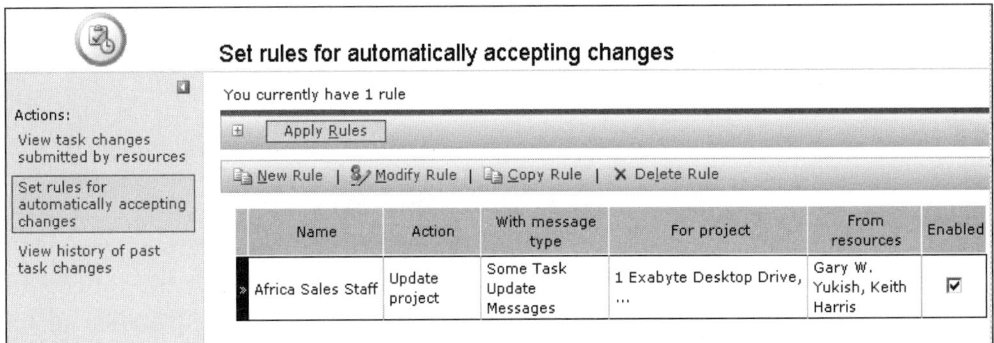

Figure 8-15: Set rules page displays a new rule

The next time you have task updates, run your automated rules first to accept all automatic updates. To run rules, click the Apply Rules tab at the top of the View task changes submitted by resources page. The system displays the Apply Rules section, shown in Figure 8-16. If you click the Apply resource change rules to pick list, you can choose to apply the rule to all projects specified in each rule or to a specific project. Click the Run Rules Now button to run the rules.

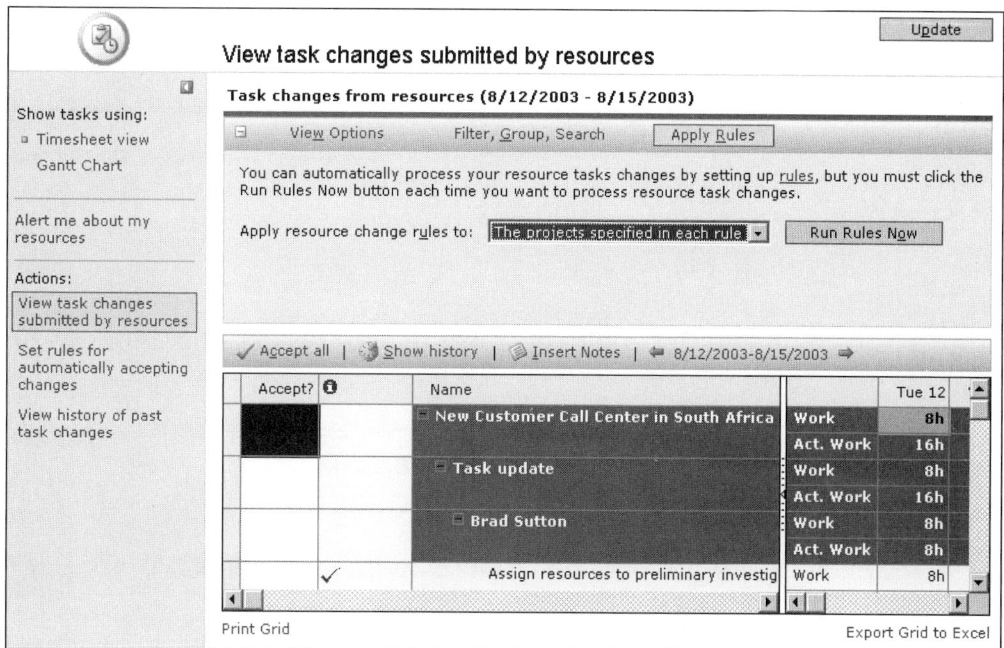

Figure 8-16: Apply Rules tab

When you click the Run Rules Now button, the system opens each project specified in your rules and updates messages for only those resources specified in your rules. When the updates are completed, the system displays the confirmation message shown in Figure 8-17.

Figure 8-17: Successful update using rules

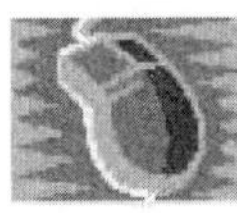

Hands On Exercise

Exercise 8-3

Create a new Rule for processing task updates.

1. Click on the Set rules for automatically accepting changes link in the actions pane
2. In the Set rules for automatically accepting changes page, click the New Rule button in the toolbar
3. Select a type of task to which the rule applies
4. Explore the field options available and click Next
5. Select a rule for selecting projects or select specific projects and click Next to continue
6. Select a rule for selection resources or select specific resources and click Finish to continue

Exercise 8-4

Apply your new Rule to one or more task updates.

1. Click the View task changes submitted by resources link in the actions pane
2. Click on the Apply Rules tab
3. Select the Apply resource changes rules to pick list and explore your options
4. Click the Run Rules Now button
5. Click the OK button to save changes to the active project
6. Click the OK button in the confirmation message in Project Web Access

Timesheet Approval

A new feature of Project Server 2003 is the timesheet approval process. This process allows people like resource managers, line managers, or team leaders to approve the timesheets of resources before the project manager processes the actuals contained in each resource's timesheet.

Before you can use the timesheet approval process, your Project Server administrator must enable timesheet approval within Project Server.

If you are a manager who was been granted timesheet approval authority within Project Server, the system displays a Timesheet section on your Home Page in Project Web Access, as shown in Figure 8-18.

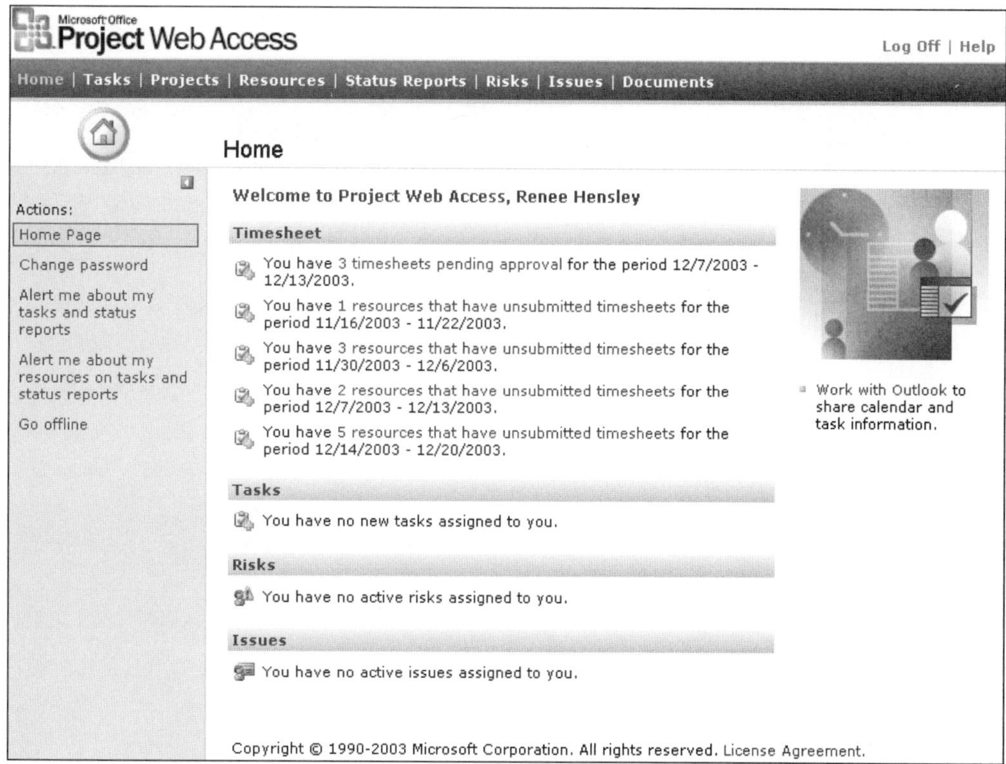

Figure 8-18: Timesheet section of Home page

The Timesheet section of the Home page contains information about the number of timesheets pending approval and the number of resources that have unsubmitted timesheets for specific reporting periods. To begin the timesheet approval process, click the Timesheet link at the beginning of the section or click the ___ timesheets pending approval link. The system displays the Approve timesheets page shown in Figure 8-19.

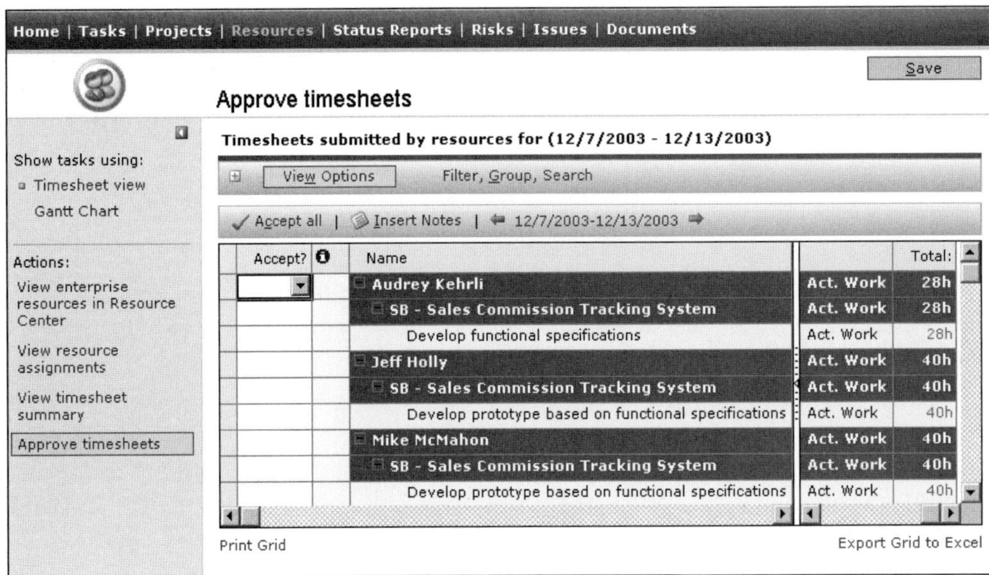

Figure 8-19: Approve timesheets page

You can find the Approve timesheets page in the Project Web Access Resource Center. The page displays each task submitted for approval, grouped by the assigned resource and then by project. As with other pages in Project Web Access, the Approve timesheets page contains a View Options tab and a Filter, Group, Search tab at the top of the grid. The View Options tab offers options to display Overtime Work and to select an outline level, as shown in Figure 8-20.

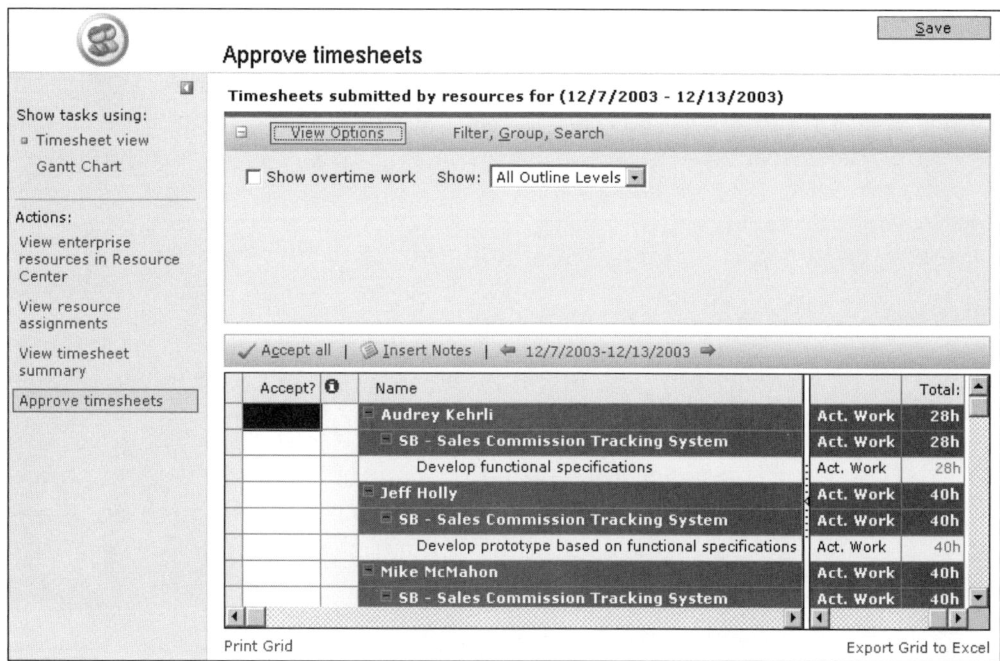

Figure 6:20 Approve timesheet page
View Options tab

The Filter, Group, Search tab, shown in Figure 8-21, offers filtering by all assignments or by a custom filter, along with grouping and searching capabilities covered in previous modules.

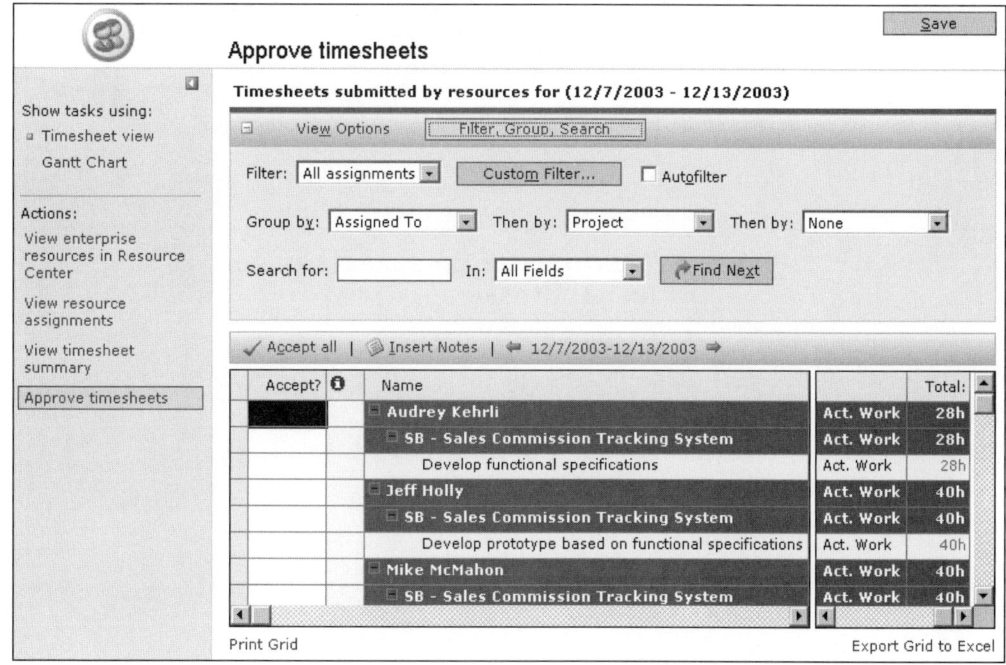

Figure 8-21: Approve timesheets page
Filter, Group, Search tab

As with the approval of task updates on the Updates page, you can select an Accept or Reject value for each timesheet task on the Approve timesheets page. The page includes an Accept All button, an Insert Notes button, and a date selector button, as are also included on the Updates page. In Figure 8-22, notice that I have approved each task submitted by all resources. Click the Save button when you have accepted or rejected each timesheet task.

When you reject any timesheet tasks, it has the following consequences:

- The affected resources see a special indicator for each rejected task in the Indicators column of their View my tasks page.
- The resource's project manager will see the Timesheet not approved indicators for the resources task update on the Updates page, previously shown in Figure 8-3.

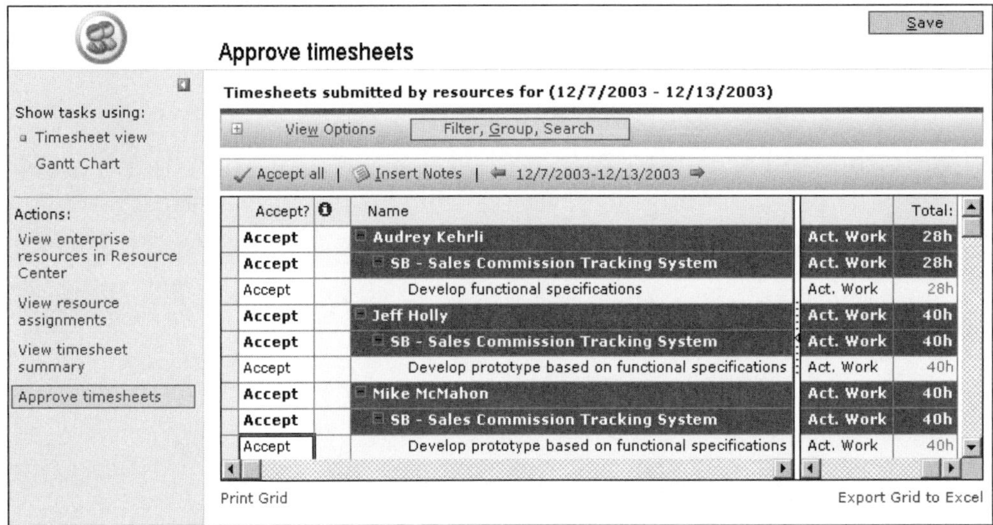

Figure 8-22: Approve timesheets page Timesheet tasks approved

Once you have approved or rejected all timesheets, the system redisplays the page indicating that your resources have not submitted any timesheet changes for the current period, as shown in Figure 8-23.

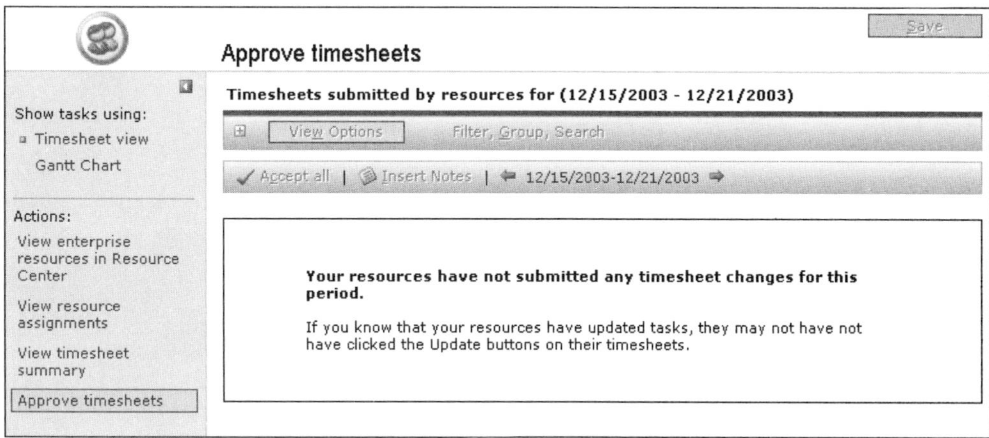

Figure 8-23: Approve timesheets page No timesheets to approve

By default, a project manager can update a task even when you have *rejected* the timesheet containing the task, thus allowing the project manager to overrule your rejection of a timesheet. If your organization is using a timesheet approval process, then msProjectExperts recommends that you establish standard procedures for handling timesheets that are either unapproved or rejected.

Viewing Unsubmitted Timesheets

Timesheet section of the Home page shows you both timesheets pending approval and unsubmitted timesheets. If you click the ___ resources that have unsubmitted timesheets link for a specific period, the system displays the View timesheet summary page shown in Figure 8-24. The display includes each task that is scheduled during the selected period, grouped by the assigned resource and then by project.

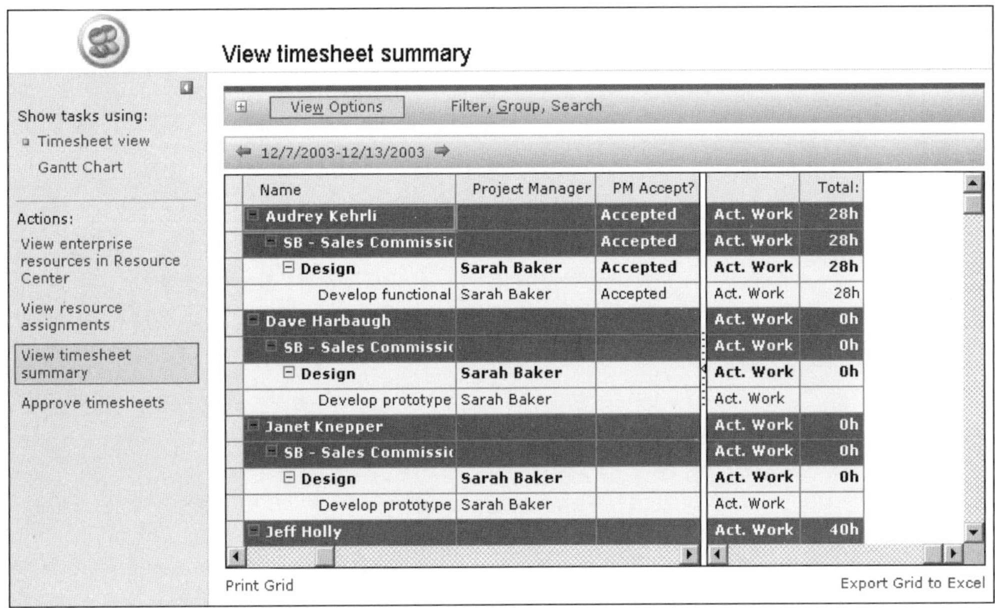

Figure 8-24: View timesheet summary page

As with the Approve timesheets page, the View timesheet summary page contains a View Options tab and a Filter, Group, Search tab. The View Options tab is identical on both pages. The Filter, Group, Search tab shown in Figure 8-25 contains the following filters:

- All timesheets
- All approved timesheets
- All rejected timesheets
- All submitted timesheets not yet approved
- All unsubmitted timesheets
- Custom filter

The Filter, Group, Search tab offers the same grouping and searching capabilities covered in previous modules.

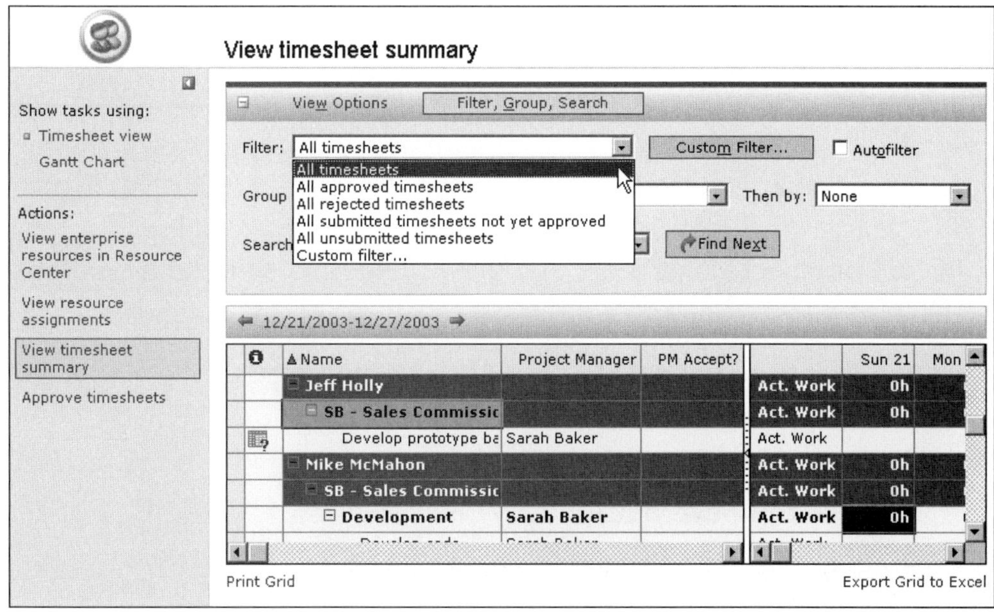

Figure 8-25: View timesheet summary page Filter, Group, Search tab

The View timesheet summary page does not allow you to take any action on any user's timesheet, and is for informational purposes only. The left portion of the grid contains a number of columns that you can use for determining the update and approval status of each task. These columns include the following:

- Indicators
- Name
- Project Manager
- PM Accept?
- Assigned To
- Project
- Timesheet Status

You can use the PM Accept? column to determine whether the project manager has approved or rejected a task update, regardless of whether you have approved or rejected the user's timesheet. You can use the Timesheet Status column to determine whether the resource has submitted the timesheet to you for approval.

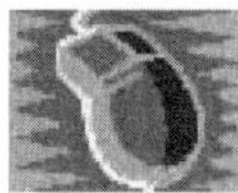

Hands On Exercise

Exercise 8-5

Accept or reject timesheets and view unsubmitted timesheets for your resources.

1. Click the Timesheet link in the content area of the Home page in Project Web Access
2. Accept or reject a timesheet
3. Click the Save button
4. Click the Home menu
5. Click a link in the Timesheet section for an unsubmitted timesheet during a specific time period
6. Examine the information shown in the View timesheet summary page

Axioms for Success with Tracking

To be successful in tracking project progress using Project Server, your organization should keep the following in mind:

- Everyone in your organization who is responsible for reporting progress should enter their time and send their updates on a standard day each week.
- Managers should deal appropriately with anyone who is responsible for reporting progress, but who fails to cooperate or participate fully in the process. You must take all necessary steps to ensure the full participation of everyone in your organization in order to validate the project data in the system.
- Your organization should track and manage the absence of resources during each update cycle. If necessary, you can implement surrogate processes for absent resources.
- Project managers should enter time for absent resources directly in the project plan and then push the changes back to the resources by republishing the updated assignments.
- Your organization should also track and manage the absence of managers during each update cycle. For updating purposes, other managers can take over tasks owned by absent managers and process the updates.
- Stay current with progress reporting and updates to make sure that you are managing your projects with current data.

Module 09

Using the Home Page

Learning Objectives

After completing this module, you will be able to:

- Change your password for Project Server authentication
- Set alerts and reminders for yourself
- Set alerts and reminders for resources that you manage
- Go offline with Project Web Access
- Go online with an offline copy of Project Web Access

Using Features from the Home Page

When a project manager logs into Project Web Access, the system displays a Home page similar to the one shown in Figure 9-1. Because the navigation system is adaptive in Project Web Access, the system displays menu selections according to your group membership. The main menu bar displayed across the top of Steve Master's home page shows only those menus that a project manager has permission to view. If Steve had an administrator's account, the system would also display an Admin menu selection in addition to the menus displayed for a project manager. By default, Team Members do not see the menu choices for Resources, Updates, or Admin.

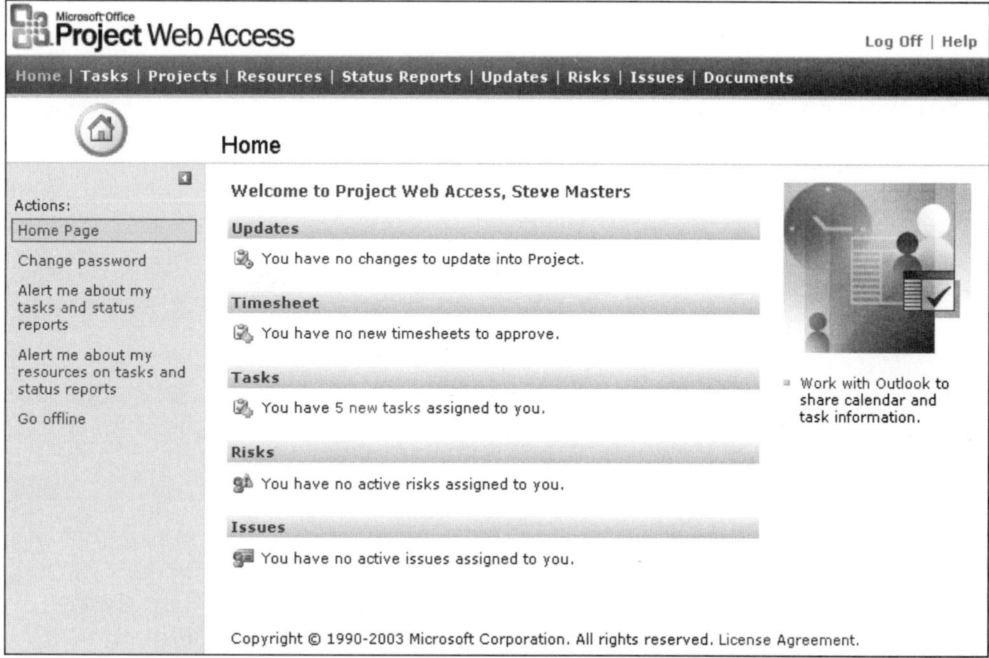

Figure 9-1: Project Web Access home page for a project manager

In the Actions pane on the left, the system displays the available actions according to group membership. The available actions for a project manager are as follows:

- Home Page
- Change password
- Alert me about my tasks and status reports
- Alert me about my resources on tasks and status reports
- Go offline

Changing Your Password

Click the Change password link in the Actions pane to change your password. Only users defined with Project Server authentication can change their passwords in Project Server. Windows users change passwords according to domain policy. If you logon with a Project Server account, clicking Change password from the Actions pane displays the Change Password page shown in Figure 9-2.

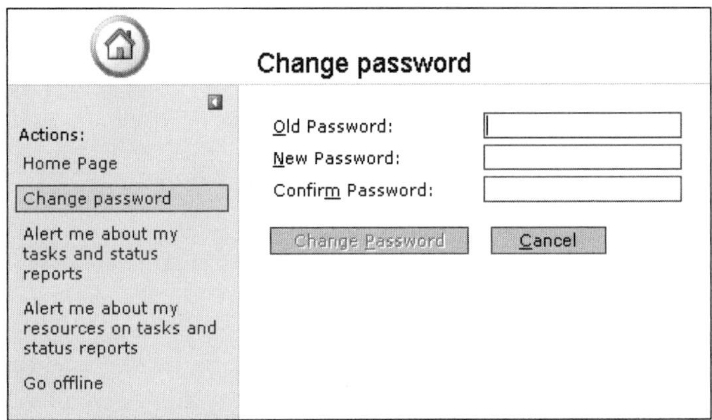

Figure 9-2: Change password page

The system displays an error message on the Change password page if you attempt to change your password while logged on as a Windows authenticated user.

To change your password, enter your old password, type a new password and confirm it, and then click the Change Password button. The system reports success displaying the confirmation dialog shown in Figure 9-3.

Figure 9-3: Password change is successful

Setting Alerts and Reminders for Yourself

Project Web Access allows you to receive alerts and reminders via e-mail messages using its alerts and reminders engine. You can determine whether the system sends you immediate notification of certain events and you can create personalized criteria-based reminders for yourself. Click the Alert me about my tasks and status reports link in the Actions pane to display the Alert me about my tasks and status reports screen shown in Figure 9-4.

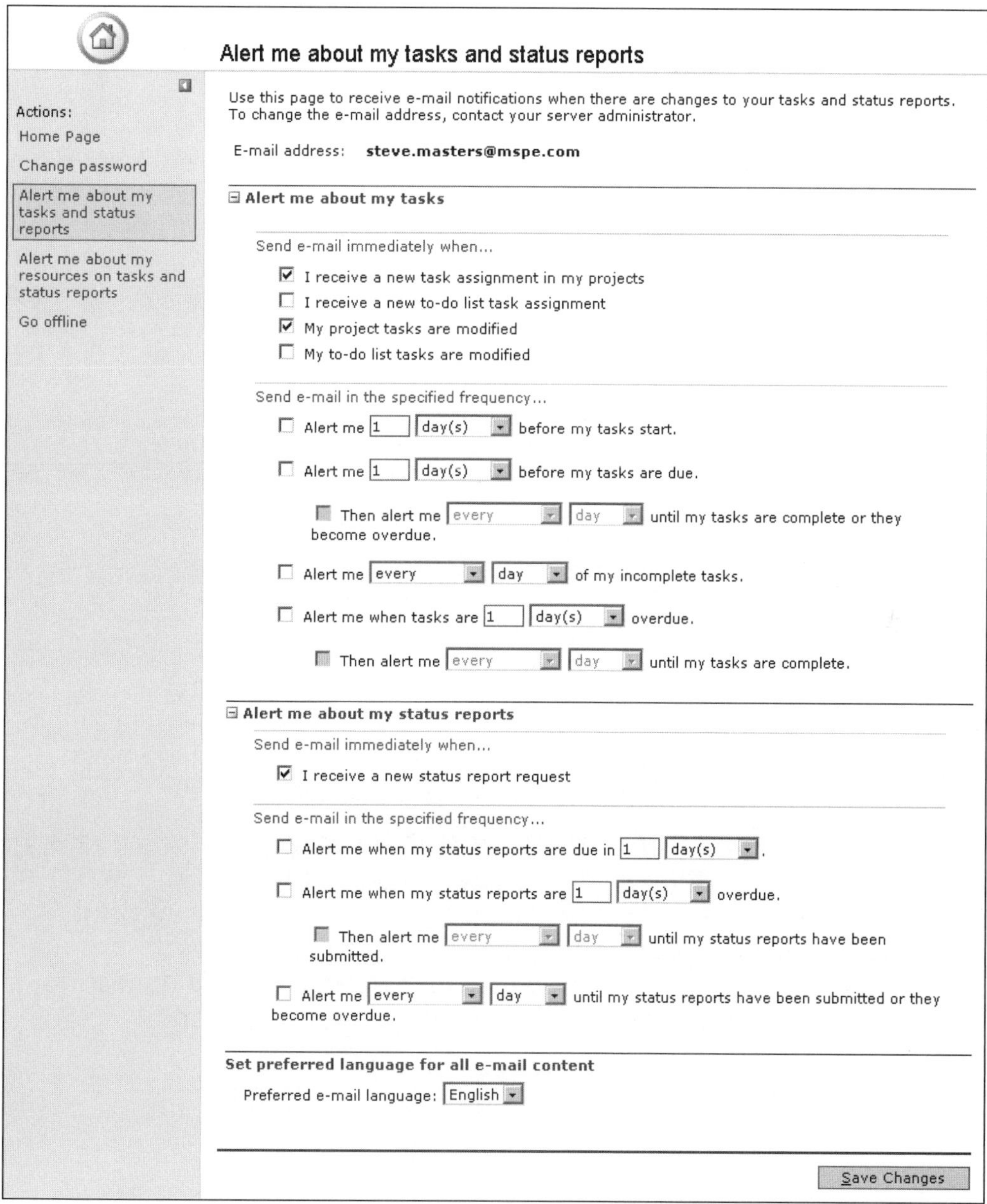

Figure 9-4: Alert me about my tasks and status reports

The first set of options in the Alert me about my tasks section allows you to subscribe to e-mail messages that the system sends immediately when certain events occur. These events are:

- When you receive a new task assignment in a project
- When you receive a new task assignment in a to-do list
- When one of your task assignments is modified in a project
- When one of your task assignments is modified in a to-do list

Notice in Figure 9-4 that the default settings cause the system to alert you only when you receive new task assignments in a project or when your resources modify their project task assignments.

The second set of options allows you to create reminders related to specific task criteria for project work and to-do lists. Each night the system tests your criteria and generates an email message containing the task reminders you've set. You receive an email only if you have both set criteria and the system finds an appropriate match between your tasks in the system and your criteria. You can think of the criteria as triggering conditions. These include:

- Before a task starts
- Before a task is due
- Until a task is complete or becomes overdue
- When you have an incomplete task
- When you have an overdue task
- Until an overdue task is complete

Notice in Figure 9-4 that the default settings include none of these options. When you select one or more of these options, you should also set your desired frequency, as you do not have to receive these nightly.

The first option in the Alert me about my status reports section causes you to receive an immediate e-mail message whenever you receive a new status report request. The second set of options causes you to receive e-mail messages at a specified frequency whenever your status reports are due or overdue. You can also set your language preference in the final section. Click the Save Changes button when you have made your selections.

Setting Reminders for your Resources

Select the Alert me about my resources on tasks and status reports link in the Actions pane to display the pages shown in Figure 9-5. The Alert me about my resources on tasks and status reports page offers you alerts that the system sends immediately when they occur. You can set an alert to trigger when a resource submits a new task, submits a new task assignment, delegates a task, or updates a task. All of these options are selected by default. Select and deselect these options as you wish.

This page also allows you to set up reminders for your resources about their project work. When you set reminders for your resources, you may choose to have the reminder go to your resource only, to yourself only, or to both you and your resource.

Keep in mind that "my resources" means that each resource is attributed with an RBS value in a subordinate leaf to your own value, or that the resource is managed by you on a project.

Select the reminders you want for your resources. You can also set your language preference in the final section. Click the Save Changes button when your selections are complete.

If a resource deselects a reminder option, and the resource's manager selects the same reminder option for the resource, the manager's selection will trump the user's selection.

Alert me about my resources on tasks and status reports

Actions:
Home Page
Change password
Alert me about my tasks and status reports
Alert me about my resources on tasks and status reports
Go offline

Use this page to receive e-mail notifications when there are changes to your resources' tasks and status reports. To change the e-mail address, contact your server administrator.

E-mail address: **steve.masters@mspe.com**

Alert me about my resources' tasks

Send e-mail immediately when my resources...

- [x] Submit new tasks and assignments
- [x] Delegate tasks
- [x] Update tasks

Send e-mail in the specified frequency for upcoming tasks...

- [ ] Alert resources 1 day(s) before their tasks are due.
  - (•) e-mail me only
  - ( ) e-mail my resources
  - ( ) e-mail me and my resources

Send e-mail in the specified frequency for overdue tasks...

- [ ] Alert resources when their tasks are 1 day(s) overdue.
  - [ ] Then alert resources every day until their tasks are complete.
  - (•) e-mail me only
  - ( ) e-mail my resources
  - ( ) e-mail me and my resources

Send e-mail in the specified frequency for tasks requiring updates...

- [ ] Alert resources when their tasks have started for 1 day(s) but have no actual work.
  - (•) e-mail me only
  - ( ) e-mail my resources
  - ( ) e-mail me and my resources

Alert me about my resources' status reports

Send e-mail immediately when my resources...

- [x] Submit a status report

Send e-mail in the specified frequency for upcoming status reports...

- [ ] Alert resources when their status reports are due in 1 day(s).
  - (•) e-mail me only
  - ( ) e-mail my resources
  - ( ) e-mail me and my resources

Send e-mail in the specified frequency for overdue status reports...

- [ ] Alert resources when their status reports are 1 day(s) overdue.
  - [ ] Then alert resources every day the status reports are submitted.
  - (•) e-mail me only
  - ( ) e-mail my resources
  - ( ) e-mail me and my resources

Set preferred language for all e-mail content

Preferred e-mail language: English

Save Changes

Figure 9-5: Alert me about my resources on tasks and status reports

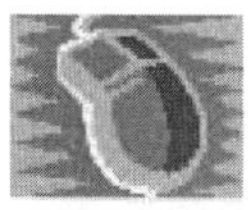

Hands On Exercise

Exercise 9-1

Explore the setting of alerts and reminders to yourself, and reminders to your resources.

1. Click the Alert me about my tasks and status reports link in the Actions pane
2. Explore the selections
3. Click the Alert me about my resources on tasks and status reports in the Actions pane
4. Explore the selections

Taking Project Web Access Offline

Microsoft Project Web Access leverages the offline capabilities of Microsoft Internet Explorer and the Windows operating system to provide timesheet and status report functionality offline. Offline functionality is limited to the date range you select and allows you to perform only the following actions:

- Enter timesheet information for later posting to the server
- Create and/or edit Status Reports that you can later uploaded to the server

When you click the Go offline link in the Actions pane, your system may first display the ActiveX warning dialog shown in Figure 9-6.

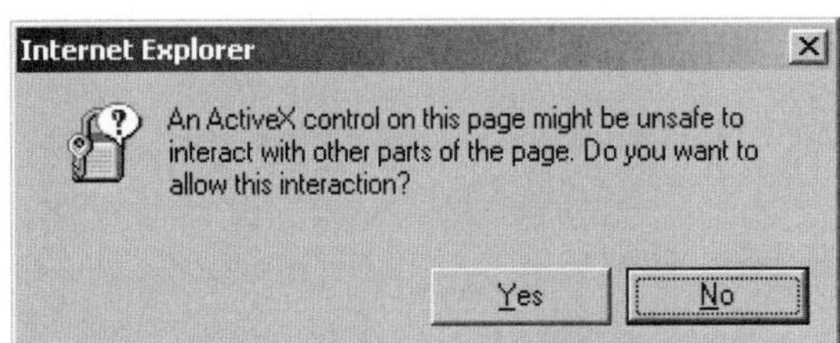

Figure 9-6: ActiveX warning dialog

The appearance of the ActiveX warning dialog is dependent on the security settings in your Internet Explorer browser

Click the Yes button in the warning dialog to display the Go offline page shown in Figure 9-7.

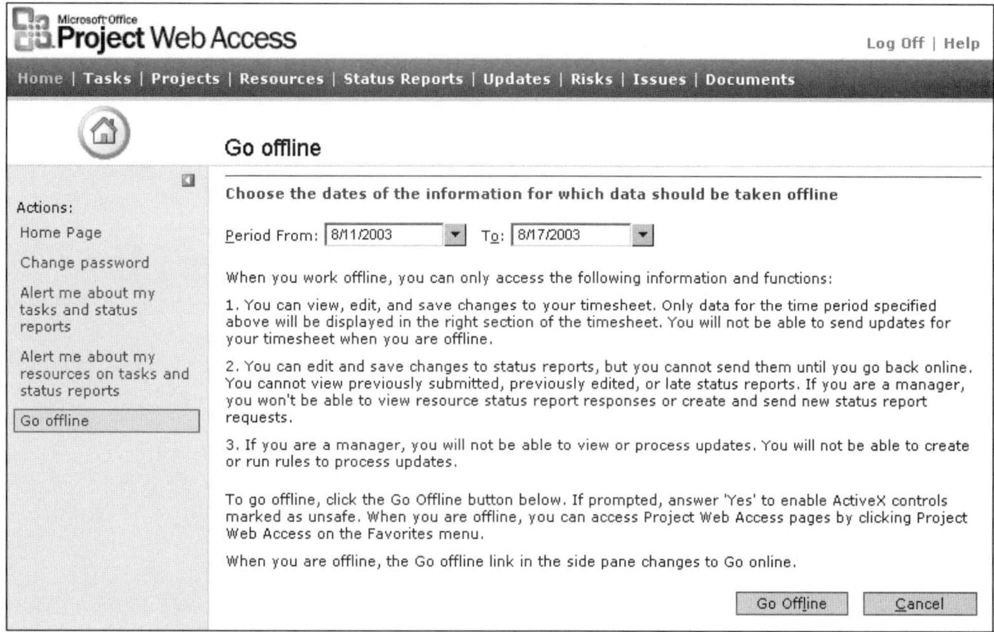

Figure 9-7: Go offline page

To go offline with Project Web Access, select the date range desired by setting values in the Period from and To pick lists, then click the Go Offline button.

The dates in the Period from and To pick lists default to the one-week period from the current date. If your organization uses managed time periods, the system will not allow you to enter progress in your timesheet during closed time periods while working offline.

When you click on the Go Offline button, the display continues to change while the system takes a snapshot of your Project Web Access information and copies it into your offline folders. The system reports progress as it saves each page, as shown in Figure 9-8.

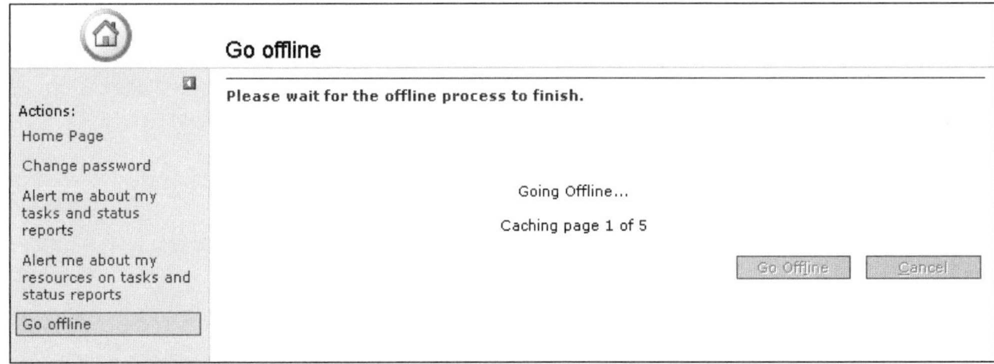

Figure 9-8: Interim information while taking Project Web Access pages offline

Upon completion of the process, the system displays the confirmation alert box shown in Figure 9-9.

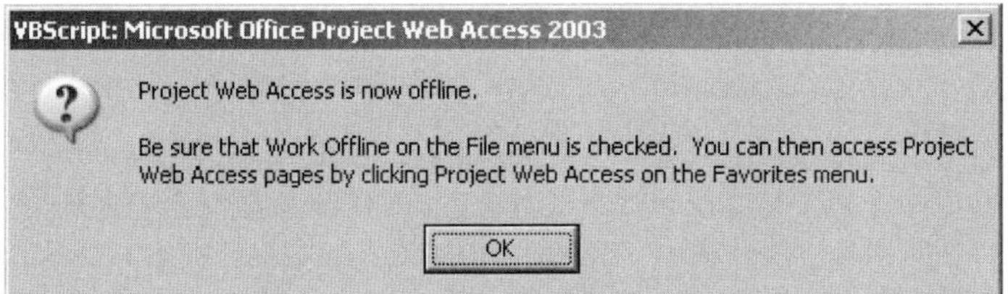

Figure 9-9: Offline mode confirmed

Click the OK button in the alert dialog and the system will redisplay the Home page, which now has a very limited menu selection available as shown in Figure 9-10. Note that the selection that once was Go offline is now Go online.

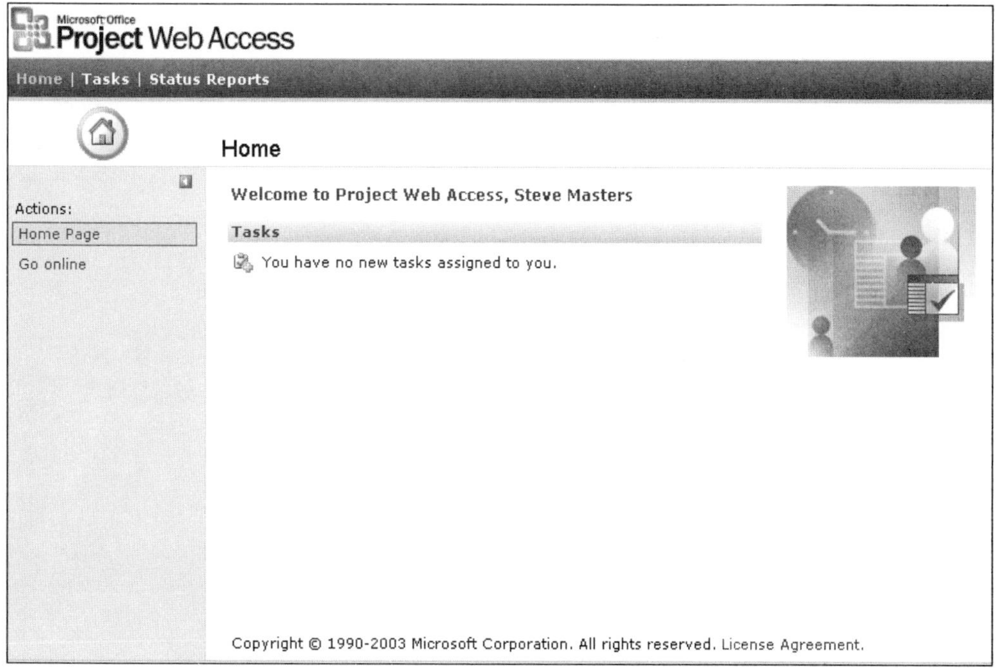

Figure 9-10: Project Web Access Home page while working Offline

Taking Project Web Access offline adds a link to your Favorites menu in as shown in Figure 9-11. To access your Offline pages, use this link.

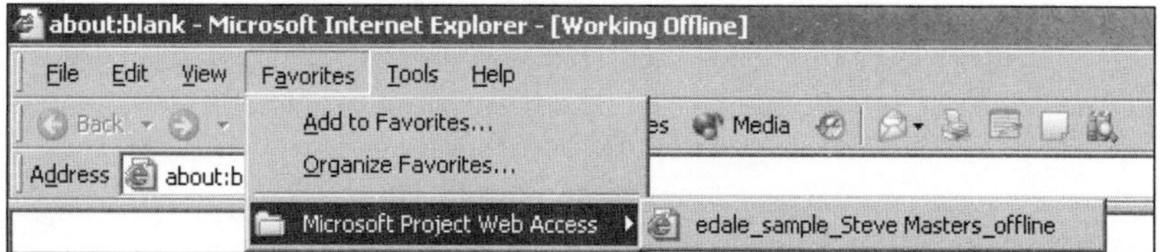

Figure 9-11: Access Offline pages from the Favorites menu

While working in Offline mode, you can enter progress in your timesheet in the View my tasks page as shown in Figure 9-12. You can also edit and create status reports in the Status Reports page. These remain local to your machine until you reconnect to Project Server and choose to go online.

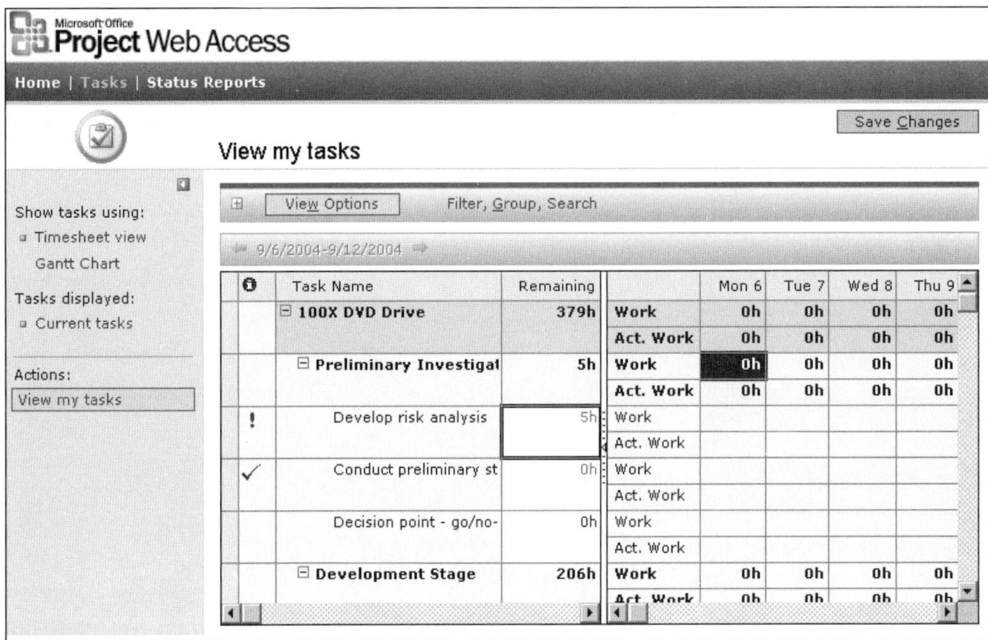

Figure 9-12: View my tasks page while in Offline mode

Once you are back in the office and can establish a connection with your Project Server, you can return to working online by clicking the Go online selection in the Actions pane, as shown previously in Figure 9-10. When you click the Go online link, the system displays the Offline Mode page shown in Figure 9-13.

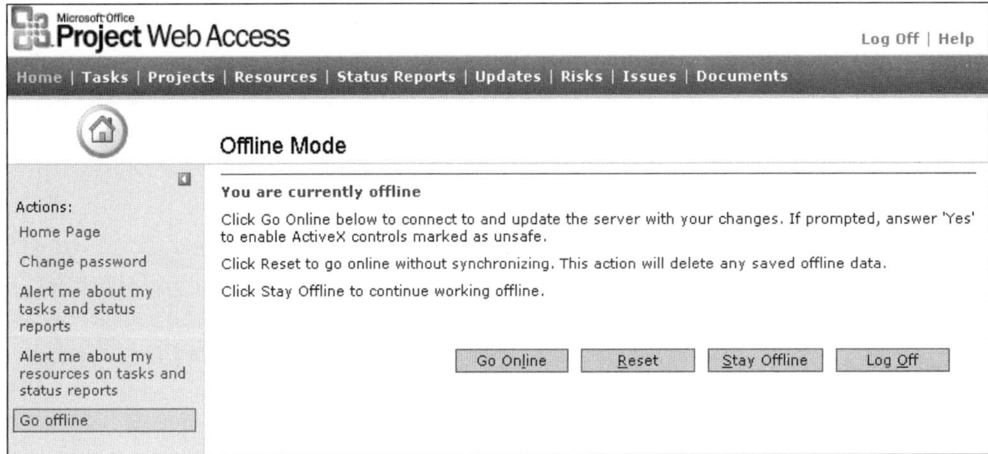

Figure 9-13: Offline Mode page

Click the Go Online button to update any data you have entered while in Offline mode and synchronize your data with the server. Keep in mind that although going online saves your data to the server, it doesn't automatically update time entries in your timesheet or send your offline status reports to their respective managers. You must perform these actions after the system is online.

Click the Reset button to discard any data entered while in Offline mode and reconnect as if you were never Offline. Click the Stay Offline button to remain in Offline mode. Click the Log Off button to log out of Project Web Access.

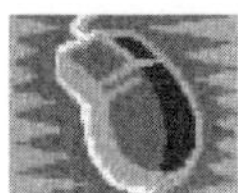

Hands On Exercise

Exercise 9-2

Take Project Web Access offline and then go back online again.

1. From the Home page, click the Go Offline link in the Actions pane
2. In the Go offline resulting display, select a date range for your offline activities
3. Click the Go Offline button when done
4. Click OK when the system prompts
5. Explore the Offline version of Project Web Access
6. Click the Go online link from the Actions pane on the Home page
7. Click the Go online button from the resulting Offline Mode page
8. Verify that you are back online with Project Web Access

Module 10

Working with Risks, Issues, and Documents

Learning Objectives

After completing this module, you will be able to:

- Create and submit a new risk or issue
- Edit issues and risks
- Filter the Risks or Issues page
- Link risks to tasks, issues, documents, and other risks
- Link issues to tasks, risks, documents, and other issues
- Open a document library
- Create a new document library
- View documents contained in a document library
- Create new documents and upload documents to libraries
- View and use the project workspace for a selected project

Working with Risks, Issues, and Documents

The management of risks, issues, and documents is an important aspect of your organization's project management methodologies. Windows SharePoint Services (previously called SharePoint Team Services) provides the platform and services for managing risks, issues, and documents within Project Server. All three services function correctly for users who have Windows credentials and use Windows authentication to access Project Server. Users who access Project Web Access with Project Server accounts are not able to access these services through Project Web Access.

When you log into Project Web Access, the Home page announces both active and changed risks, and active and changed issues. Notice in Figure 10-1 that I have one active risk and one active issue assigned to me.

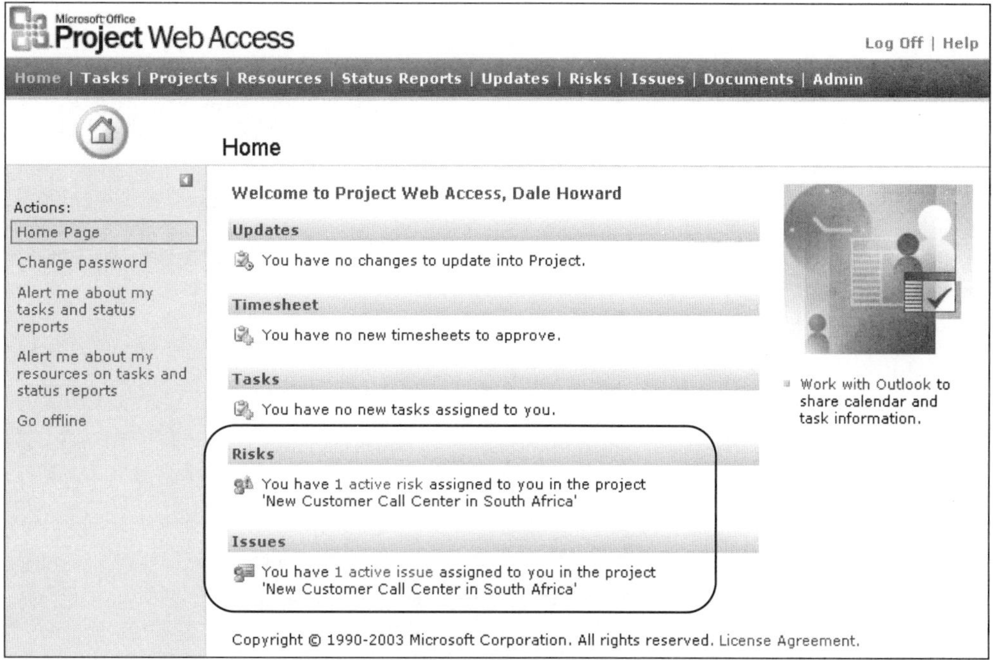

Figure 10-1: Home page with Issues information

Working with Risks

The Project Management Institute defines a risk as "an uncertain event or condition that, if it occurs, has a positive or negative effect on a project objective." Risks have both causes and consequences. If a risk occurs, the consequence can be either negative or positive. As a part of your organization's risk management methodologies, you may need to log and document anticipated risks to your project work.

Viewing Risks

On the Home page, you can either click the Risks link in the center of the page or click the Risks menu at the top of the page. To access the active risks assigned to you in a particular project, click the ___ active risks link the Risks section in the middle of the page. As you saw in the Tracking module, you can also access Risks through the timesheet interface in the View my tasks page.

When you click either the Risks link or the Risks menu, the system displays the View and submit risks in all projects page as shown in Figure 10-2.

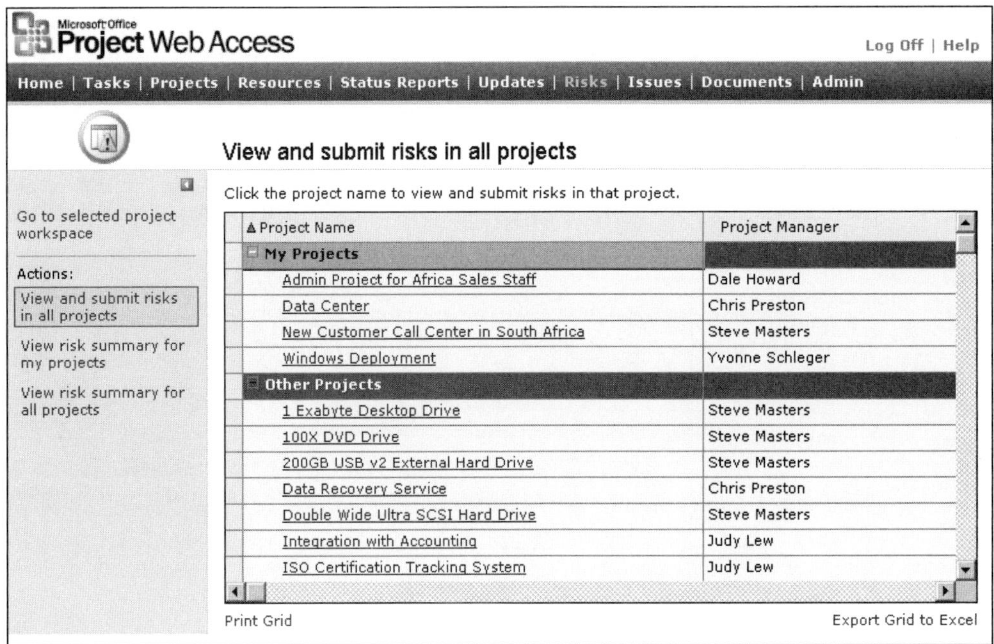

Figure 10-2: View and submit risks in all projects page

In the View and submit risks in all projects page, the phrase "all projects" refers to the all of the projects to which you have access. The system automatically gives you access to any project in which you have an assignment or to any project for which you are the manager. In addition, the system may also give you access to additional projects based on your security permissions.

Notice in Figure 10-2 that there are two sections of projects: My Projects and Other Projects. The My Projects section contains projects in which you have an assignment or for which you are the manager. The Other Projects section contains projects to which you have access by your security permissions.

Click the View risk summary for my projects link in the Actions pane to view the risk statistics for projects in the My Projects section. The system displays the View risk summary for my projects page, as shown in Figure 10-3. This page gives you the latest statistics on Active, Postponed, and Closed risks in your projects. Notice that there is one Active risk and one Postponed risk in the New Customer Call Center in South Africa project.

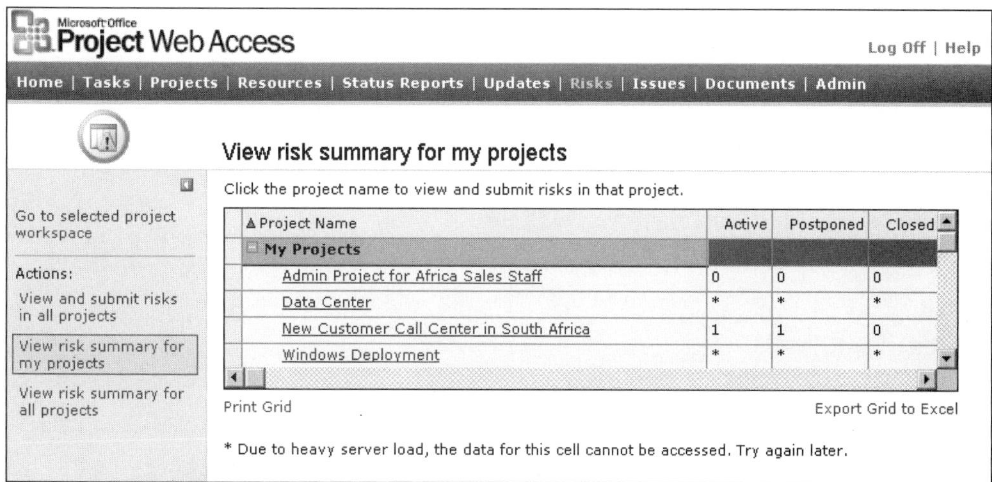

Figure 10-3: View risk summary for my projects

You can also click the View risk summary for all projects link in the Actions pane to display a statistics page for the projects listed in both the My Projects and Other Projects sections.

Click the link for any project in the grid to display the Risks page for the selected project. As shown in Figure 10-4, the project name displays above the page title. In the Select a View section of the Actions pane, notice that you can select a number of views based on standard criteria, such as all risks assigned to me or all risks owned by me. Click one of the links in the Actions pane to redisplay the page with the conditions applied. Click the All Risks link in the activities menu to return the Risks page to the full selection of project risks.

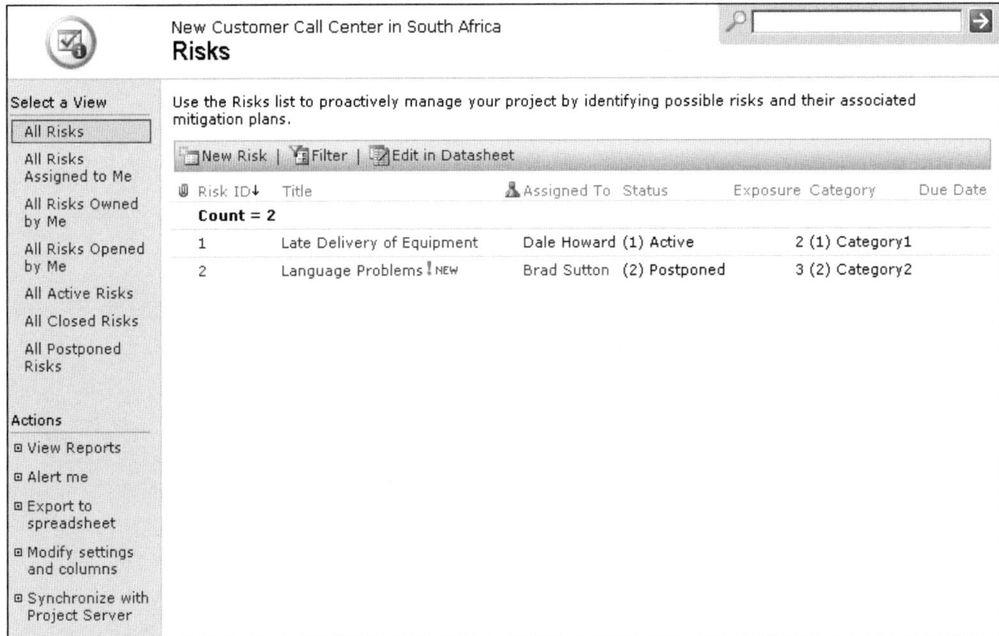

Figure 10-4: Risks page for a single project

You can use filtering to determine the list of risks displayed on the Risks page. Click the Filter link in the toolbar to activate autofiltering on the list of risks, as shown in Figure 10-5. Each field in the display becomes a pick list allowing you to set a value to filter on any column. Making a selection applies it to the view. Click the Hide Filter Choices button on the toolbar to cancel filtering.

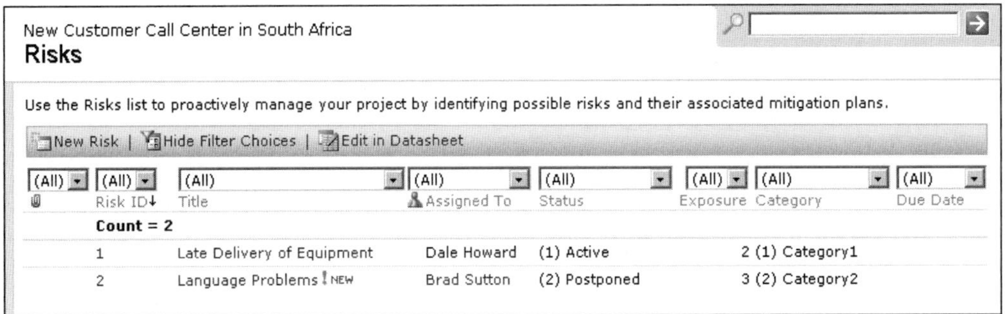

Figure 10-5: Risks page in ad hoc filter mode

You can also view the list of risks in an Excel-like view by clicking the Edit in Datasheet button on the toolbar. The system displays the list of risks in a grid of rows and columns, as show in Figure 10-6.

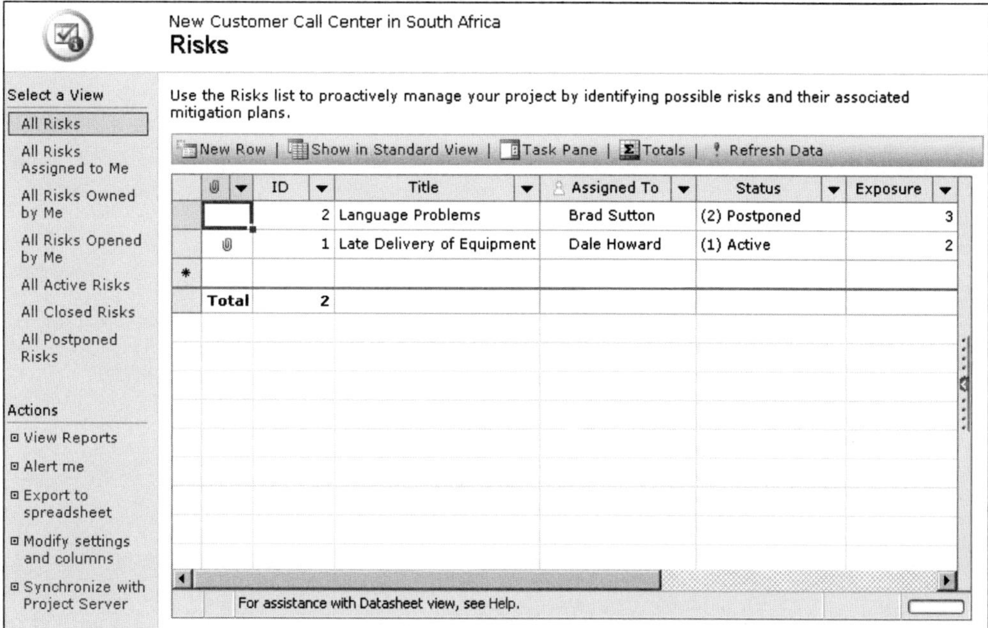

Figure 10-6: Risks page in datasheet view

While in the datasheet view of your project risks, you can create a new row and add a risk by clicking the New Row button. Click the Task Pane button to display a pane with choices for working with your datasheet in Excel or Access, as is shown in Figure 10-7. The choices available include being able to export and link the risk list to either an Excel spreadsheet or to an Access table. Click the Totals button to shown and hide totals at the bottom of the datasheet.

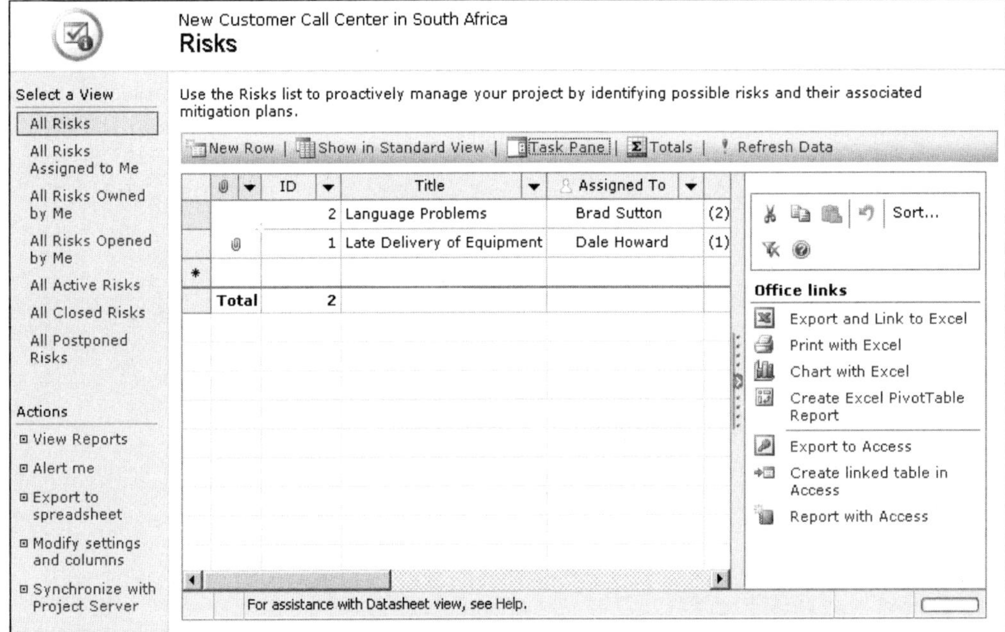

Figure 10-7: Datasheet view of Risks page with Task Pane displayed

To return to the standard view of your project risks, click the Show in Standard View button on the toolbar. Click the name of the risk in the list to display the risk details page shown in Figure 10-8.

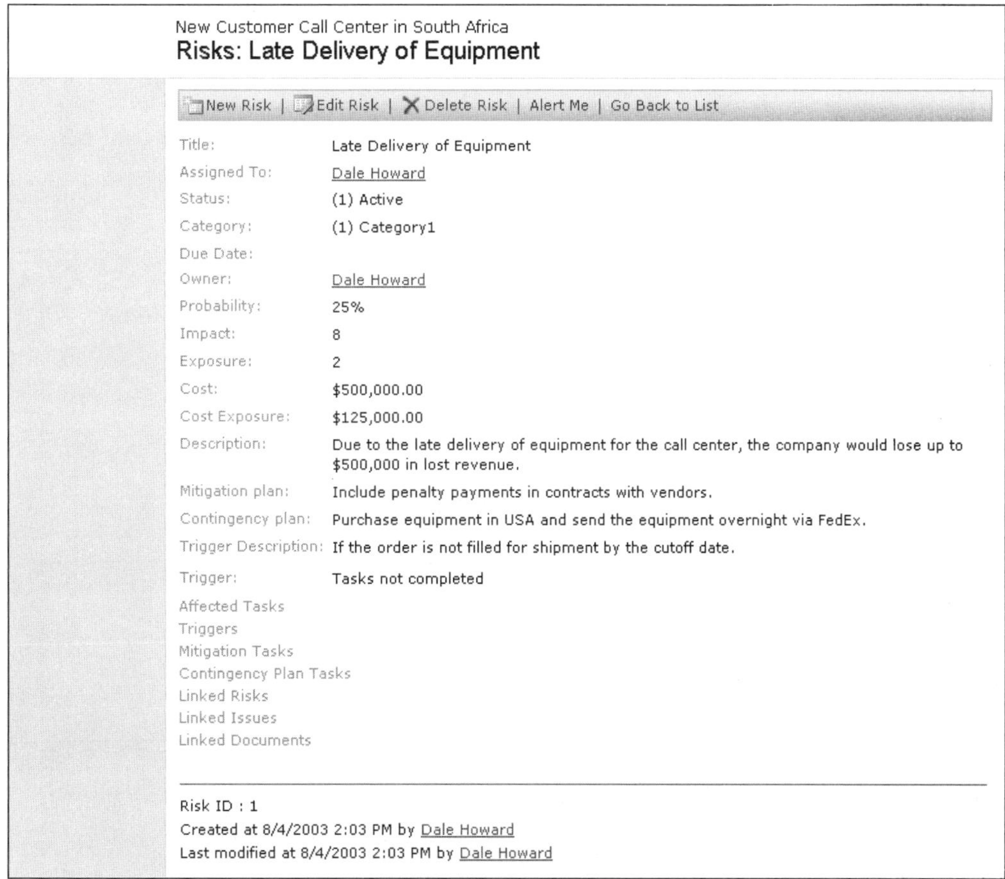

Figure 10-8: View risk details

Creating and Editing Risks

Click the Edit Risk button at the top to open the risk for editing as shown in Figure 10-9. You can make changes to any of the risk details from this page.

When you click the New Risk button, a page displays that is similar to the page shown in Figure 10-9, except the fields on the page are blank.

New Customer Call Center in South Africa
Risks: Late Delivery of Equipment

Save and Close | Attach File | Delete Risk | Go Back to List

Title * — Late Delivery of Equipment
Assigned To — Dale Howard
Status — (1) Active
Category — (1) Category1
Due Date — 12 AM 00
Enter date in M/D/YYYY format.
Owner — Dale Howard
Probability * — 25 %
Impact * — 8
The magnitude of impact should the risk actually happen
Cost — 500,000
The cost impact should the risk actually happen
Description — Due to the late delivery of equipment for the call center, the company would lose up to $500,000 in lost revenue.
The likely causes and consequences of the risk
Mitigation plan — Include penalty payments in contracts with vendors.
The plans to mitigate the risk
Contingency plan — Purchase equipment in USA and send the equipment overnight via FedEx.
The fallback plans should the risk occur.
Trigger Description — If the order is not filled for shipment by the cutoff date.
Trigger — Tasks not completed
Specify your own value:
The condition that triggers the contingency plan

Affected Tasks	Select project tasks that are impacted by this risk
Triggers	Select project tasks that are triggers for this risk
Mitigation Tasks	Select project tasks that are part of the mitigation plan
Contingency Plan Tasks	Select project tasks that are part of the risk contingency plan
Linked Risks	Select other related risks in this project
Linked Issues	Select project issues that are related to this risk
Linked Documents	Select project documents that are related to this risk

* indicates a required field

Risk ID : 1
Created at 8/4/2003 2:03 PM by Dale Howard
Last modified at 8/4/2003 2:03 PM by Dale Howard

Related Risks

Risk ID	Title	Remove Related ID
2	Language Problems ! NEW	Remove

Figure 10-9: Edit risk page

Attaching Risks to Tasks, Issues, Documents, and Other Risks

In the Edit risk page, click the Attach file button to attach documents to the risk. The system displays the Attach File page shown in Figure 10-10.

Figure 10-10: Attach file to a risk

To attach a file to a risk, click the Browse button to open the Choose file dialog. Navigate to the desired file, select the file, and then click the Open button as shown in Figure 10-11. Click OK to complete the attachment of the file.

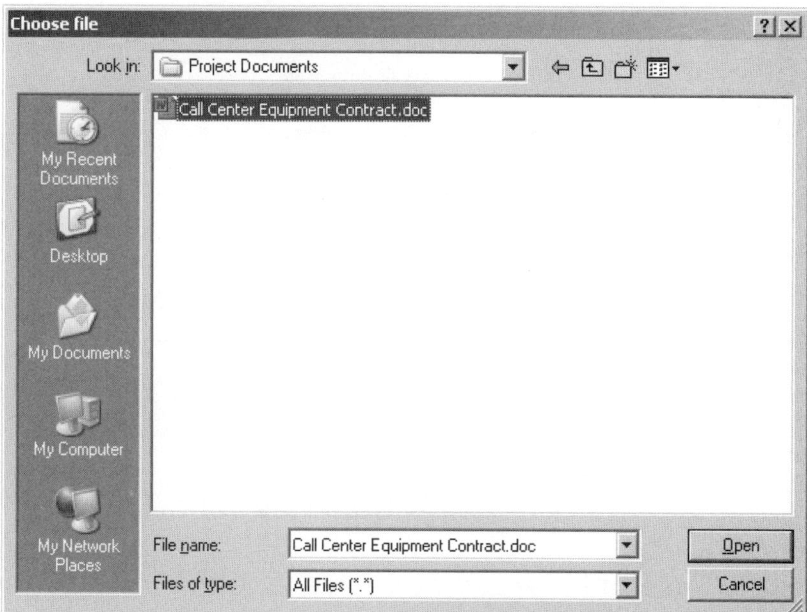

Figure 10-11: Choose file dialog

The system displays a paperclip icon on the Risks page for each risk with one or more attached files.

At the bottom of the Edit risk page is a section of options that allow you to cross-link your risk to the following:

- Affected Tasks
- Triggers
- Mitigation tasks
- Contingency Plan Tasks
- Linked Risks
- Linked Issues
- Linked Documents

Selecting any of these options opens the appropriate dialog for the situation. For example, I have clicked the Affected Tasks link and the system opens the Link to the selected tasks dialog, as shown in Figure 10-12.

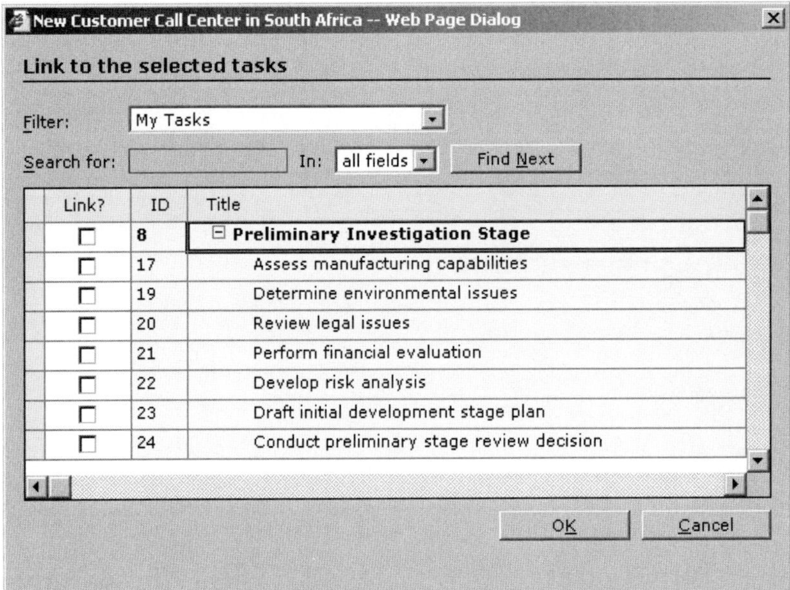

Figure 10-12: Link to the selected tasks dialog

Note the filtering tools and search feature available to help you narrow the selection. Select the checkbox in the Link column for one or more items and then click the OK button.

While in the Edit risk page, you can delete a risk by clicking the Delete Risk button. The system displays a confirmation dialog. Click the OK button in the confirmation dialog to delete the risk, or click the Cancel button to cancel the deletion.

When you have finished editing a risk, click the Save and Close button to save any changes you made. Click the Go Back to List button to abandon your changes without saving.

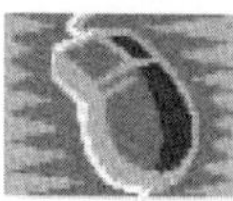

Hands On Exercise

Exercise 10-1

Create a new Risk in Project Web Access.

1. Select Risks from the Project Web Access main menu
2. Click the name of a project that you created or to which you are assigned
3. Click the New Risk button on the toolbar
4. Enter relevant information about the new risk
5. Click Save and Close button on the toolbar

Exercise 10-2

Edit and link a risk to a task.

1. Select the risk you created in Exercise 10-1
2. Click the Edit Risk button on the toolbar
3. Select the Affected Tasks link near the bottom of the page
4. Select one or more tasks impacted by the risk
5. Click OK when finished
6. Click Save and Close button on the toolbar

Working with Issues

An issue is any type of problem or concern which you might have during the life of the project, and which you want to communicate to those who have an interest in the project. Examples of project issues could include a shortage of the necessary resources to complete the project on time, or an unanticipated hardware upgrade that you need to move forward with project work.

Viewing Issues

Because the Risks, Issues, and Documents are very similar, you will find the features of the Issues pages very familiar. To access Issues, you can either click the Issues menu at the top of the page or the Issues link in the center of the Home page. The system displays the View and submit issues in all projects page shown in Figure 10-13.

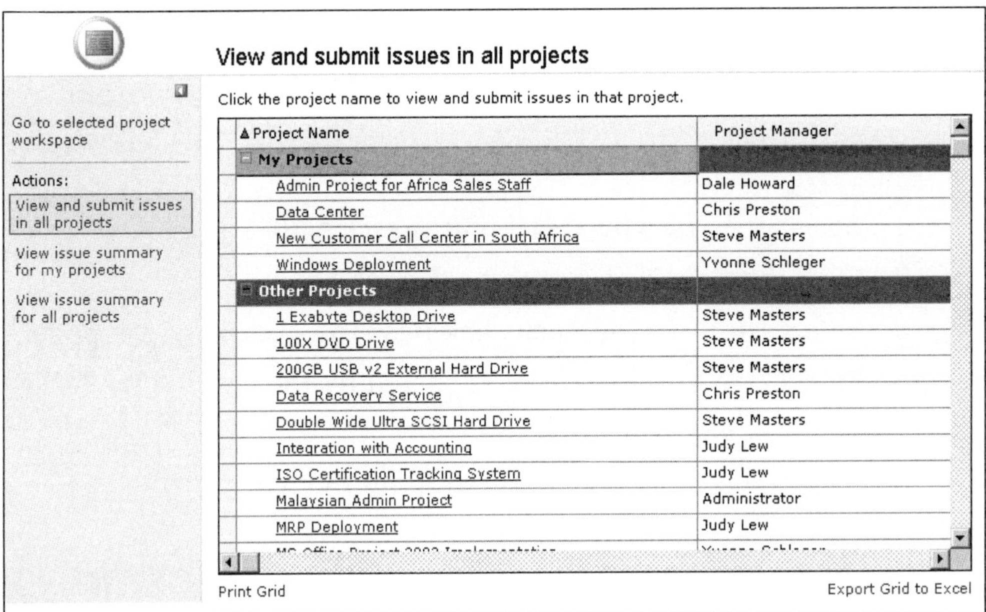

Figure 10-13: View and submit issues in all projects page

As with the Issues page, you can click the View issues summary for my projects link in the Actions pane to view the issues statistics for projects in the My Projects section. You can also click the View issues summary for all projects link in the Actions pane to display a statistics page for the projects listed in both the My Projects and Other Projects sections.

Click the name of any project in the grid to display the Issues page for the selected project, as shown in Figure 10-14. Similar to Risks, the Select a View section of the Actions pane contains a number of views based on standard criteria.

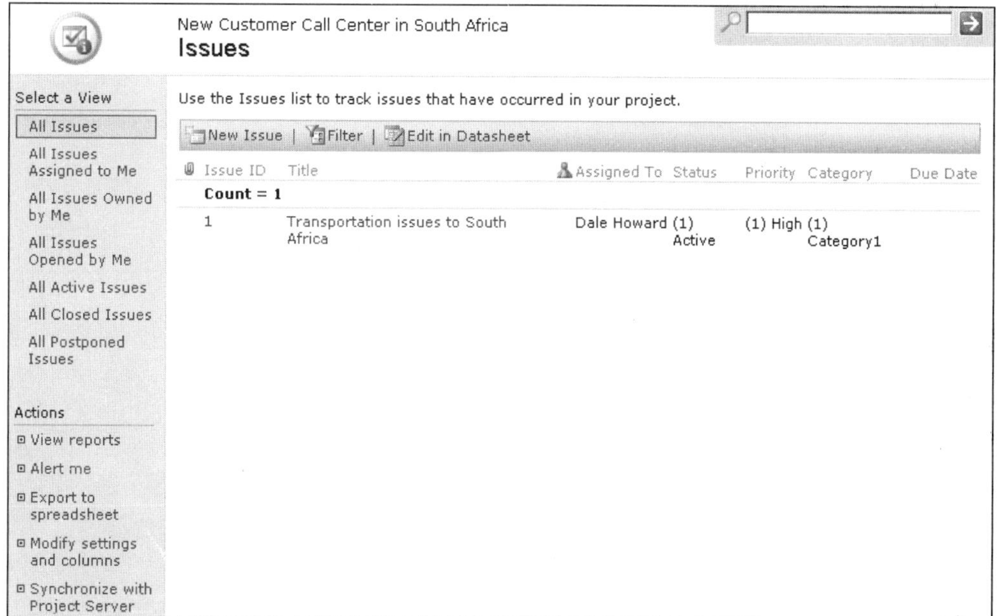

Figure 10-14: Issues page for a single project

You can click the Filter button on the toolbar to restrict the list of issues displayed on the Issues page. You can also view the list of issues in an Excel-like view by clicking the Edit in Datasheet button on the toolbar. Click the name of the issue in the list to display the issue details page, shown in Figure 10-15.

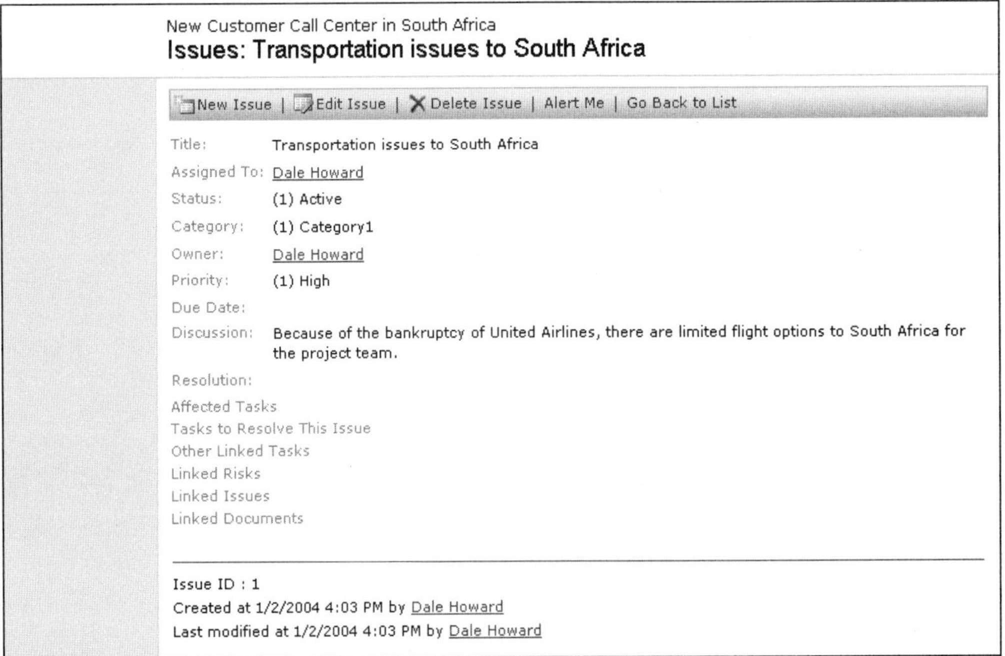

Figure 10-15: View issue details

Creating and Editing Issues

Although there are a fewer number of details available for an issue than for a risk, the interface functions are the same. You can click the Delete Issue button to remove the issue, or click the New Issue button to create a new issue. Click the Edit Issue button to open the issue for editing, as shown in Figure 10-16. You can make changes to any of the issue details from this page.

When you click the New Issue button, a page displays that is similar to the page shown in Figure 10-16, except the fields on the page are blank.

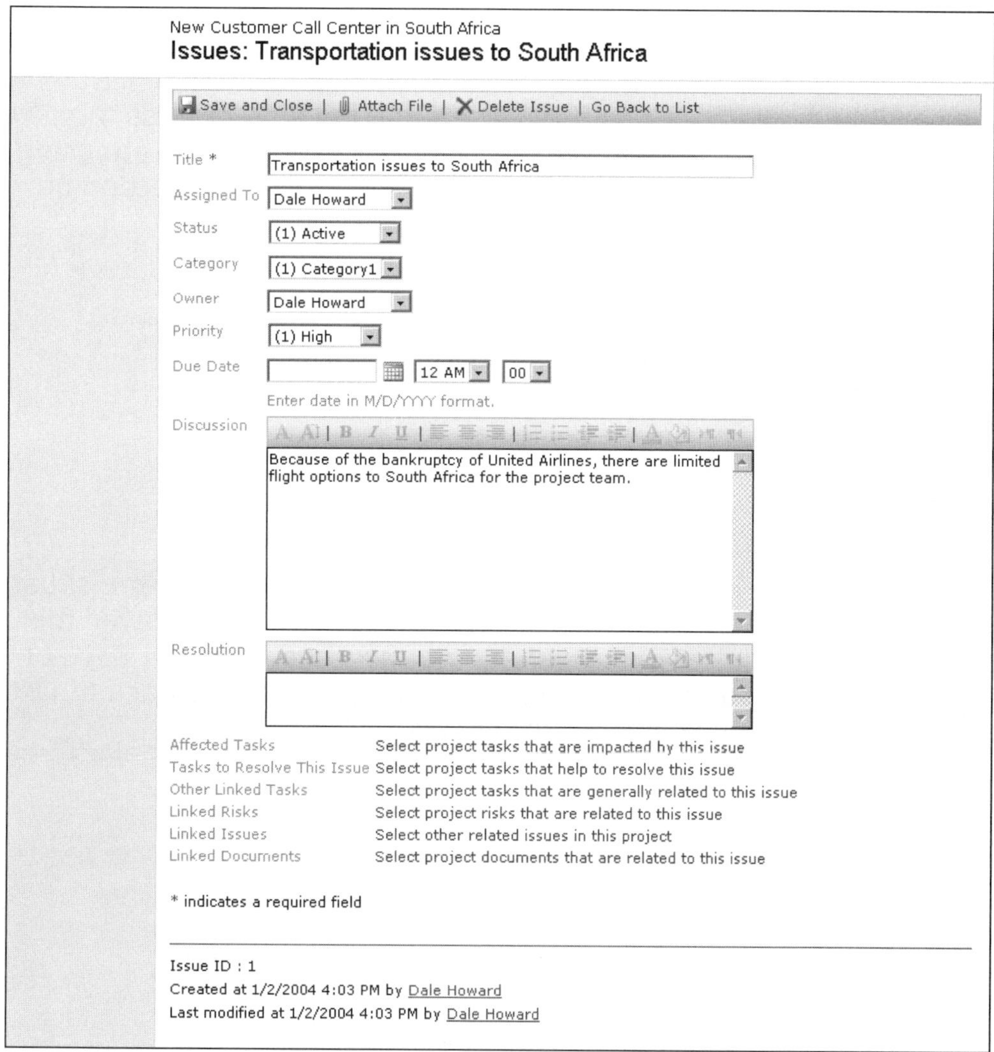

Figure 10-16: Edit issue page

Attaching Issues to Other Issues, Tasks, Risks, and Documents

As you learned to do with risks, you can attach documents to an issue by clicking the Attach File button in the Edit issue page. The process for attaching a document to an issue is identical to the process for attaching a document to a risk. At the bottom of the Edit issue page is a section of options that allow you to cross-link the issue to the following:

- Affected Tasks
- Tasks to Resolve this Issue
- Other Linked Tasks
- Linked Risks
- Linked Issues
- Linked Documents

Selecting any of these options opens the appropriate dialog for the situation. The dialogs displayed for linking issues are identical those displayed for linking risks. When you have finished editing the issue, click the Save and Close button to save any changes made editing. Click the Go Back to List button to abandon the changes without saving.

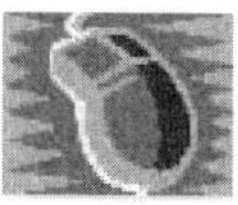

Hands On Exercise

Exercise 10-3

Create a new issue in Project Web Access.

1. Select Issues from the Project Web Access main menu
2. Click the name of a project that you created or to which you are assigned
3. Click the New Issue button on the toolbar
4. Enter relevant information about the new issue
5. Click Save and Close button on the toolbar

Exercise 10-4

Edit and link an issue to a task.

1. Select the issue you created in Exercise 10-1
2. Click the Edit Issue button on the toolbar
3. Select the Affected Tasks link near the bottom of the page
4. Select one or more tasks impacted by the issue
5. Click OK when finished
6. Click Save and Close button on the toolbar

Working with Document Libraries

During the life cycle of a typical project, you may create multiple documents such as templates, deliverables, and items of information associated with the project. During project definition, you might create a Project Charter and a Statement of Work document. During the execution stage of the project, you might create Change Control documents and expense reports. At the closure of a project, you might create a Lessons Learned document to capture the knowledge gained during the life of the project to name a few. Regardless of which type of project documents you create, each document is a part of your project's "electronic paper trail."

Viewing Document Libraries

To manage project documents, click the Documents menu at the top of the Project Web Access page. As you saw in the Tracking module, you can also access Documents through the timesheet interface in the View my tasks page. When you click the Documents menu, the system displays the View and upload documents in all projects page shown in Figure 10-17.

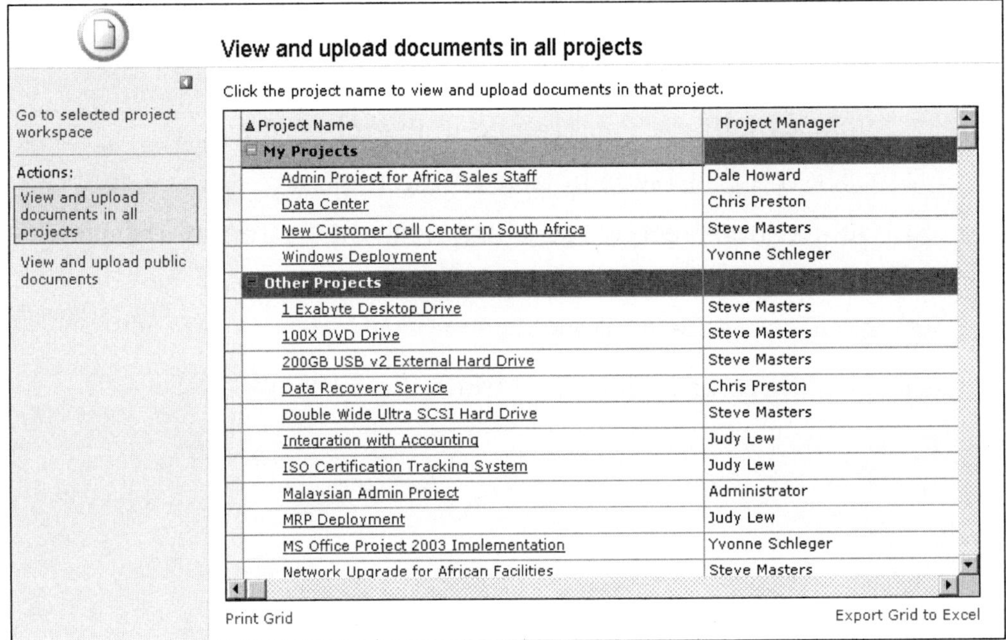

Figure 10-17: View and upload documents in all projects page

As with risks and issues, the system automatically grants you access to any project in which you have an assignment or to any project for which you are the manager. In addition, the system may also give you access to additional projects based on your security permissions and your position in your organization's RBS structure. Following he same pattern as risks and issues, notice in Figure 10-17 that there are two sections of projects: My Projects and Other Projects.

To give Windows users access to risks, issues, and document libraries for specific projects, give them a small assignment in each project. These are typically tasks with a token effort.

The Actions pane of the View and upload documents page offers two possible actions:

- View and upload documents in all libraries
- View and upload public documents

When you apply the first action, remember that the phrase "all libraries" refers to the libraries associated with all of the projects to which you have access. When you apply the second action, the phase "public libraries" refers to those that are available to every user in the system. To view the public libraries, click the View and upload public documents link and the system displays the Public Document Libraries page shown in Figure 10-18.

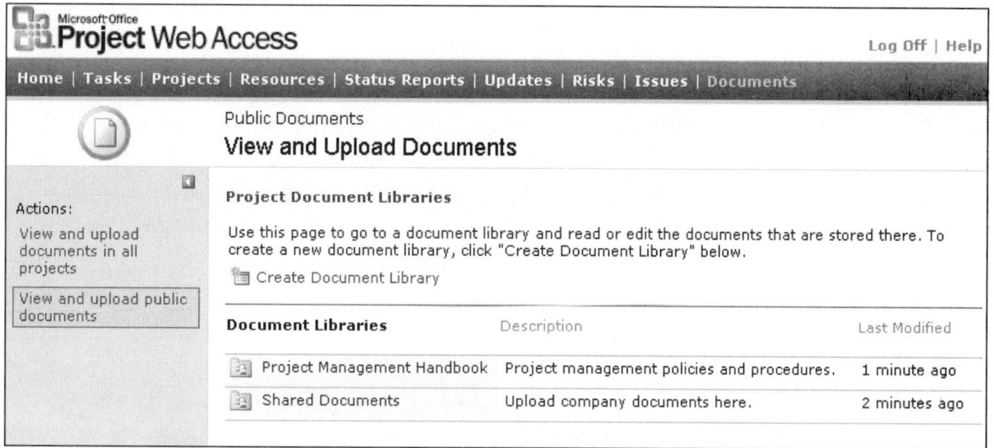

Figure 10-18: Public Document Libraries page

Figure 10-18 shows two public libraries to which I can upload documents. One is the Project Management Handbook library, which is a custom library I created. The other is the Shared Documents library, which is the default public library for documents. To return to the all projects page, click the View and upload documents in all projects link in the Actions pane.

Click the project name in the grid to open the Project Document Libraries page for the selected project, as shown in Figure 10-19. As with risks and issues, the name of the project displays above the page title.

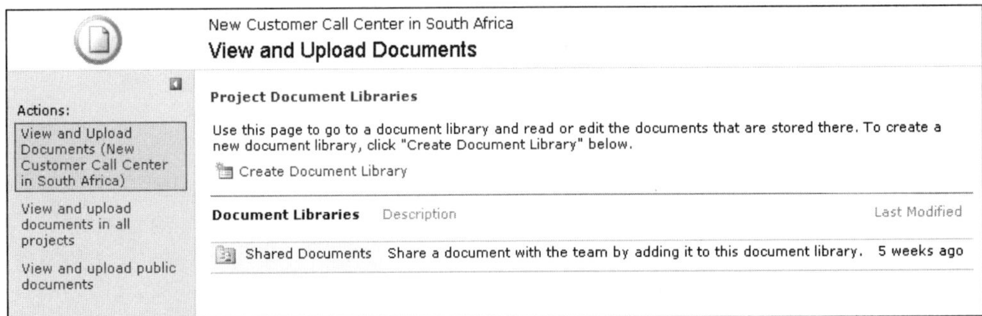

Figure 10-19: Project Documents Library page for a selected project

Each project includes one default document library, which is the Shared Documents library. The Project Document Libraries page for each project displays this library and any other libraries that the team has added.

Creating a New Document Library

Click the Create Document Library link to generate a new library for your project. The system displays the New Document Library page shown in Figure 10-20. Give your new library a name and a description, and select your desired options in the Navigation and Document Versions sections of the page.

Document versioning is a new feature of Project Server 2003. This feature allows you to keep multiple versions of a document. If you enable this feature for your document library, the system automatically creates a new version of a document each time a user edits the document. If you need to reverse changes needs to a document, you can restore the previous version and continue working.

In the Document Template section, select the default template used for creating all new documents in the library. Your choice of templates includes the following:

- Microsoft Word document
- Microsoft FrontPage Web page
- Microsoft Excel spreadsheet
- Microsoft PowerPoint presentation
- Basic page

- Web Part page
- None

The reason for selecting a blank template relates to features available only if you have a Microsoft Office 2003 client application license installed on your workstation. The full version of the Office 2003 web components, available only to users of Office 2003, allows you to create, open, and edit Office documents in the web browser, avoiding the need to download and upload the document each time. This feature will not work for users of earlier Office versions.

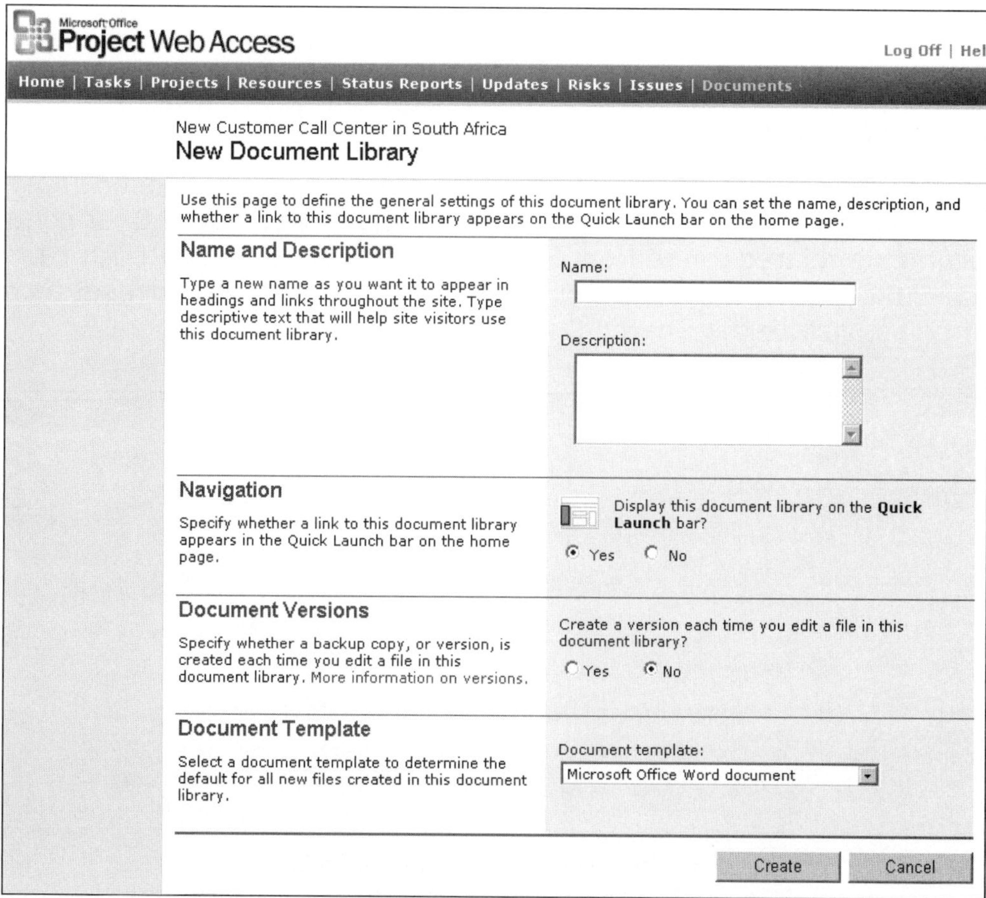

Figure 10-20: New Document Library page

When you click the Create button, the system creates the new library and adds it to your Project Document Libraries page, as shown in Figure 10-21.

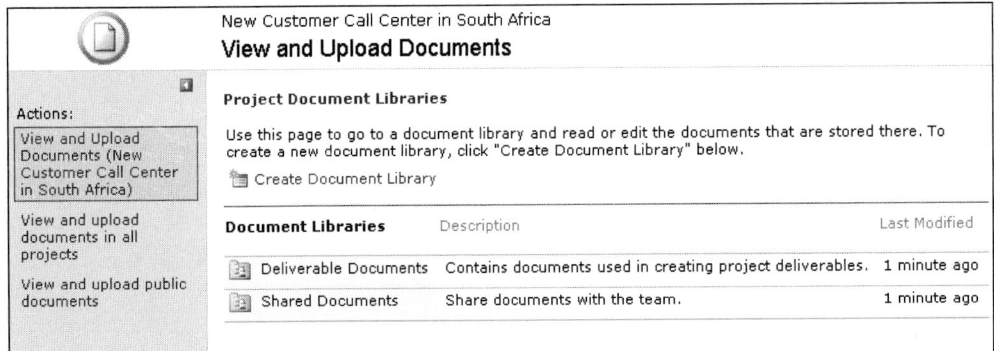

Figure 10-21: New library added

Using a Document Library

Click on the name of a document library to open it and view the documents in the library. The Shared Documents library shown in Figure 10-22 contains six documents related to the New Customer Call Center in South Africa project. Notice that the system flags the Project Budget spreadsheet as new since my last visit to the Shared Documents library.

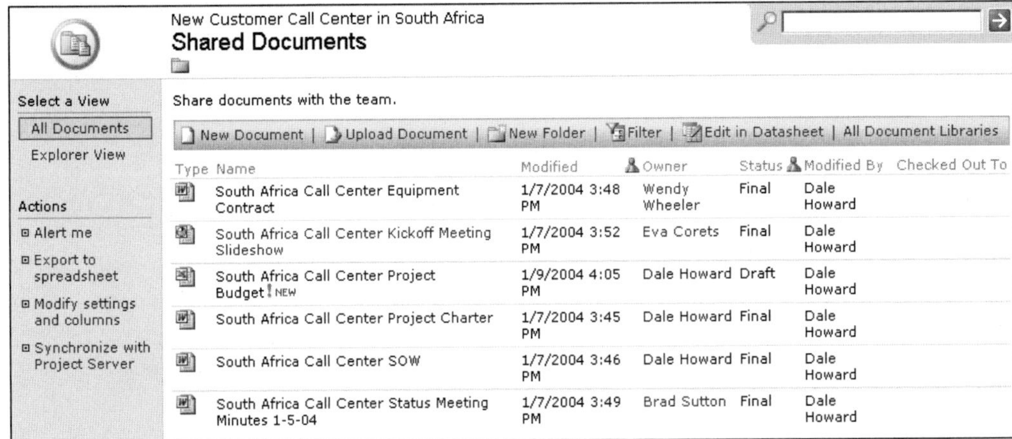

Figure 10-22: Documents in the Shared Documents library

The system offers you two default views of your document library through the Select a View section at the top of the Actions pane. The default view for a documents library is the All Documents view. Click the Explorer View link to apply the folders view shown in Figure 10-23.

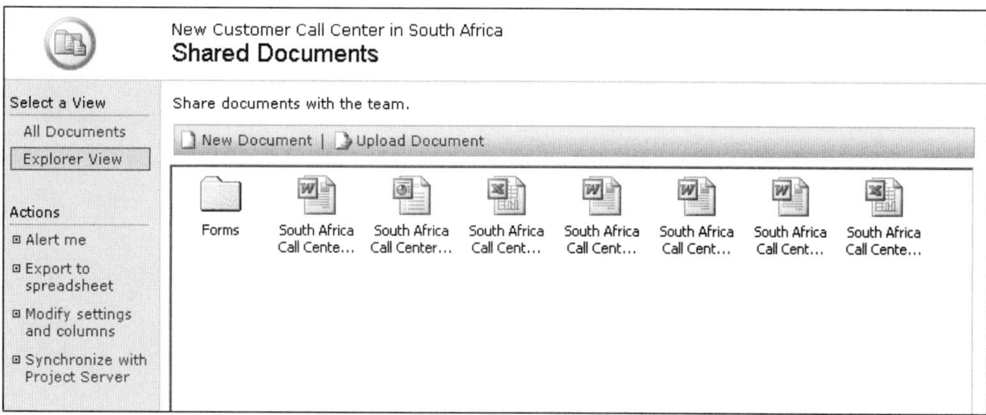

Figure 10-23: Explorer View of the document library

Notice in Figure 10-23 that the toolbar for the document library contains only two buttons when you apply the Explorer view. When you apply the All Documents view, the toolbar for the document library contains several familiar buttons, such as the Filter and Edit in Datasheet buttons, which you saw in the Risks and Issues pages. The toolbar also offers buttons to create a new document in the library, upload an existing document to the library, to create a new folder within the library, and to return to the list of all document libraries.

Uploading Documents to a Library

Click the Upload Document button to upload an existing document to your project document library. The system displays the Upload Document page shown in Figure 10-24. As with linking documents to risks and issues, click the Browse button and navigate to the location of the document. Select the existing file in the Choose file dialog and then click the Open button.

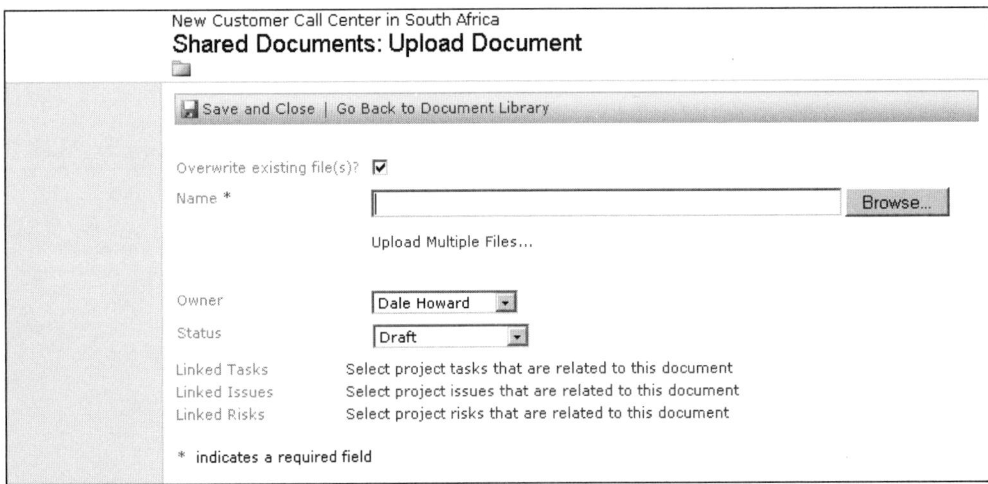

Figure 10-24: Upload Document page

When you have selected the file you wish to upload to the document library, you can also specify an Owner and a Status for the document. By default, the system sets the Owner value to your user account and the Status value to Draft. You can also link the document to any tasks, issues, and risks to which the document is related.

The system selects the Overwrite existing files option by default in the Upload Document page. If you are uploading an updated version of a document previously uploaded, you may wish to deselect the Overwrite existing files option to save multiple versions of your document.

If you wish to upload more than one document simultaneously, click the Upload Multiple Files link. The system displays the Upload Documents page reconfigured to select multiple documents, as shown in Figure 10-25. You can upload multiple documents by navigating to the location of each document and then selecting the checkbox to the left of the document name.

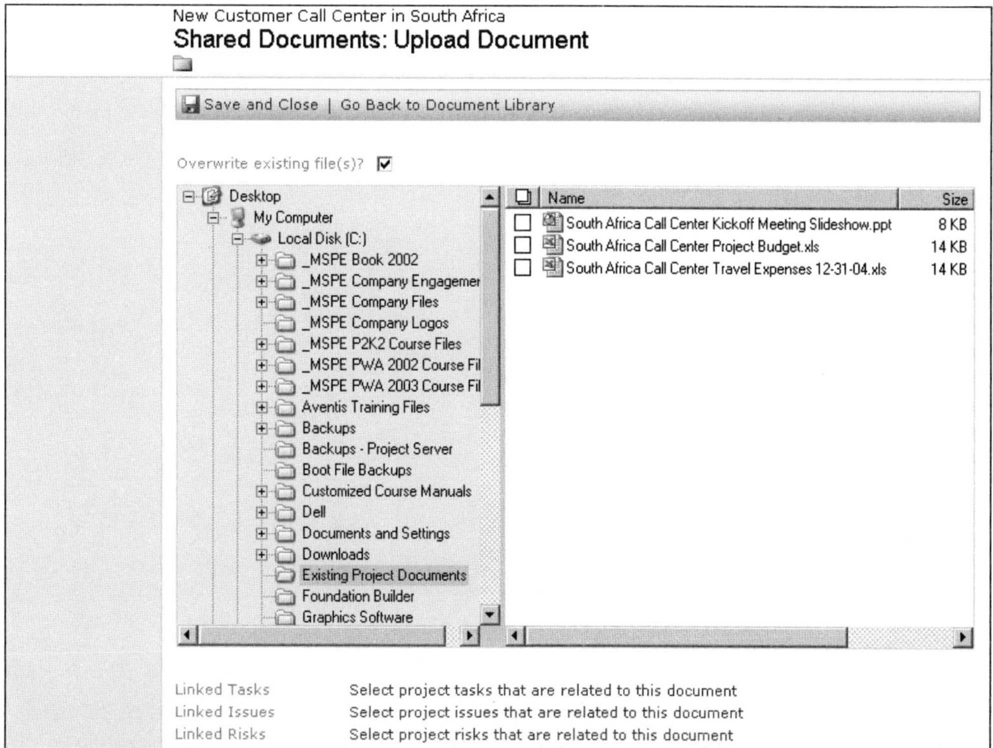

Figure 10-25: Upload Document page to upload multiple documents

When you have selected the documents that you wish to upload, click the Save and Close button to return to the document library page. The system displays the newly uploaded documents and flags them as new documents.

When you upload multiple files simultaneously, the system sets the Owner value to None and the Status value to Draft for each document. If you wish to specify an Owner or Status value for these documents, you must edit the Properties for each document individually.

Creating a New Document in a Library

Click the New Document button on the toolbar to create a new document. The system automatically opens a new document based on the template type specified as the default for the document library. The default template in each project's Shared Documents folder is the Microsoft Word document template.

Create the document and then click the Save button in the application. The system displays the Save As dialog shown in Figure 10-26. Notice that the system pre-selects the Shared Documents folder in the Save in pick list.

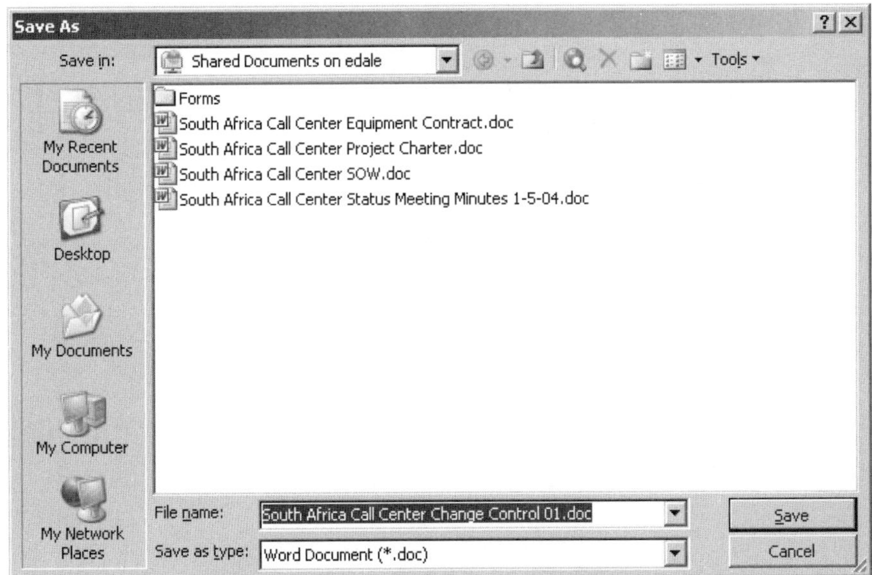

Figure 10-26: Save as dialog for new document in a library

Click the Save button in the Save As dialog box and the system presents the Web File Properties dialog shown in Figure 10-27. Select the Owner and Status of the new document and then click the OK button. The system displays the new document in the document library and flags it as a new document.

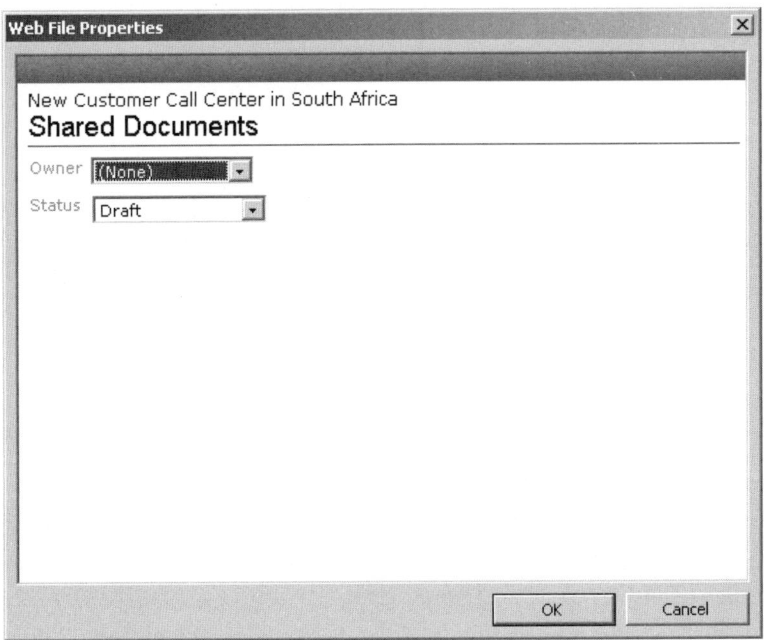

Figure 10-27: Web File Properties dialog

Creating a New Folder in a Library

It is now possible to create new folders within libraries in Project Server 2003.These function as sub-libraries to the libraries in which you create them To create a folder in the project library, click the New Folder button on the toolbar. The system displays the New Folder page, shown in Figure 10-28.

Figure 10-28: New Folder page

Give the folder a name and then click the Save and Close button. The system displays the new folder in the document library, as shown in Figure 10-29.

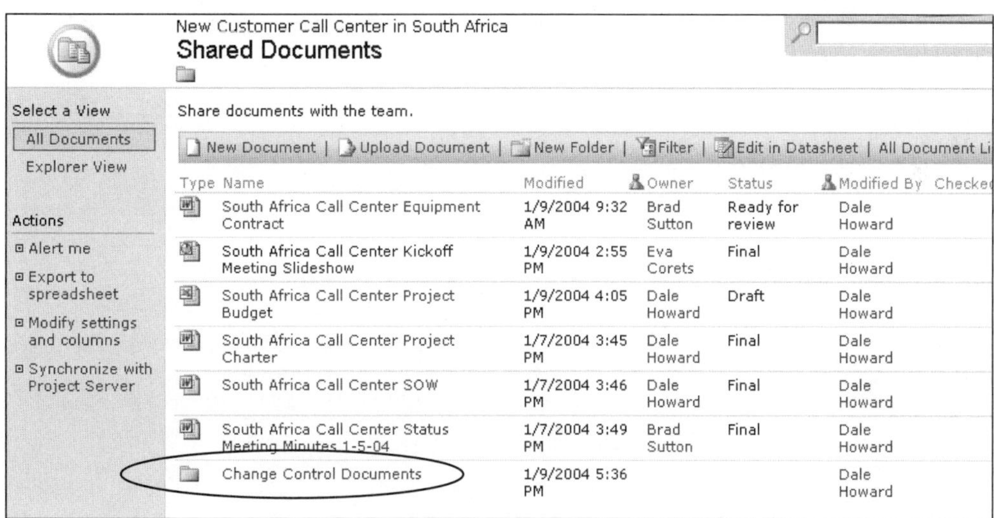

Figure 10-29: New folder created in document library

To add documents in the new folder, simply click the folder to open it. The system displays a document library page for the new folder

Working with Existing Documents in a Library

To work with an existing document in a document library, float your mouse pointer over the name of the document. The system displays a pick list indicator for the selected project, as shown in Figure 10-30.

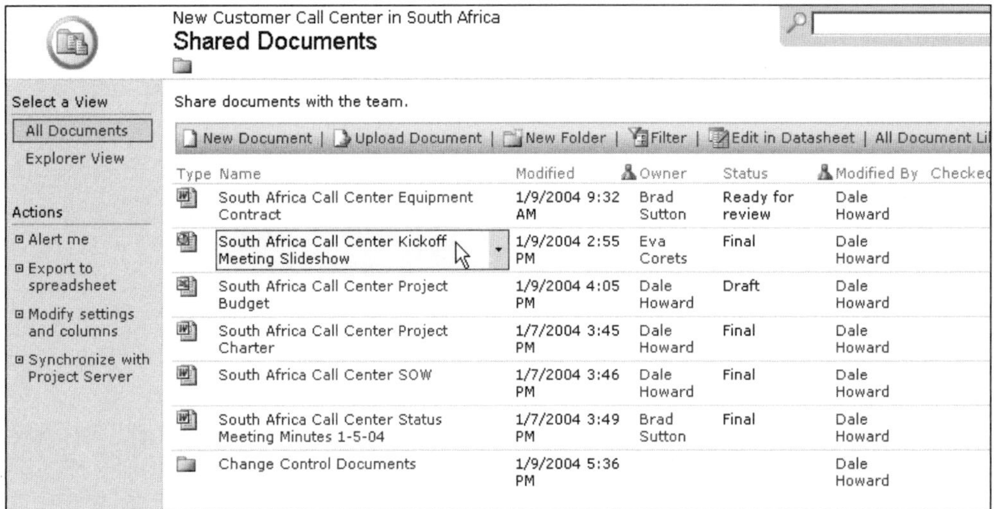

Figure 10-30: Preparing to edit a document

Click the pick list indicator to view the list of options for working with the document, as shown in Figure 10-31.

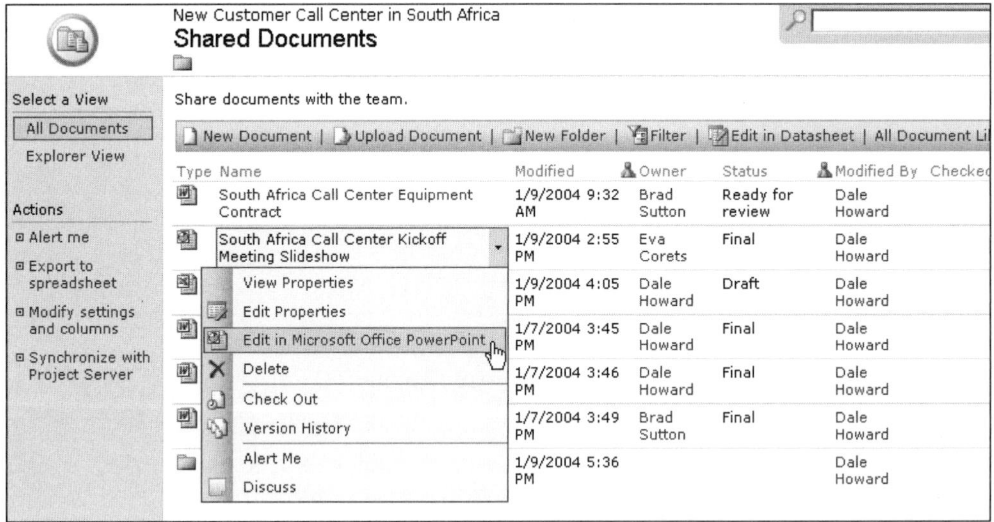

Figure 10-31: Options for working with a document in the library

Viewing Document Properties

Click View Properties from the pick list menu for the selected project to view the Properties of the document, as shown in Figure 10-32. Notice that the buttons on the toolbar offer the remaining selections found on the pick list shown previously in Figure 10-31. Click the Go Back to Document Library button when you are finished.

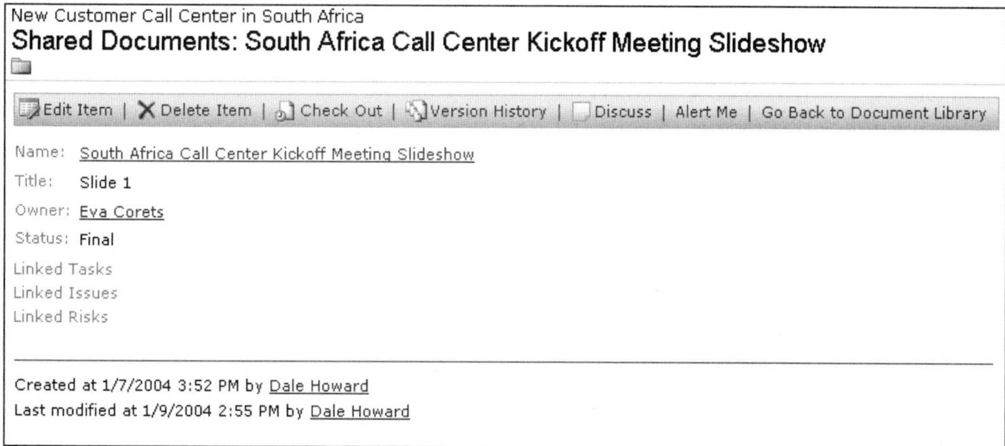

Figure 10-32: Properties of the selected document

Editing Document Properties

Click Edit Properties from the pick list menu for the selected project to edit the selected document's Properties as shown in Figure 10-33. When you finish editing the document properties click the Save and Close button to save the changes and return to the document library. Click the Go Back to Document Library button to discard the changes and return to the document library.

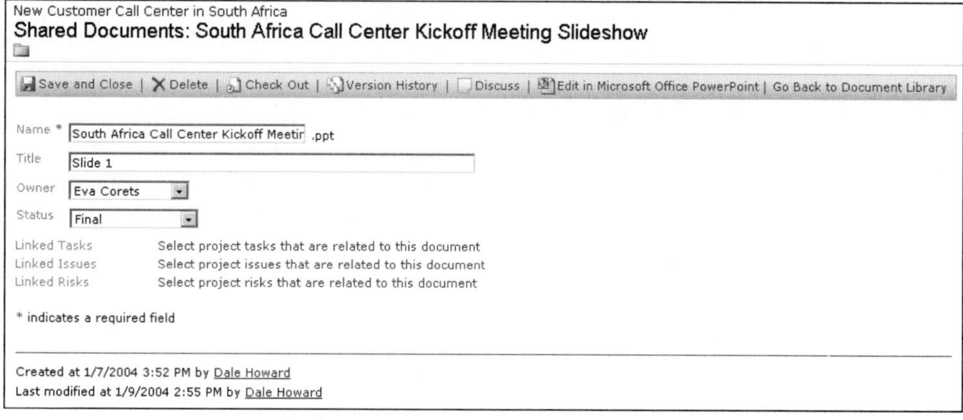

Figure 10-33: Edit the Properties of the selected document

Editing in a Microsoft Office Application

Click Edit in Microsoft Office application from the pick list menu for the selected project to open the document in the application used to create it. The system opens both the application and the document, and displays the Shared Workspace sidepane on the right side of the screen, as shown in Figure 10-34.

Figure 10-34: PowerPoint slideshow in editing mode with Shared Workspace sidepane on the right

The Shared Workspace sidepane shows information about the status of your document, along with additional information such as presence of team members, related links, related documents, and tasks. The Shared Workspace feature also allows team collaboration in which multiple members team members can open and edit the same document simultaneously. While editing the document, each team member can click the Update button to update their copy of the document with latest saved changes made by other team members.

As you work with the document in editing mode, click the Save button to save the latest changes to the document, and click File ➢ Close to close the document and click File ➢ Exit to close the application.

Deleting a Document

Click Delete from the pick list menu for the selected project to remove the selected document from the document library. The system displays a confirmation dialog to confirm your action. Click the Yes button to delete the document, or click No to cancel the action.

Checking Out/Checking In a Document

Click Check Out from the pick list menu for the selected project to prevent others from editing the document while you have it open. Because the system allows multiple users to edit a document simultaneously, you must check out the document if you wish to edit it exclusively. When you click the Check Out button, the system displays the document's checked out status in the documents folder as shown in Figure 10-35.

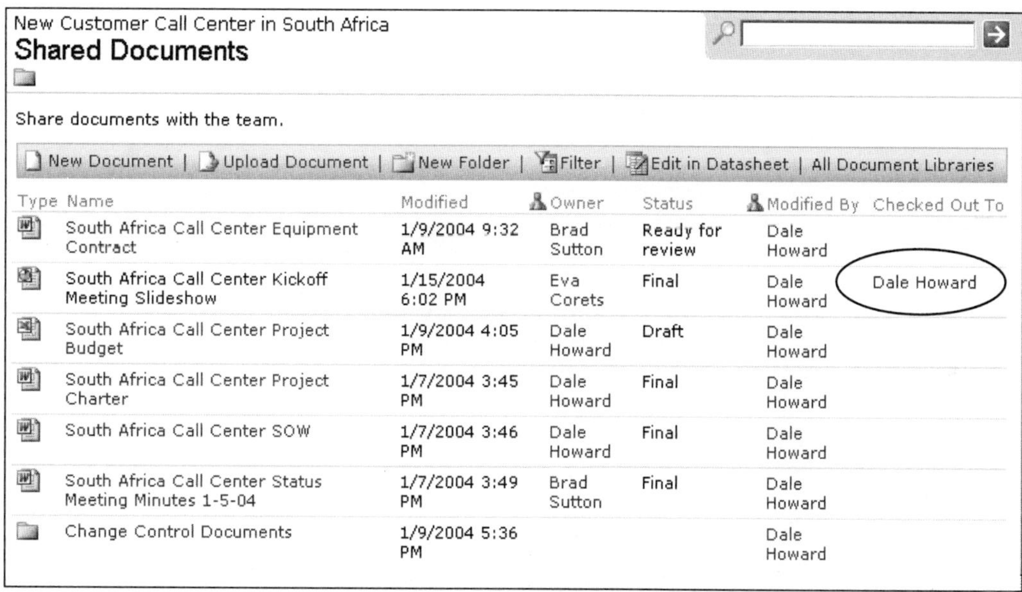

Figure 10-35: Document checked out

You will normally use the document check out feature in conjunction with document editing, so click the Edit in Microsoft Office application menu item to open the document. The Shared Workspace sidepane shows the checked out status of the document, as shown in Figure 10-36.

Figure 10-36: Shared workspace shows checked out document

You can also check out a document by clicking File ➢ Check Out in the application used to open the document.

When you finish editing the checked out document, click the Save button to save it. When you close the document, the system may display the Check In dialog as shown in Figure 10-37.

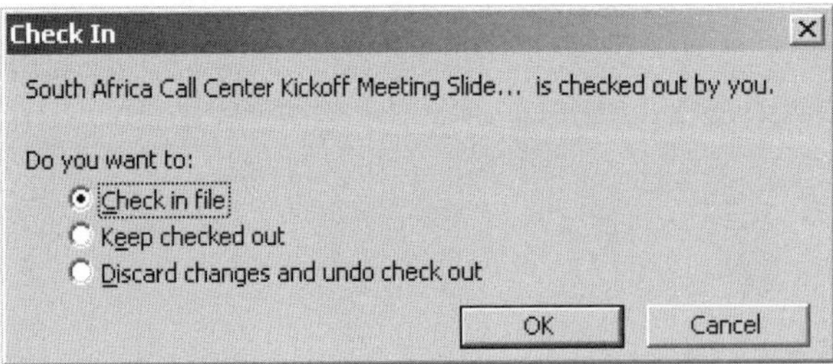

Figure 10-37: Check In dialog

The system automatically displays the Check In dialog when you close the file if you opened the document first and then checked out the document from the File menu. The dialog does not display if you checked out the document first and then opened it for editing.

Select the first option in the Check In dialog to check in the file. You can choose to leave the file in its checked out condition if you plan to edit the file again later and do not want anyone to edit it in your absence. You can also choose to discard your changes and undo the checked out condition of the document. Make your selection and click the OK button. The system displays the Check In Comments dialog shown in Figure 10-38. Add any comments you wish to make and click the OK button to return to the document library.

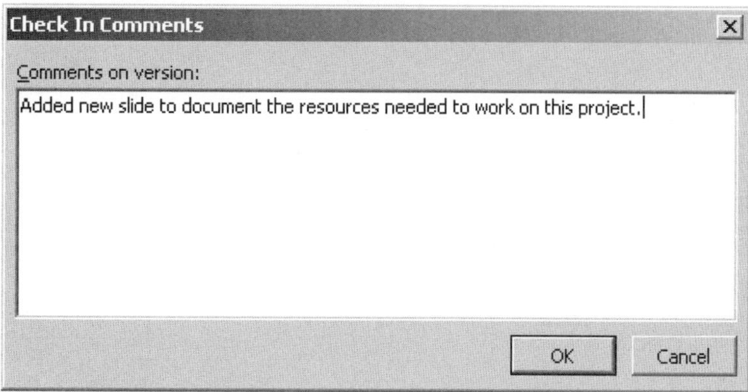

Figure 10-38: Check In Comments dialog

Prior to saving the document, you can also check in the document by clicking the Check in link in the Shared Workspace sidepane.

Working with the Versions History

Click Version History from the pick list menu for the selected project to view your document's version history. The system displays the Versions page with the version history by date in descending order. Notice in Figure 10-39 that there are four versions of the project budget spreadsheet file.

Figure 10-39: Versions page for the selected document

The system always displays the current version of the document at the top of the versions list. You can revert to a previous version of the document in just a few steps. Float your mouse pointer over the version date to expose a pick list selector. Click the pick list button to the right of the version date and select the Restore option from the menu. In Figure 10-40, for example, I am preparing to restore my PowerPoint slideshow version number three.

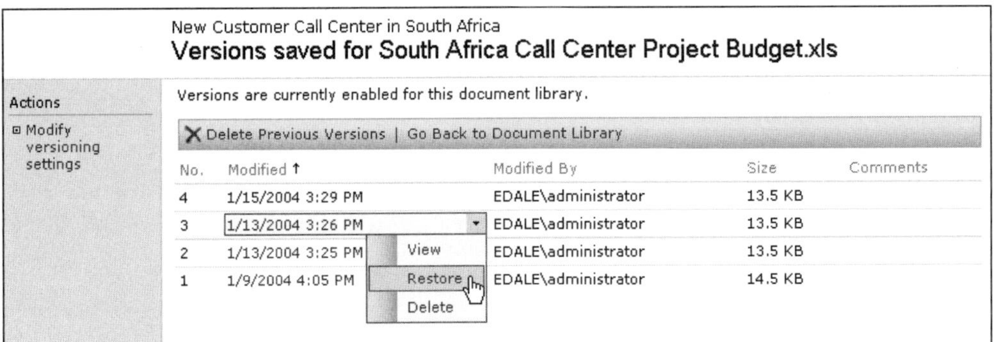

Figure 10-40: Preparing to restore the fifth version of the slideshow

When you select the Restore menu option, the system displays the confirmation dialog shown in Figure 10-41. Click the OK button to complete the restoration of the version, or click the Cancel button to cancel the operation.

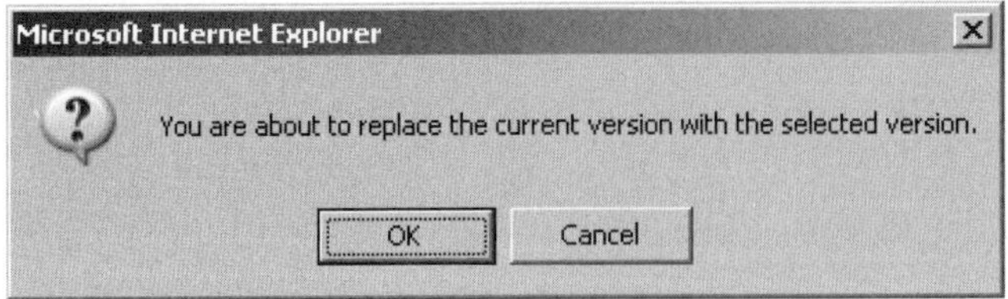

Figure 10-41: Restore version confirmation dialog

When you restore a previous version of a document, the system adds the restored version at the top of the versions list. In Figure 10-42, what is now version five is actually the restored version 3.

Figure 10-42: Version 3 restored as version 5 of the budget spreadsheet

The system always opens the current version of a document when you click the Edit in Microsoft Office application pick list menu selection for any document in a document library. In the previous illustration, the system would open version 5 of the budget spreadsheet and you would not see the changes made in version 4.

Click the Go Back to Document Library button to return to your selected document library.

Before you can use version control with a document, your Project Server administrator must enable Versions for the selected document library.

Discussing a Document

You can only discuss a document from within the project workspace for the selected project. I will discuss the document discussions feature in the next section of this module.

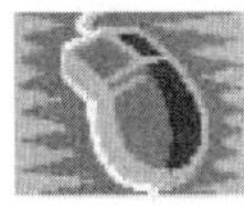

Hands On Exercise

Exercise 10-5

Create a new document library.

1. Select Documents from the Project Web Access main menu
2. Click the name of a project that you created or to which you are assigned
3. Click the Create Document Library button on the toolbar
4. Give your new library a name and description
5. Make your desired selections in the Navigation, Document Versions, and Document Template sections
6. Click the Create button

Exercise 10-6

Upload a document to a Library.

1. Open the document library created in Exercise 10-5, if necessary
2. Select Upload Document on the tool bar
3. Use the Browse button to navigate to an existing file
4. Set the Owner and Status selections for the document
5. If you would care to do so, link the document to one or more tasks, issues, or risks
6. Click the Save and Close when you are finished
7. Verify that the uploaded document appears in the document library
8. Notice the icon indicating that the document is new

Using the Project Workspace

New to Project Server 2003 is full access to the SharePoint project workspace created by the system for each project published to the Project Server database. To access the project workspace for any project, select a project in the data grid on the Risks, Issues, or Documents page and then click the Go to selected project workspace link at the top of the Actions pane, as shown in Figure 10-43.

Figure 10-43: View and submit risks page with Project Workspace link

Warning: When you select a project in the grid, do not click the hyperlink for the actual project. Instead, select either the row header to the left of the project name or the Project Manager cell to the right of the project name.

The system opens a new Internet Explorer window and displays the project workspace for the selected project, as shown in Figure 10-44.

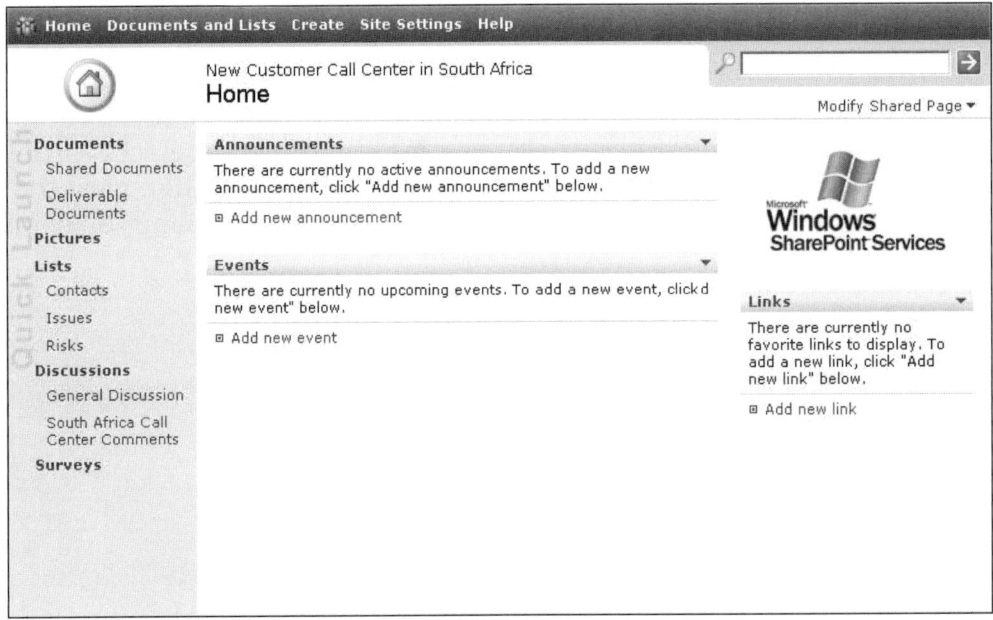

Figure 10-44: Project workspace for the New Customer Call Center in Africa project

The project workspace page provides a single location for accessing project documents, pictures, contacts, issues, risks, discussions, and surveys. The page displays each of these options in the Quick Launch bar on the left side of the page. The project workspace page offers sections for project-related announcements and events, and even links to other project-related Web pages.

Your organization could use the project workspace page as a single point of communication within the Project Server environment.

Discussing a Document

To discuss a project document, select a document library in the Documents section of the Quick Launch bar. In the list of documents in the document library, float your mouse pointer over the desired document, click the pick list button and select Discuss from the menu. In Figure 10-45, notice that I am choosing to discuss the February 2004 Team Status Report document.

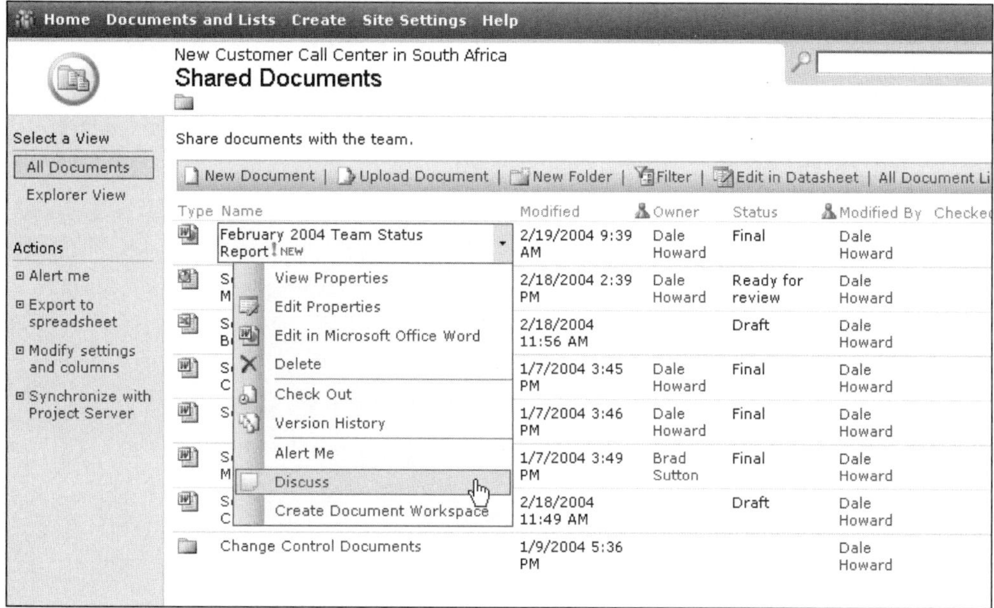

Figure 10-45: Discuss a document

The system displays the document with a Discussion toolbar at the bottom of the document, as shown in Figure 10-46. The Discussions toolbar allows you to insert discussions *in* the document or *about* the document. The difference between the two options is how the system handles the discussion thread, whether internally or externally to the document.

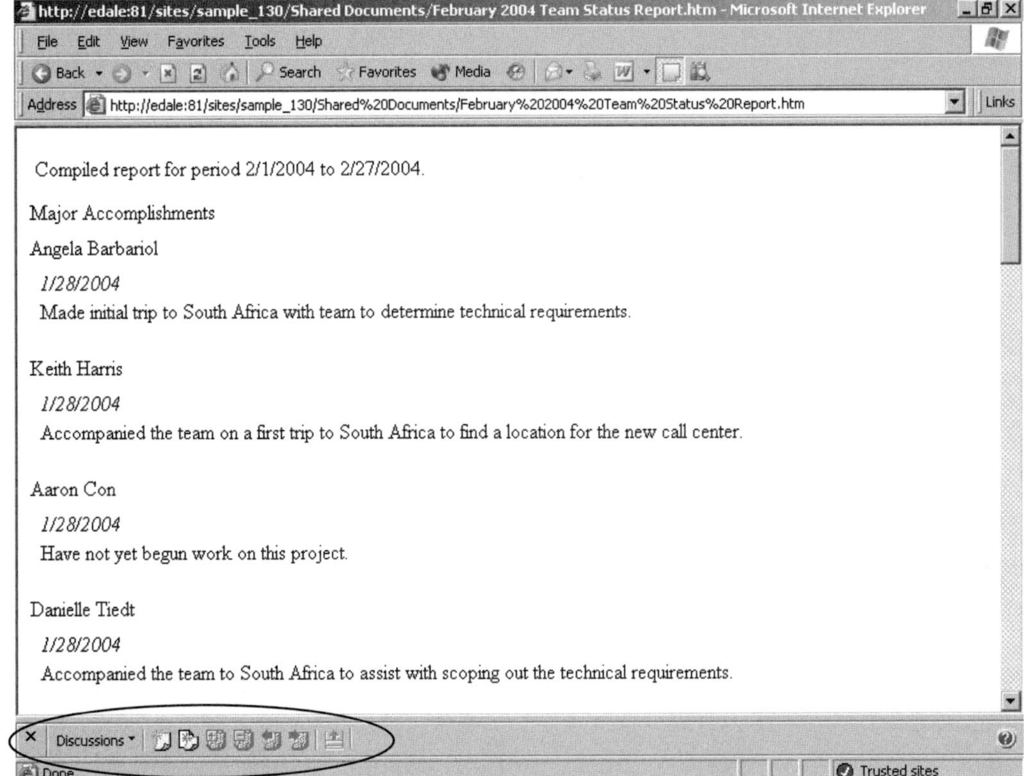

Figure 10-46: Discussions toolbar for the selected document

To insert a discussion in the document, use either of the following options:

- Click the Insert Discussion in the Document button on the toolbar
- Click the Discussions button on the toolbar and then select the Insert in the Document option from the popup menu

The system displays a Discussion marker in the document and also displays additional information in the Discussions toolbar, as shown in Figure 10-47.

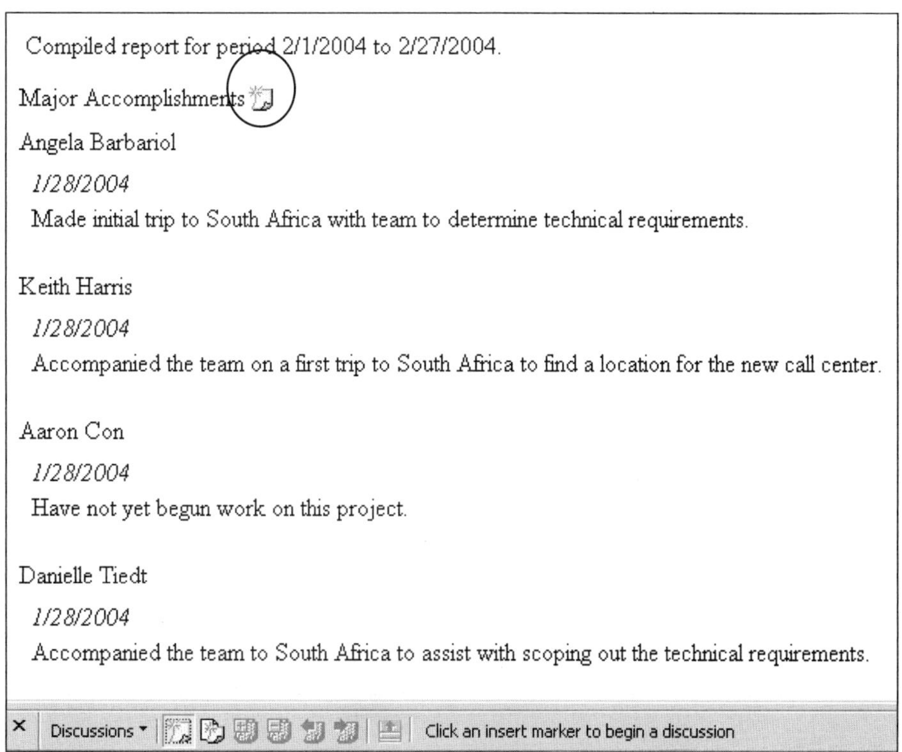

Figure 10-47: Insert Discussion in the document

To add to the discussion in the document, click the discussion marker in the document. The system displays the Enter Discussion Text dialog as shown in Figure 10-48.

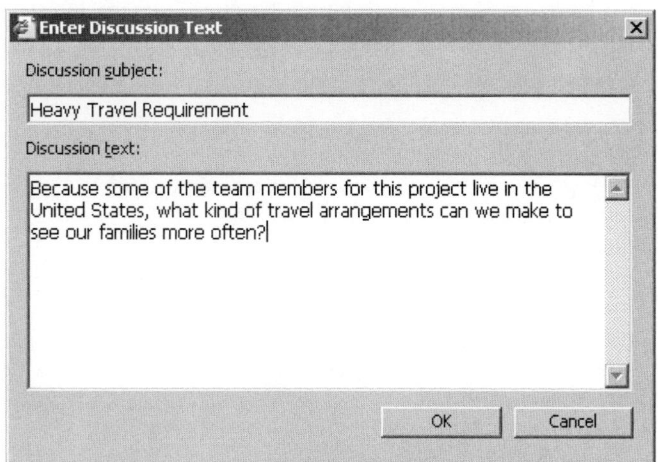

Figure 10-48: Enter Discussion Text dialog

Enter your discussion text and then click the OK button. The system displays your discussion within the document, along with additional discussion buttons on the Discussions toolbar, as shown in Figure 10-49.

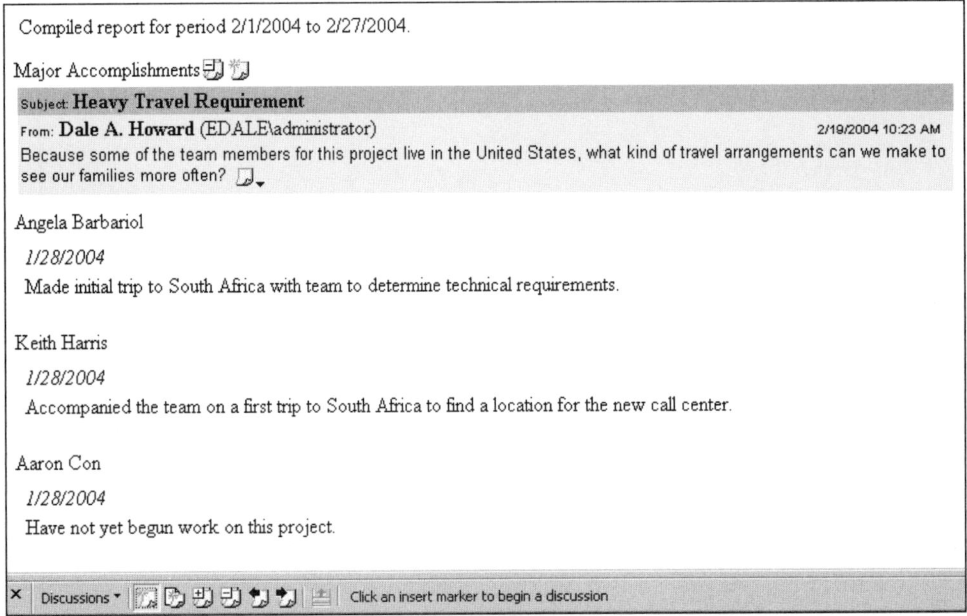

Figure 10-49: Discussion in a document

To view all discussions in the document, click the Expand all Discussions button on the Discussions toolbar. To hide the discussions, click the Collapse all Discussions button. Click the Previous button or the Next button to navigate between discussion items.

To add your thoughts to an existing discussion, click the Show a menu of options icon at the bottom of the existing discussion and select the Reply option, as shown in Figure 10-50. Notice that the system offers you several other options as well, such as editing, deleting, or closing the discussion.

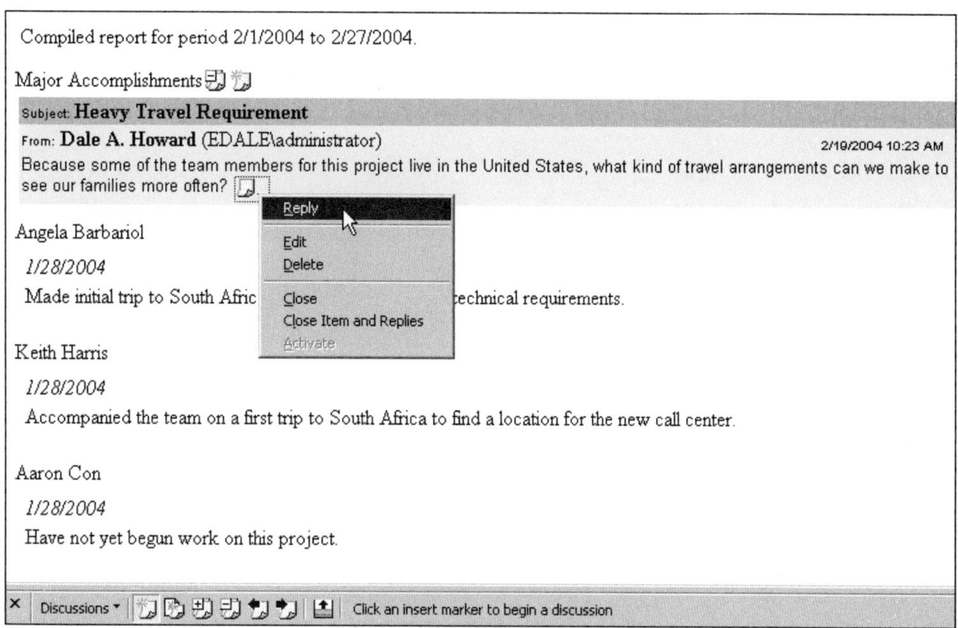

Figure 10-50: Reply to an existing discussion

> **Warning:** You can only insert discussions *in* an HTML document. The system will generate an error message if you attempt to insert a discussion in a non-HTML document such as PowerPoint slideshow. The system will allow you to insert discussions *about* any type of document, however.

To insert a discussion about the document, use either of the following options:

- Click the Insert Discussion about the Document button on the toolbar
- Click the Discussions button on the toolbar and then select the Insert about the Document option from the popup menu

The system displays the Enter Discussion Text dialog previously shown in Figure 10-48. Enter your discussion text and then click the OK button. The system opens a discussion pane at the bottom of the document, as shown in Figure 10-51.

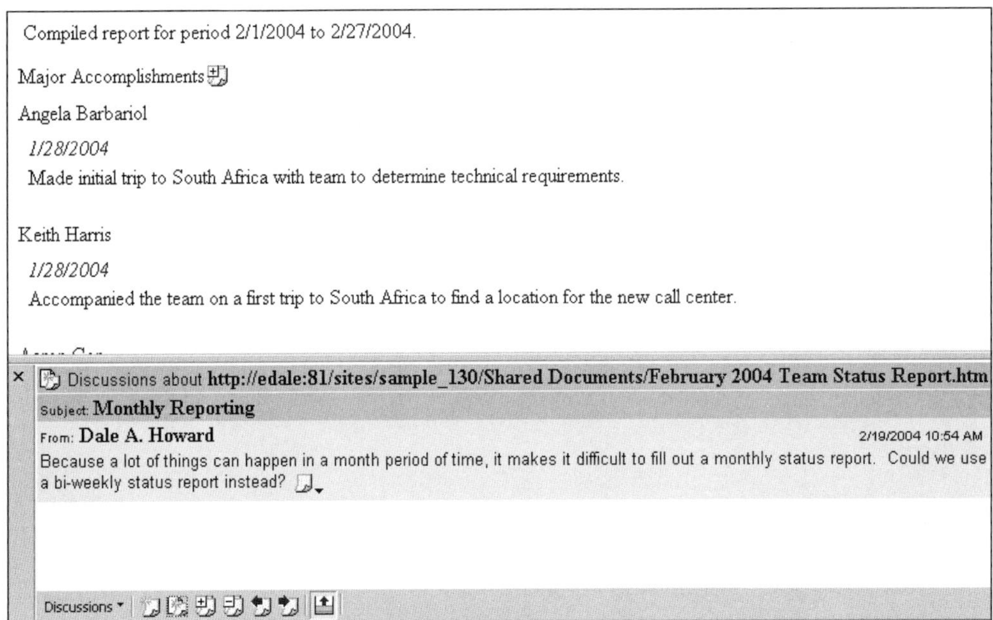

Figure 10-51: Discussion about the document

The system activates the Show/Hide Discussion Pane button on the Discussions toolbar. Click this button to show or hide the pane containing discussions about the document.

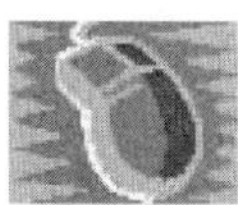

Hands On Exercise

Exercise 10-7

Explore the project workspace for a selected project.

1. Select Risks, Issues, or Documents from the Project Web Access main menu
2. Select a project that you created or to which you are assigned
3. Click the Go to selected project workspace link at the top of the Actions pane
4. Explore the project workspace for your selected project
5. Close the project workspace window

Module 11

Working with Advanced Features of Risks, Issues, and Documents

Learning Objectives

After completing this module, you will be able to:

- View reports for Risks, Issues, and Documents lists
- Set alerts for Risks, Issues, and Documents lists
- Export a list of Risks, Issues, or Documents to an Excel spreadsheet
- Modify settings and columns for Risks, Issues, and Documents lists
- Synchronize the Project Server database with Risks, Issues, and Documents lists that were exported as linked files to Excel or Access

Using Actions Pane Features

The Risks, Issues, and Documents pages of Project Web Access offer you a number of advanced features, such as exporting to Excel and modifying the layout of Views. You will find these features in the Actions section of the Actions pane on the Risks, Issues, and Documents pages. These advanced features include:

- View Reports (Risks and Issues only)
- Alert Me
- Export to spreadsheet
- Modify settings and columns
- Synchronize with Project Server

Figured 11-1 shows the Actions section of the Actions pane for the Risks page.

Figure 11-1: Actions section of Actions pane on Risks page

Viewing Reports

Click the View Reports link to display the Reports page for either Risks or Issues. The Risks - Reports page shown in Figure 11-2.

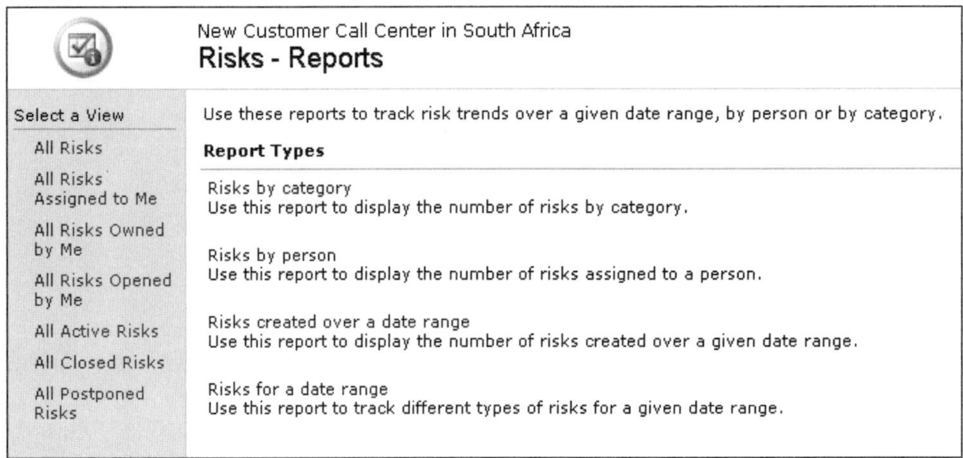

Figure 11-2: Reports page for a selected project

The Report Type section of the Reports page for either Risks or Issues offers four options for creating a report in the selected project:

- By category
- By person
- Created over a date range
- For a date range

When you click the link for the type of Report you desire, the system displays the report in a grid of rows and columns. For example, I have selected the Risks by person report shown in Figure 11-3.

Figure 11-3: Risks by person report

For each type of report, the Report Settings section of the Actions pane displays two or more pick lists that you can use to customize your report. Notice in Figure 11-4 that I can narrow the number of names displayed in the report by selecting a value from the Assigned To pick list. After you select an item from any of the pick lists, click the Create report button to create your customized report.

Figure 11-4: Customize the Risks by person report

Click the Go to Report Home button on the toolbar to return to the Reports page for either Risks or Issues. You can also click the Go Back to List button to return to the Risks page for the selected project.

Hands On Exercise

Exercise 11-1

View a Report for a Risks or Issues list.

1. Click either Risks or Issues from the Project Web Access main menu
2. Select a project which you created or to which you are assigned
3. In the Actions pane, click the View Reports link
4. Select one of the Report Types
5. Modify the Report, if necessary

Setting Alerts

Click the Alert Me link in the Actions pane of the Risks, Issues, or Documents pages to display the New Alert page shown in Figure 11-5.

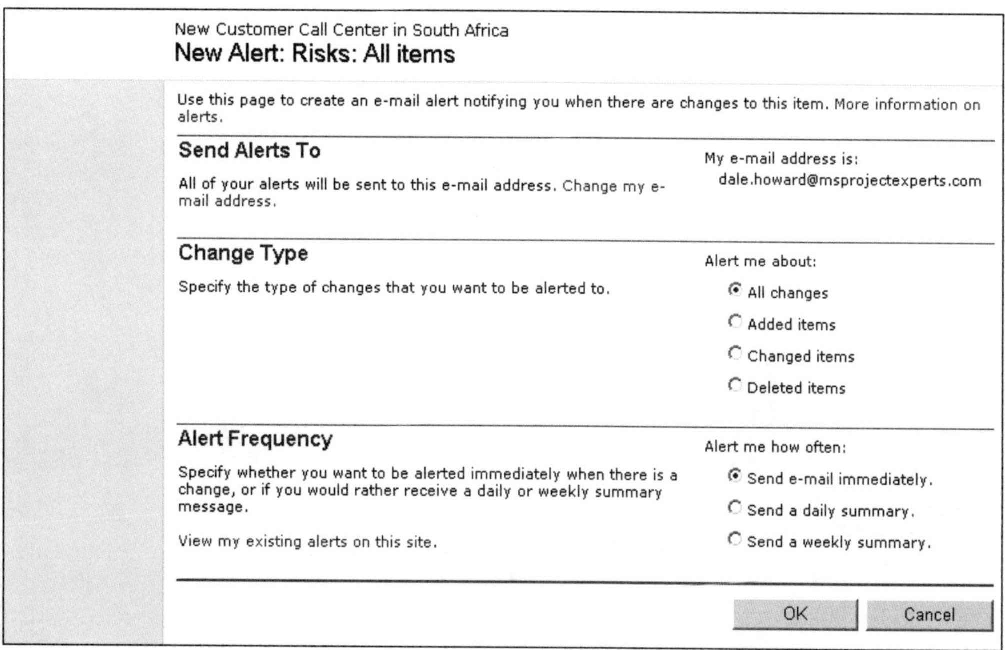

Figure 11-5: New alert page

Select an option in the Change Type section to determine what type of activity will trigger an e-mail alert to you. These activities include the following:

- All changes
- Added items
- Changed items
- Deleted items
- Web discussion updates (Documents only)

Select an option in the Alert Frequency section to determine how often you want the system to send you alerts. The system can alert you immediately, or send you a daily or weekly summary of changes. Click the OK button to confirm your alert selections, or click the Cancel button to cancel the alert.

Exporting to an Excel spreadsheet

Click the Export to spreadsheet link in the Actions pane to export the selected project's list of Risks, Issues, or Documents to an Excel workbook. The system creates an Excel query file and then displays the File Download dialog shown in Figure 11-6.

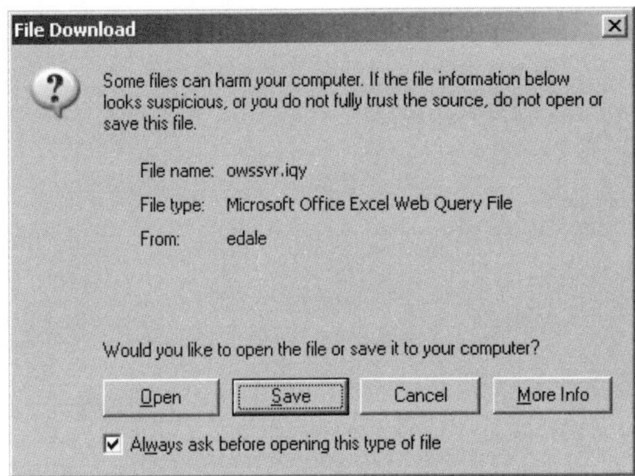

Figure 11-6: File Download dialog

Click the Save button to save the file, and open it later in Excel. If you click the Open button to open the query file in Excel, the system displays the Opening Query dialog shown in Figure 11-7. Click the Open button to open the query file in Excel.

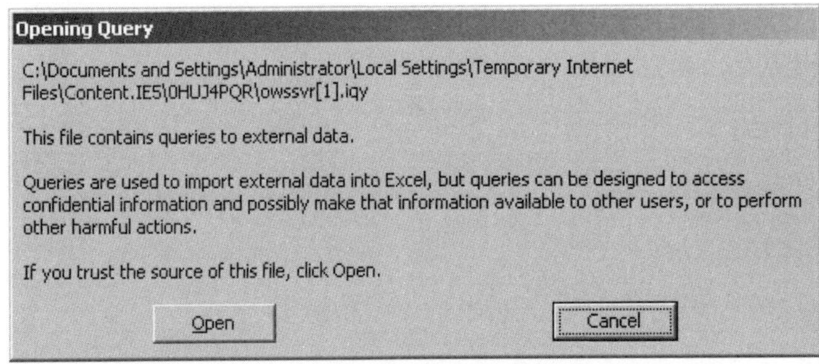

Figure 11-7: Opening query dialog

The system opens the query file in Excel and displays a floating List toolbar to help you to manipulate the query data. Figure 11-8 shows the exported Risk list for a project as an Excel query file.

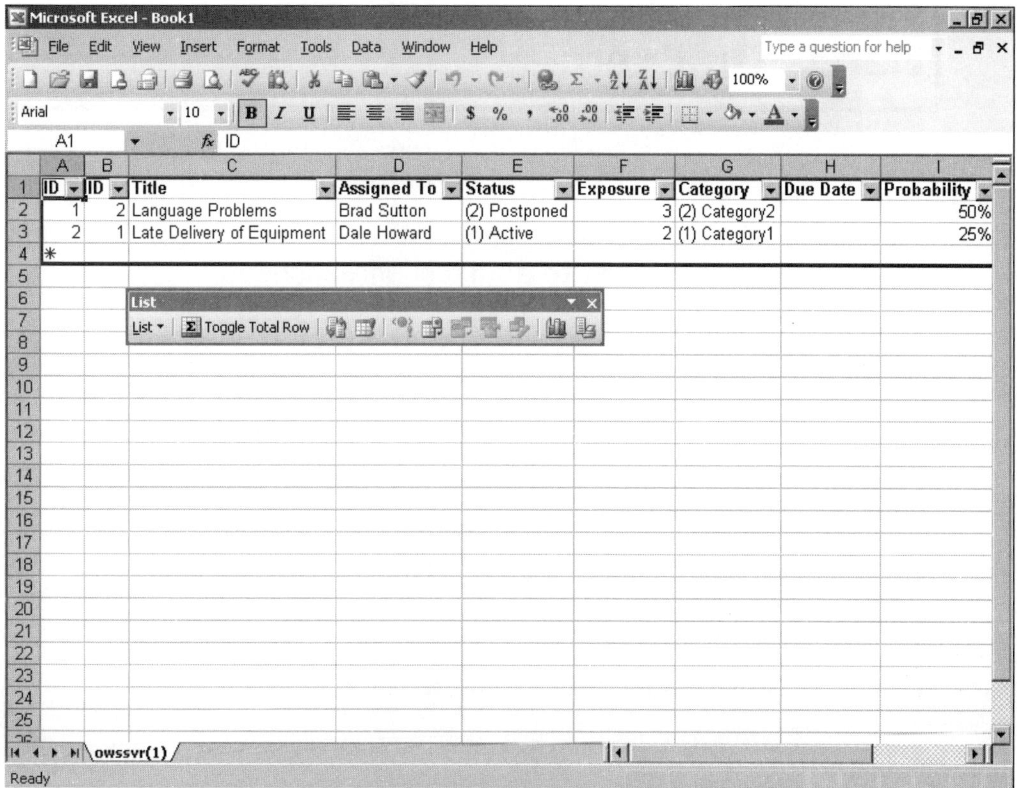

Figure 11-8: Risk query for a selected project opened as an Excel workbook

When you export a Document library list to Excel, the system displays the warning dialog shown in Figure 11-9. The warning indicates that you can edit rows of information in the query, such as the information contained in the Status or Owner fields, but you may not add additional records to the query.

Figure 11-9: Excel warning dialog

Hands On Exercise

Exercise 11-2

Export a Risks or Issues list to an Excel spreadsheet.

1. Click either Risks or Issues from the Project Web Access main menu
2. Select a project which you created or to which you are assigned
3. In the Actions pane, click the Export to spreadsheet link
4. In the File Download dialog, click the Open button
5. In the Opening Query dialog, click the Open button
6. Examine the spreadsheet file in Excel
7. Close the spreadsheet file and exit Excel

Modifying Settings and Columns

Click the Modify settings and columns link in the Actions pane to customize the display characteristics of the Risks, Issues, or Documents pages. Clicking this option on the Risks page displays the Customize Risks page shown in Figure 11-10.

The Customize page for Risks, Issues, and Documents contain the same three sections: General Settings, Columns, and Views. Naturally, the options in each section are slightly different and vary according to the function of the page.

The options available in the General Settings section for both Customize Risks and Customize Issues are:

- Change general settings
- Change permissions for this list

The options available in the General Settings section for Customize Documents are:

- Change general settings
- Save document library as template
- Change permissions for this document library
- Delete this document library

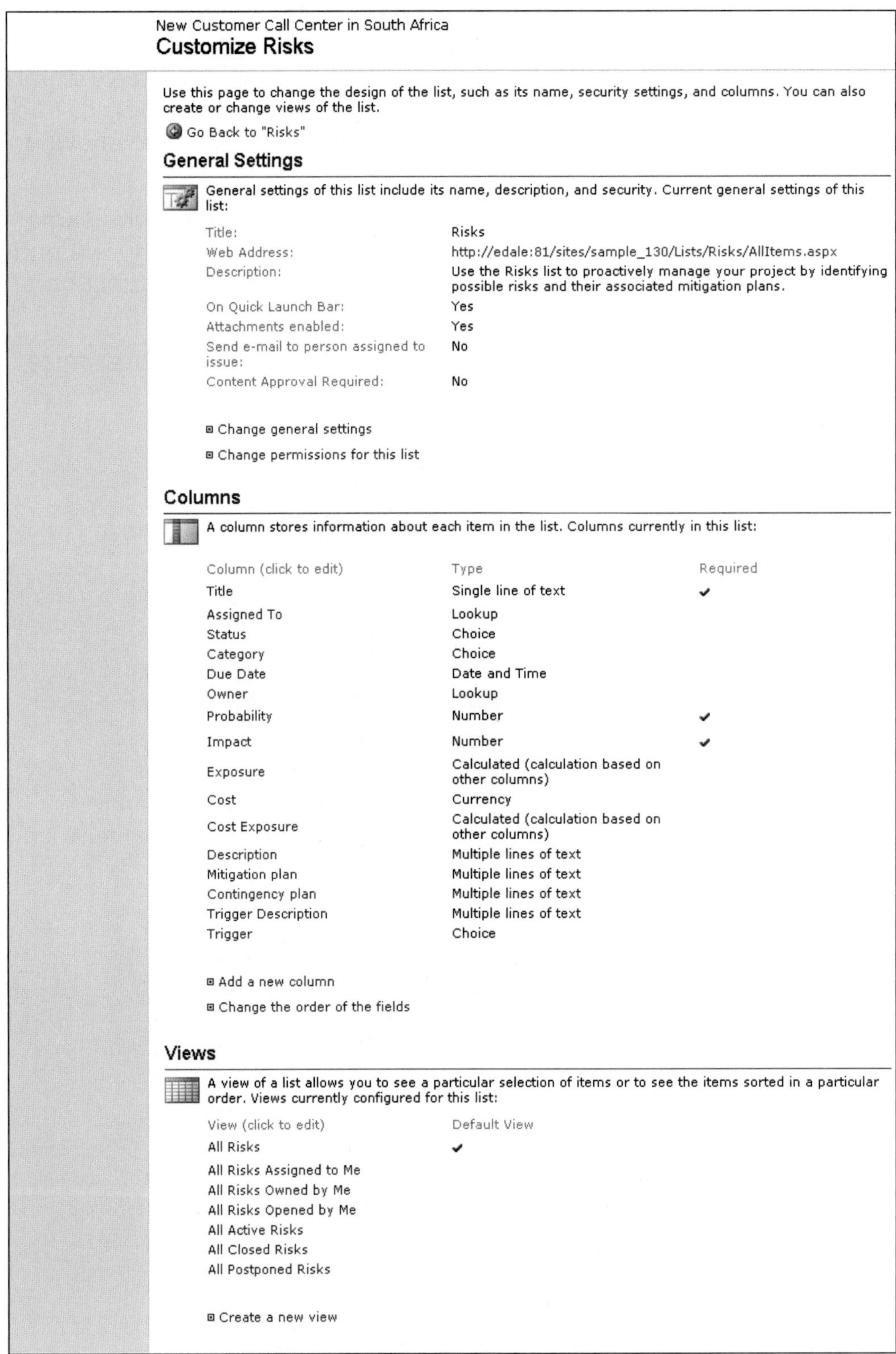
New Customer Call Center in South Africa

Customize Risks

Use this page to change the design of the list, such as its name, security settings, and columns. You can also create or change views of the list.

Go Back to "Risks"

General Settings

General settings of this list include its name, description, and security. Current general settings of this list:

Title:	Risks
Web Address:	http://edale:81/sites/sample_130/Lists/Risks/AllItems.aspx
Description:	Use the Risks list to proactively manage your project by identifying possible risks and their associated mitigation plans.
On Quick Launch Bar:	Yes
Attachments enabled:	Yes
Send e-mail to person assigned to issue:	No
Content Approval Required:	No

Change general settings

Change permissions for this list

Columns

A column stores information about each item in the list. Columns currently in this list:

Column (click to edit)	Type	Required
Title	Single line of text	✔
Assigned To	Lookup	
Status	Choice	
Category	Choice	
Due Date	Date and Time	
Owner	Lookup	
Probability	Number	✔
Impact	Number	✔
Exposure	Calculated (calculation based on other columns)	
Cost	Currency	
Cost Exposure	Calculated (calculation based on other columns)	
Description	Multiple lines of text	
Mitigation plan	Multiple lines of text	
Contingency plan	Multiple lines of text	
Trigger Description	Multiple lines of text	
Trigger	Choice	

Add a new column

Change the order of the fields

Views

A view of a list allows you to see a particular selection of items or to see the items sorted in a particular order. Views currently configured for this list:

View (click to edit)	Default View
All Risks	✔
All Risks Assigned to Me	
All Risks Owned by Me	
All Risks Opened by Me	
All Active Risks	
All Closed Risks	
All Postponed Risks	

Create a new view

Figure 11-10: Customize Risks page

Modifying General Settings for Risks and Issues

In the General Settings section for Risks or Issues, click the Change general settings link and the system displays the List Settings page shown in Figure 11-11.

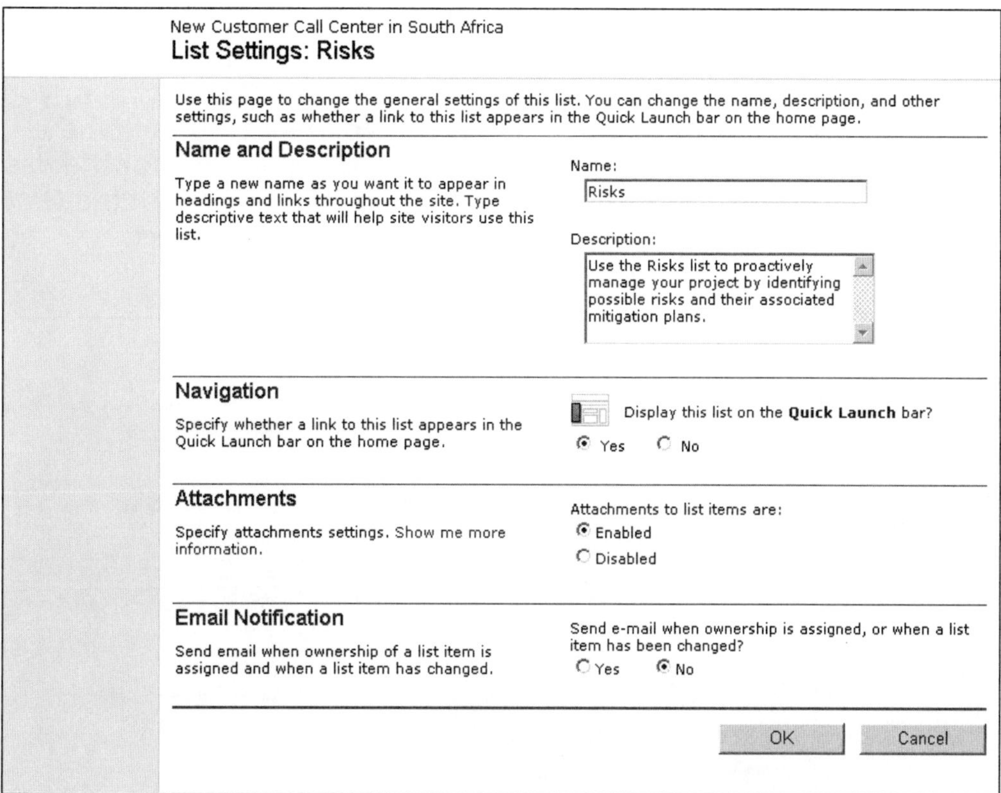

Figure 11-11: List Settings page for Risks

The options in the List Settings page allow you to specify the name and description of the Risks or Issues page, and to determine how the system handles navigation, attachments, and e-mail notifications for the selected project only. Select your desired options and then click the OK button to apply the changes or Cancel to discard the changes.

The Navigation section of the List Settings page offers the option to display the list on the Quick Launch bar. You can find the Quick Launch bar in the project workspace page for the selected project.

In the General Settings section for Risks or Issues, click the Change permissions for this list link to open the Change Permissions page shown in Figure 11-12. Use this page to determine who has access to the Risks page for the selected project. The page displays a description of each user group to which you can assign users. The description lists the permissions for each group. To edit the permissions for any of the groups listed, click the name of the group or select the checkbox for the desired group and then click Edit Permissions of Selected Users on the toolbar. After selecting a group, you can also add users to the group by clicking the Add Users button on the toolbar. You can delete user groups by selecting the checkbox for the desired group and then clicking the Remove Selected Users button. Click the Go Back to List button to return to the Risks page for the selected project.

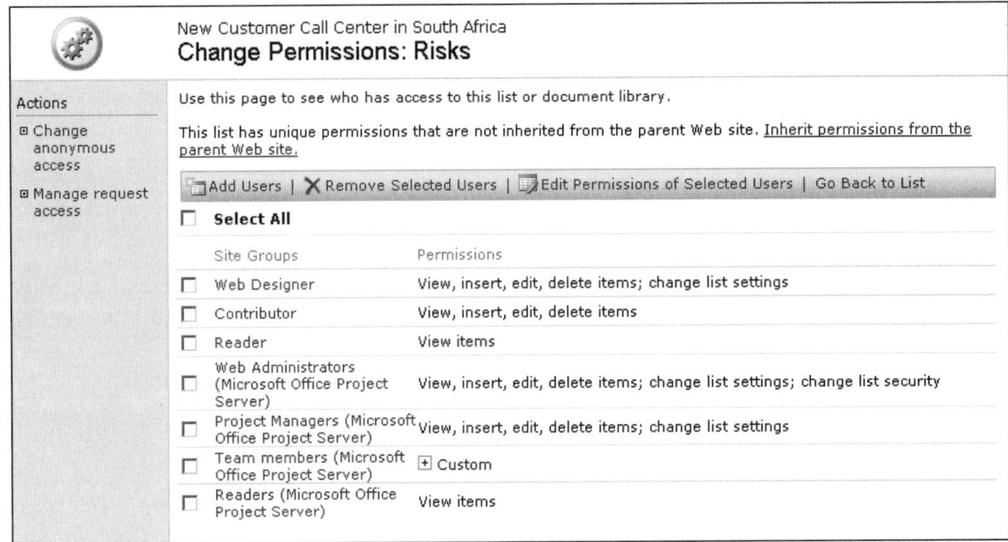

Figure 11-12: Change Permissions page

Because making changes in permissions potentially affects many users in your organization, msProjectExperts recommends that your Project Server administrator be responsible for making all changes to permissions.

Modifying General Settings for Documents

In the General Settings section for Documents, click the Change general settings link and the system displays the List Settings page. The List Settings page for Documents contains sections at the bottom of the page for Document Versions and the Document Template, as shown in Figure 11-13. I previously discussed the options on this page in Module 10 in the section on creating a new document library.

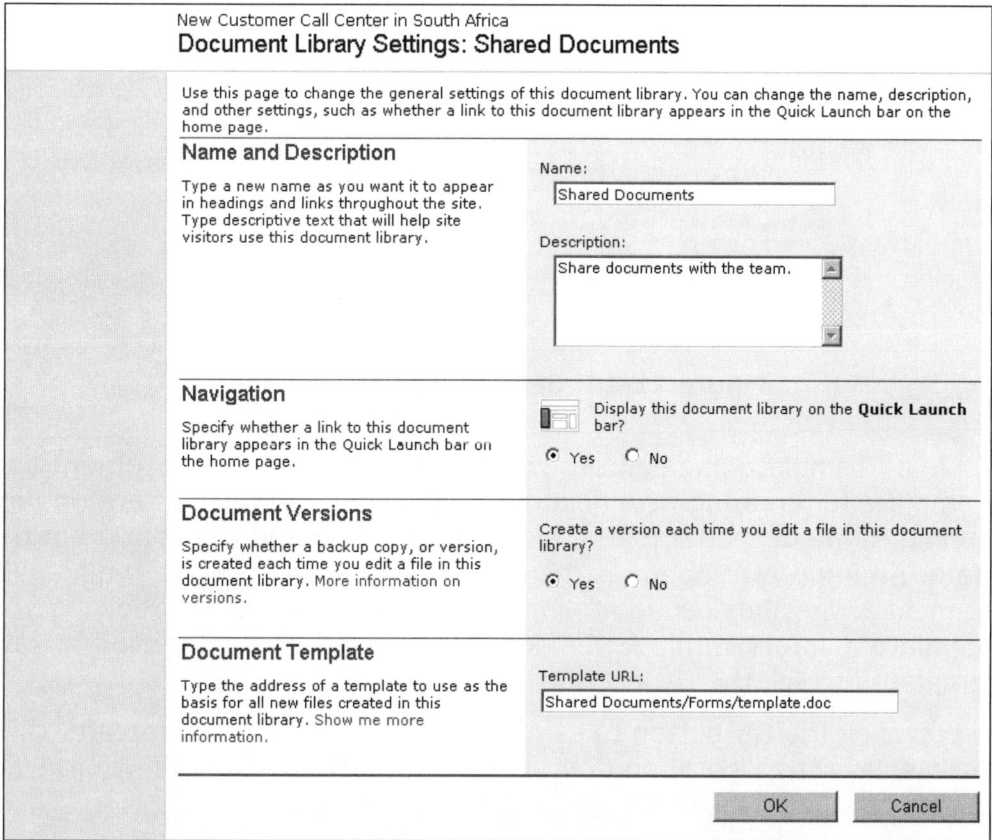

Figure 11-13: List Settings page for Documents

In the General Settings section for Documents, click the Save document library as template link and the system displays the Save as Template page, as shown in Figure 11-14.

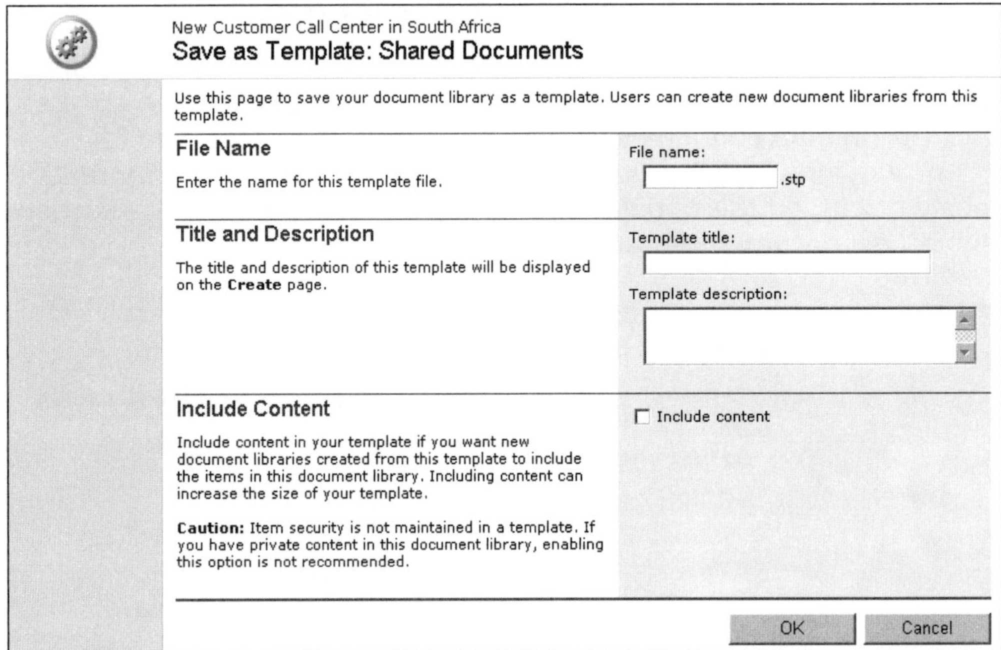

Figure 11-14: Save as Template page

The Save as Template page allows you to save the selected document library as a template for creating new document libraries. The page offers options for the File Name of the template, along with a Title and Description of the template. An important option is the Include content checkbox, which allows you to include specific documents in your document template allowing you to pre-populate a library with specific documents. Click the OK button to save the template or click the Cancel button to discard your changes.

When you click the OK button to save the document library template, the system displays the Operation Completed Successfully page shown in Figure 11-15.

Figure 11-15: Operation Completed Successfully page

To return to the list customization page, click the OK button. To manage the templates in the gallery, click the List template gallery link. The system displays the List Template Gallery page for the selected project shown in Figure 11-16.

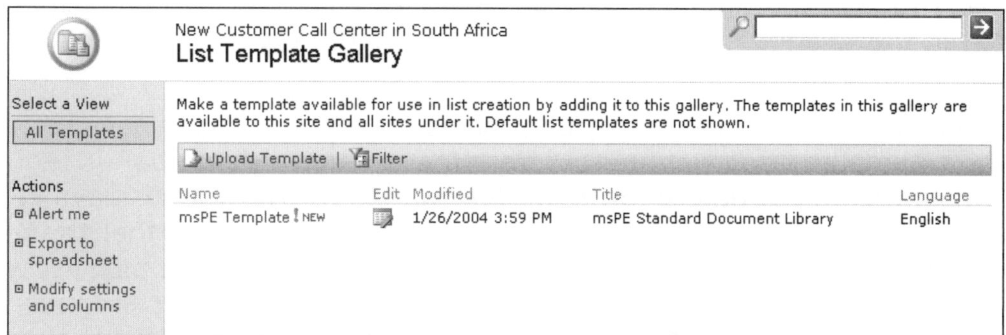

Figure 11-16: List Template Gallery page

Use the options on the List Template Gallery page to take the following actions:

- Upload a new template to the gallery
- Apply filtering to the templates in the gallery
- Set up alerts
- Export the gallery to an Excel spreadsheet
- Modify the settings and columns for the gallery

In the General Settings section for Documents, you can change the user permissions for the library by clicking the Change permissions for this document library link. The options on the Change permissions page are identical to the options available for Risks and Issues list.

In the General Settings section for Documents, click the Delete this document library link to remove the library for the selected project. The system displays the confirmation dialog shown in Figure 11-17. Click the OK button to delete the document library or click the Cancel button to cancel the deletion process.

Figure 11-17: Confirmation dialog to delete a document library

Modifying Columns Settings

You make changes to any of the columns displayed on the Risks, Issues, or Documents pages by clicking the link for the name of the column. Figure 11-18 shows the Change Column page for the Status column. To get this display, you click the Status column in the Risks page. The system displays options in the Change Column page according to the type of column you select.

Notice in Figure 11-18 that the system gives you options to change the column's name and description, to determine whether information is required in the column, and to determine what information the system displays in the column as well as how it displays the information. You can see that the system displays information in the Risks Status column using a pick list with options for Active, Postponed, and Closed. If you want to add, change or delete a status value, you do it here. Edit the column to your liking, and then click the OK button to save the changes for the selected column or click the Cancel button to discard the changes.

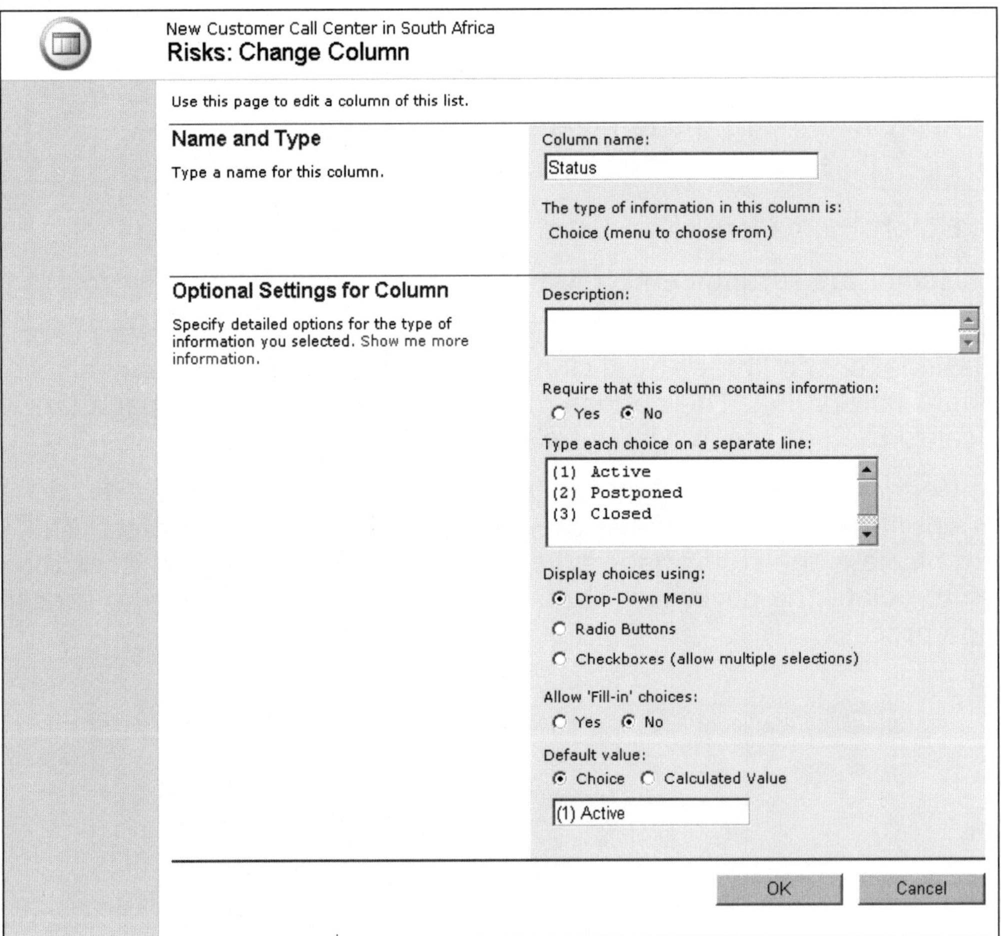

Figure 11-18: Change Column page for the Status column

When you click the Add a new column link in the Columns section, the system opens the Add Column page shown in Figure 11-19. This page is virtually identical to the Change Column page and requires you to enter the name of the column along with the type of type of information displayed in the column. Based on the type of column you choose, the system redraws the page to include options for the column type. Notice in the figure that I chose to display Choice as my information type (menu to choose from) and the system displayed the selections in the Optional Settings for Column section accordingly. Make your selections about the new column and then click OK to add the new column, or click Cancel to discard the changes.

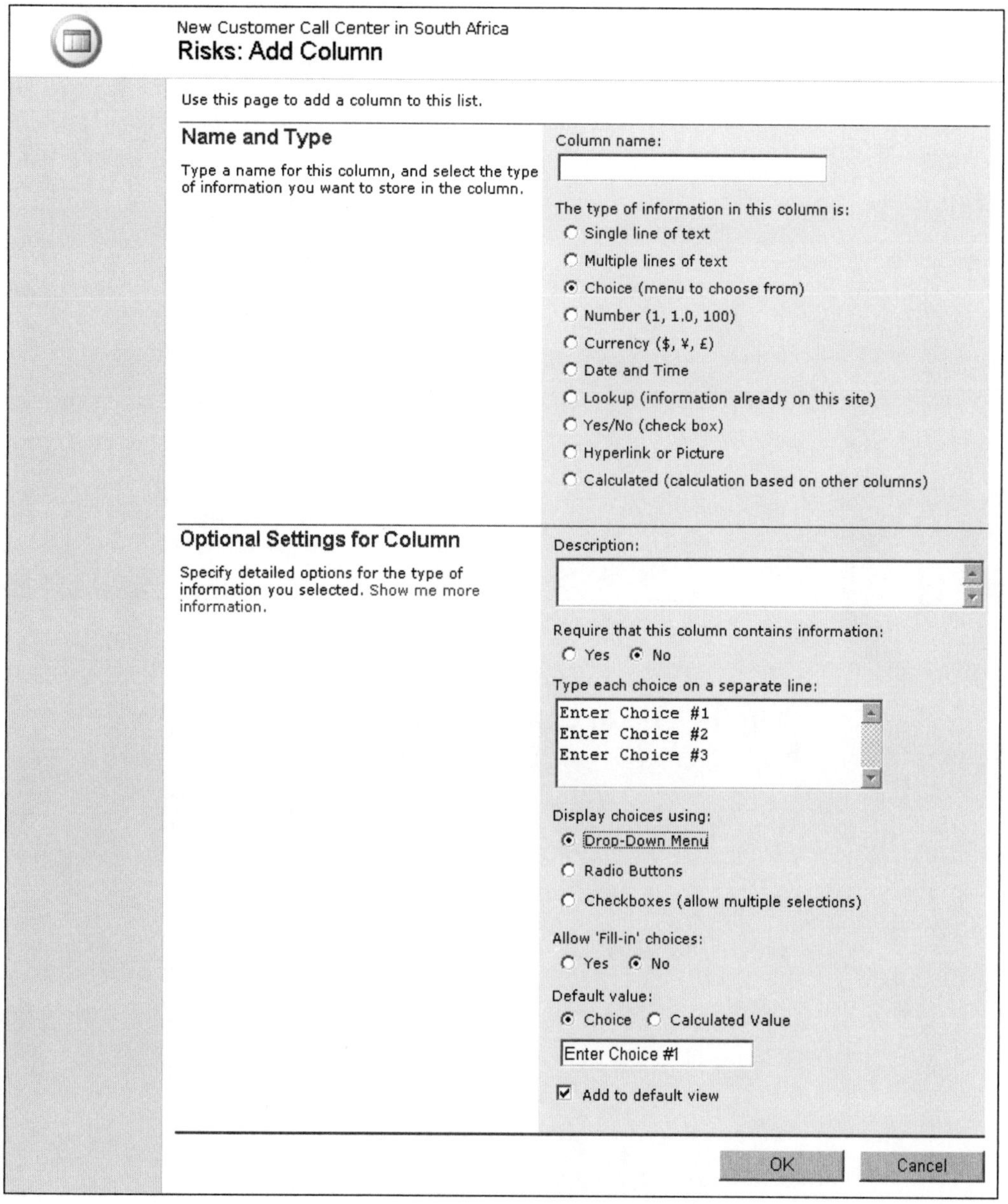

Figure 11-19: Add Column page with Choice information selected

Click the Change the order of the fields link in the Columns section to open the Change Field Order page. Notice in Figure 11-20 that the page displays the current order of fields listed in the Risks page for the selected project. A numbered pick list to the right of each field name indicates the position of the field from the top of the list. When you change the position number for a field, the system automatically renumbers the remaining fields. Make any changes you desire to the order of the fields, and then click the OK button to save the changes. Click the Cancel button to discard the changes.

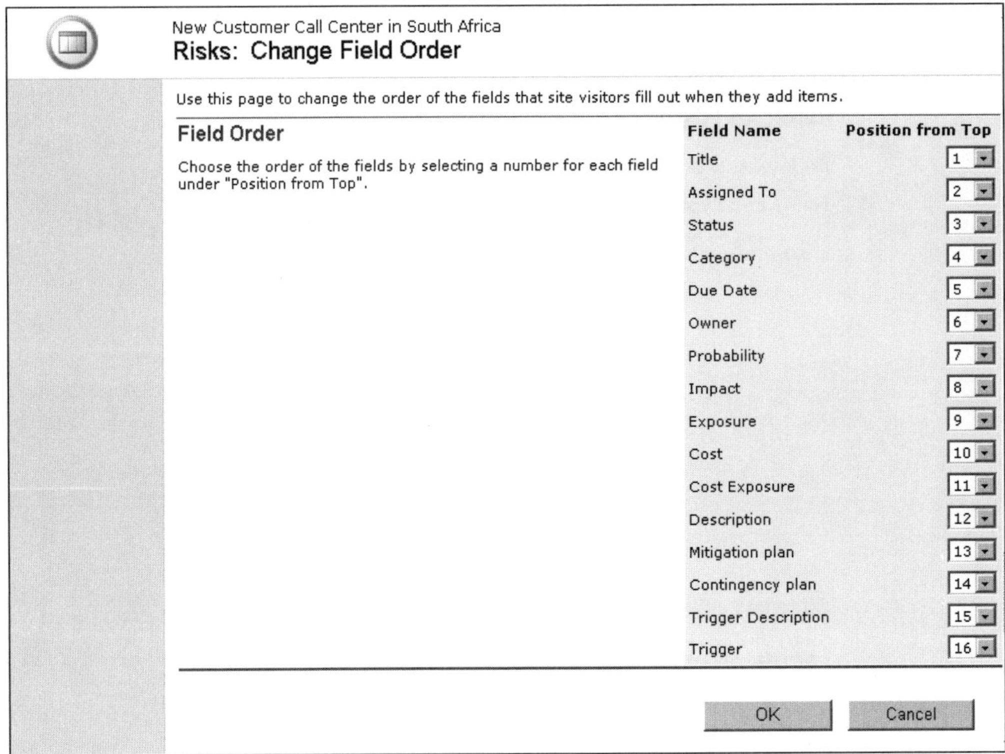

Figure 11-20: Change Field Order page

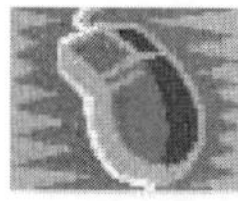

Hands On Exercise

Exercise 11-3

Add an extra column to a Document library.

1. Select Documents from the Project Web Access main menu
2. Select a project and click the document library which you wish to modify
3. Click the Modify settings and columns link in the Actions pane
4. In the Columns section, click Add a new column
5. Enter a name for your column and choose a data type
6. Set optional settings for the column
7. Click OK when done
8. View the new column in the document library

Modifying Views

When you a click a View listed in the Views section, the system presents the Edit View page. Notice in Figure 11-21 that I selected the All Risks Assigned to Me view for editing. The Name section of the Edit View page allows you to rename the view, specify the Web address for the view, or set this view as the default view. The Columns section of the Edit View page allows you to select which columns the system displays in the view and in what order. The Sort section allows you to apply two levels of sorting to the selected view. The Filter section allows you to apply multiple levels of filtering to the view. By default, the system displays only two levels of filtering, but you can click the Show More Columns link to add more columns to the filter.

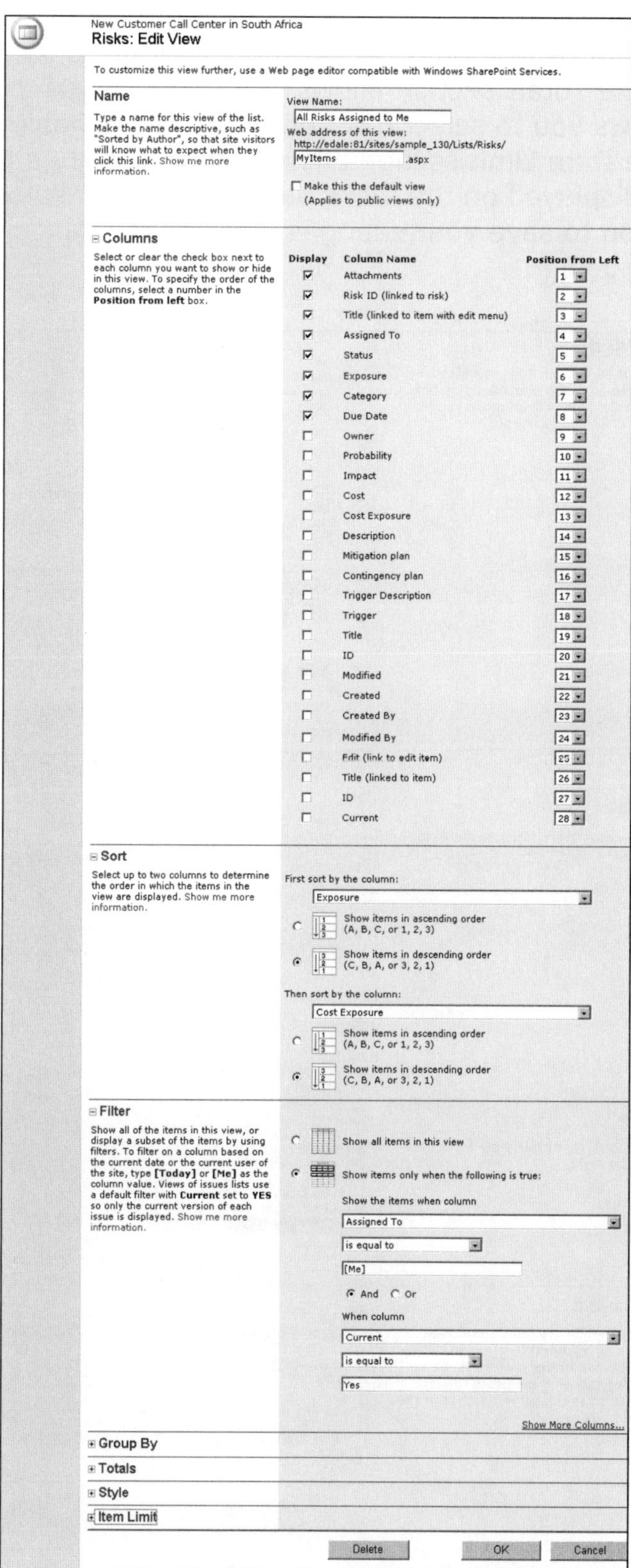

Figure 11-21: Edit View page

By default, the system displays the Group By, Totals, Style, and Item Limit sections collapsed. In Figure 11-22, I expanded the contents of these four sections. The Group By section allows you to apply up to two levels of grouping, while the Totals section allows you to add totals to the display. The Style section allows you to select from one of eight available styles for the display, while the Item Limit section allows you to specify a limit on the number of risks displayed on the Risks page. Make your selections and then click the OK button to save your changes, or click the Cancel button to discard your changes.

⊟ **Group By**

Select up to two columns to determine what type of group and subgroup the items in the view will be displayed in. Show me more information.

First group by the column:

None

(•) Show groups in ascending order (A, B, C, or 1, 2, 3)

( ) Show groups in descending order (C, B, A, or 3, 2, 1)

Then group by the column:

None

(•) Show groups in ascending order (A, B, C, or 1, 2, 3)

( ) Show groups in descending order (C, B, A, or 3, 2, 1)

By default, show groupings:

(•) Expanded ( ) Collapsed

⊟ **Totals**

Select one or more totals to display.

Column Name	Total
Assigned To	None
Status	None
Category	None
Due Date (Average supported in datasheet view only)	None
Attachments	None
Title	None
Risk ID	Count

⊟ **Style**

Choose a style for this view from the list on the right.

View Style:

Shaded
Issues Boxed
Issues Boxed, no labels
Custom
Default

⊟ **Item Limit**

Use an item limit to limit the amount of data that is returned to users of this view. You can either make this an absolute limit, or allow users to view all the items in the list in batches of the specified size.

Number of items to display:

100

(•) Display items in batches of the specified size.

( ) Limit the total number of items returned to the specified amount.

Delete | OK | Cancel

Figure 11-22: Last four sections expanded on the Edit View page

You can also delete the current view while in the Edit View page by clicking the Delete button. The system displays a confirmation dialog to make certain you want to delete the view.

When you click the Create a new view link in the Views section, the system presents the Create View page shown in Figure 11-23. The system allows you to create three kinds of Views: Standard, Datasheet, and Calendar.

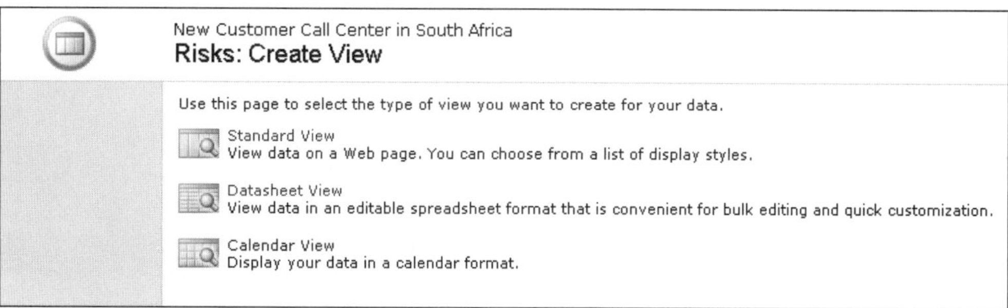

Figure 11-23: Create View page

All default view selections in the Actions pane are Standard views for Risks, Issues, and Documents. Click the Standard View button to create a new Standard view, or click the Datasheet View link to create a new Datasheet view. Because the Create View pages for both selections are virtually identical to the Edit View pages you've previously worked with, I will not go into depth on how to create new Standard and Datasheet views.

If the source list for which you want to create a custom view contains a column with date information, you can create a Calendar View to display information on a standard calendar. Click the Calendar View link to display the Create Calendar View page shown in Figure 11-24. In the Name section of the page, enter a name for your new Calendar View and select the checkbox if you wish to make this new view the default view for the list page you're applying it to. In the Audience section, select an option to make this new view either a Personal view or a Public view. Personal views are for your own personal use, while Public views are available to everyone within the system.

The Make this the default view option applies only to Public views. The system will not allow you to set a Private view as the default view.

New Customer Call Center in South Africa
Risks: Create Calendar View

Use this page to create a view of this list.

Name

Type a name for this view of the list. Make the name descriptive, such as "Sorted by Author", so that site visitors will know what to expect when they click this link. Show me more information.

View Name:

Make this the default view
(Applies to public views only)

Audience

Select the option that represents the intended audience for this view. Show me more information.

View Audience:

Create a Personal View

Personal Views are intended for your use only. However, if given the correct URL, others may use, modify or delete your personal view.

Create a Public View

Public views can be visited by anyone using the site.

Columns

Select the column(s) on which the calendar will be based.

Base calendar on: Due Date / Modified / Created

Base calendar on the following interval:
Between Due Date / Modified / Created and Due Date / Modified / Created

Calendar Settings

Choose the calendar settings for this view.

Calendar opens in: Month View / Week View / Day View

You can change this at any time while using the calendar.

Filter

Show all of the items in this view, or display a subset of the items by using filters. To filter on a column based on the current date or the current user of the site, type **[Today]** or **[Me]** as the column value. Views of issues lists use a default filter with **Current** set to **YES** so only the current version of each issue is displayed. Show me more information.

Show all items in this view

Show items only when the following is true:

Show the items when column

Current

is equal to

Yes

And Or

When column

None

is equal to

Show More Columns...

OK Cancel

Figure 11-24: Create a Calendar View page

In the Columns section, select an option to base the calendar on a single date or on a date range. Both options allow you to choose whether to display the Risk, Issue, or Document according to date criteria. In the Calendar Settings section, you choose whether to display a monthly, weekly, or daily calendar. The Filter section, gives you options to display all items or to apply a filter to the list. If you select the option to filter your list, create the filter with one or two columns of data. When you have finished creating your custom Calendar view, click the OK button to save your view or click the Cancel button to discard the view.

When your new custom view is complete, it appears in the Actions pane for the Risks, Issues, or Documents page. Click on your new view to apply it. Figure 11-25, shows the new custom Calendar view I created to show all risks in a calendar format, based on the creation date of the risk.

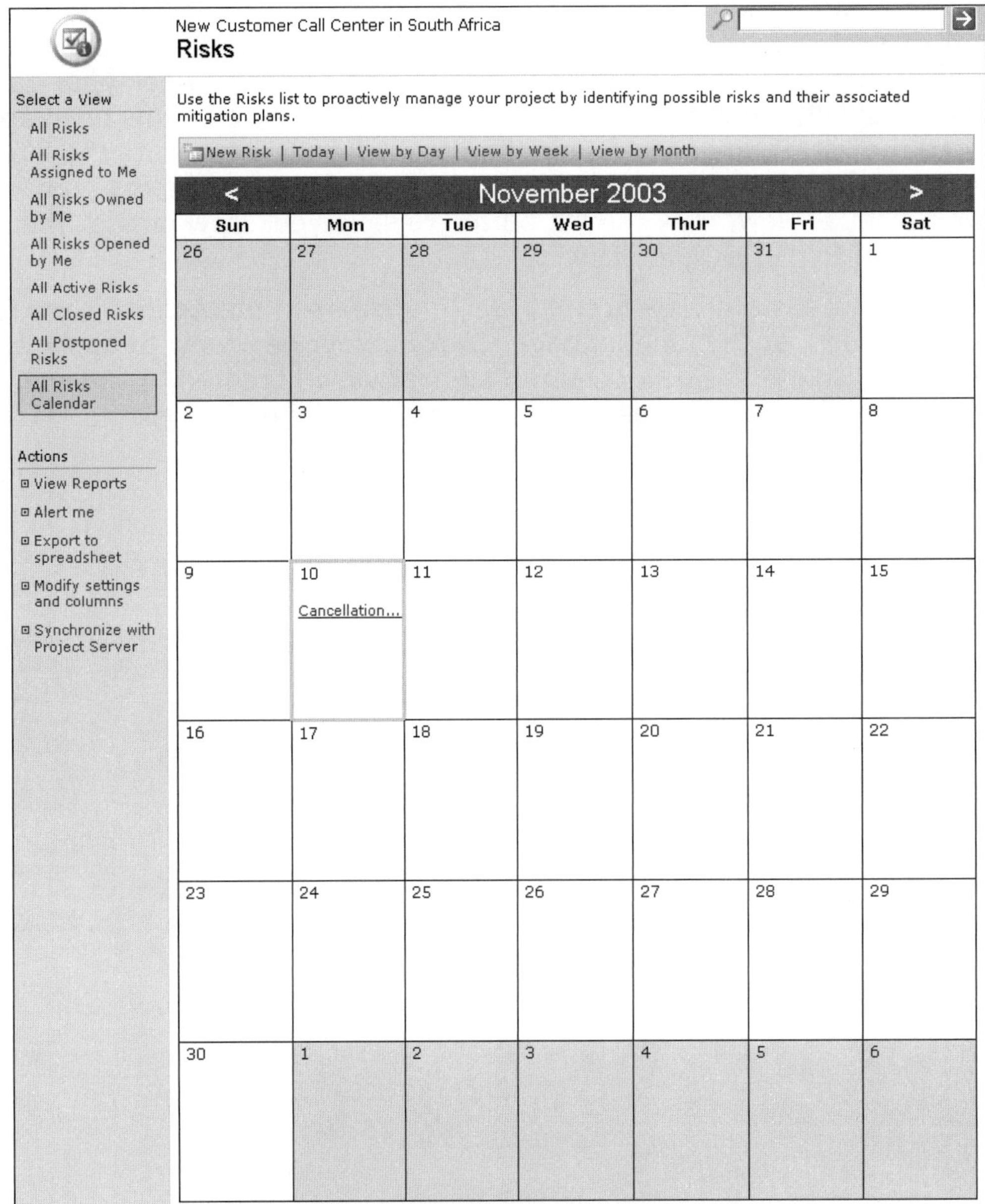

Figure 11-25: Custom Calendar View

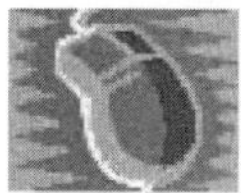

Hands On Exercise

Exercise 11-4

Add a new view to a Document library.

1. Select Documents from the Project Web Access main menu
2. Select a project and then select the document library in which you wish to create a new view
3. Click the Modify settings and columns link in the Actions pane
4. In the Views section, click Create a new view and select a Standard View
5. Enter a Name for your new view, select an Audience, and determine the columns to display and the order to display them
6. Select additional options as you desire
7. Click the OK button when you are finished creating the new view
8. Try your new view in the document library

Synchronizing with Project Server

Project Server 2003 gives you the means to export and link a Risks, Issues, or Document list to an Excel spreadsheet or to an Access table. To use this feature, apply the Datasheet view of any project's Risk, Issue, or Documents list and then click the Task Pane button in the toolbar to display to open the Task Pane shown in Figure 11-26.

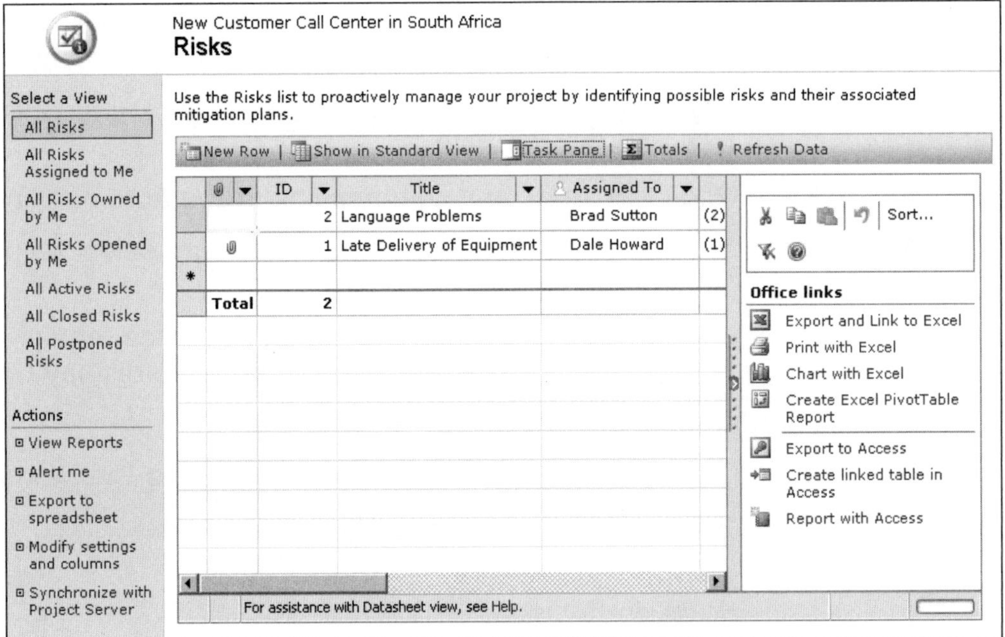

Figure 11-26: Task pane for Risks list

If you export a Risks, Issues, or Documents list to either Excel or Access, and subsequently make changes to the exported file in these applications, you can synchronize the changes with the SharePoint database. In fact, both Excel and Access warn you at the time you save by displaying the dialog shown in Figure 11-27.

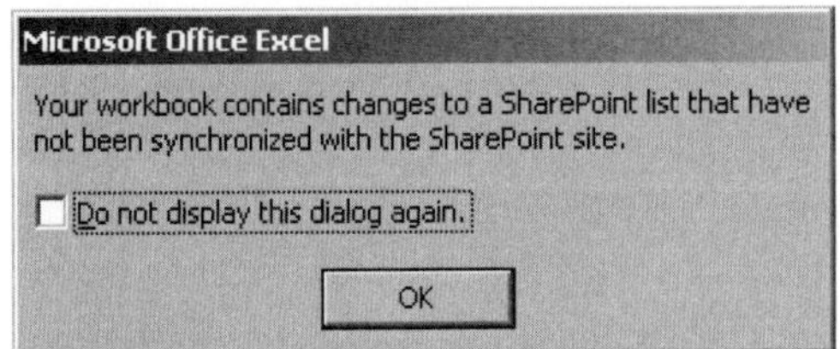

Figure 11-27: Synchronization warning dialog

To synchronize the changes in a linked Excel spreadsheet or Access table, click the Synchronize with Project Server link at the bottom of the Actions list in the Actions pane. The system displays a confirmation dialog box shown in Figure 11-28. Click the OK button to synchronize the data.

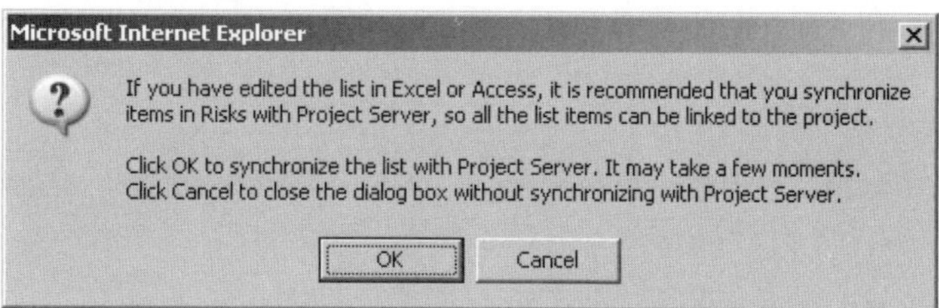

Figure 11-28: Synchronize to Project Server dialog

Once the system synchronizes the changes between Excel or Access and the SharePoint database, it displays the confirmation dialog shown in Figure 11-29.

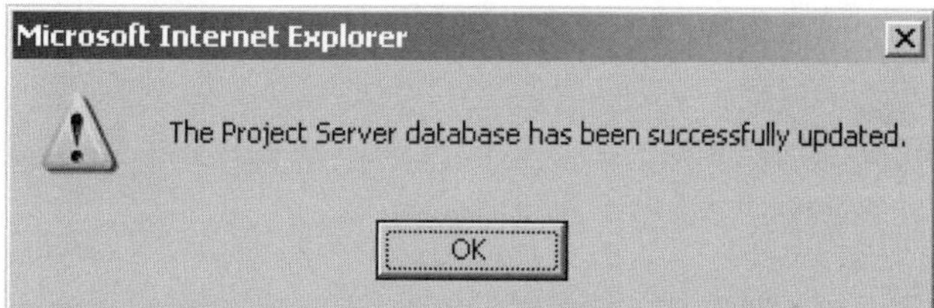

Figure 11-29: Synchronization is successful

Module 12

Working with Status Reports

Learning Objectives

After completing this module, you will be able to:

- Create a new status report request
- Save and send a status report request
- Edit and delete a status report
- Respond to a status report request
- Submit an unrequested status report
- View individual status report responses
- View a merged team status report
- View unrequested status reports

Requesting a Status Report

Select Status Reports from the main menu in Project Web Access to begin working with the Status reports overview page shown in Figure 12-1. Team members do not see the Request a status report section of the page or the option in the Actions pane.

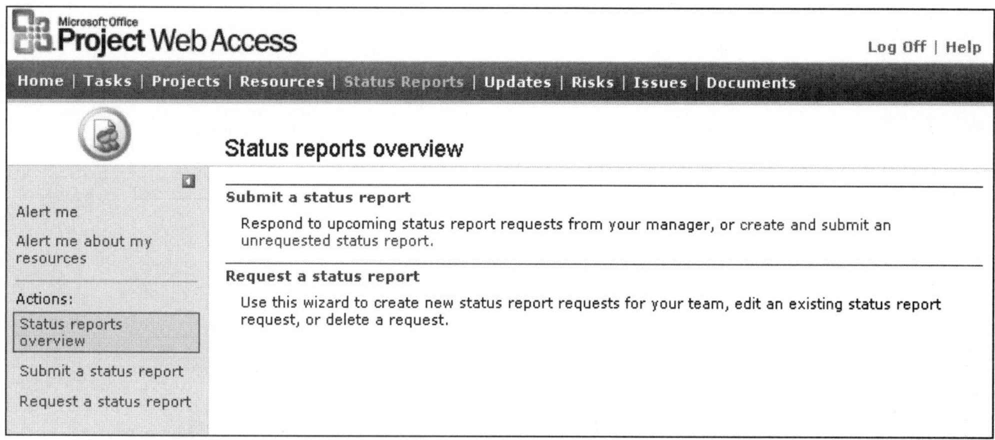

Figure 12-1: Status Reports overview page

The Request a status report feature is dependent on permissions granted in Groups in Project Web Access. By default, it is available only to the following Groups: Executives, Project Managers, Resource Managers, Team Leads, and Administrators.

You can use the Request a status report feature to create periodic Status Reports due on a regular basis. Click the Request a status report link to display the Request a status report page shown in Figure 12-2. Note that the selections on this page not only allow you to create a new status report request, they also allow you to modify or delete an existing status report request. You must select an action before continuing.

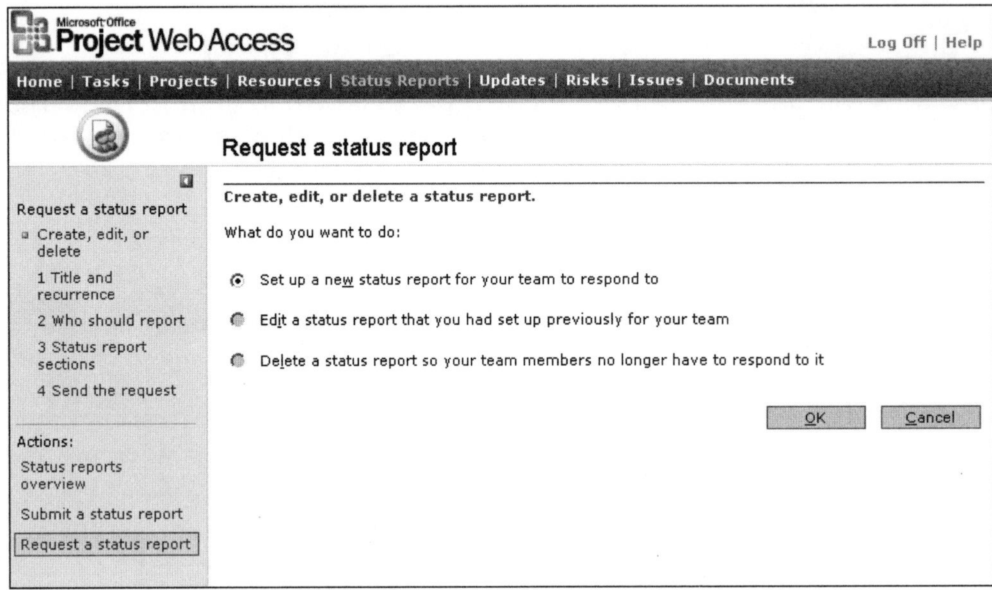

Figure 12-2: Select Status Report page

Creating a New Status Report Request

To create a new status report request, select Set up a new status report for your team to respond to on the Request a status report page shown previously in Figure 12-2, and click the OK button. The system displays the Step 1 page of a four-step wizard, as shown in Figure 12-3. Give the status report a name, determine its recurrence rate and due date, and set the start date of the first reporting period on this page. Notice in Figure 12-3 that my new status report is due on a monthly basis on the last Friday of every month and the first reporting period begins February 1, 2004. In other words, team members must submit their first response on the last Friday of February.

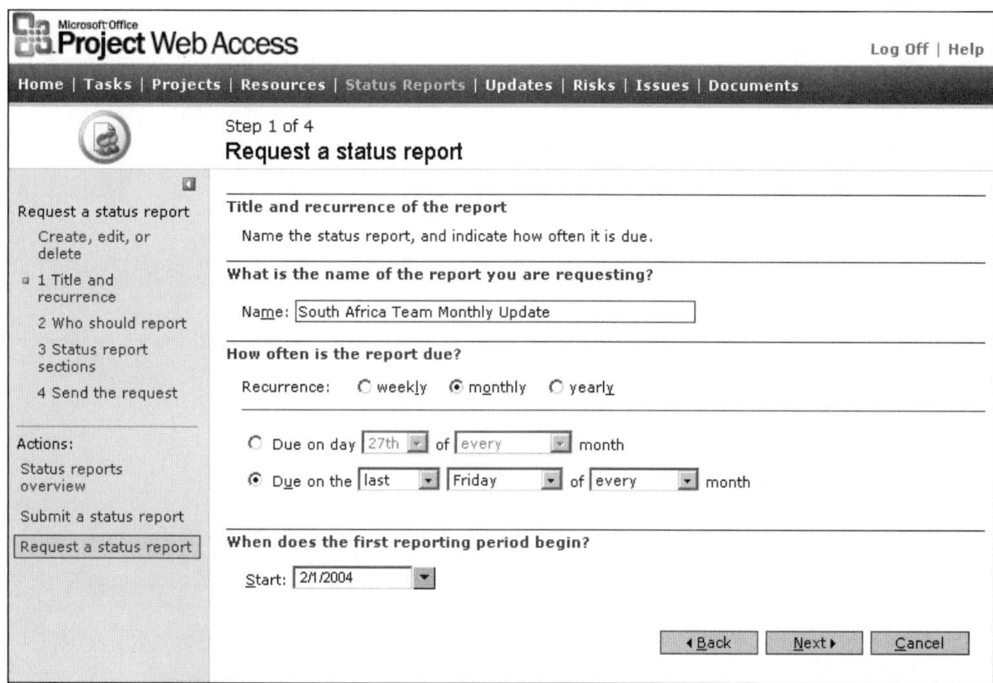

Figure 12-3: Request a Status Report – Step 1
Set the Title and Recurrence

Click the Next button to display the Step 2 page and select the resources who must respond to the status report. Notice in Figure 12-4 that I selected four resources. Notice that system selects the checkbox to the left of each name by default as you add resources to the respondent list. The checkbox is an indication to the system to merge the responses from each individual resource into a single consolidated Status Report. Deselecting the checkbox removes the individual from the merged report.

Figure 12-4: Request a Status Report – Step 2 Select the resources who should respond to the status report request

Click the Next button to display the Step 3 page, where you configure status report's topical sections. By default, the system offers the three sections shown in Figure 12-5. You can delete, reorder, rename, add to them, or accept them as they are.

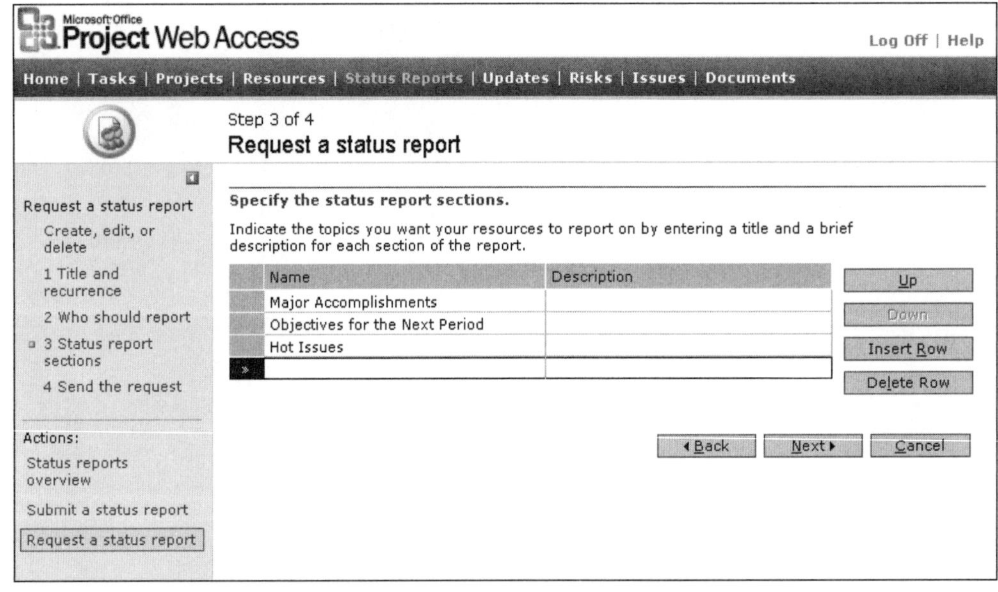

Figure 12-5: Request a Status Report – Step 3 Determine status report sections

Click the Next button to display Step 4 shown in Figure 12-6. This page gives you an opportunity to go back and edit your selections, or to confirm the Status Report creation. Click the Save button to create and save the status report in the system without sending it to the respondents or click the Send button to save the status report and send it to the respondents immediately. If you save without sending, you can send the report later. Click the Cancel button to cancel the operation.

Figure 12-6: Request a Status Report – Step 4 Confirm status report creation

After you save or send your status report the system redisplays the Status reports overview page as shown in Figure 12-7. Notice that your new status report request displays in the Requested reports section.

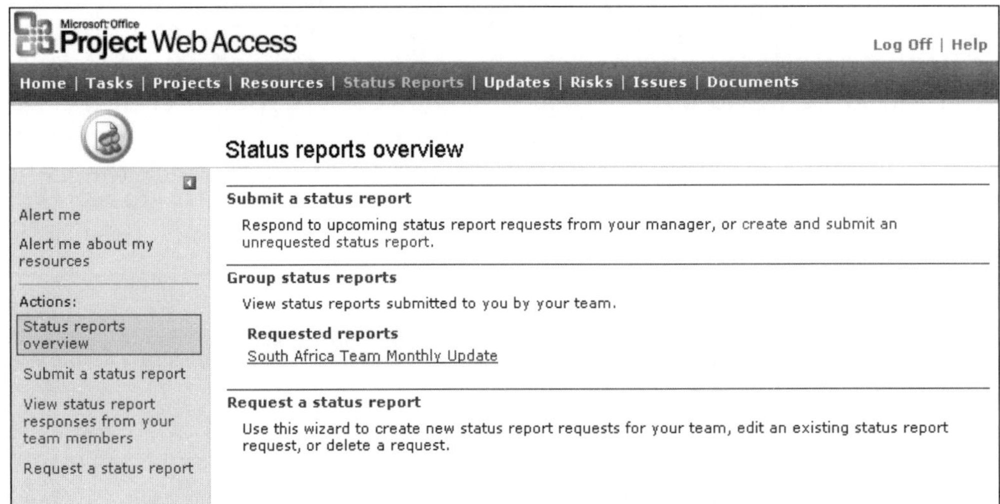

Figure 12-7: Status reports overview page with new status report request

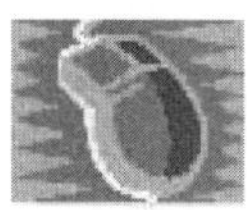

Hands On Exercise

Exercise 12-1

Create a new Status Report request.

1. Select Status Reports from the Project Web Access main menu
2. Click the Request a Status Report link
3. Select the Set up a new Status Report for your team option button and click the OK button
4. Set the Name and Reoccurrence options for the new status report and click the Next button (use a past date for the first reporting period)
5. Select yourself and members of your class as resources who must respond to the Status Report
6. Verify that the merge checkbox is selected for each name, and then click Next to continue
7. Specify the section headings for the Status Report and click the Next button to continue
8. Click the Send button to send the Status Report
9. Navigate to the Project Web Access Home page to verify the status report request

Editing and Deleting Status Reports

To edit an existing status report, you must first click the Request a status report link on the Status reports overview page. The system displays the Request a status report page. When you click the Edit a status report that you had set up previously for your team option the system displays a pick list of your previously created status reports. Notice in Figure 12-8 that I am selecting the Steve Masters Team Weekly Report for editing. Once you select a status report for editing, click the OK button to continue through all four steps of the wizard.

Figure 12-8: Edit a status report request

To delete a status report request, select the Delete a status report so your team members no longer have to respond to it option. As with the Edit a status report selection, the system displays your previously created status reports in a pick list. Select a status report for deletion and click the OK button. The system displays the confirmation dialog shown in Figure 12-9.

Figure 12-9: Status report deleted

Responding to a Status Report Request

When a project manager sends a status report request the selected resources see the status report request in Status Reports section of their Home page, as shown in Figure 12-10. Resources may see multiple status report requests created by multiple managers.

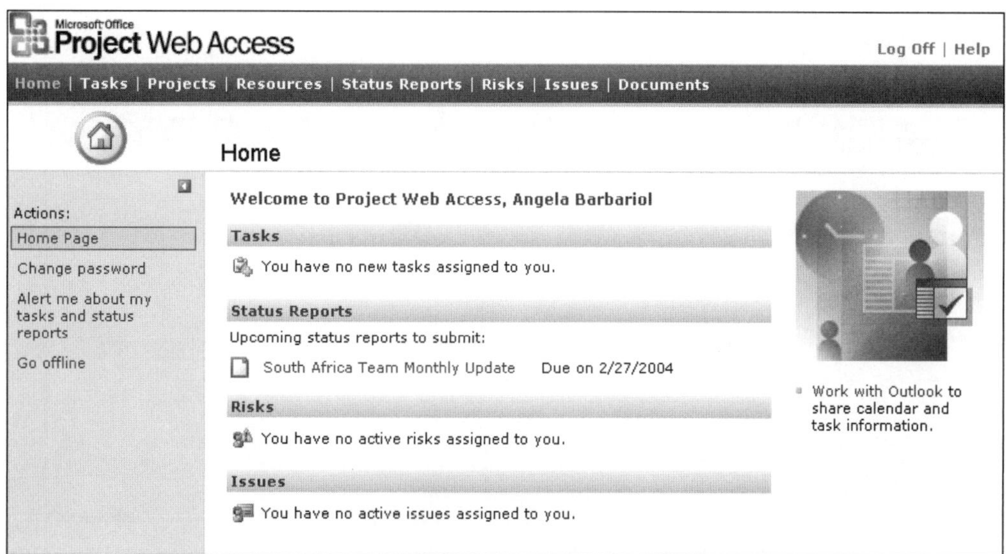

Figure 12-10: Project Web Access Home page Upcoming status report

To respond to a status report request, click the Status Reports link on the Project Web Access menu or in the Status Reports content area of the Home page that allows you to navigate to the Status reports overview page or allows you to select a specific status report. If you select either of the first two methods, the system displays your personal Status Reports page with a list of all upcoming status reports shown in Figure 12-11.

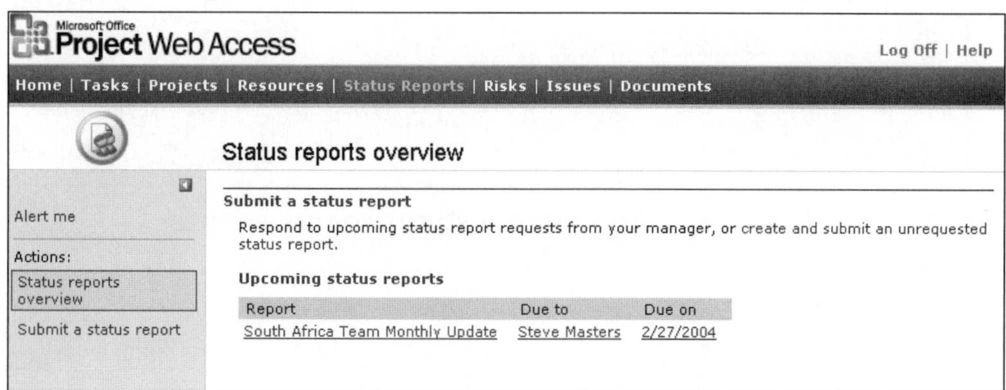

Figure 12-11: Status reports overview page

To respond to a specific status report request from the Home page, click on the named status report link.

When you click the link for a specific status report from your Home page or Status reports overview page the system displays the Submit a status report page shown in Figure 12-12.

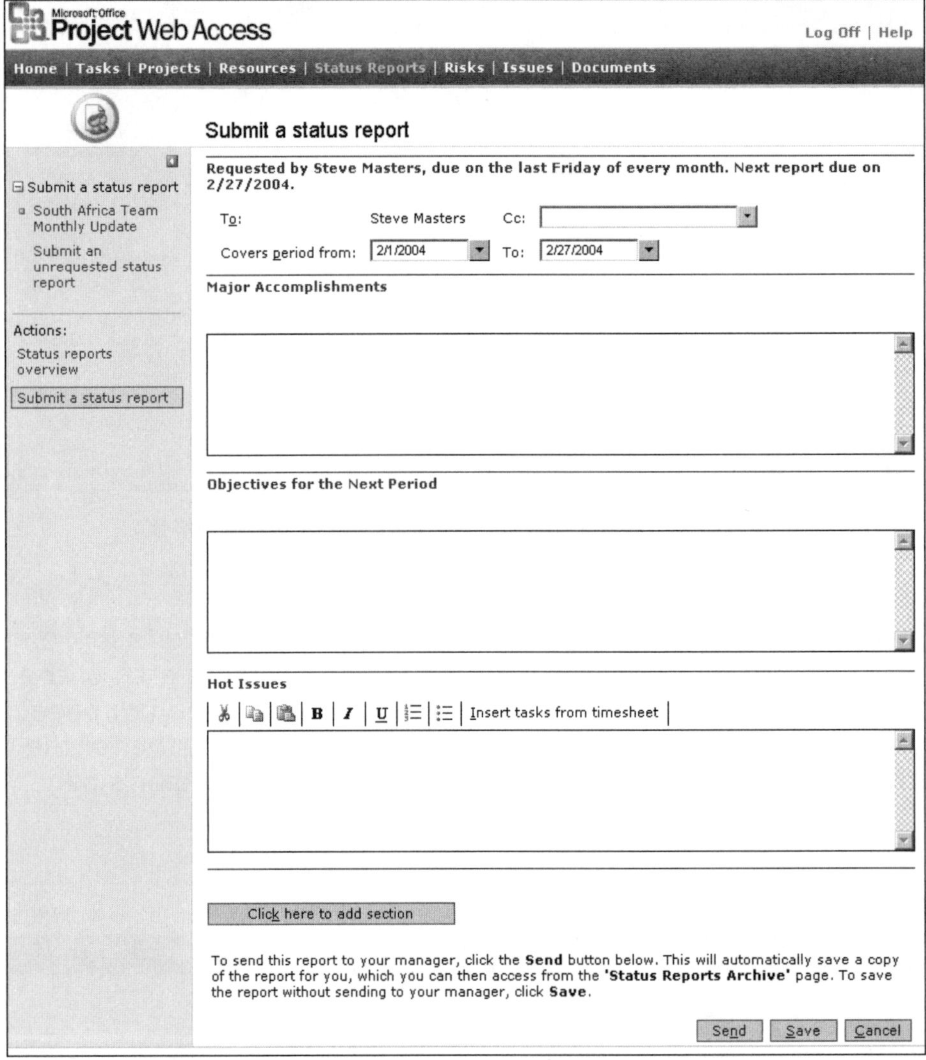

Figure 12-12: Submit a status report page

Text in the upper section of the Submit a status report page describes the status report and indicates the manager who requested it. You can select one or more names from the Cc: pick list to send a carbon copy of the status report. If you desire, you can select a reporting period different from the one indicated by selecting different dates in either of the two date fields.

To select multiple values from the Cc: pick list, select the first name, press the Control key on your keyboard, and then select the additional names.

To enter information into your status report, click the text field in any of the topic sections. When you do, the editing toolbar displays for that section. Notice in Figure 12-13 that I selected the Major Accomplishments text field.

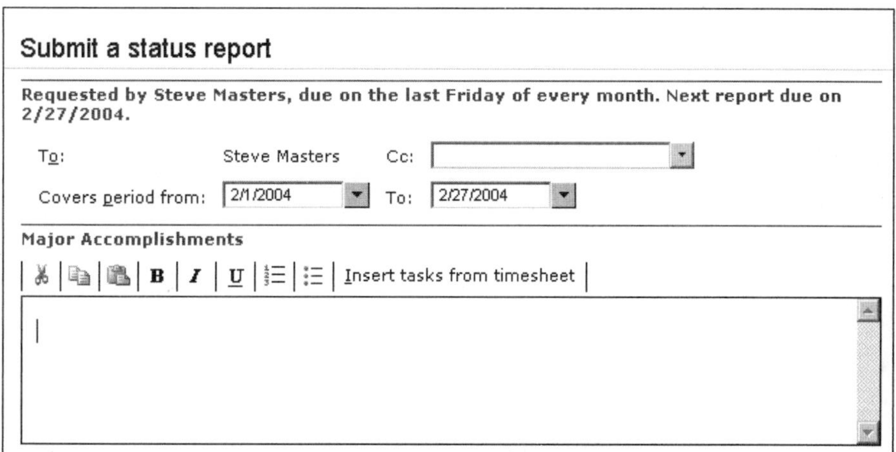

Figure 12-13: Ready to type enter text in the Major Accomplishments field

Use the toolbar for each text field to apply rich text formatting to your entries. Click the Insert tasks from timesheet button to bring display your timesheet in the Submit a Status report page. Select the checkbox to the left of each task you want displayed in your status report, and then click the Insert Tasks button at the bottom of the page. Notice in Figure 12-14 that I have selected and inserted each of the tasks in the Review Current Infrastructure section of my timesheet.

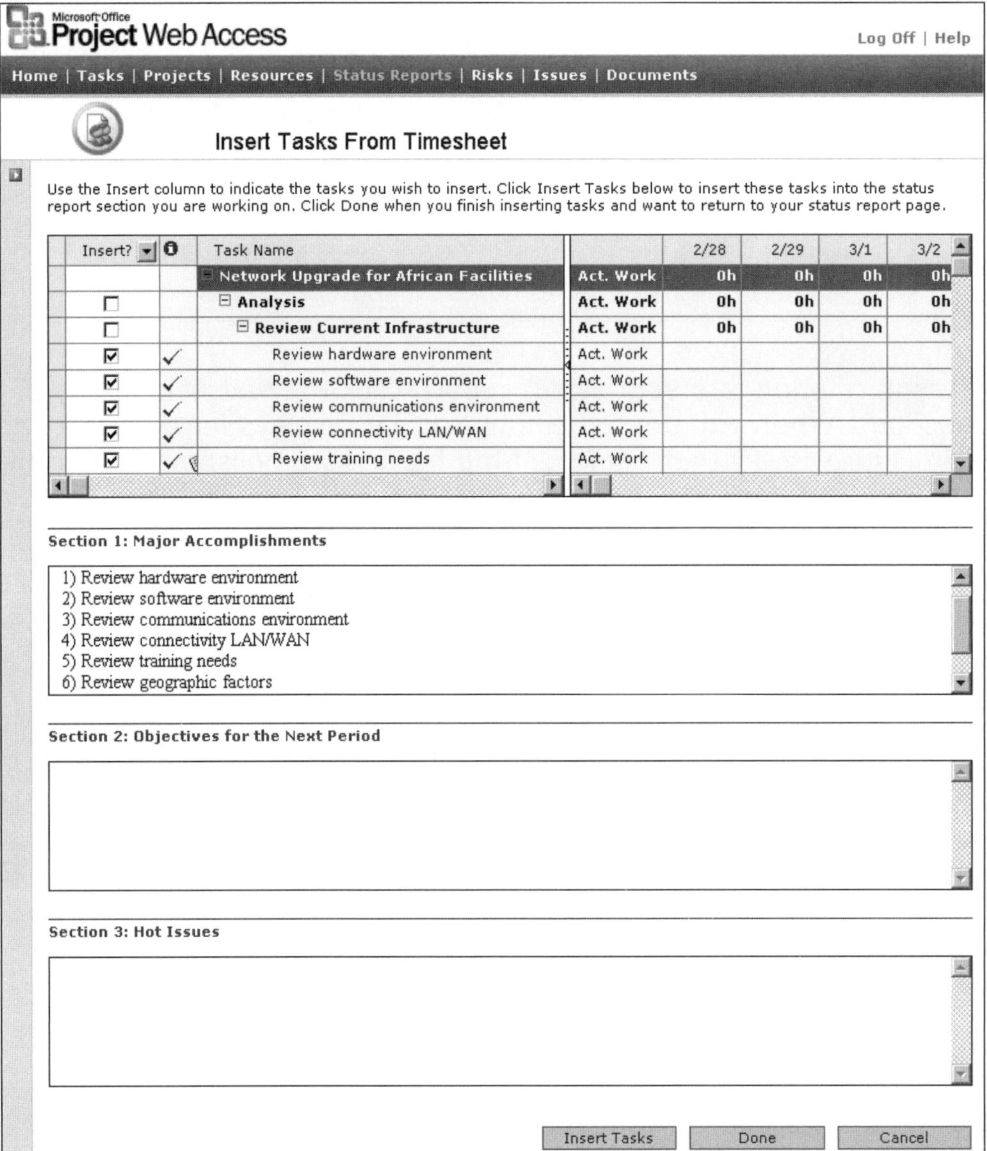

Figure 12-14: Insert Tasks from Timesheet page

Click the Done button to close the Insert Tasks from Timesheet page and return to the Submit a status report page.

At the bottom of the Submit a status report page, click the Click here to add section button to create an additional topic section. Name the new topic section and then click the OK button. A new topic section will appear at the bottom of the page. Click the Send button when you are ready to submit the status report or click the Save button to save the Status Report to send later.

Submitting an Unrequested Status Report

You can create and send an ad hoc status report without a manager requesting a status report from you. To submit an unrequested status report, first click the Status Reports menu to display the Status reports overview page. Click the Create and submit an unrequested status report link in the Submit a status report section of the page. The system displays a Submit a status report page, shown in Figure 12-15, allowing you to create your own custom report.

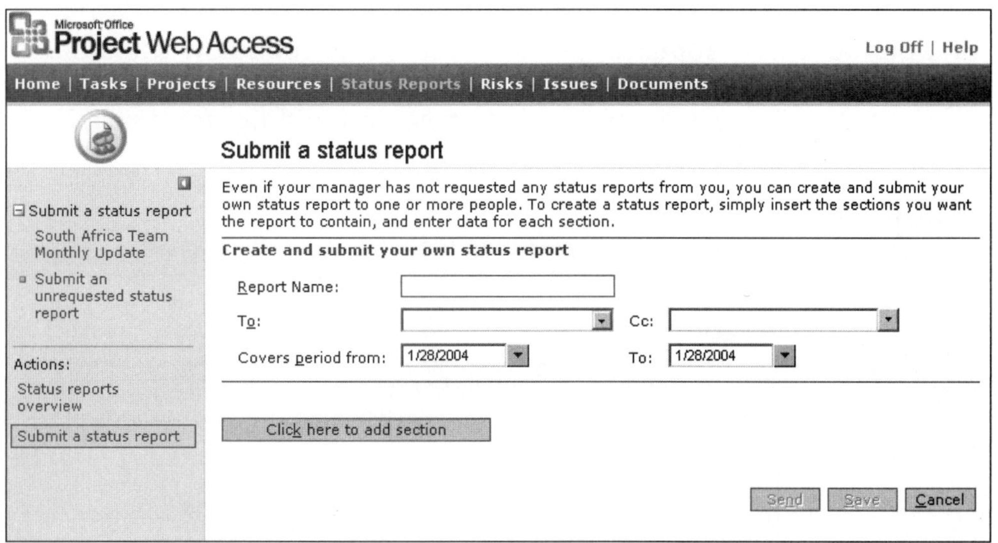

Figure 12-15: Create a status report page
Create an unrequested status report

To create the unrequested status report, first give your status report a name and then select the primary status report recipient as well as anyone you wish to receive a carbon copy of the status report from the respective pick lists. Next, select the reporting period that your status report covers. Click the Click here to add section button and give your new topic section a name, and then click the OK button. Insert additional topic sections as you wish. Enter data into your status report the same way you enter data into a requested status report using the same system provided tool set. Click the Send when you are ready to submit the status report. Otherwise, click the Save button to save the status report and send it later.

Viewing the Status Reports Archive

The Status Reports Archive page provides you access to view your saved status reports and any previously submitted status reports. Click the Status Reports menu and then click the Status Reports Archive link in the Actions pane of the Status reports overview page. Note that this link does not appear on your Status reports overview page until you submit your first status report. The system displays the Status Reports Archive page shown in Figure 12-16, indicating that there are two status reports in the archive. The first is a submitted status report for the February 2004 reporting period while the second is a saved status report not yet submitted for the March 2004 reporting period. Icons appearing in the report column below the status report name indicate the status of the reports. In the figure, I'm floating my mouse over the indicators to reveal their meaning in a popup display.

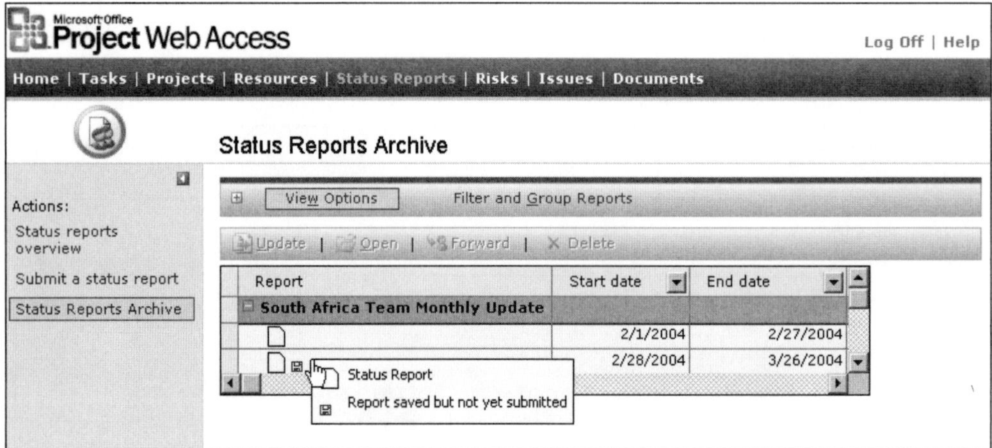

Figure 12-16: Status Reports Archive page

To view either status report, click its icon in the Report column. The system displays the status report, as shown in Figure 12-17.

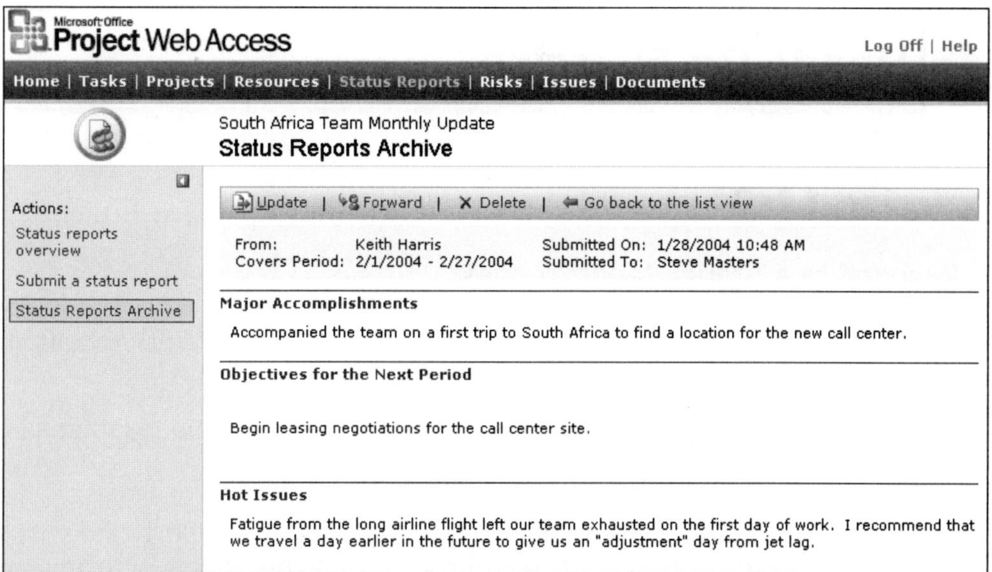

Figure 12-17: Submitted status report

If you wish to edit the status report and then resubmit it, click the Update button on the toolbar. The system opens the status report page, ready for editing. Click the Save or Send button when you are finished. If you simply wish to forward the status report to another manager, click the Forward button on the toolbar. Select one or more people from the Forward To pick list and then click the Send button.

To submit a saved status report, first open the status report in the Status Reports Archive page by clicking its icon in the Report column. Finish editing your report as necessary and then click the Send button.

Hands On Exercise

Exercise 12-2

Respond to a Status Report request.

1. Click the Status Reports option on the Project Web Access main menu
2. Select the Status Report request created for this class session
3. Fill out the Status Report using your own data
4. Click into one of the topic sections, click the Insert tasks from timesheet button on the toolbar, and experiment with inserting tasks
5. Click Send when you have completed your Status Report response

Viewing Status Report Responses

The system alerts managers to new status report responses on their Home page in Project Web Access. Figure 12-18 shows the relevant alert section of the Home page.

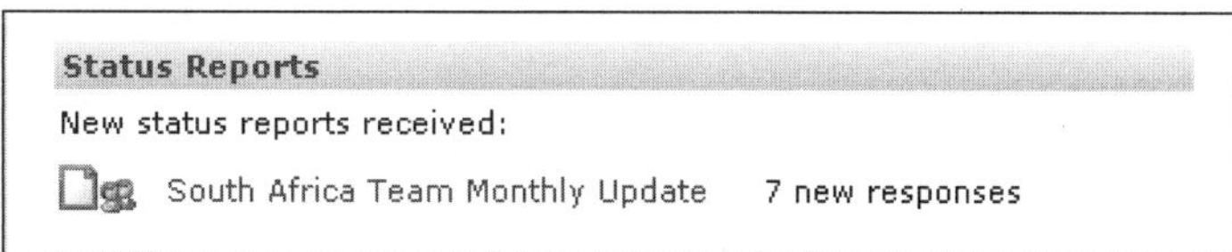

Figure 12-18: Status Reports section of Home page

To view status report responses, click the link for the specific status report on the Home page. You can alternately click the Status Reports menu to navigate to the Status reports overview page and then select the specific status report. Selecting a status report opens the View status report responses from your team members page shown in Figure 12-19. Note the title of the report displays at the top of the page.

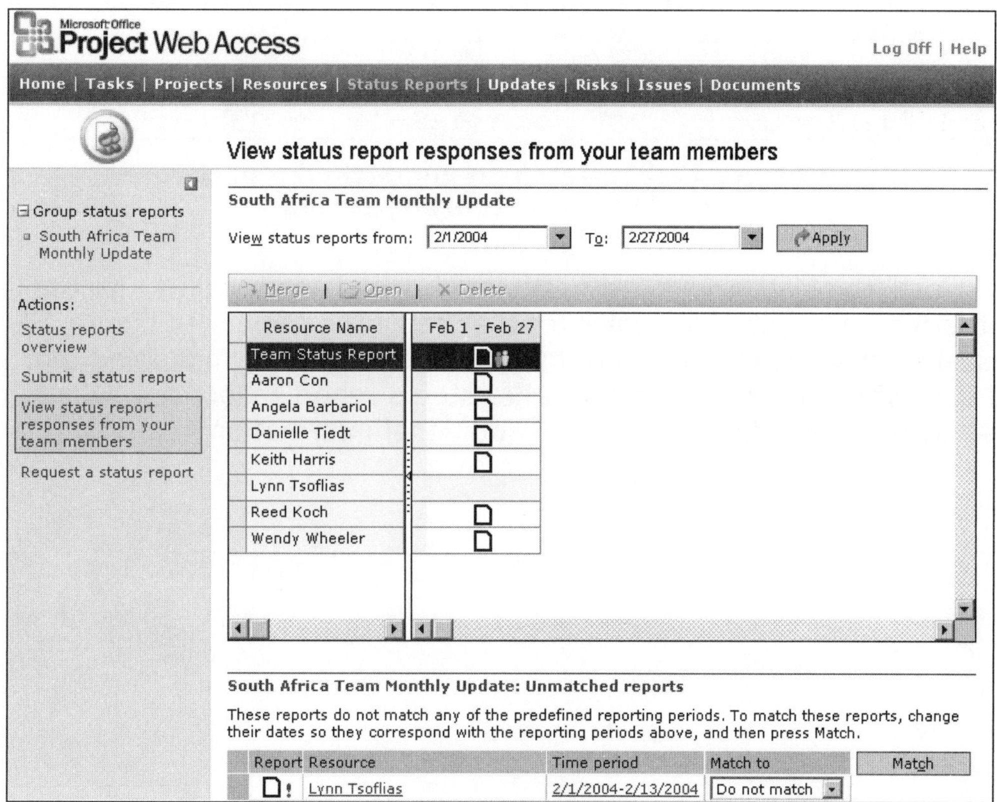

Figure 12-19: View status report responses

This page uses a data grid to show the responses from each resource for each reporting period. The data grid lists resources by name in the Resource Name column and indicates the date range for each reporting period in the column header at the top of each response column. As the months accrue, you see more columns in the display representing additional reporting periods. You can scroll through the columns for each reporting period to view previously submitted reports. The data grid indicates a response to the status report request in each cell using an icon that looks like a blank piece of paper and indicates no response from a resource with a blank cell. The top row in the data grid is the merged Team Status Report.

Notice that Figure 12-19 shows that there are responses from all of the team members except for Lynn Tsoflias. At the bottom of the page, in the Unmatched reports section, notice that Lynn did respond to the status report request, however, she reported for a non-standard reporting period.

Before viewing the compiled team report, I want to bring Lynn's report into the team report. To do this, I click the Match To pick list button, select a standard reporting period, and then click the Match button. Notice in Figure 12-120 that I selected the standard reporting period for the February 2004 status report.

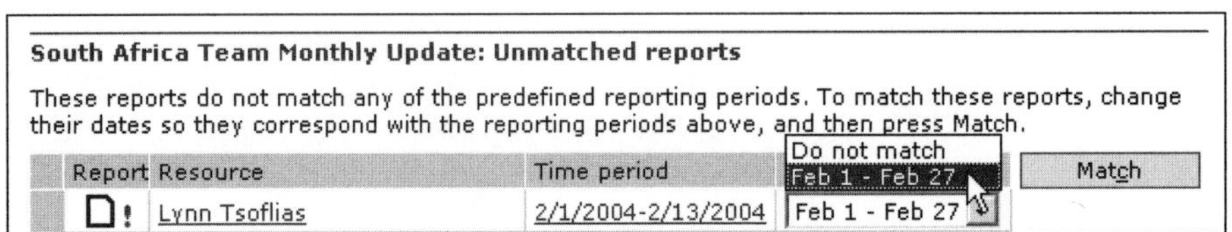

Figure 12-20: Match an unmatched report to a standard reporting period

When I click the Match button, the system brings Lynn's report into the list with the rest of the status reports for that reporting period. In Figure 12-21 that system now displays an icon for Lynn's status report indicating that I need to merge her report with the other status report responses. Floating my mouse pointer over the icon displays additional information in a popup.

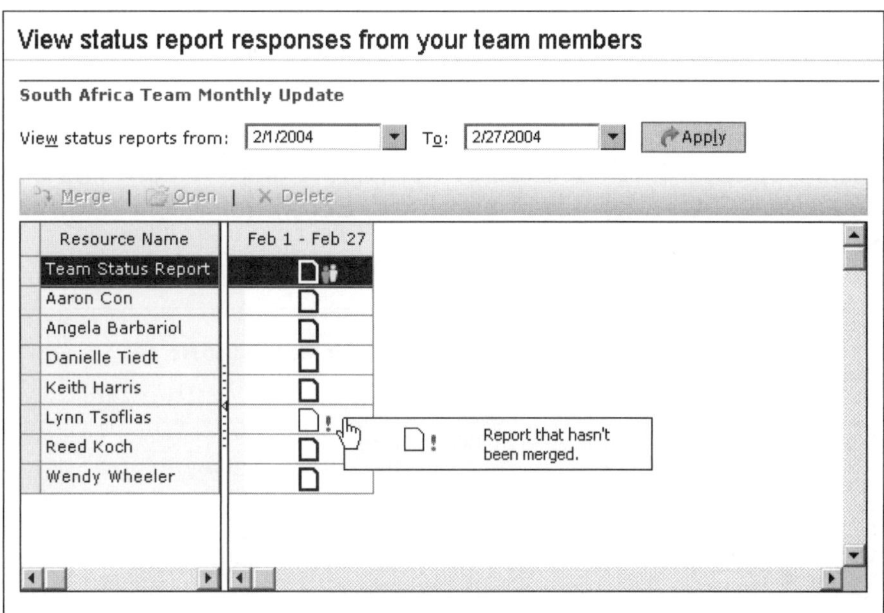

Figure 12-21: Unmerged status report response

To merge Lynn's status report with the others, I click the icon for her Feb 1 – Feb 27 reporting period. The system displays Lynn's individual status report, as shown in Figure 12-22. When I click the Merge button in the toolbar at the top of the status report, the system merges her report into the combined Team Status Report.

Figure 12-22: Click the Merge button to merge this status report

As with opening an individual's status report, you open the merged team status report by clicking the icon in the Team Status Report row. The system merges the reports based on the options you chose when you selected the responding resources for the status report request.

Figure 12-23 displays the merged Team Status Report for the South Africa Team Monthly Update. Each section of the report display contains each team members response listed by name and date. Scroll down the page to read responses in all sections.

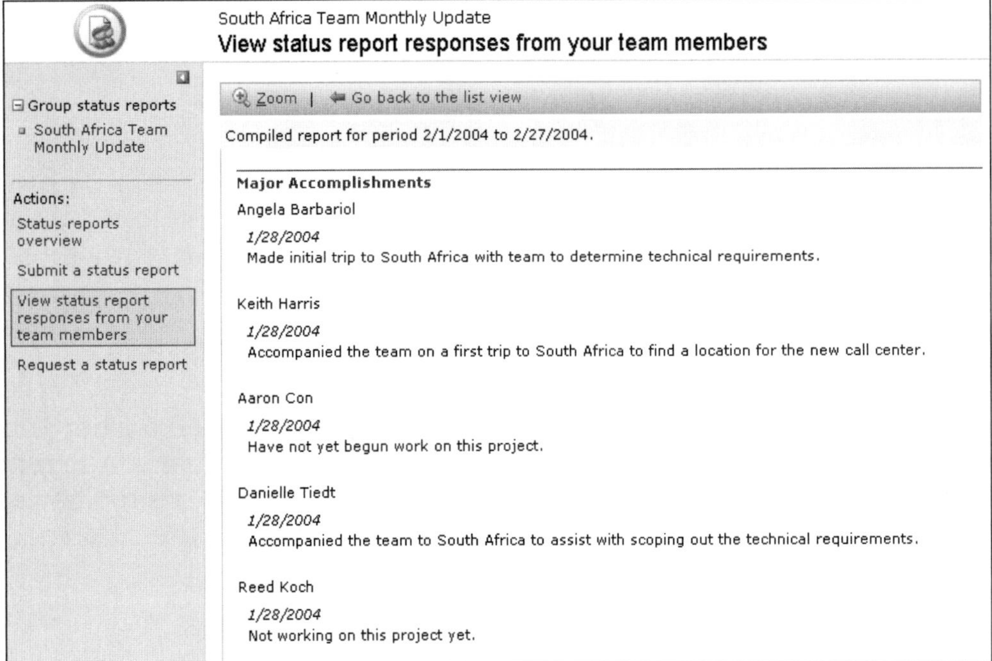

Figure 12-23: Team Status Report

Click the Zoom button at the top of the compiled Status Report to open the report in a new window. In the new window, select File ➢ Save As and save the Team Status Report in HTML format. You can then open this file in Word or FrontPage for editing.

msProjectExperts recommends that you upload the saved copy of the Team Status Report to the document library for the project team. Doing so will allow you to share the status reports with the team and with other stakeholders. You can also distribute these reports by email.

Viewing Unrequested Status Reports

When a team member sends you an unrequested status report, the system does not alert you in the Status Reports section the Project Web Access Home page. In fact, the only indication you will receive is an additional link in the Actions pane for the Status reports overview page. The Miscellaneous reports link shown in Figure 12-24, appears only when you receive unrequested status reports.

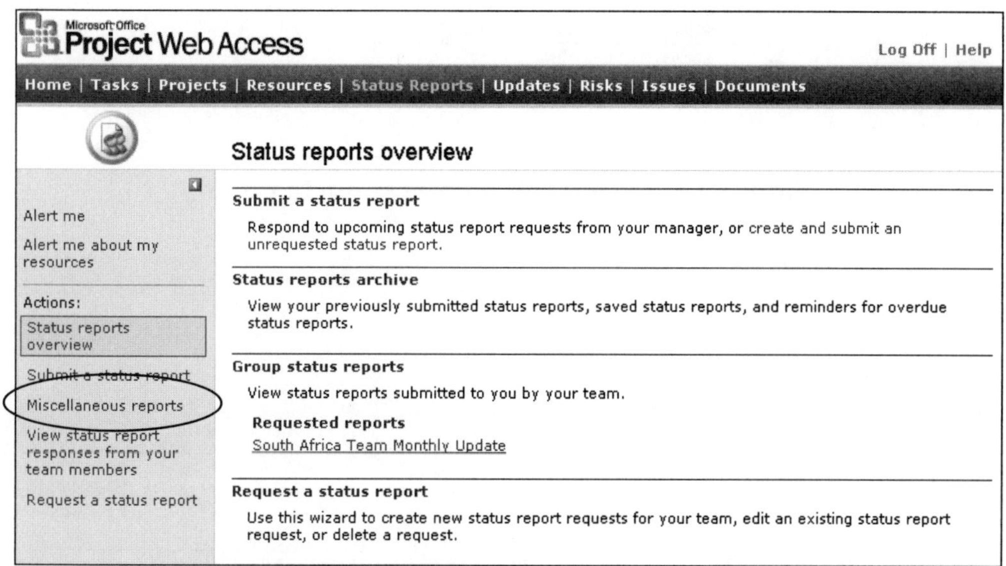

Figure 12-24: Miscellaneous reports link in Actions pane

To view unrequested status reports, click the Miscellaneous reports link. The system opens the Miscellaneous status reports page shown in Figure 12-25. To view the report, click on the links in any of the columns of the report. You cannot merge unrequested reports into any previously requested status reports.

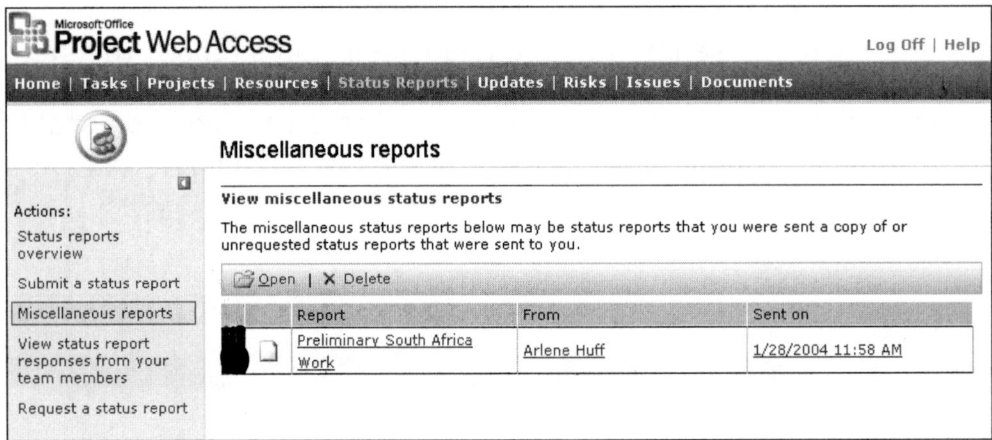

Figure 12-25: Miscellaneous reports page

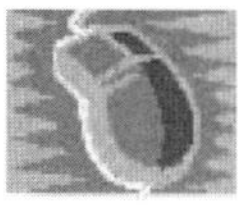

Hands On Exercise

Exercise 12-3

View Status Report responses.

1. Select Status Reports from the main menu
2. Select a Status Report to view
3. Click the icon for an individual resource to view an individual report
4. Click the icon for the Team Status Report to view the merged team status report
5. Click the Zoom Button on the tool bar
6. In the new Internet Explorer window, click File ➢ Save As and save the zoomed report as an html document

Module 13

Working in the Resource Center

Learning Objectives

After completing this module, you will be able to:

- Apply Resource Center views
- View resource availability
- Edit resource details
- Open a resource for editing in Microsoft Project 2003
- View resource assignment information
- Adjust actuals for your resources
- View a timesheet summary for your resources

Using the Resource Center

When you click Resources on the Project Web Access menu, the system displays the Resource Center page shown in Figure 13-1. The Resource Center contains a data grid that displays all of the resources your security permissions allow you to see in the Enterprise Resource Pool. The default display lists all resources in the system.

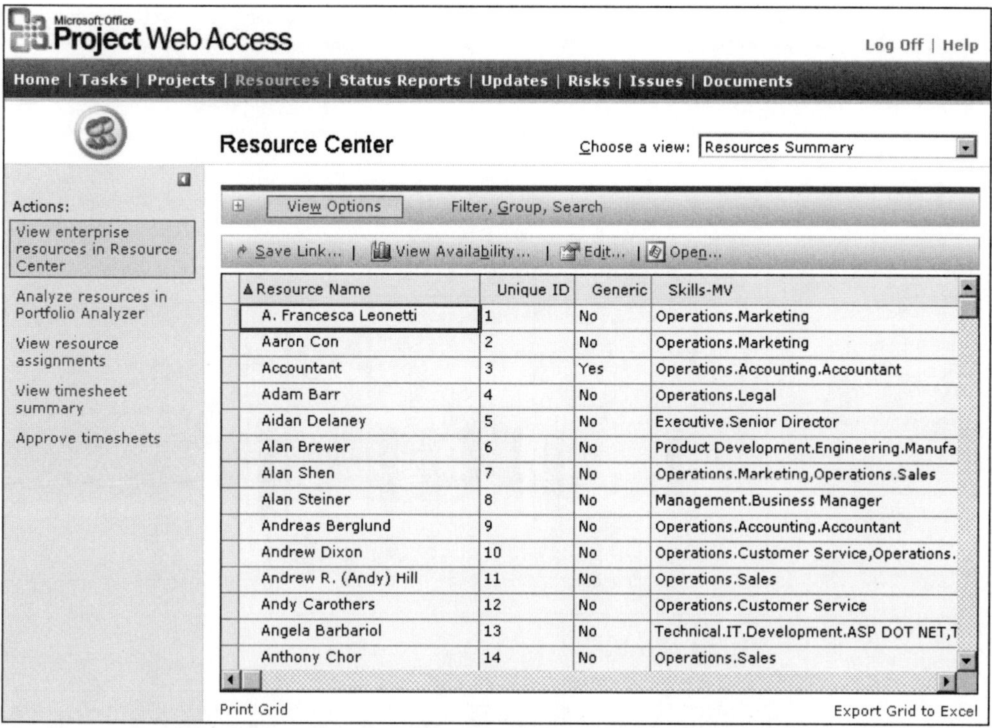

Figure 13-1: Resource Center default view

The Resource Center displays only enterprise resources. It does not display local resources.

To select a view, use the Choose a view pick list in the upper right hand corner of the page. You can choose any view defined in the system for the Resource Center that you have permission to see. The Resources Summary view is the only view included in the Resource Center by default.

Your Project Server administrator controls the views available in the Resource Center. If you need a custom view in the Resource Center, contact your Project Server administrator.

Viewing Resource Availability

You can use the Resource center to analyze the availability of one or more resources by first selecting the resources in the data grid, and then clicking the View availability button on the toolbar. The system displays the View Resource Availability page shown in Figure 13-2.

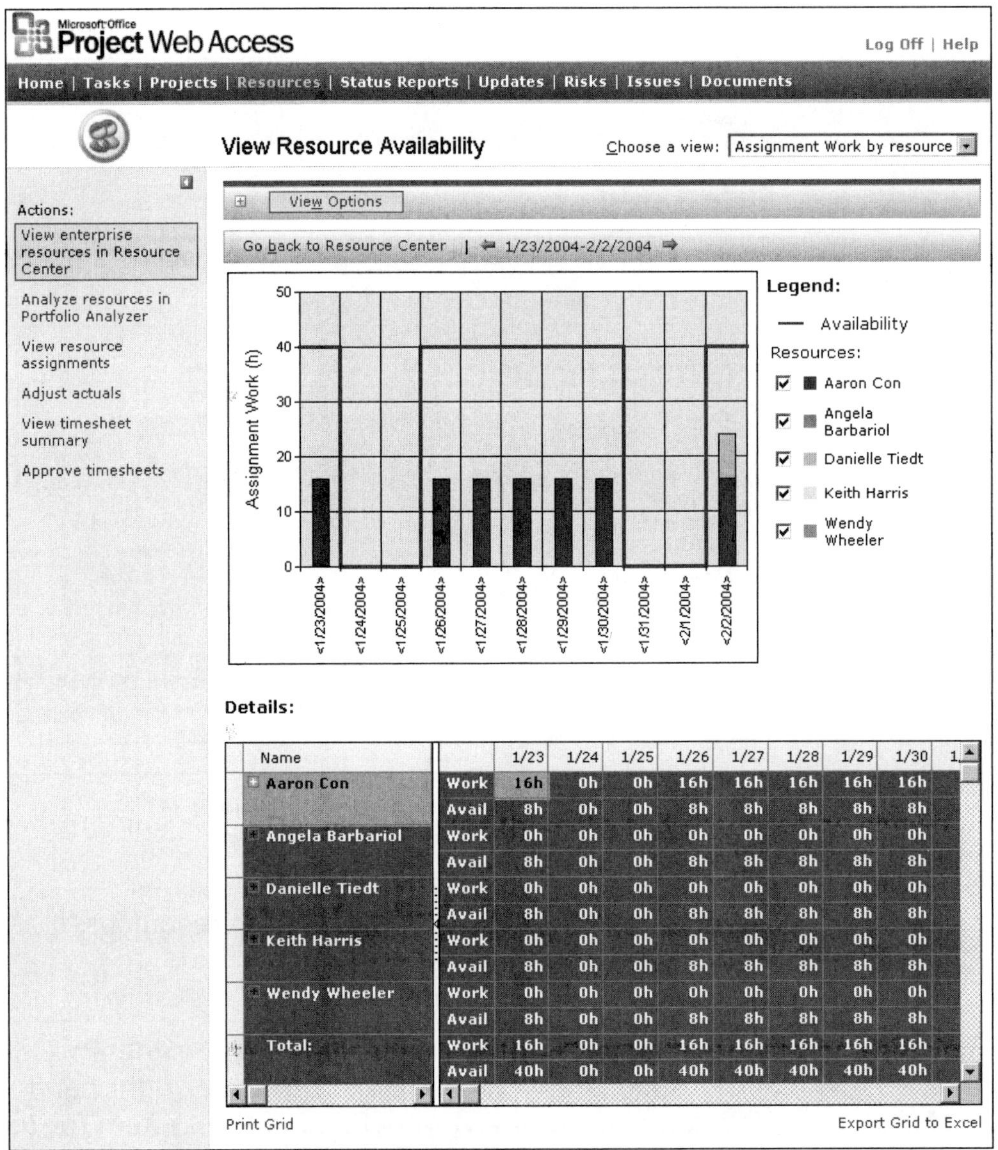

Figure 13-2: View Resource Availability page Assignment Work by resource view

The page contains two sections; a chart and a timesheet. The chart displays a graphic representation of the data displayed in the timesheet. By default, the chart shows Assignment Work and Availability for each resource across time.

The Choose a view pick list displayed in the View Resource Availability page allows you to select one of four default views:

- Assignment Work by resource
- Assignment Work by project
- Remaining Availability
- Work

The Assignment Work by resource view displays a stacked bar chart for each time period, with each bar portion representing the assignment work of an individual resource. This view also displays a line chart representing the total Availability for all of the selected resources. Shown previously, Figure 13-2 displays the Assignment Work by resource view is in Figure 13-2.

Figure 13-3 shows the Assignment Work by project view. This view displays a stacked bar chart for each time period, with each bar portion representing the total assignment work for the selected resources in an individual project. The line chart in the view represents the total Availability for all of the selected resources.

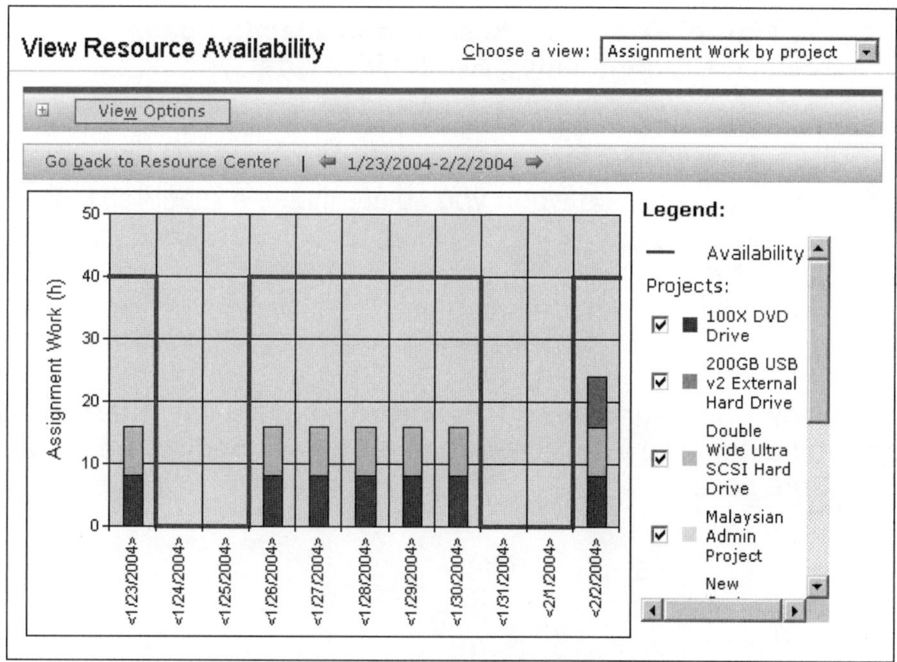

Figure 13-3: View Resource Availability page Assignment Work by project view

Figure 13-4 shows the Remaining Availability view that displays a line chart for each selected resource, with each line showing the remaining availability for each resource during each time period.

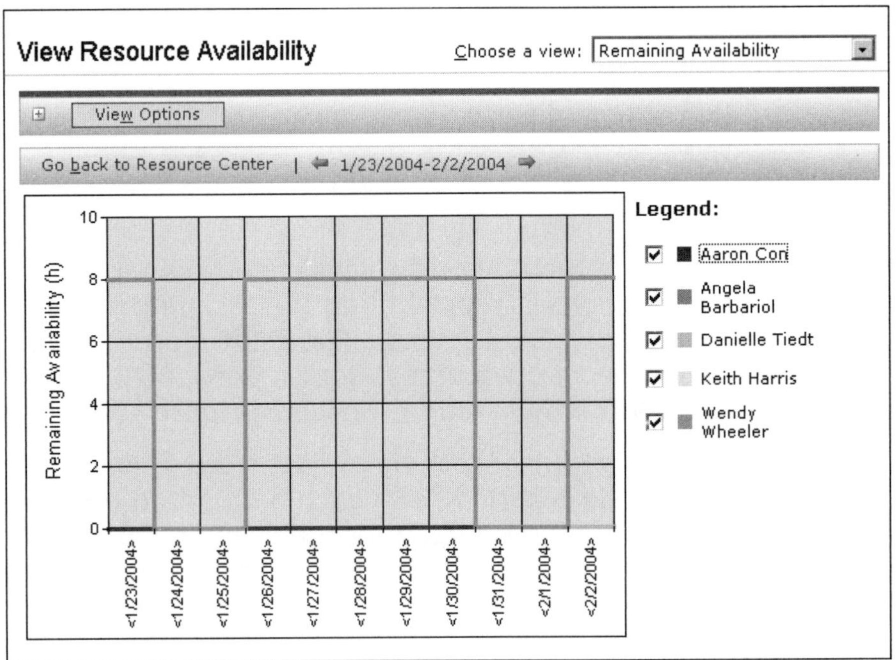

Figure 13-4: View Resource Availability page Remaining Availability view

It can be difficult to see the remaining availability for a specific resource when you select multiple resources. To make it easier you can deselect one or more resources using the check boxes in the Legend section until you see the line chart for your specific resource.

Figure 13-5 shows the Work view. This view displays a line chart for each resource representing the total amount of work assigned to the resource during each time period.

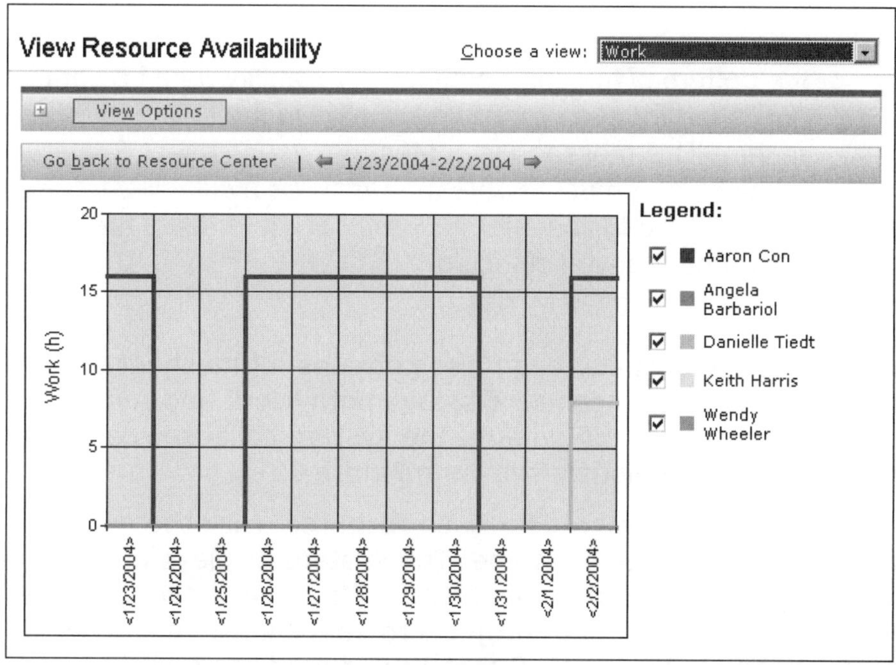

Figure 13-5: View Resource Availability page Work view

While you work in the View Resource Availability page, you can change the date range of the view using the date tool in the toolbar. Click the View Options tab shown in Figure 13-6 to broaden or narrow the date window thereby changing the scale of the graph. Select the Include Proposed Bookings option to include proposed bookings for the selected resources in the graph and timesheet.

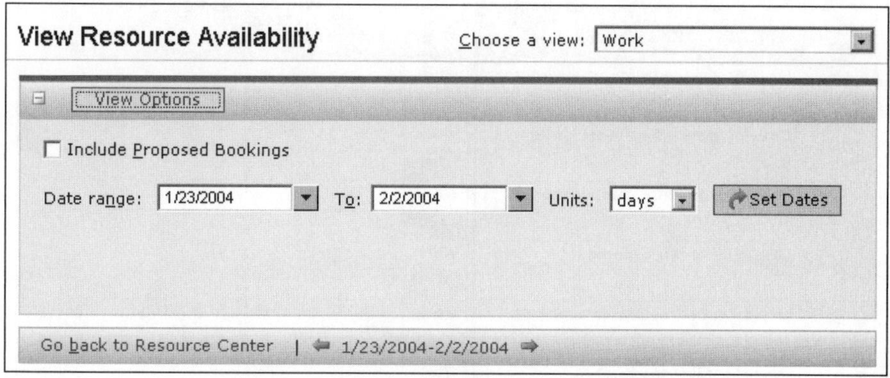

Figure 13-6: View Options tab

Warning: You may occasionally see a message in red text at the bottom of the chart stating, "Availability data has not been published for one or more resources in the selected date range." This message indicates that your Project Server administrator must update the resource availability tables before you can see information for some or all of the dates in the range that you selected.

The View Resource Availability page also contains a timesheet grid at the bottom of the page. The timesheet displays both Work and Availability values for each selected resource. By default, the system collapses each resource's task assignments, as previously shown in Figure 13-2.

To expand the task assignments for each resource, click the expand symbol (+) to the left of the resource's name. The system displays each project in which the resource has assignments along with a line showing the resource's Availability. Expand one or more projects to see specific resource assignments. Notice in Figure 13-7 that I expanded the New Server Farm for Africa Region project for Danielle Tiedt.

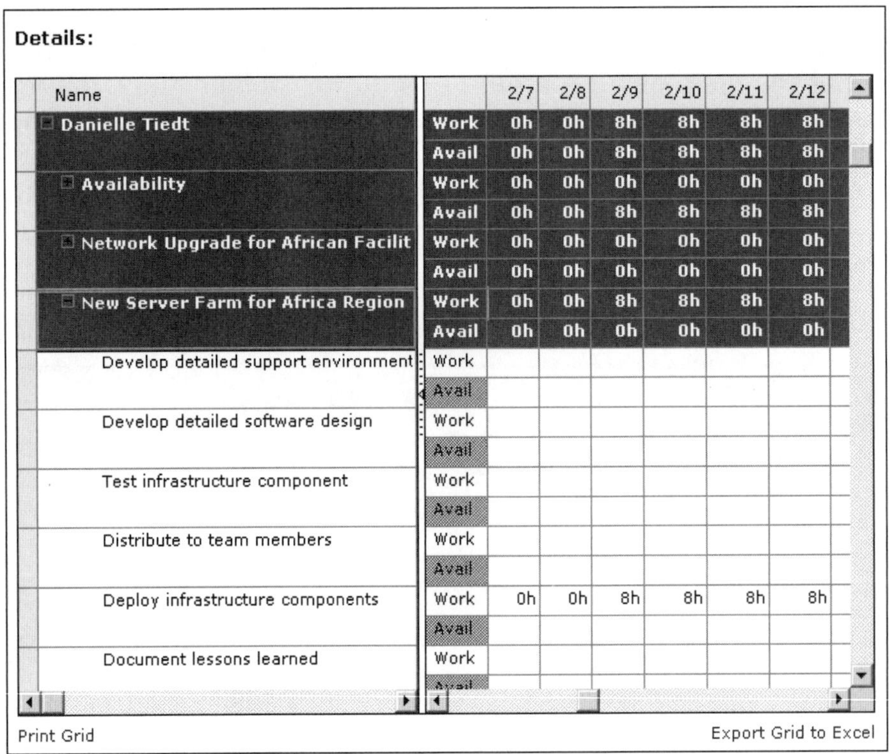

Figure 13-7: Timesheet grid with resource assignments expanded

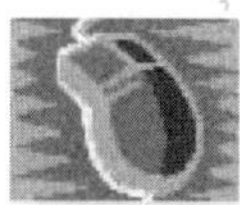

Hands On Exercise

Exercise 13-1

Explore the Resource Center and then determine current work levels and availability for a resource.

1. Select Resources from the Project Web Access main menu
2. Select one or more resources by clicking in the grid. Use the control key to select multiple resources.
3. Click View Availability on the toolbar
4. Use the Choose a view pick list to change the views
5. Select and deselect projects or resources in the various detailed displays
6. Select each of the available views and examine the information presented about each resource or project

Editing Resource Details

If you have the proper Project Server security permissions, you can edit the custom enterprise details for a resource by selecting a single resource and then clicking the Edit button on the Resource Center toolbar. The system displays the Resource Details page for the selected resource as shown in Figure 13-8.

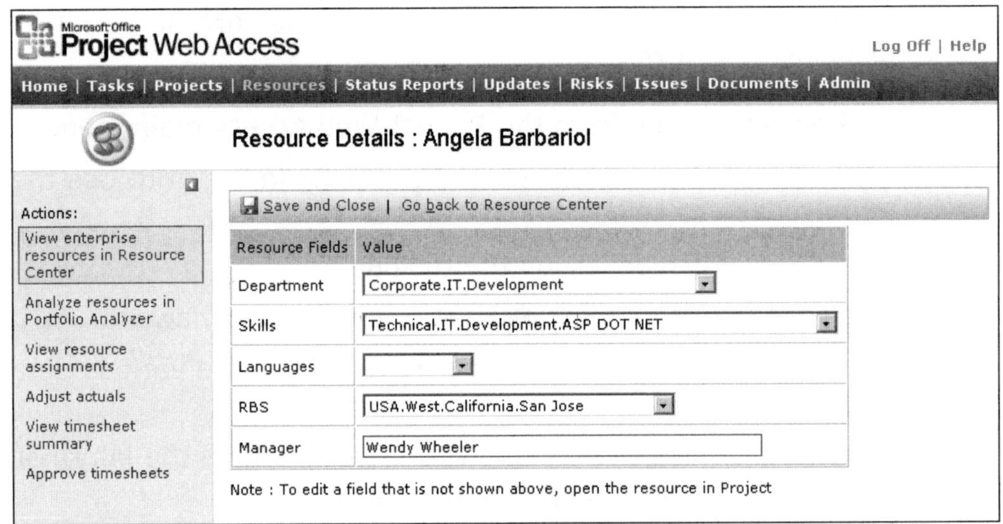

Figure 13-8: Resource Details page for a selected resource

The Resource Details page displays all of the custom enterprise resource fields and outline code fields set up for resources in your organization's Project Server implementation. Edit your fields, then click the Save and Close button to commit the changes. Click the Go back to Resource Center button to discard the changes.

To edit standard fields for the resource, such as Group or Standard Rate, you must checkout the resource from the Enterprise Resource Pool for editing using Microsoft Project 2003 Professional Edition.

Hands On Exercise

Exercise 13-2

Edit resource details for a selected resource.

1. Select Resources from the Project Web Access main menu
2. Select a resource by clicking in the grid
3. Click Edit Resource Details on the toolbar
4. Note that only Enterprise Resource Outline Codes can be edited in this area

Opening a Resource for Editing

If you have the proper Project Server security permissions, you can open a resource for editing in Microsoft Project 2003 by selecting a single resource and clicking the Open button on the Resource Center toolbar. The system launches Microsoft Project 2003 and checks out the single resource for editing in the Enterprise Resource Pool file as shown in Figure 13-9. Edit the resource as desired, then save and close the checked out resource.

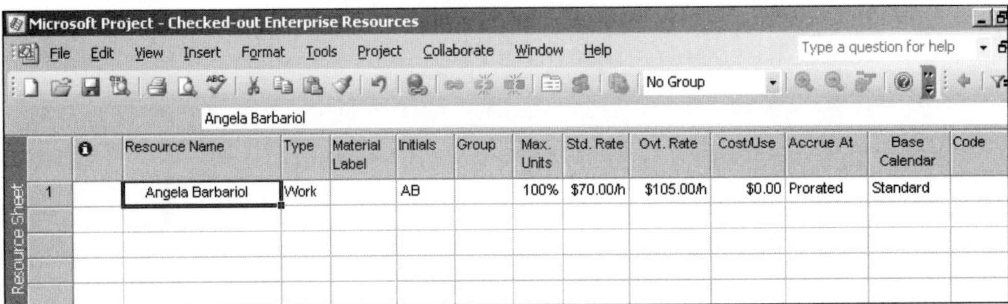

Figure 13-9: Single resource checked out for editing

When a resource is open for editing in Microsoft Project 2003, you can change both standard and custom information about the resource. You can change the information in standard fields such as Group and Standard Rate and can change the information in enterprise custom fields established for your organization.

Viewing Resource Assignments

Select the View resource assignments link in the Actions pane of the Resource Center to display the View resource assignments page shown in Figure 13-10. The View resource assignments page allows you to select up to 100 resources for viewing. Select your desired resources from the Available resources list on the left and copy them to the Resources to display list on the right by clicking the Add button. Click the Add All button to add all of the resources to the Resources to display list.

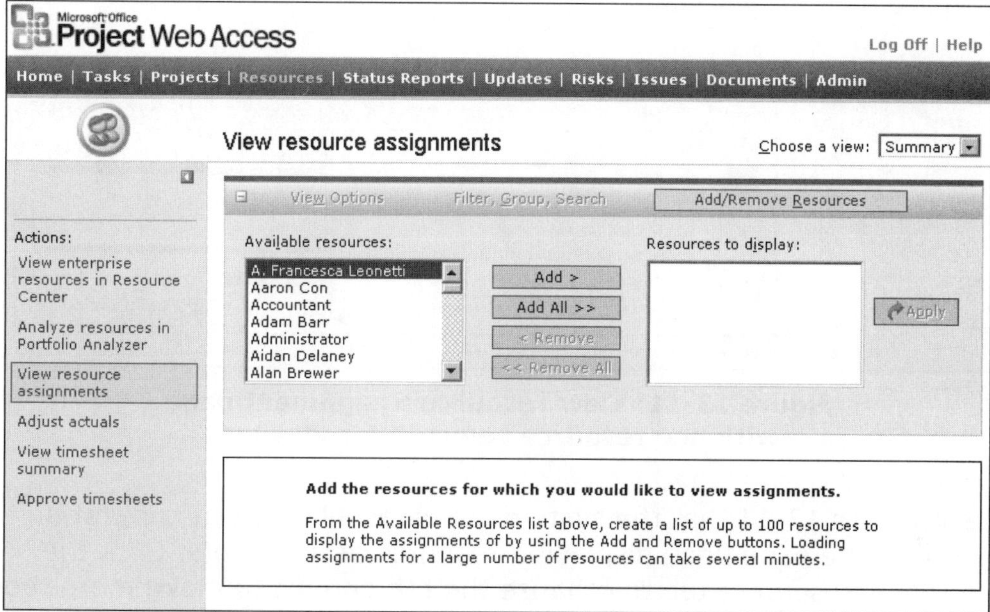

Figure 13-10: View resource assignments page

After selecting your list of resources to display, click the Apply button. The View resource assignments display changes as shown in Figure 13-11.

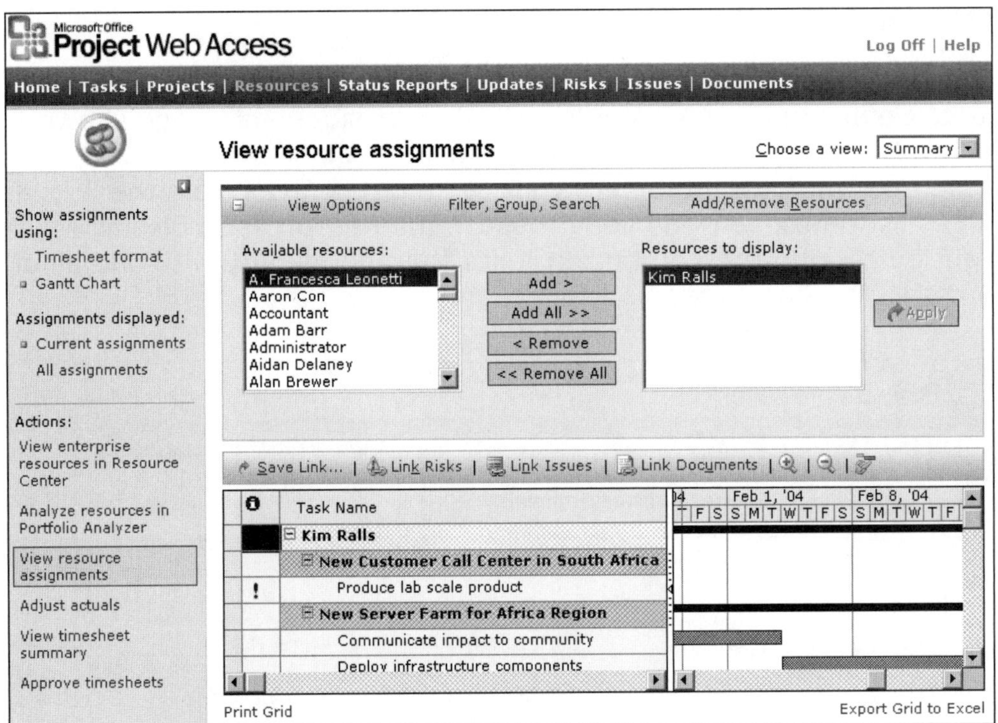

Figure 13-11: View resource assignment page with one resource selected for viewing

Notice in Figure 13-11 that the system activates all three customization tabs at the top of the page upon displaying resource assignments. Click the Add/Remove Resources tab to collapse the tab options to make more room for displaying assignments.

The options in the Actions pane on the left side of the page allow you to apply a Timesheet or Gantt Chart format to the assignments, and to show either Current assignments or All assignments. By default, the system displays Current assignments and applies the Gantt Chart format. Click the Timesheet format to view each resource's timesheet. Click the All assignments link if you want to see both completed and future assignments, as well as current assignments.

The View resource assignments page includes a toolbar with buttons to link Issues, Risks, or Documents to an assignment. You can link risks, issues, and documents to tasks in exactly the same way as in the View my tasks or the Updates pages. The system displays additional toolbar buttons that are appropriate to either the Gantt Chart or Timesheet format.

The View Options allows you to select the Show scheduled work option to show the planned work for each task assignment in a separate row for each task. The default grouping in the Filter, Group, Search tab is by Resource and then by Project. Figure 13-12 shows the View resource assignments page with Timesheet format, All assignments, and Show scheduled work options selected.

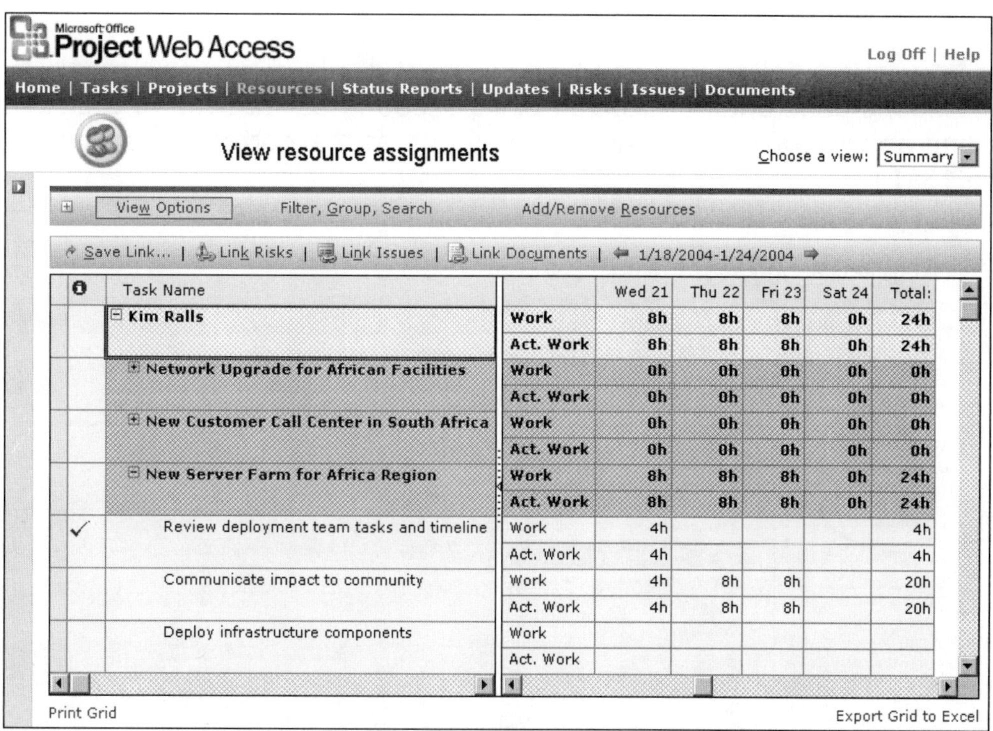

Figure 13-12: View resource assignments page configured for ease of use

By default, the Summary view is the only available selection on the Choose a view pick list unless your Project Server administrator has created additional views for your organization. Notice that the same task indicators that display in the View my tasks and Updates pages also appear in this view. This is not surprising since the View resource assignments page is a window into user assignments and timesheet information.

Click the Save Link button on the toolbar to save a link that can recall your view with the custom grouping and filtering you applied in the Filter, Group, Search tab. Enter a name for your new link in the save link dialog shown in Figure 13-13. When you subsequently click the link, the system displays the view with your custom formatting changes.

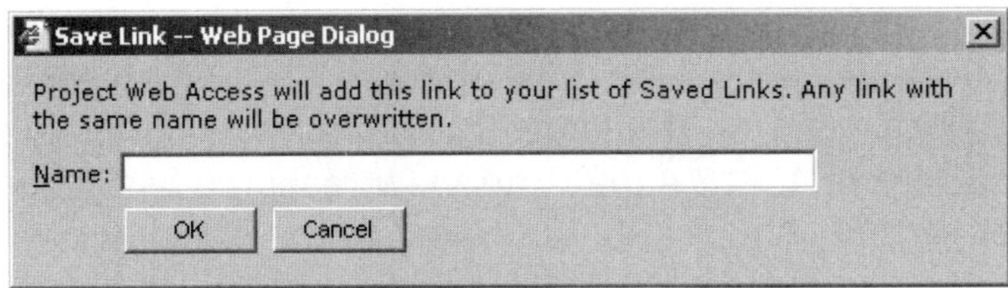

Figure 13-13: Save link dialog box

When you save a link in any page, the system displays two new menu items in the Actions pane adding a Saved Links section near the top of the Actions pane and an Organize your saved links option at the bottom as shown in Figure 13-14.

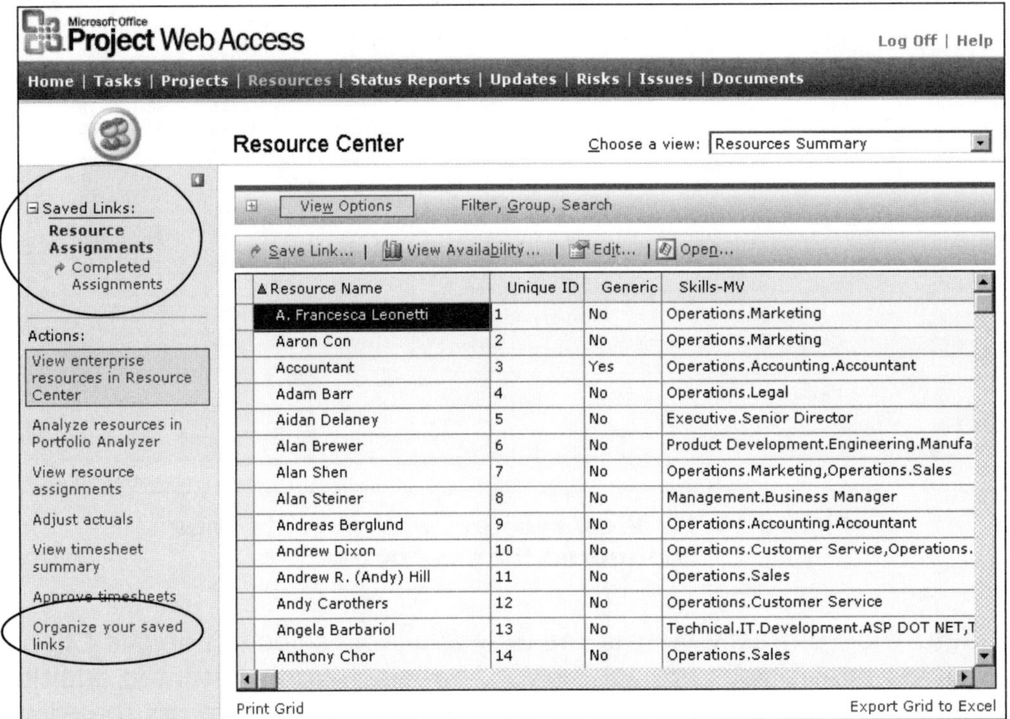

Figure 13-14: Saved links options

Click the Organize your saved links option to display the Organize your saved links page shown in Figure 13-15. You can delete or rename your links from this page. Note you cannot reverse a link deletion.

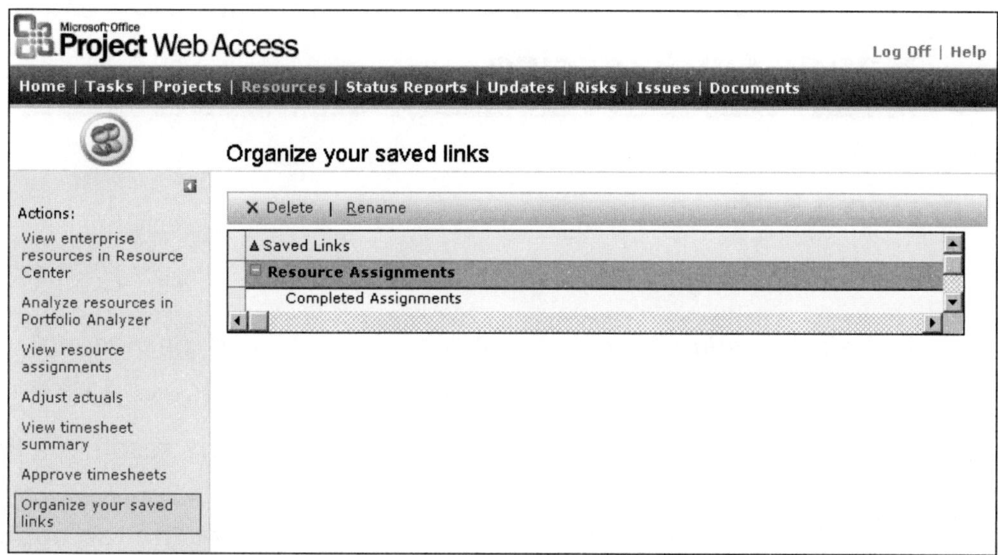

Figure 13-15: Organize your saved links page

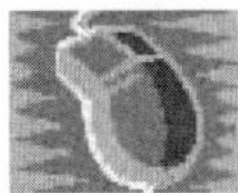

Hands On Exercise

Exercise 13-3

View resource assignments.

1. Select Resources from the Project Web Access main menu
2. Select View resource assignments from the Actions pane
3. Select one or more resources from the Available resources list, then click the Add button and the Apply button
4. Click the Add/Remove resources tab to collapse the tab options
5. Apply the Timesheet format with All assignments displayed
6. Examine the resource assignments for your resources

Adjusting Actuals for Resources

Project Server 2003 allows resource managers and other authorized individuals to enter and adjust actual progress for their resources. This is useful to your organization if you use Project Server's timesheet approval process, as it allows you to correct errors on timesheets prior to approving them.

To adjust actuals for a resource, click the Adjust actuals link in the Actions pane in the Resource Center. The system displays the Adjust actuals page shown in Figure 13-16. Notice that the layout of this display is very similar to the View resource assignments page.

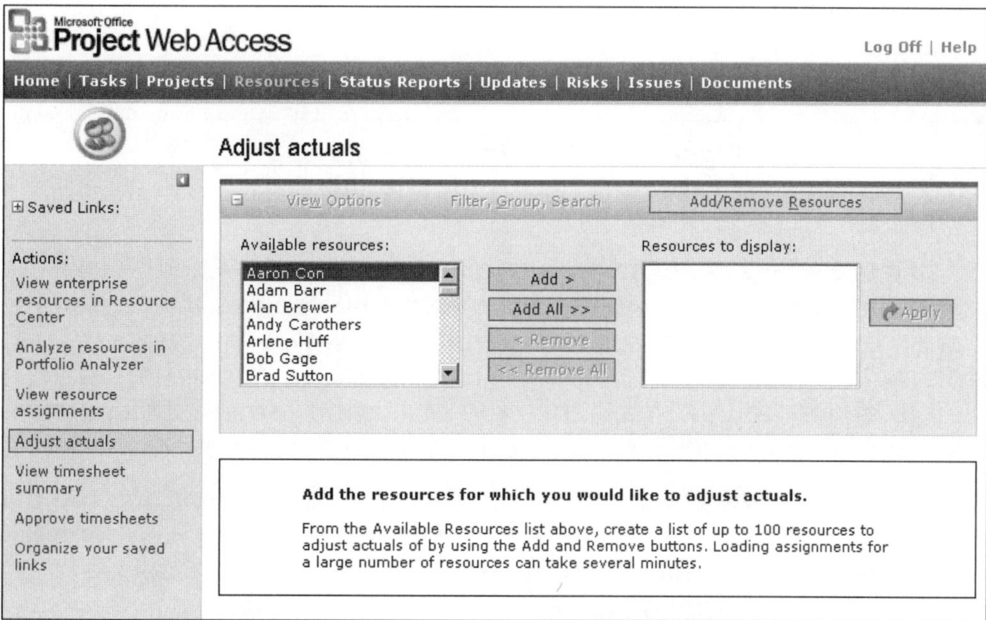

Figure 13-16: Adjust actuals page

As with the View resource assignments page, the Adjust actuals page allows you to pre-select up to 100 resources. Select resources from the Available resources list on the left and copy them to the Resources to display list on the right by clicking the Add button. Click the Add All button to add all of the resources to the Resources to display list. Click the Apply button to display your resources and then click the Add/Remove Resources tab to collapse the options on the tab to increase the page area available to display data as shown in Figure 13-17.

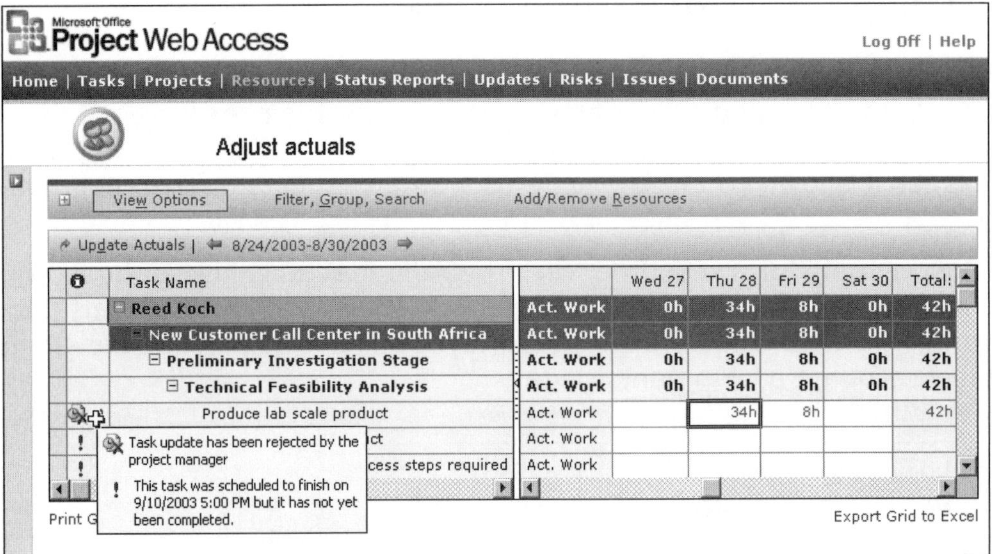

Figure 13-17: Adjust actuals page "Fat finger" error on Thursday 28

Notice in Figure 13-17 that the project manager rejected Reed Koch's task update on the task *Produce lab scale product*. You can see the reason for the rejection in the timesheet portion of the page, in which the resource has accidentally "fat fingered" 34 hours of Actual Work on August 28, when he intended to type 4 hours. This is the type of situation where it's appropriate for a manager to intervene and adjust a resource timesheet.

To adjust actuals for any resource select the task assignment and the date in the timesheet, and edit the numbers entered by the resource. When finished, click the Update Actuals button on the toolbar. The system displays the confirmation dialog shown in Figure 13-18.

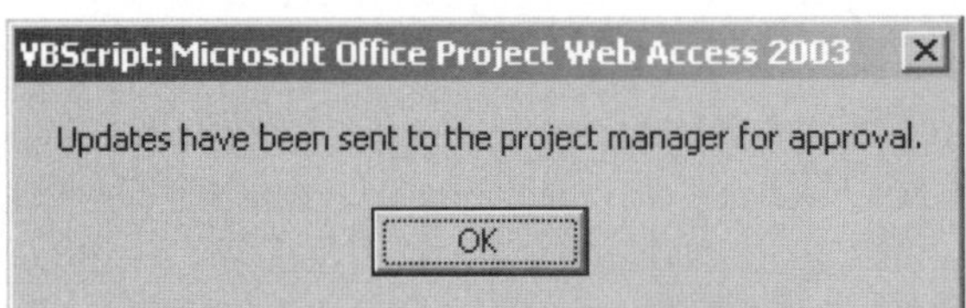

Figure 13-18: Updated actuals send to project manager

Viewing the Timesheet Summary

Project Server 2003 allows individuals with the proper authority, such as resource managers, to view resource timesheets. This may be useful to your organization, as it allows managers to oversee resource entry of actual work in the system. To view the Timesheet summary for your resources click the View timesheet summary link in the Actions pane in the Resource Center. The system displays the View timesheet summary page shown in Figure 13-19.

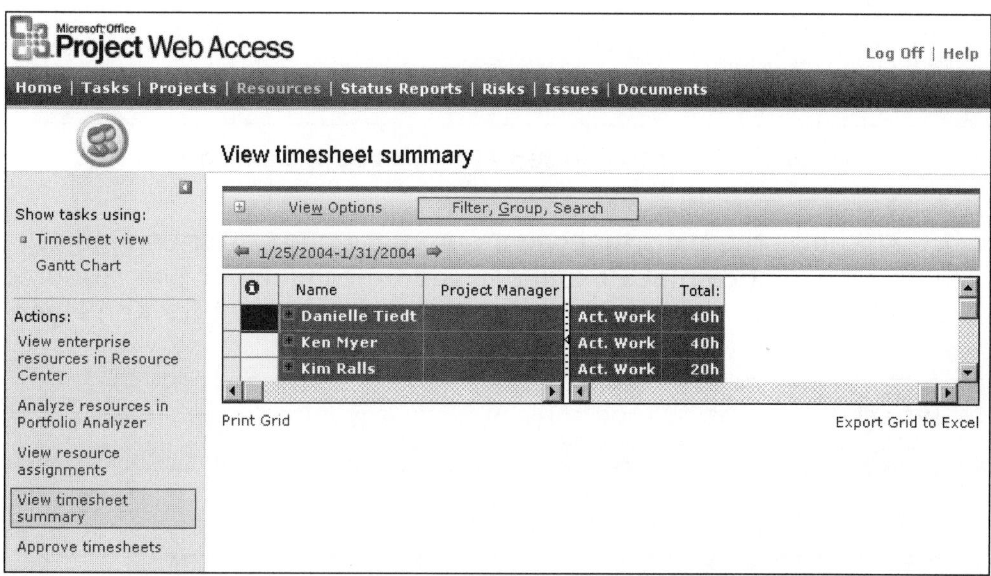

Figure 13-19: View timesheet summary page

The View timesheet summary page is for viewing of timesheet information only. You must perform actions such as approving timesheets or adjusting actuals on other pages. To make best use of the View timesheet summary page set up your page as follows:

- Collapse the Actions pane to see more of the timesheet
- Expand the name of each resource whose timesheet you wish to see
- Collapse any project assignments you do not wish to see
- Position the split bar as you desire between the resource list and the timesheet
- Use the date selector tool to select the desired date range for the timesheet summary
- Using the scroll bar in the timesheet portion of the grid, scroll to the left until you see the days in the desired time period
- Apply a filter from the Filter, Group, Search tab

The Filter pick list on the Filter, Group, Search tab contains five preformatted filters, such as the All unsubmitted timesheets filter, that allow you to view only the timesheets meeting the criteria you choose. Notice in Figure 13-20 that I am selecting the All approved timesheets filter.

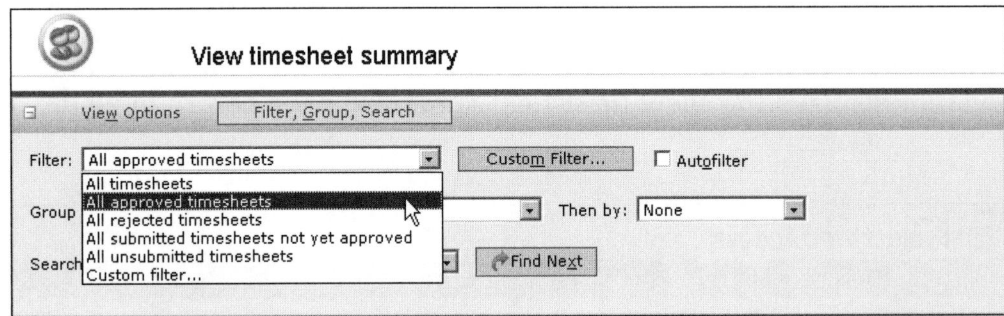

Figure 13-20: Expanded Filter, Group, Search tab

Figure 13-21 shows the View timesheet summary page after configuring it to optimize viewing. Notice that I expanded the timesheets for two resources, Danielle Tiedt and Kim Ralls, and I collapsed the timesheet for Ken Myer.

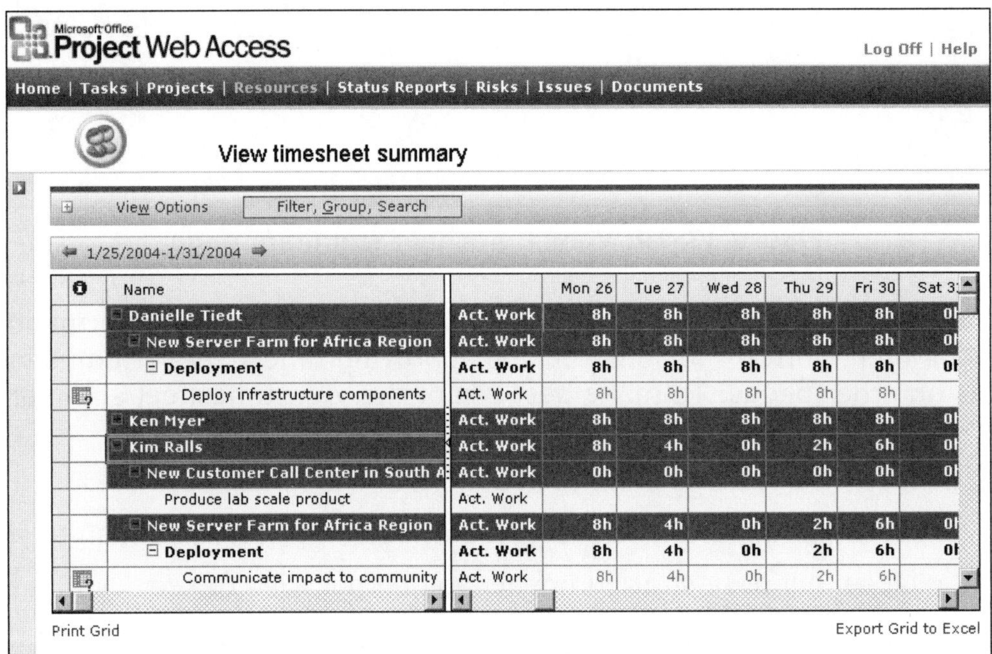

Figure 13-21: View timesheet summary page configured for best viewing

Module 14

Working in the Project Center

Learning Objectives

After completing this module, you will be able to:

- Work in the Project Center
- Access Risks, Issues, and Documents from the Project Center
- Work with Project Center views
- Build a project team in the Project Center
- Edit project details and open a project in the Project Center
- Check in a project
- Work with detailed Project views
- Organize and manage saved links
- Create and manage to-do lists

Working in the Project Center

The Project Center is the distribution hub for project information and project analysis in Project Web Access. The Project Center home page displays portfolio-level views across all projects in your organization's portfolio. In addition, you can select an individual project from any Project Center view to open a detailed project view allowing you to drill down into the project detail. You can also access core Project Server analysis features from the Project Center using the Portfolio Analyzer and the Portfolio Modeler. Figure 14-1 shows the Project Center page with Steve Master's portfolio of projects displayed.

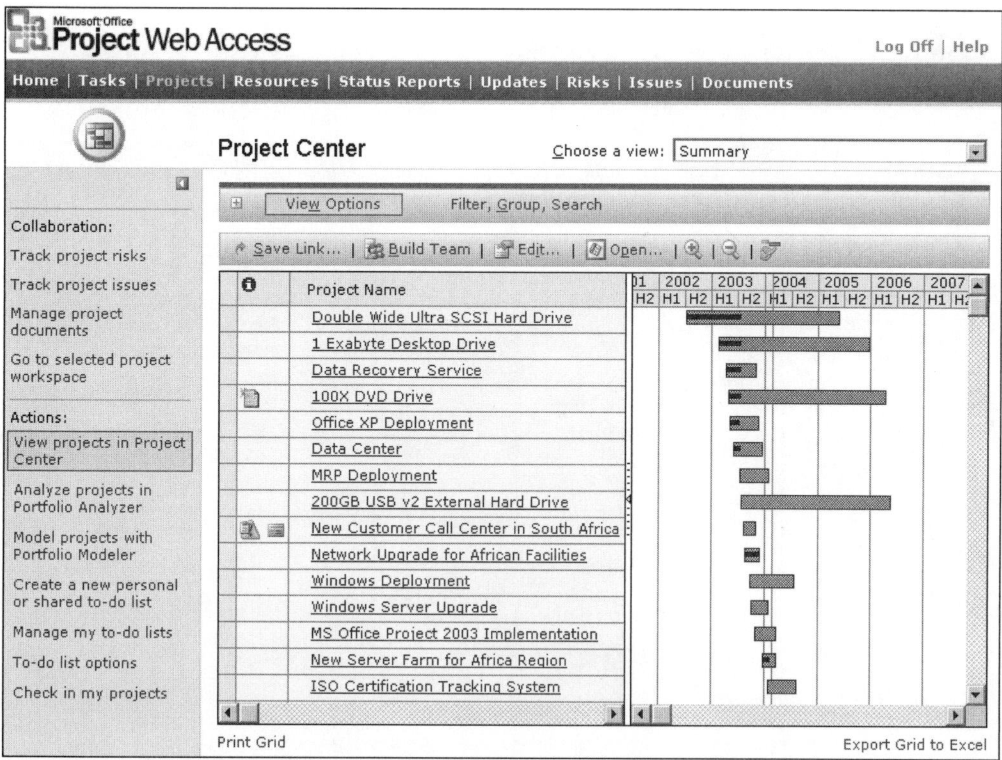

Figure 14-1: Project Center page

The Project Center page displays a data grid with a project list on the left and a Gantt Chart on the right. The project list displays a single line of information about each project with multiple columns of information about each project, depending on the current view selected from the Choose a view drop down list.

The Gantt Chart displays one or two Gantt bars representing the life span of the project. When the system displays two Gantt bars, one represents the baseline schedule while the other represents the current schedule of the project.

Accessing Risks, Issues, and Documents from the Project Center

You can use the Project Center page to access Risks, Issues, or Documents for any of the projects in the portfolio. Notice in Figure 14-1 that the Indicators column reveals that 100X DVD Drive project has Documents associated with it, while the New Customer Call Center in South Africa project has Risks and Issues associated with it. You can quickly see the meaning of the indicators by floating your mouse over the Indicators column for any project, as shown in Figure 14-2.

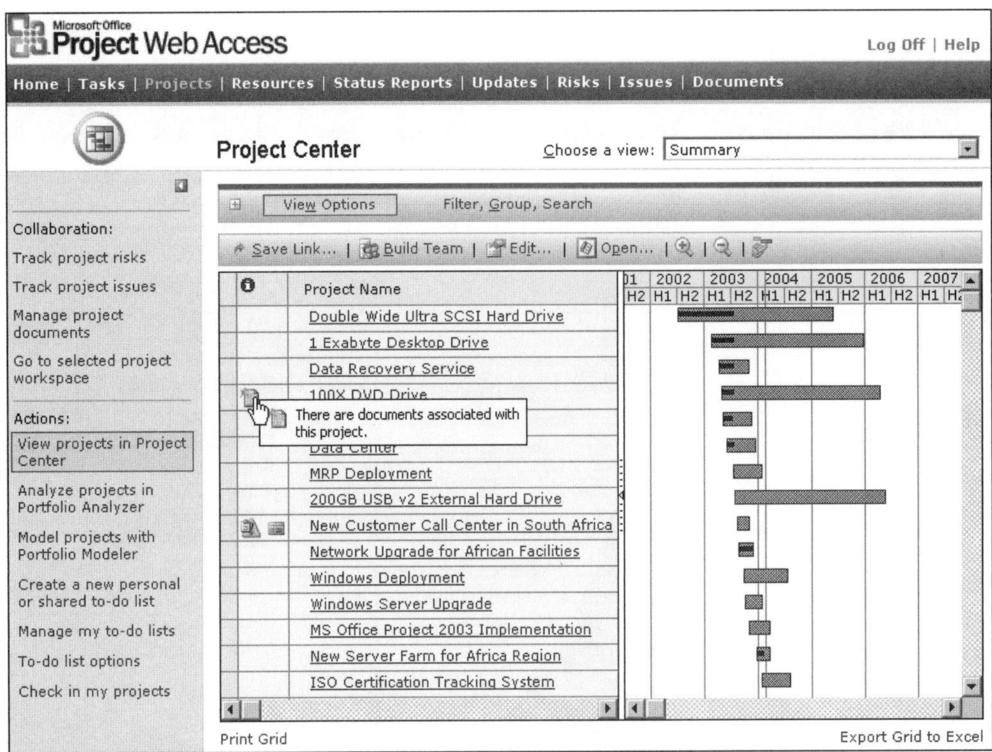

Figure 14-2: Documents associated with the 100X DVD Drive project

To access the Risks, Issues, or Documents page for any project, do one of the following:

- Click the Risk, Issue, or Document icon in the Indicators column to the left of the project
- Select any cell for a project in any column other than the Project Name column, and then click one of the first three links in the Collaboration section of the Actions pane

The Collaboration section of the Actions pane also contains a link that takes you to the project workspace for the selected project.

Using Project Center Views

The Project Center page is your primary source for a two-dimensional presentation of your project portfolio. The system provides five standard views that you select from the Choose a view pick list in the upper right corner of the page:

- Summary
- Tracking
- Cost
- Earned Value
- Work

The Project Center Summary view displays the "vital statistics" for each project, with columns showing the project's Version, Duration, Start date, Finish date, Percent Complete, and Owner. The Summary view includes a Gantt Chart with a single Gantt bar for each project, using a unique color for each project version, and with a black stripe in the Gantt bar indicating project progress. Notice in Figure 14-3 that the system displays the 200GB USB v2 External Hard Drive project twice, once for the Target (baseline) version and once for the Published (production) version of the project. Notice also that the system displays a different colored Gantt bar for each version.

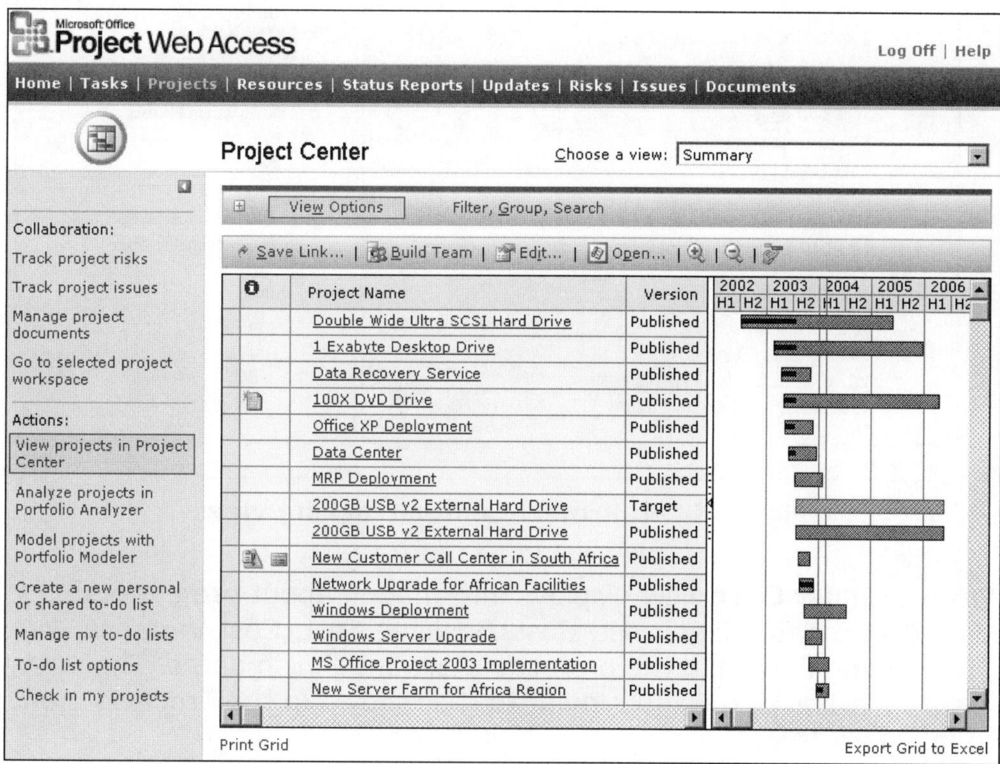

Figure 14-3: Project Center Summary view

To use the Version feature in Project Server, your Project Server administrator must first set up versions according to your company's methodologies.

The Project Center **Tracking** view displays schedule variance information about each project, including the scheduled Start and Finish dates, Actual Start and Actual Finish dates, Baseline Start and Baseline Finish dates, Percent Complete, Duration, Actual Duration, Remaining Duration, Actual Cost, and Actual Work fields. The Tracking view displays a Tracking Gantt Chart with two Gantt bars for each project, as is shown in Figure 14-4. The top Gantt bar represents the current schedule of each project, while the bottom Gantt bar depicts the baseline schedule for each project. The black stripe in the top Gantt bar indicates project progress.

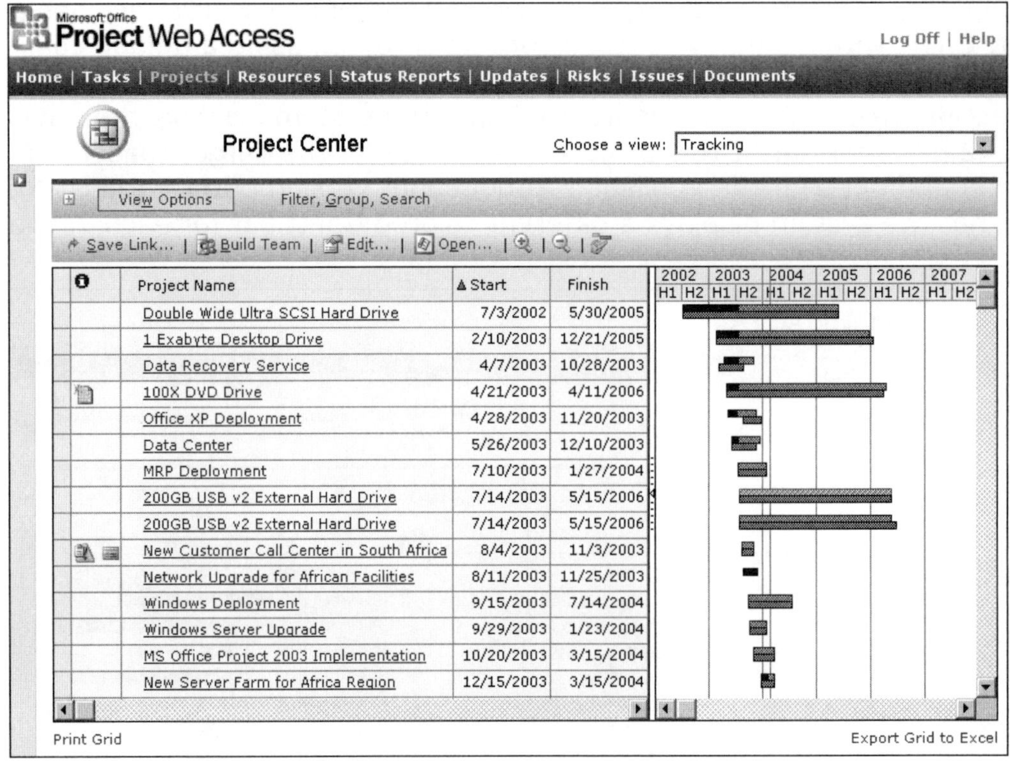

Figure 14-4: Project Center Tracking view

The Project Center **Cost** view displays information about project costs, including columns for Fixed Cost, Cost, Baseline Cost, Cost Variance, Actual Cost, Remaining Cost, and the project's Start and Finish dates. The Cost view also displays a Tracking Gantt similar to that shown in the Tracking view, as shown in Figure 14-5.

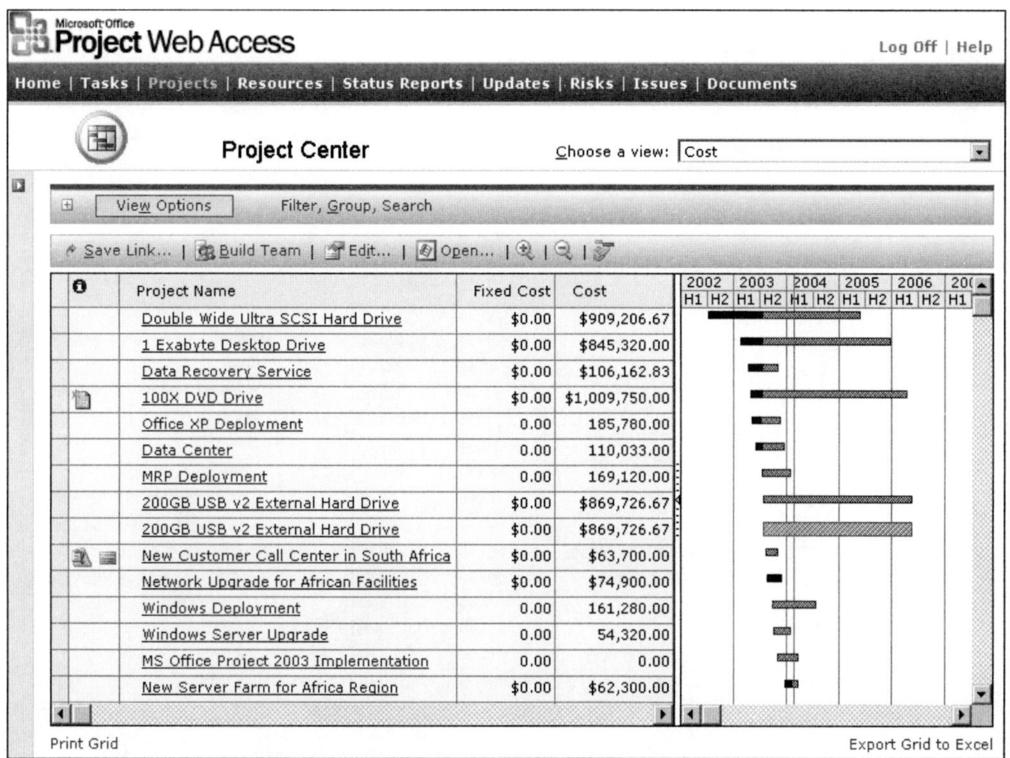

Figure 14-5: Project Center Cost view

The Project Center **Earned Value** view displays the calculated earned value at the project level for each project. This view includes columns for BCWS, BCWP, ACWP, SV, CV, Cost, Baseline Cost, VAC, and the Start and Finish dates. The Earned Value view, shown in Figure 14-6 includes the same Tracking Gantt as the Cost view. Notice in the figure that only the Published version of any project displays tracking information.

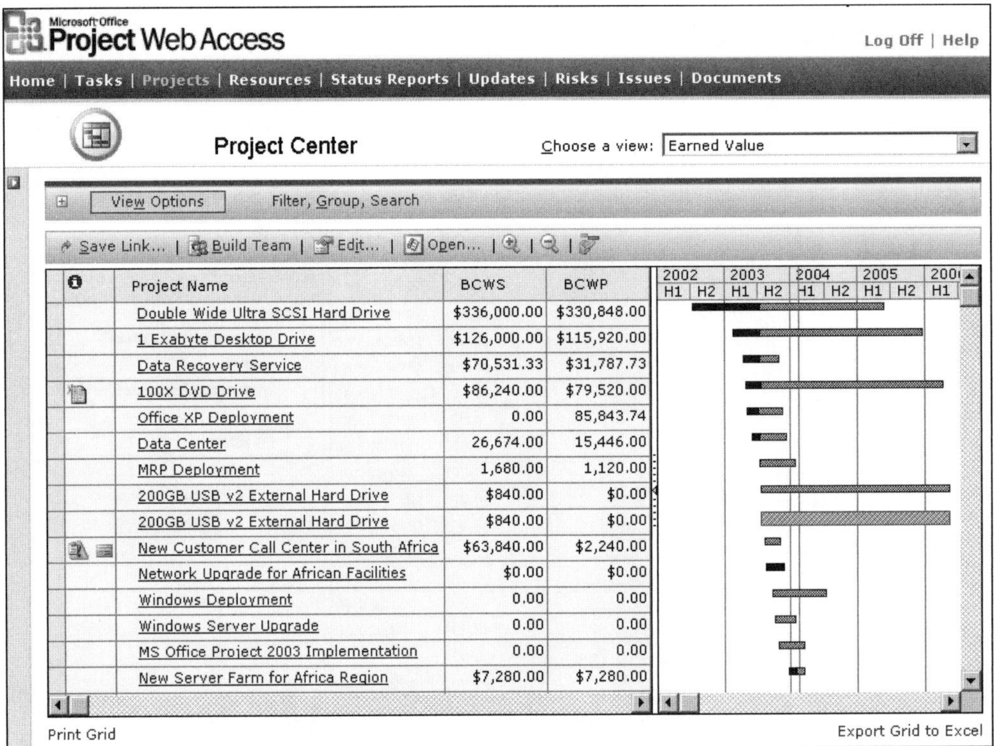

Figure 14-6: Project Center Earned Value view

The Project Center **Work** view displays information about the expenditure of project work hours, with columns for Work, Baseline Work, Work Variance, Actual Work, Remaining Work, % Work Complete, and the project's Start and Finish dates. The Work view displays the same Tracking Gantt found in the Cost and Earned Value views, as shown in Figure 14-7.

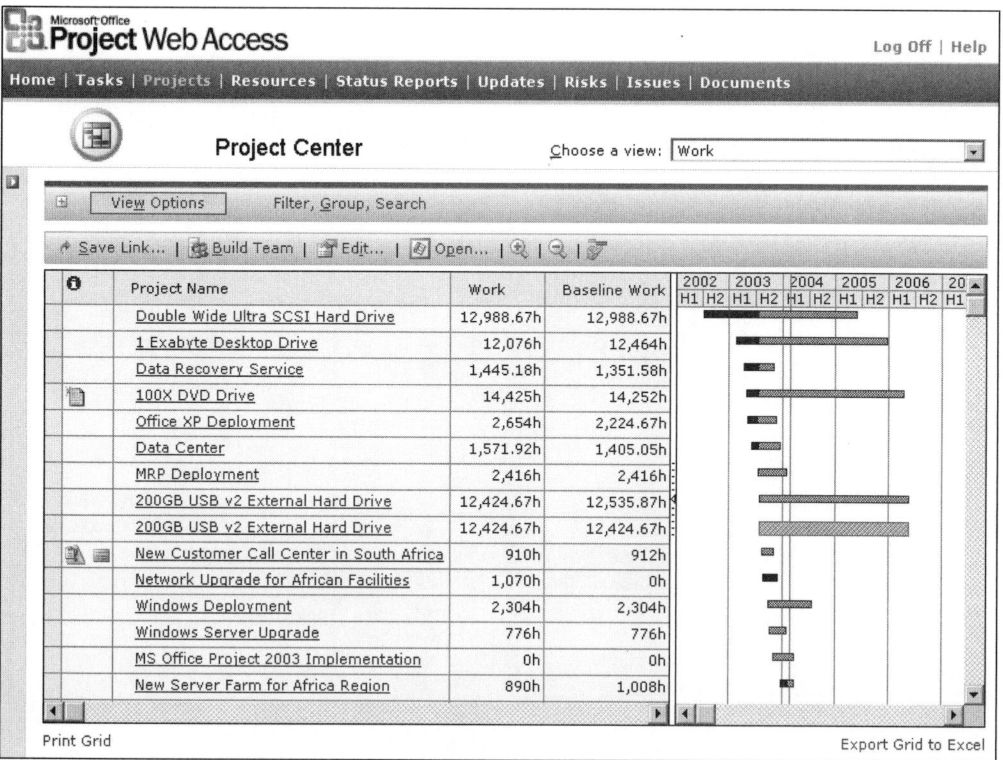

Figure 14-7: Project Center Work view

In addition to the five standard views, the Choose a view pick list may also include custom views added by your Project Server administrator. The Project Center is a great forum for the use of graphical indicators in custom views. Figure 14-8 shows the A Datum Executive Summary view that displays several columns containing custom graphical indicators.

The Budget column shows the cost variance for each project using a red, yellow, or green stoplight indicator. The Schedule column reveals schedule variance for each project using the same three stoplight indicators. The Exposure column contains a red, yellow, or green flag indicating High, Medium, or Low exposure for each project.

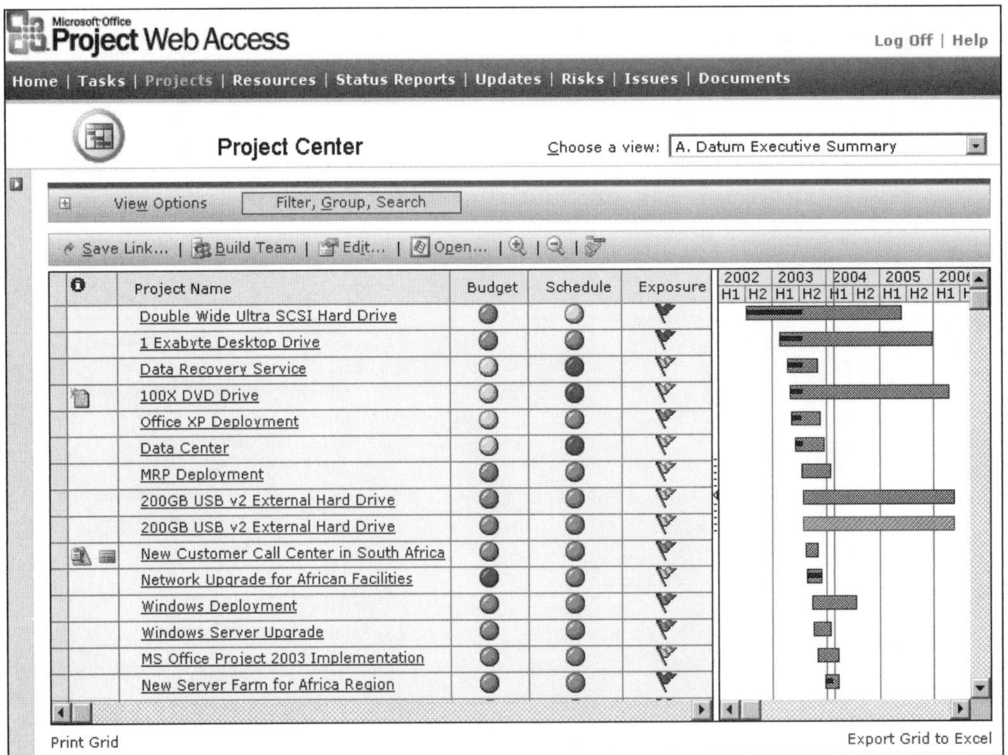

Figure 14-8: Custom Project Center view

As with the Resource Center, you can apply Filtering and Grouping to the Project Center views. In Figure 14-9, I have grouped the projects by Owner and filtered for all High exposure projects. Notice that two project managers, Chris Preston and Steve Masters, handle the lion's share of the difficult projects from an exposure perspective. Contrary to what you might expect, most of the projects for each of these project managers are on track from both a budget and a schedule perspective. This fact might reveal a high level of competency for these two project managers.

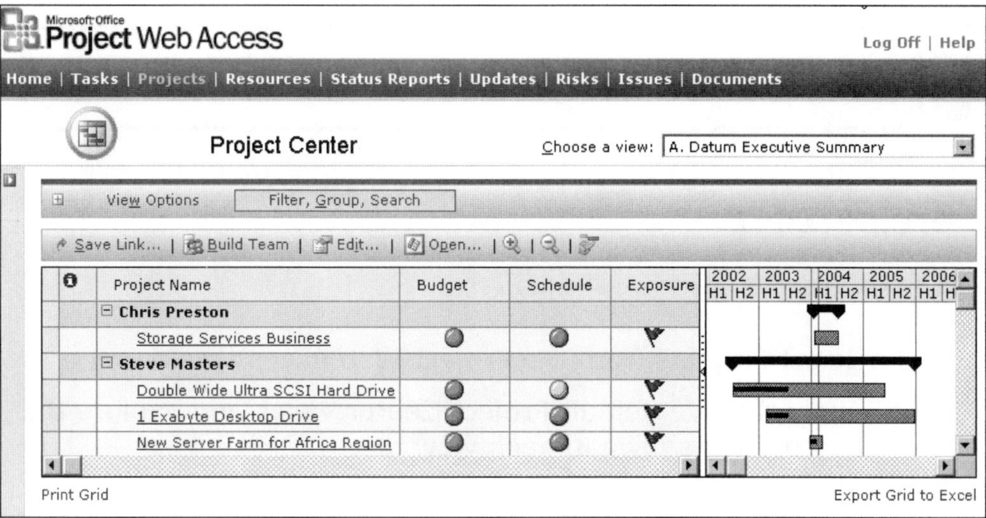

Figure 14-9: A.Datum Executive Summary view with grouping and filtering

When you use the Save Link feature in the Project Center, your saved link will include both the Group and the Filter that you have applied.

Use the Zoom In and Zoom Out buttons to change the timescale of the Gantt Chart. You can change the timescale to periods as small as 15-minute time intervals or as large as years. Use the Go To Task button, represented on the far right hand icon on the tool bar above the data grid, to scroll the Gantt Chart to the start date of the selected project.

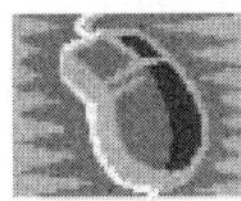

Hands On Exercise

Exercise 14-1

Explore the Project Center views.

1. Select Projects from the Project Web Access main menu
2. Apply the five default Project Center views and explore the information shown in each view
3. Reapply the Summary view
4. Click the Filter, Group, Search tab
5. In the Group by field, select the Owner field
6. Note that the display changes to the grouped view
7. Create your own custom Filter and note the results

Building a Project Team

The Project Center includes a Build Team feature that you can use to build a project team from within Project Web Access. This feature is especially useful for Resource Managers who do not have the full version of Microsoft Project. In the 2002 version, you could only build a team for a project using the full client tool.

To use the Build Team feature, to which Microsoft refers as Team Builder Lite, select a project in the Project Center view and then click the Build Team button on the toolbar. The system displays the Build Team page shown in Figure 14-10.

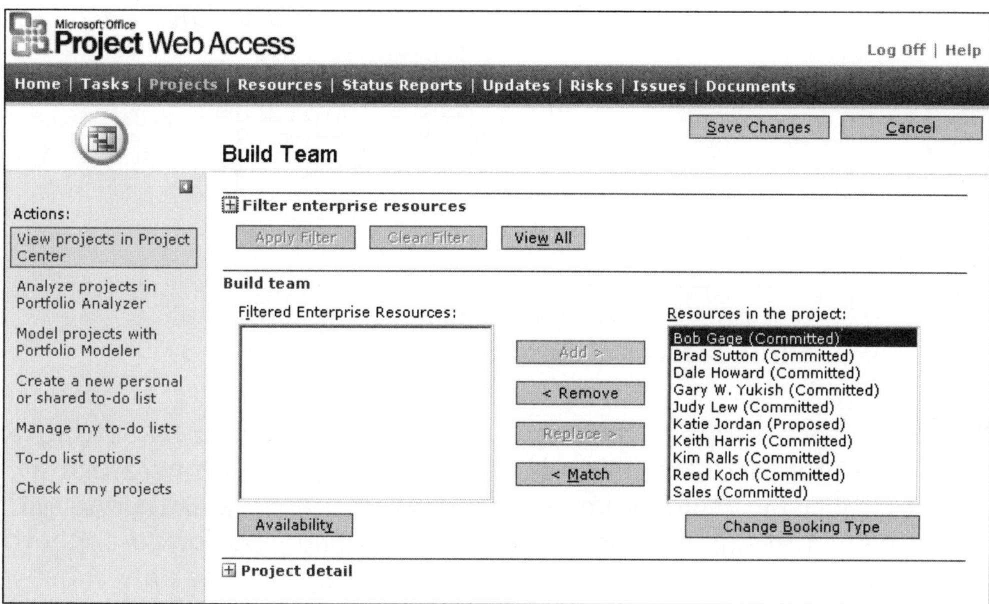

Figure 14-10: Build Team page

By default, the Build Team page does not display any resources in the Filtered Enterprise Resources list on the left side of the page. Click the View All button to display all of the resources in the Enterprise Resource Pool. If you wish to pre-filter the list of resources that the system displays, click the expand button (+) in the Filter enterprise resources section. The system displays the Filter enterprise resources section shown in Figure 14-11.

If your organization has a large resource pool, the Filter enterprise resources option allows you to narrow the field using the custom attributes assigned to your resources. Loading many hundreds of resources into the selection list can consume a lot of time. Use filtering to speed up the performance of the tool.

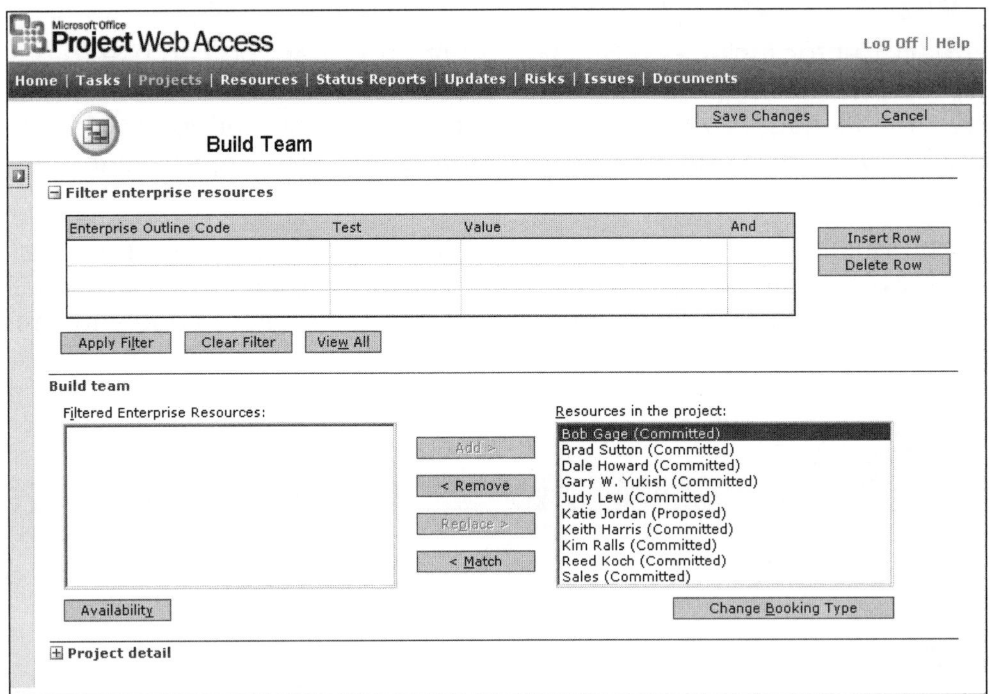

Figure 14-11: Build Team page with Filter enterprise resource section expanded

To filter the list of enterprise resources, build a custom filter by setting values in the Enterprise Outline Code, Test, and Value columns. Build a compound filter using multiple lines of fields, tests, and values along with and/or values in the And column. Click the Apply Filter button to apply the filter. In Figure 14-12, I filtered the list of resources to show only those in the Marketing Department.

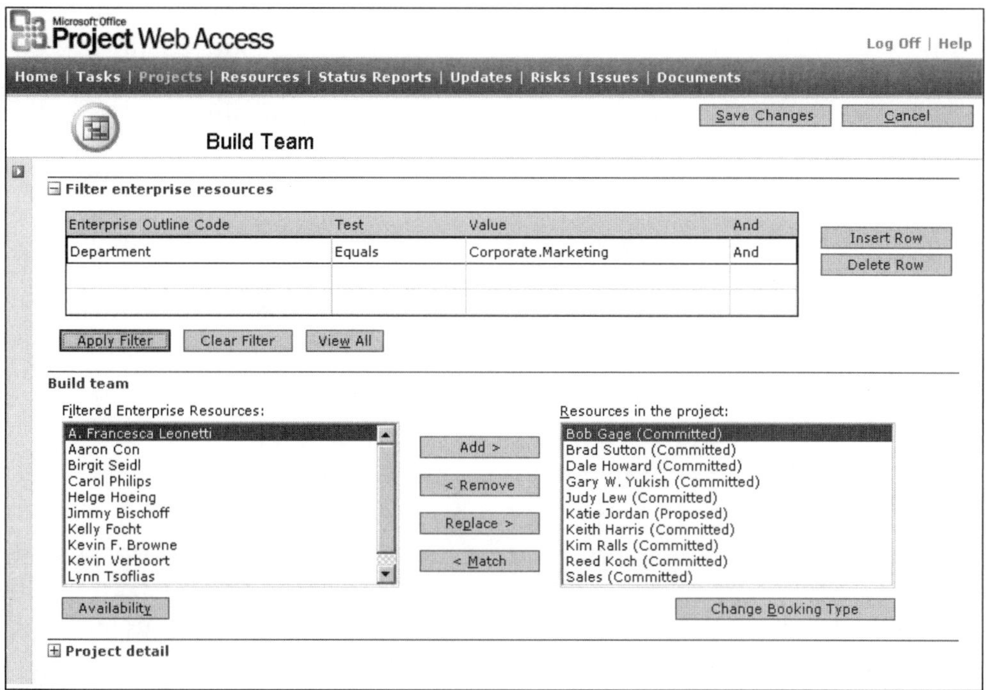

Figure 14-12: Build team page with Filter applied

When using Build Team, you may wish to see the selected project as a guide in selecting team members. Click the expand button (+) in the Project detail section at the bottom of the page and the system displays project details as shown in Figure 14-13. The project details displayed include the Task Name, Duration, Start and Finish dates, % Complete, and Resource Names for each task in the project.

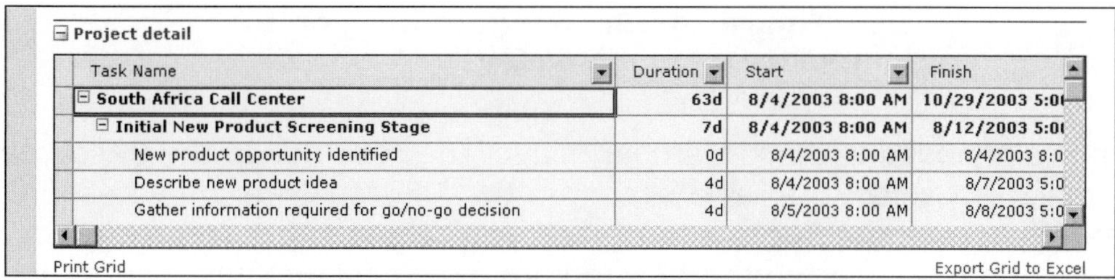

Figure 14-13: Project detail section expanded on Build Team page

To build your project team, select the names of resources in the Filtered Enterprise Resources list and click the Add button. To remove members from the team, select the names of team members in the Resources in the project list and click the Remove button. If you remove a team member who has not reported progress on any task assignments, the system displays the confirmation dialog shown in Figure 14-14.

Figure 14-14: Changes to project team saved successfully

If you attempt to remove a team member who has reported progress on any task assignments, or who has actual progress pending, the system will deny the removal with the dialog shown in Figure 14-15. At this point, your best option is to use the Assign Resources dialog in Microsoft Project Professional to replace the resource only on task assignments with remaining work.

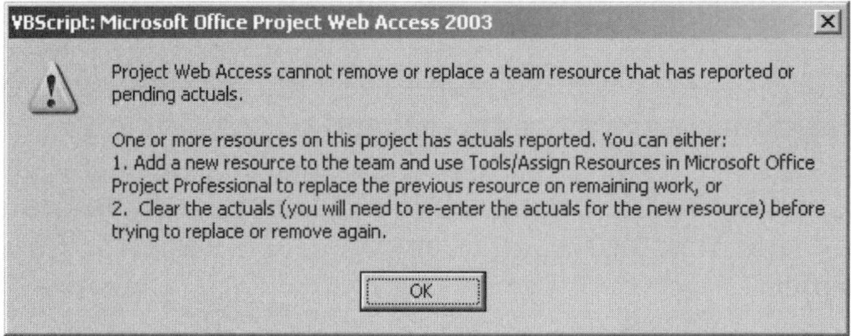

Figure 14-15: Cannot remove or replace a team member with actuals

To replace an existing team member, select the resource in the Resources in the project list, select the replacement in the Filtered Enterprise Resources list, and then click the Replace button. If you attempt to replace a team member who has reported progress on any task assignments, or who has actual progress pending, the system will deny the replacement with the dialog shown previously in Figure 14-15.

To match the skills of a team member such as a Generic resource, select the Generic resource from the Resources in the project list and click the Match button. The system builds a temporary filter that matches the resource attributes defined for the Generic resource. This temporary filter will replace any filter that you have already built, and will display only those resources who match the attributes of the Generic resource.

To change the booking type for any member of the project team, select the resource from the Resources in the project list and then click the Change Booking Type button. The system toggles the Booking Type for the selected resource, such as changing a resource from Committed to Proposed.

Remember from Module 3 that a Proposed booking indicates a tentative commitment for the resource, while a Committed booking indicates a firm commitment. The default Booking type for each project team member is Committed.

Editing Project Details and Opening Projects

If you have the proper security permissions, you can edit the enterprise custom fields for any project you can see in the Project Center. Select a single project in the data grid and then click the Edit button on the Project Center toolbar. The system displays the Project Details page shown in Figure 14-16.

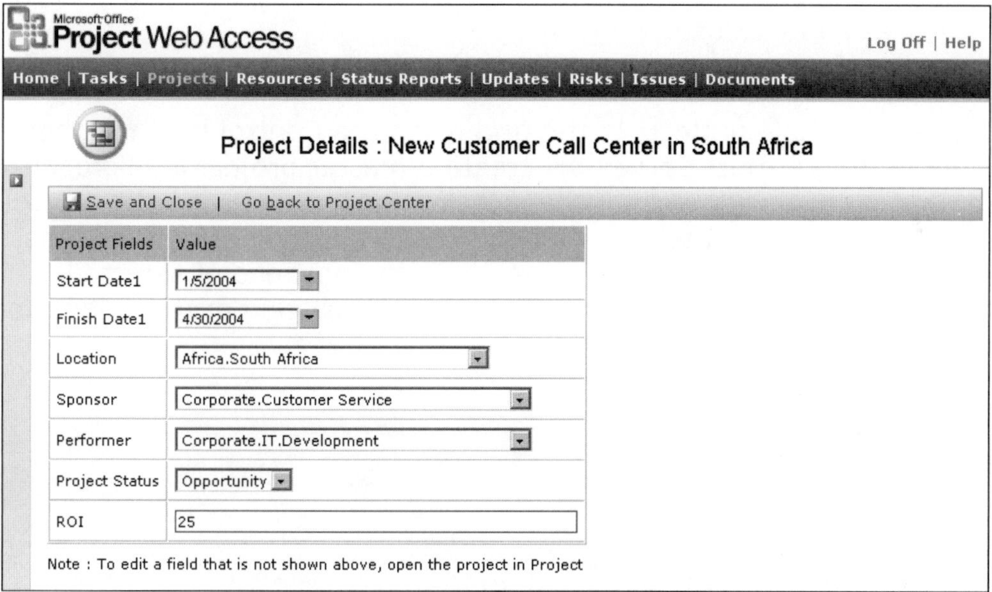

Figure 14-16: Project Details page for a selected project

The Project Details page displays all custom enterprise project outline codes plus only those enterprise project fields that do not contain either a value list or a formula. Enterprise project outline codes and fields are the only project-level information that you can edit through Project Web Access. Edit any of the displayed fields and then click the Save and Close button to commit the changes. Click the Go back to Project Center button to return to the Project Center page.

To edit any custom enterprise project field not displayed in the Project Details page, you must open the project in Microsoft Project Professional, and then click Project ➤ Project Information. You must edit custom enterprise project fields that contain a value list or formula using this method.

Clicking the Open in Microsoft Project icon on the toolbar launches Microsoft Project Professional, if you have not already launched it, and then checks out and loads the project that you selected in the grid. After completing the logon ritual according to the preferences you set, you can proceed to edit your project.

Because you can access Project Center views from within Microsoft Project Professional, you can use the Open in Microsoft Project feature to locate files in a very large portfolio. Because the Open dialog box in Microsoft Project Professional allows you to group but does not provide filtering capabilities, use the filtering capabilities of the Project Center views instead.

If you select multiple projects in the grid using the Control key and then click the Open button, Project Server will create a master project in Microsoft Project Professional with each of the selected projects as subprojects. You can use a master project to set cross-project dependencies between tasks in the selected projects, or to analyze trends in the portfolio of selected projects. Figure 14-17 shows a master project consisting of five subprojects managed by Steve Masters.

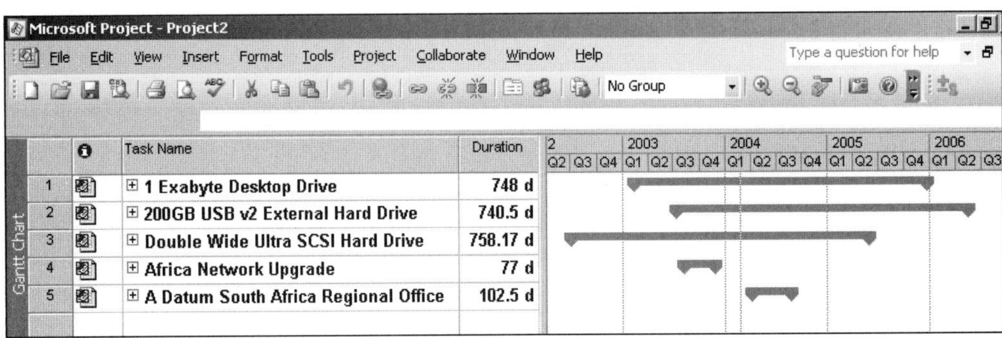

Figure 14-17: Master project with five subprojects managed by Steve Masters

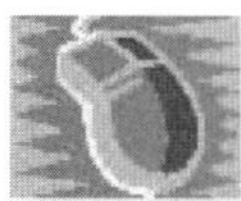

Hands On Exercise

Exercise 14-2

Edit the Project Details for a project.

1. Select Projects from the Project Web Access main menu
2. Select a project in the grid
3. Click the Edit button on the toolbar
4. Examine the fields available for editing
5. Click the Go back to Project Center button

Checking In Projects

Project Server 2003 allows you to check in projects that you own. Occasionally you may find that the system leaves a project in a checked out state because of network problems or a workstation crash. To check in a project, click the Check in my projects link at the bottom of the Actions pane. The system displays the Check in my projects page shown in Figure 14-18.

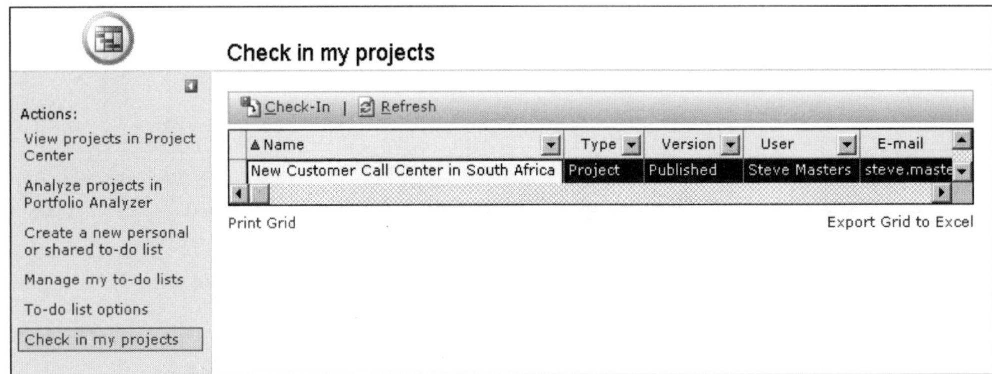

Figure 14-18: Check in my projects page

Notice that the system indicates that Steve Masters has checked out the New Customer Call Center in South Africa project, even though he does not have the project currently open in Microsoft Project Professional. To check in a project, select the desired project and click the Check-In button on the toolbar. The system displays the warning message shown in Figure 14-19.

Figure 14-19: Warning dialog about checking in a checked out project

If you accidentally check in a project that you current have checked out in Microsoft Project Professional, when you attempt to save or close the project, Microsoft Project displays the warning dialog shown in Figure 14-20.

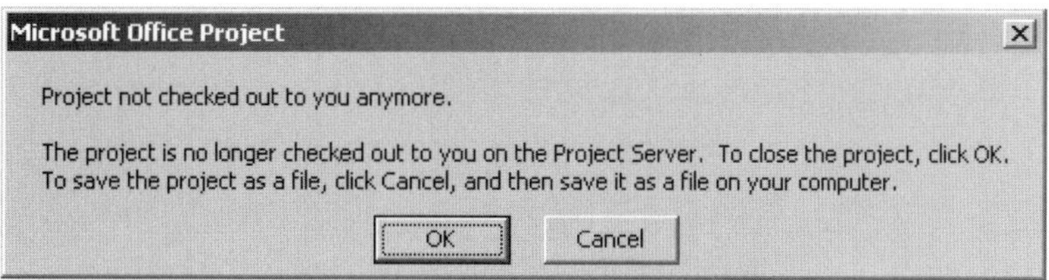

Figure 14-20: Project not checked out warning

Working with Detailed Project Views

In addition to viewing a single line of information about each project in the portfolio, the Project Center gives you the ability to view the details of any project. Click the name of any project in the data grid of the Project Center page. The system displays a detailed Project view as shown in Figure 14-21.

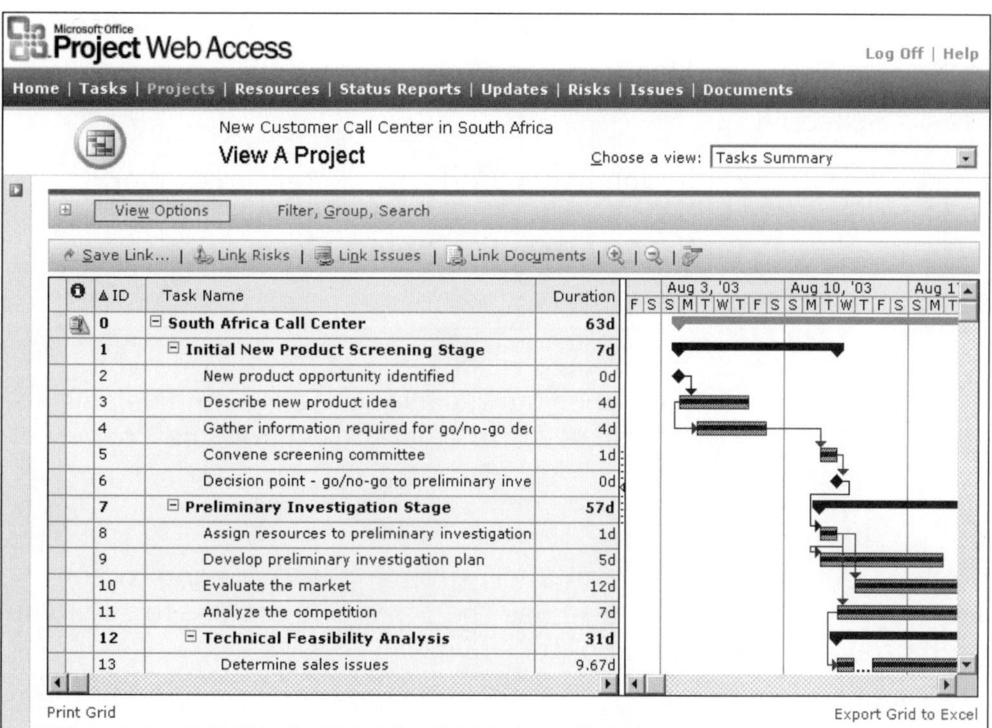

Figure 14-21: Detailed Project view of the selected project

The Choose a view pick list offers three types of detailed Project views consisting of tasks, assignments, and resources. The system includes nineteen default views organized within the three types as shown in Table 14-1.

Task Views	Assignment Views	Resource Views
Tasks Summary	Assignments Summary	Resources Summary
Tasks Top-Level		
Tasks Detail	Assignments Detail	
Tasks Leveling		
Tasks Tracking	Assignments Tracking	
Tasks Cost	Assignments Cost	Resources Cost
Tasks Earned Value	Assignments Earned Value	Resources Earned Value
Tasks Schedule		
Tasks Work	Assignments Work	Resources Work

Table 14-1: Detailed Project views

The system remembers which detailed Project view you selected the last time you displayed the page, and defaults to that view when you select another project from the Project Center.

Like Project Center views, you can apply grouping and filtering to any detailed Project view. You can also use the Save Link feature to save your preferred grouping and filtering of these views.

Use the Zoom In and Zoom Out buttons to change the timescale of the Gantt Chart. You can change the timescale to periods as small as 15-minute time intervals or as large as years. Use the Go To Task button to scroll the Gantt Chart to the start date of the selected task.

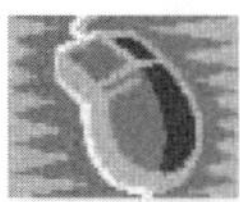

Hands On Exercise

Exercise 14-3

Explore detailed Project views from the Project Center.

1. Select Projects from the Project Web Access main menu
2. Click the name of a project in the grid
3. Select a Tasks view from the Choose a view pick list
4. Select an Assignments view from the Choose a view pick list
5. Select a Resources view from the Choose a view pick list
6. Click the View projects in the Project Center link in the Actions pane to return to the Project Center page

Organizing Your Saved Links

After you create your first saved link in any page, the system displays two new menu items in the Actions pane. A Saved Links section appears at the top of the Actions pane and an Organize your saved links option appears at the bottom as shown in Figure 14-22.

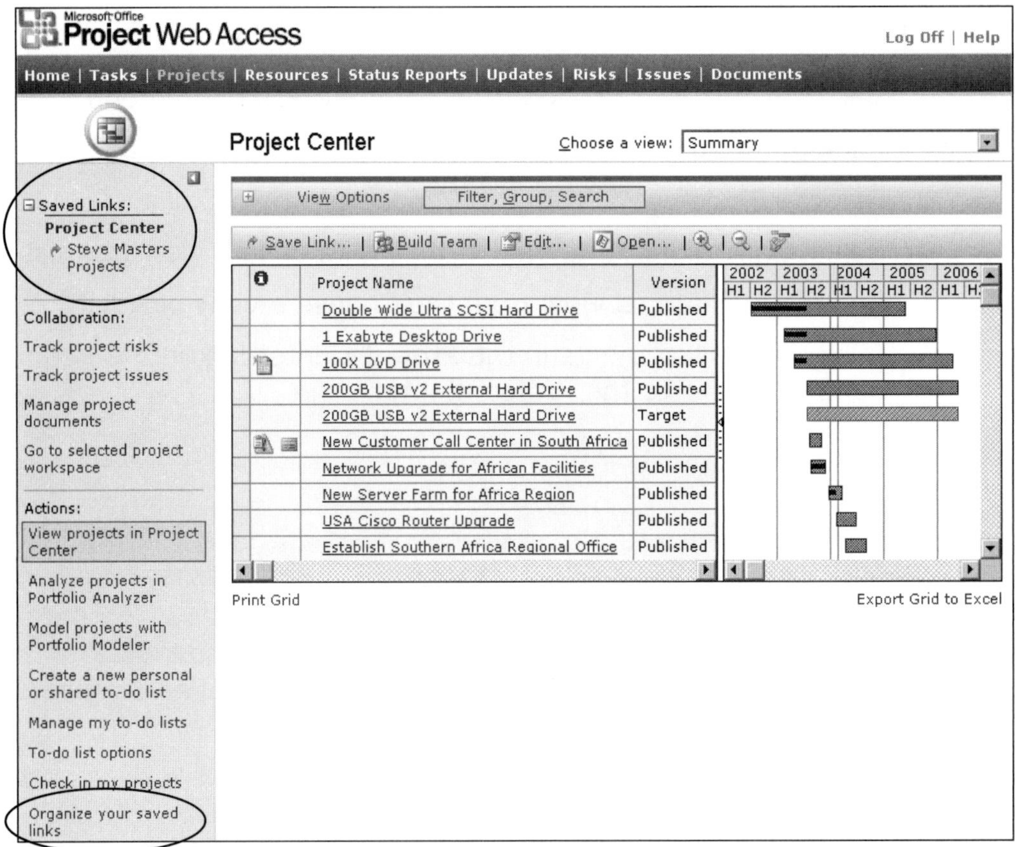

Figure 14-22: Saved links options

Notice in Figure 14-22 that I have clicked the expand button (+) to the left of the Saved Links option to display my Saved Links in the Project Center page. Click the Organize your saved links option and the system displays the Organize your saved links page shown in Figure 14-23. You can delete or rename your links from this page. Once you delete a link, you cannot undo the deletion.

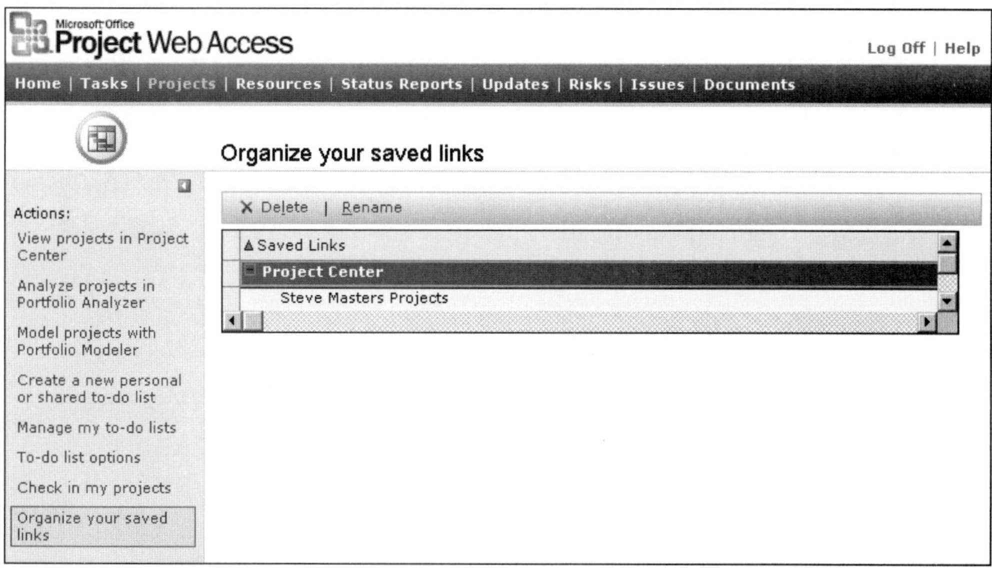

Figure 14-23: Organize your saved links page

Working with To-Do Lists

To-Do lists provide an informal task management tool within a formal project management tool. To-Do lists provide a flexible forum for managing task work that is significant enough that you want to formally record it but not formally manage it. Although tasks created on to-do lists appear in the timesheet in the View My Tasks page, to-do list tasks do not accept progress reporting like project tasks.

Click the Create a new personal or shared to-do list from the Actions pane and the system displays the Create a new personal or shared to-do list page shown in Figure 14-24.

Figure 14-24: Create a new personal or shared to-do list page

To create a new To-Do list, follow these steps:

1. Enter a name for your new to-do list.
2. Select the access rule to apply to anyone, to all resources who are assigned tasks from this to-do list, or me (only) by selecting the corresponding radio button.
3. Click the Next button to display the Create a new task page shown in Figure 14-25.

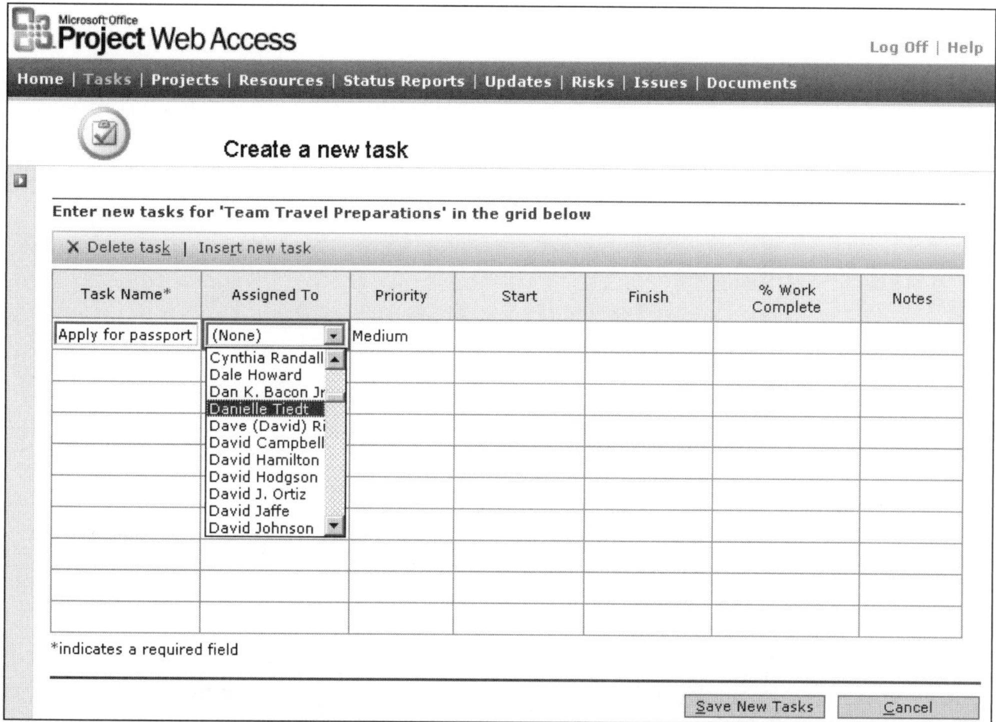

Figure 14-25: Create a new to-do list task

The Create a new task page is specific to creating tasks for to-do lists. Create new to-do list tasks by entering information in the respective columns of the data grid. The only required field is the Task Name column. Insert and delete tasks in the grid using the corresponding tools on the toolbar. Note that you can assign a resource to a task by selecting the resource name from a pick list as shown in Figure 14-25.

4. Click the Save New Tasks button to complete your entries.

The system accepts and saves your to-do list tasks and displays the Manage my to-do lists page shown in Figure 14-26. Notice that the system represents to-do lists as groupings of tasks in this view. You can also access this view directly by clicking the Manage my To-Do lists link on the Actions pane.

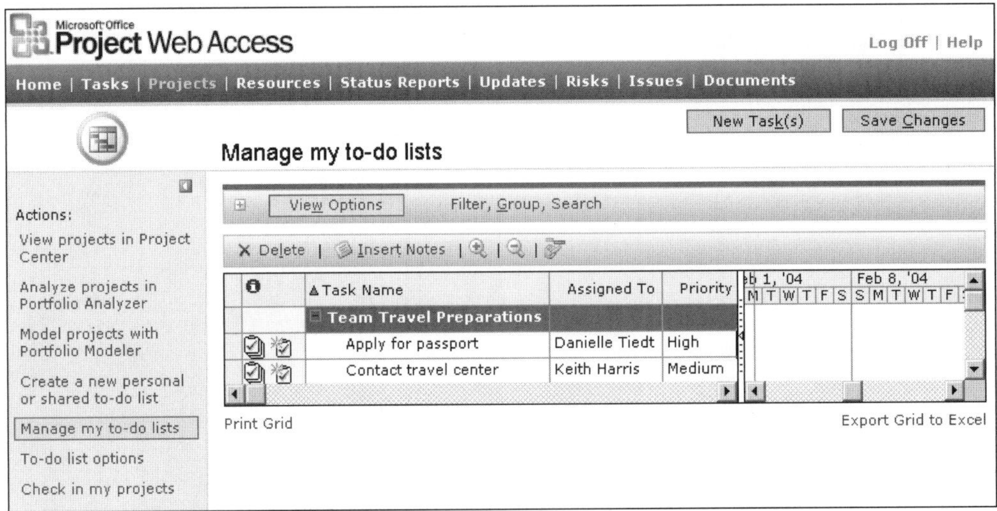

Figure 14-26: Manage my to-do lists page

Notice the icons displayed in the Indicators column in the display. The stacked clipboards icon indicates a to-do list task. The other icon indicates that the to-do task is a new assignment. To insert a note on any to-do list task, select the task and then click the Insert Notes button on the toolbar. Click the New Tasks button at the top of the page to add more tasks in the Create a new task page shown previously in Figure 14-24. Click the Save Changes button to save your to-do list to the Project Server database. The system displays the confirmation dialog shown in Figure 14-27.

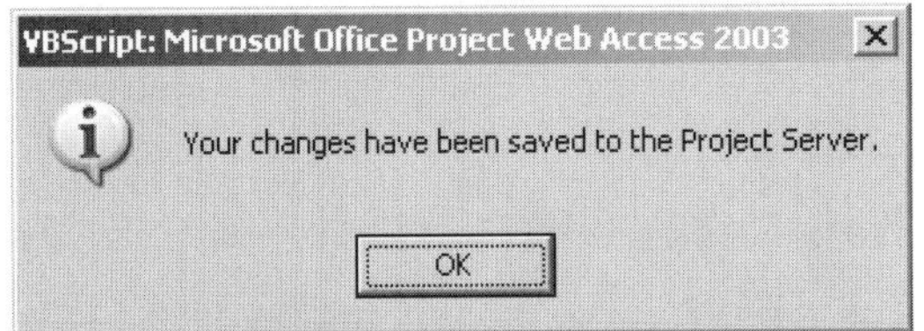

Figure 14-27: To-do list saved to Project Server

The remaining To-Do list menu selection in the Actions pane is the To-Do list options item. Click this selection and the system opens the To-Do list options page shown in Figure 14-28.

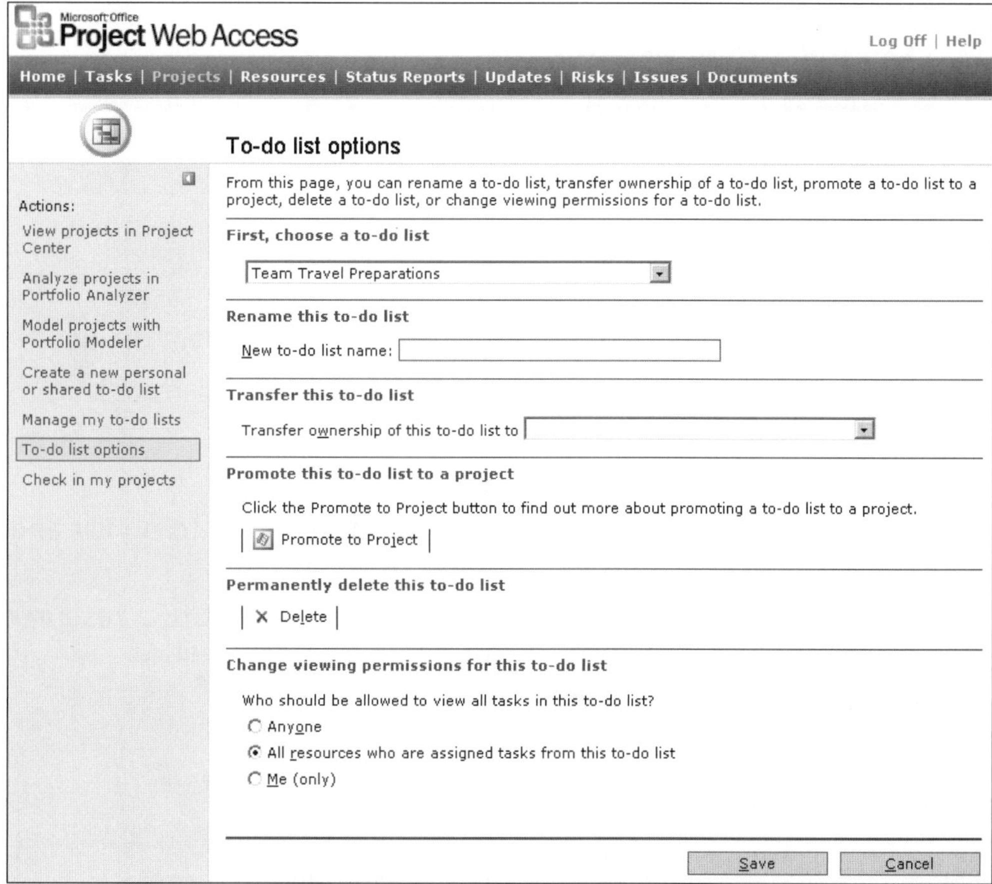

Figure 14-28: To-do list options page

Before you can use the options on this page, you must first select a to-do list. Once you select the to-do list, the system presents selections allowing you to:

- **Rename this to-do list** allows you to change a to-do list name
- **Transfer this to-do list** allows you to transfer ownership of the to-do list to another system user by selecting their name from a pick list.
- **Promote this to-do list to a project** opens Project 2003 Professional if it's not open and writes all the tasks and resource information in the to-do list into a new project file that you can then save to Project Server.
- **Permanently delete this to-do list** allows you to delete a to-do list.
- **Change viewing permissions for this to do list** allows you to change who may see the tasks in the to-do list

Click the Save button when you are satisfied with your to-do list changes.

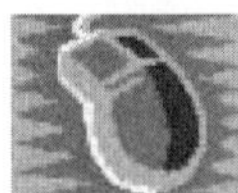

Hands On Exercise

Exercise 14-4

Create a new to-do list.

1. Select Projects from the Project Web Access main menu
2. Click Create a new personal or shared to-do list from the activities menu
3. Give your new to-do list a name
4. Select who will be allowed to view tasks in the to-do list and click Next to continue
5. Add a task in the grid, give it a name, assign it to a resource, and then enter Priority, Start and Finish information
6. Click the Save New Tasks button

Exercise 14-5

Manage to-do lists and then promote a to-do list to a project.

1. Select Projects from the Project Web Access main menu
2. Click To-do list options from the Actions pane
3. Select the to-do list you created in the previous exercise
4. Notice the options available
5. Click the Promote to Project button
6. Click the Promote to Project button at the bottom of the page
7. Click the Yes button when prompted

Module 15

Working with Project Server Analysis

Learning Objectives

After completing this module, you will be able to:

- Understand the need for Project Server analysis
- Use Portfolio Analyzer views
- Create a custom Portfolio Analyzer view and save a link to it
- Create, use, and modify Portfolio Models
- Compare Portfolio Models

The Need for Project Analysis

You will likely want to perform two types of analysis in your organization's project management environment: project analysis and resource analysis. You can use project analysis to understand what is happening across your project portfolio. For example, you might want to compare actual costs against baseline costs for a portfolio of projects in a single region.

You can use resource analysis to study resource allocation across a portfolio of projects. For example, you might want to analyze the total resource hours committed to a portfolio of projects within a single IT department.

Microsoft Project Server offers you the ability to do both project analysis and resource analysis using the Portfolio Analyzer and the Portfolio Modeler. You can find Links for both the Analyzer and Modeler in Actions pane of the Project Center page and you will notice a link to the Analyzer in the Resource Center as well.

You can access Analyzer views from either the Project Center or the Resource Center. In the Project Center the link is "Analyze projects in Portfolio Analyzer", while the Resource Center link is labeled "Analyze resources in Portfolio Analyzer." Both links take you to the Portfolio Analyzer where you can perform either type of analysis.

Using Portfolio Analyzer Views

Because Portfolio Analyzer views are highly dependent on enterprise custom data, Project Server does not include any default analyzer views. Instead, the Project Server administrator must create unique Portfolio Analyzer views to meet your organization's enterprise project analysis needs.

Portfolio Analyzer views can be used dynamically, which means that they can be modified for "on the fly" analysis. You can literally delete everything from a view and then start over, as if you were creating a new view from scratch. Because you can change anything in an analyzer view, you can create new personal views and save them simply by clicking the Save Link button.

Warning: Project Server uses Office 2003 Web Components to provide the functionality of the Portfolio Analyzer. You must have a license on your PC for Microsoft Office 2003, or Microsoft Project 2003 Standard or Professional, to get the full functionality of analyzer views. Otherwise, you will not be able to create your own personal analyzer views

To view the Portfolio Analyzer, click the Projects menu, then click the Analyze projects in Portfolio Analyzer link in the Actions pane. A Portfolio Analyzer view consists of two sections: a PivotChart and a PivotTable as shown in Figure 15-1. The PivotTable functions like an Excel worksheet, and contains the underlying data for the view. The data in the PivotTable displays graphically in the PivotChart.

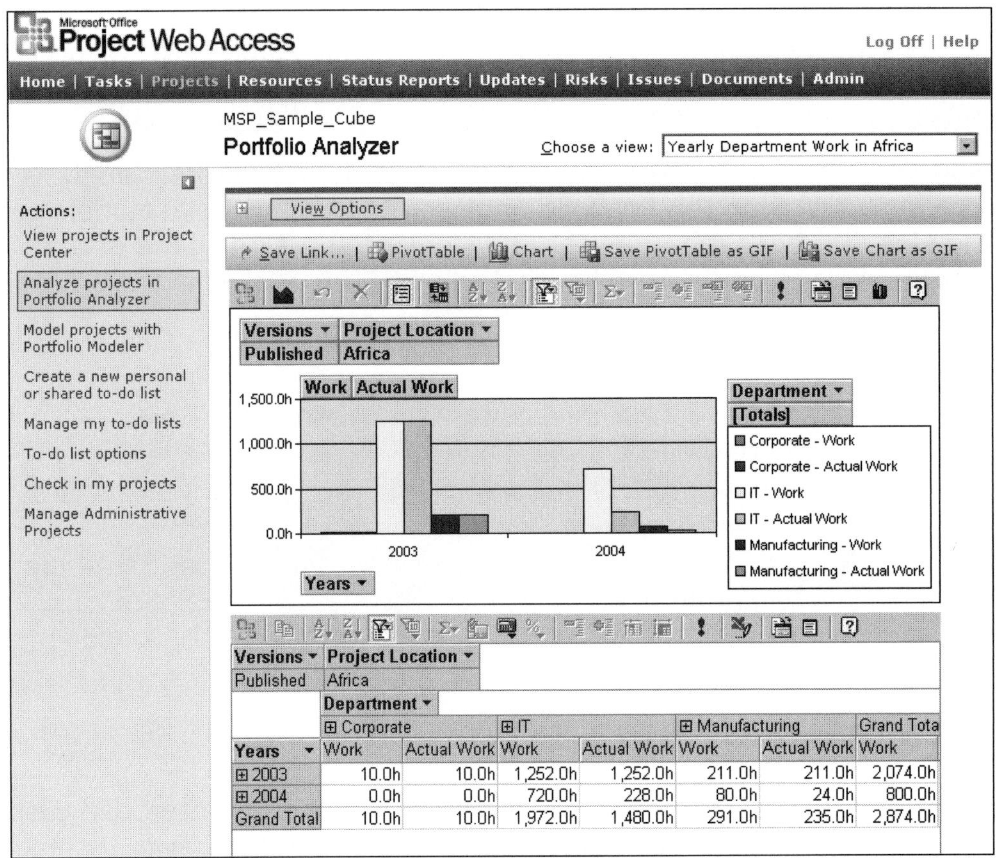

Figure 15-1: Portfolio Analyzer view Yearly Department Work in Africa

To make best use of the Portfolio Analyzer, collapse the Actions pane on the left side of the page.

In addition to the PivotTable and PivotChart areas of the view, you can access the PivotTable Field List dialog box and the Portfolio Analyzer toolbar as well. These additional features give you the ability to customize any existing Portfolio Analyzer views "on the fly" and save the new view as your own personal custom view.

You must be a Project Server administrator to create a new analyzer view that is available to everyone through the pick list. The original view creator can set view options that determine the initial state of the view, such as whether the toolbar and field list display by default or whether the view displays both the pivot table and chart or only one of these by default.

Regardless of the initial view presentation parameters, you can display the toolbar and field list by clicking the View Options tab at the top of the page and selecting the appropriate options. Figure 15-2 shows the expanded View Options tab. Select the Show Field List and Show toolbar options, then click the View Options tab to collapse it. Note that once you display the toolbar, you can toggle the display through chart and pivot table, pivot table only, or chart only.

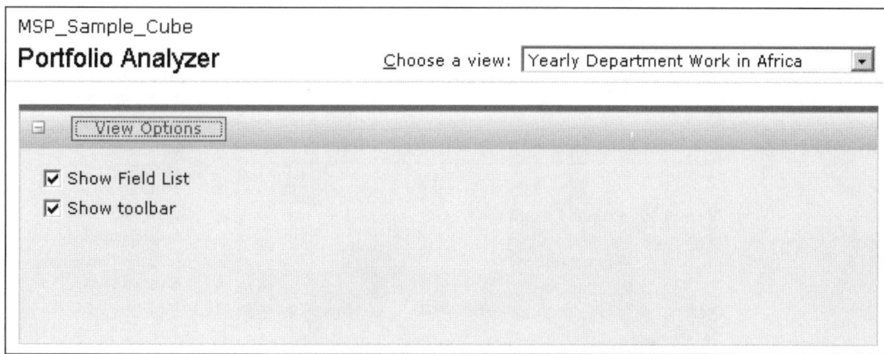

Figure 15-2: View Options tab
Portfolio Analyzer page

When you select the PivotTable Field List option, the Field List dialog box floats over the Portfolio Analyzer view as shown in Figure 15-3.

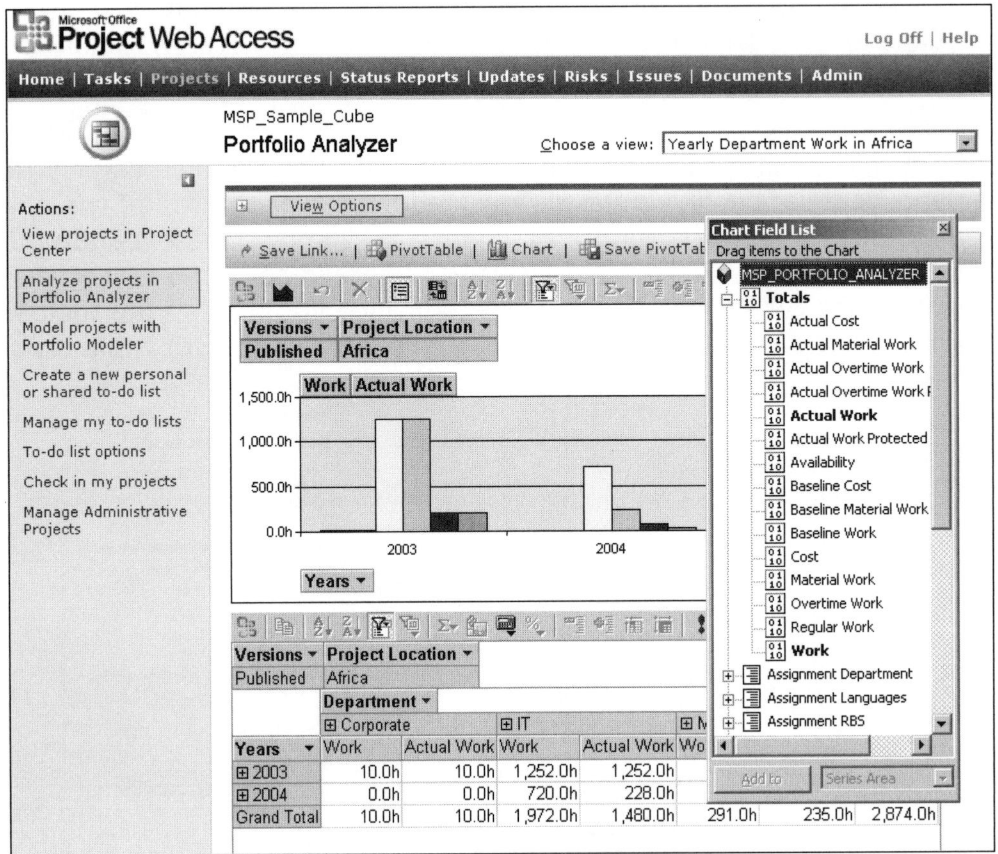

Figure 15-3: Portfolio Analyzer view with PivotTable Field List dialog box

If you accidentally hide the Field List dialog box, you can redisplay this dialog by clicking the Field List button on either the PivotTable or PivotChart toolbar.

In Figure 15-3, notice that there are two types of icons in the PivotTable Field List dialog box. The icons resembling dominos in the Totals section represent totals that you can drag into the PivotTable area. In OLAP terms, these are fact tables and contain totals for project work, availability, and costs. Figure 15-4 shows the complete list of Totals. Notice that some of the fields and dimension in the display appear in bold type; this indicates that the total or dimension is already part of the view.

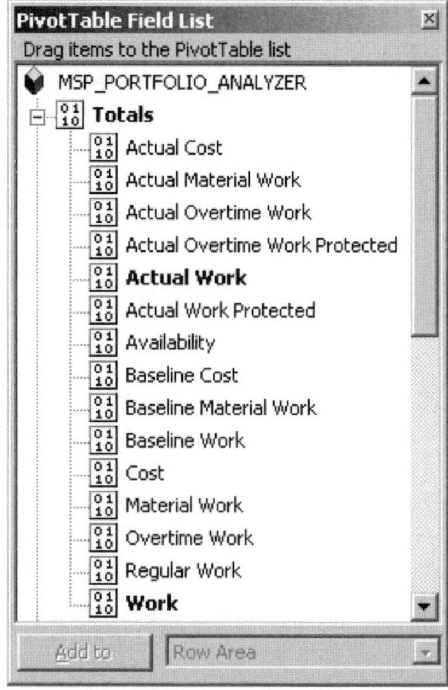

Figure 15-4: Field List with Totals list expanded

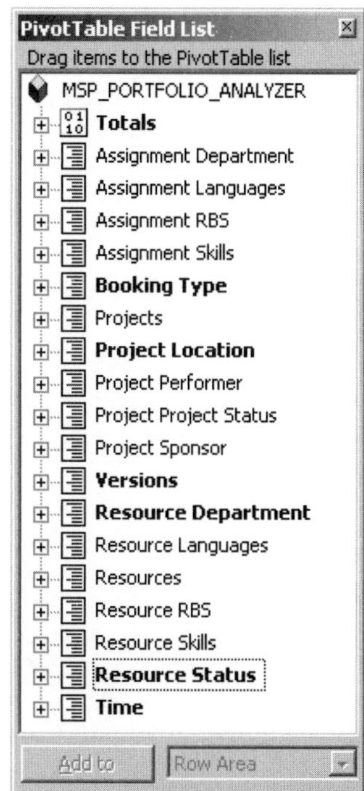

Figure 15-5: Field List shows all available fields and dimensions

The icons resembling the right-justify format text button in Word, shown in Figure 15-5, represent dimensions available in the OLAP cube. Except for a handful of default dimensions, these are the custom enterprise project outline codes and enterprise resource outline codes created by your Project Server administrator. You can drag any of the fields or dimensions into the PivotTable or chart area to create your own Portfolio Analyzer view. The default dimensions available in the OLAP Cube are:

- **Projects dimension** contains the names of all projects in the system.
- **Versions dimension** contains each project and version combination.
- **Time dimension** contains time settings, years, quarters, months, and days.
- **Resources dimension** contains all resource names.
- **Resource Status dimension** contains the types of resource information available, including Enterprise Active, Enterprise Generic Active, Local Resources, Project Fixed Costs, and Task Only Work.
- **Booking Type dimension** contains both Booking types (Proposed and Committed).

When a Portfolio Analyzer view contains both PivotTable and Chart data, the information contained in the PivotTable determines the graph in the Chart. The PivotTable contains four "drop areas" into which you can drop fields and dimensions. Figure 15-6 shows a blank PivotTable with each of these drop areas.

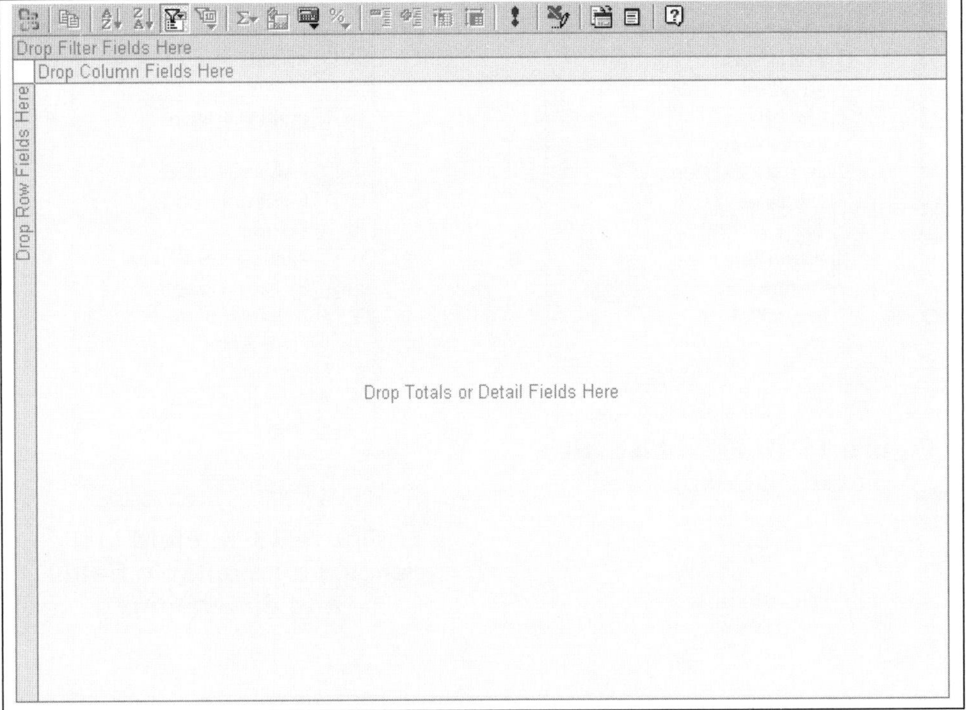

Figure 15-6: Blank PivotTable

The use of each of these drop areas is as follows:

- **Filter Fields** – Drag dimensions and total fields here to filter the data in the PivotTable.
- **Column Fields** – Drag dimensions and total fields here to group data in columns.
- **Row Fields** – Drag dimensions and total fields here to group data in rows.
- **Data Fields** – Drag total fields here to display the data grouped by row and column dimensions.

To create the PivotTable view shown in Figure 15-7, the Project Server administrator did the following:

- Dragged the Versions dimension and the Project Location field into the Filter Fields drop area
- Dragged the Department field into the Column Fields drop area
- Dragged the Years time dimension into the Row Fields drop area
- Dragged the Work and Actual Work total fields into the Data Fields drop area

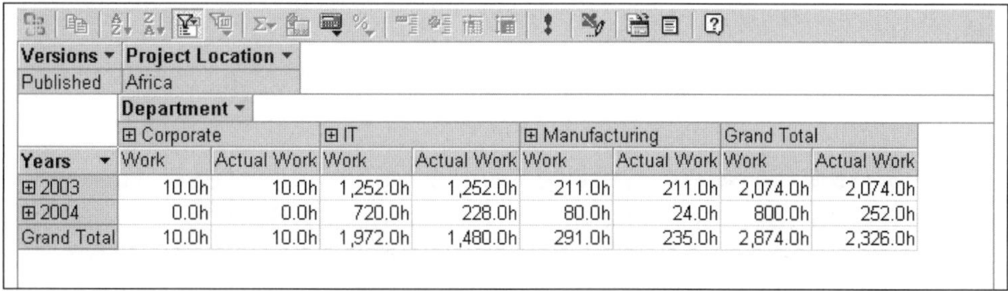

Versions	Project Location							
Published	Africa							
	Department							
	⊞ Corporate		⊞ IT		⊞ Manufacturing		Grand Total	
Years	Work	Actual Work	Work	Actual Work	Work	Actual Work	Work	Actual Work
⊞ 2003	10.0h	10.0h	1,252.0h	1,252.0h	211.0h	211.0h	2,074.0h	2,074.0h
⊞ 2004	0.0h	0.0h	720.0h	228.0h	80.0h	24.0h	800.0h	252.0h
Grand Total	10.0h	10.0h	1,972.0h	1,480.0h	291.0h	235.0h	2,874.0h	2,326.0h

Figure 15-7: PivotTable

In addition, the Project Server administrator also filtered the PivotTable data for the Versions dimension, Project Location field, and the Department field. To filter the PivotTable data, click the drop down list button on any field or dimension. In Figure 15-8, notice that I clicked the Versions drop down list and filtered the data displayed in my PivotTable view to only Published projects by deselecting the check box for target.

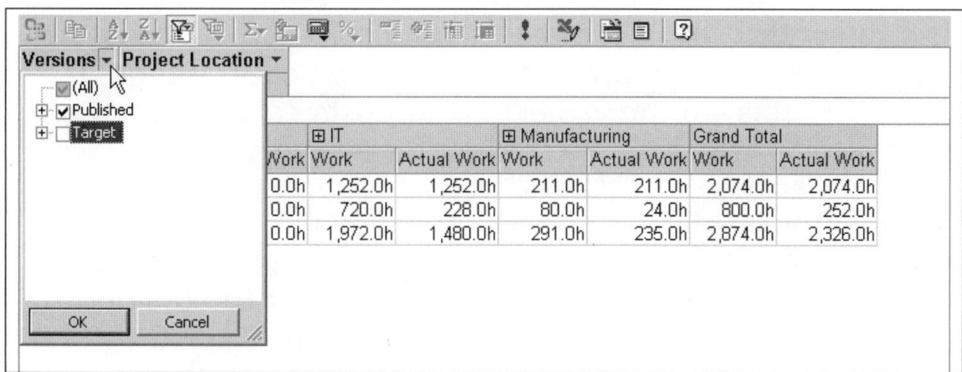

	⊞ IT		⊞ Manufacturing		Grand Total	
Work	Work	Actual Work	Work	Actual Work	Work	Actual Work
0.0h	1,252.0h	1,252.0h	211.0h	211.0h	2,074.0h	2,074.0h
0.0h	720.0h	228.0h	80.0h	24.0h	800.0h	252.0h
0.0h	1,972.0h	1,480.0h	291.0h	235.0h	2,874.0h	2,326.0h

Figure 15-8: Select only Published projects in the Versions dimension

What Is the Resource Status Dimension?

The five leaves of the Resource Status dimension allow the Portfolio Analyzer to account for every hour of Work and every dollar of Cost in the project portfolio. These five leaves function within the system as follows:

Enterprise Active refers to human resources (non-Generic and non-Local resources) assigned to tasks in all enterprise projects. In the Enterprise Active column, the Cost field displays the total costs and the Work field displays the total work for all human resources in all projects.

Enterprise Generic Active refers to Generic resources assigned to tasks in all enterprise projects. In the Enterprise Generic Active column, the Cost field displays the total costs and the Work field displays the total work for all Generic resources in all projects.

Local Resources refers to Local resources (non-enterprise resources) assigned to tasks in all enterprise projects. In the Local Resources column, the Cost field displays the total costs and the Work field displays the total work for all Local resources in all projects.

Project Fixed Costs is not a resource dimension at all, but rather, is a project dimension. It refers to the fixed costs added to each project in the Fixed Costs column of the Cost table. In the Project Fixed Costs column, the Cost field displays the total Fixed Cost for all projects.

Task Only Work is not a resource dimension at all, but rather, is a project dimension. It refers to any task in any project in which you estimated the Work for the task but did not assign a resource to the task. In the Task Only Work column, the Work field displays the total Work for tasks to which no resource is assigned in all projects.

Creating Custom Portfolio Analyzer Views

To do "on the fly" customization of any Portfolio Analyzer view, you can take a number of actions, including:

- Remove dimensions and fields from the PivotTable drop areas
- Add new dimensions and fields to the PivotTable drop areas
- Limit the data displayed in any dimension or field in the PivotTable
- Format the data in the PivotTable or the PivotChart

For example, suppose that you want to create a new custom Portfolio Analyzer view that shows project costs by project location and department, and filtered to present Published projects for 2004 only. In addition, you would like to format the resulting PivotChart as an exploded 3D pie chart.

To create this new custom Portfolio Analyzer view, first remove the Work and Actual Work fields from the Data Fields drop area. To remove a field, click and hold the gray field name and drop it anywhere outside of the PivotTable. While doing so, the mouse pointer includes a large red "X" symbol. Notice in Figure 15-9 that I am removing the Work field from the Data Fields drop area.

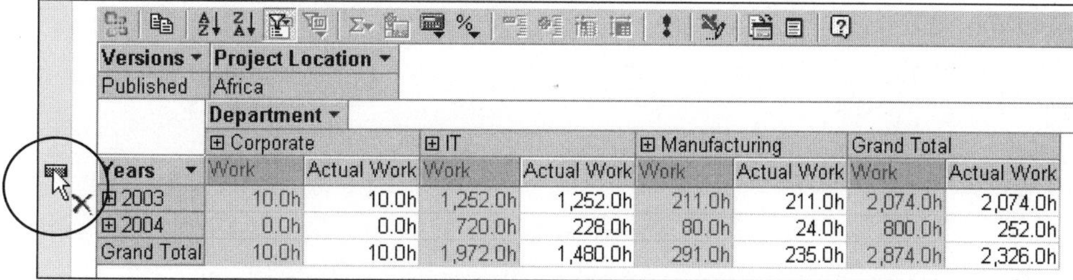

Figure 15-9: Drag the Work field from the Totals drop area of the PivotTable

After removing the Work and Actual Work fields from the PivotTable, you must add the Cost field to the Data Fields drop area. Select the Cost field in the PivotTable Field List dialog box, and drag it to the Data Fields drop area. Note that you can also double click a field or dimension to add it to the view. Double clicking a total field adds it to the Column Fields area while double clicking on a dimension adds it to the Row Fields area. Once a field or dimension is in your view, you can drag it to a new position by clicking and dragging. As you drag and drop the field, the system displays the field as a floating box and highlights the selected drop area, as shown in Figure 15-10.

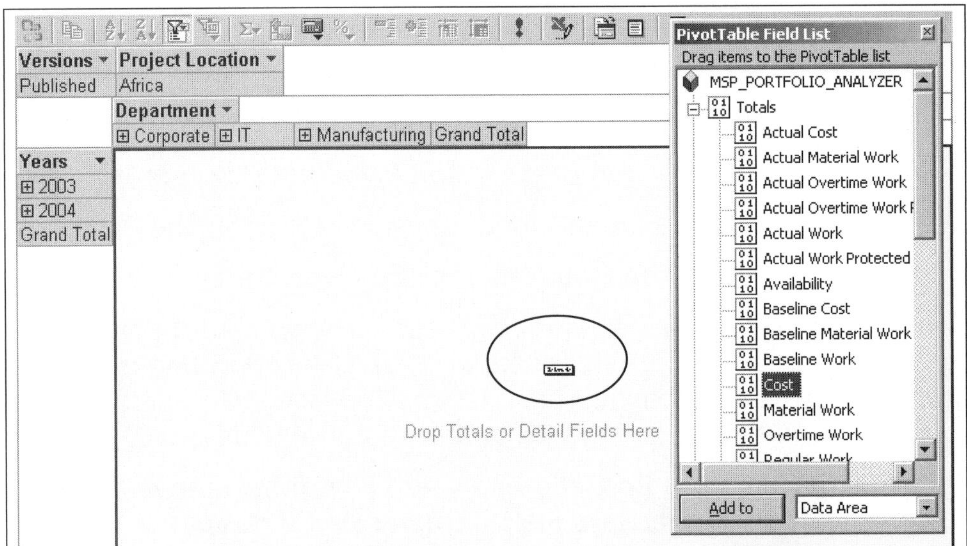

Figure 15-10: Drag the Cost total field from the Field List dialog box to the Data Fields drop area

Dragging total fields into drop areas in an Analyzer view is a very straightforward process. Either you drag a total field to the Data Fields drop area or you do not do so. Dragging dimensions is another story. With dimensions, you can select the entire dimension or a single leaf.

Next, move the Years dimension to the Filter Fields drop area, and move the Project Location field to the Row Fields drop area by dragging and dropping each of them to their new location in the PivotTable. Because the Project Location field filters the view to show Africa projects only, you need to select the other project locations you wish to display by clicking the drop down arrow button on the Project Location field and selecting all four locations. Click the OK button when your selections are complete, as shown in Figure 15-11.

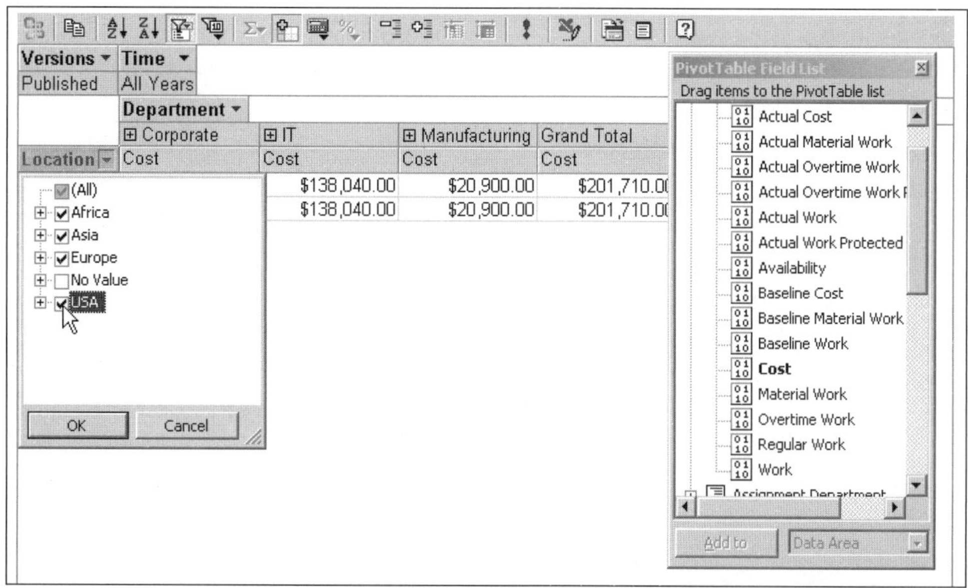

Figure 15-11: Select the desired project locations in the Locations field

To show project costs for 2004 only, you must filter the Time dimension to display 2004. To do so, click the drop down list button on the Quarters field, deselect all years other than 2004, and then click OK.

As you complete each step, not only does the PivotTable data refresh automatically, the system redraws the PivotChart as well. Figure 15-12 displays the completed PivotTable and PivotChart.

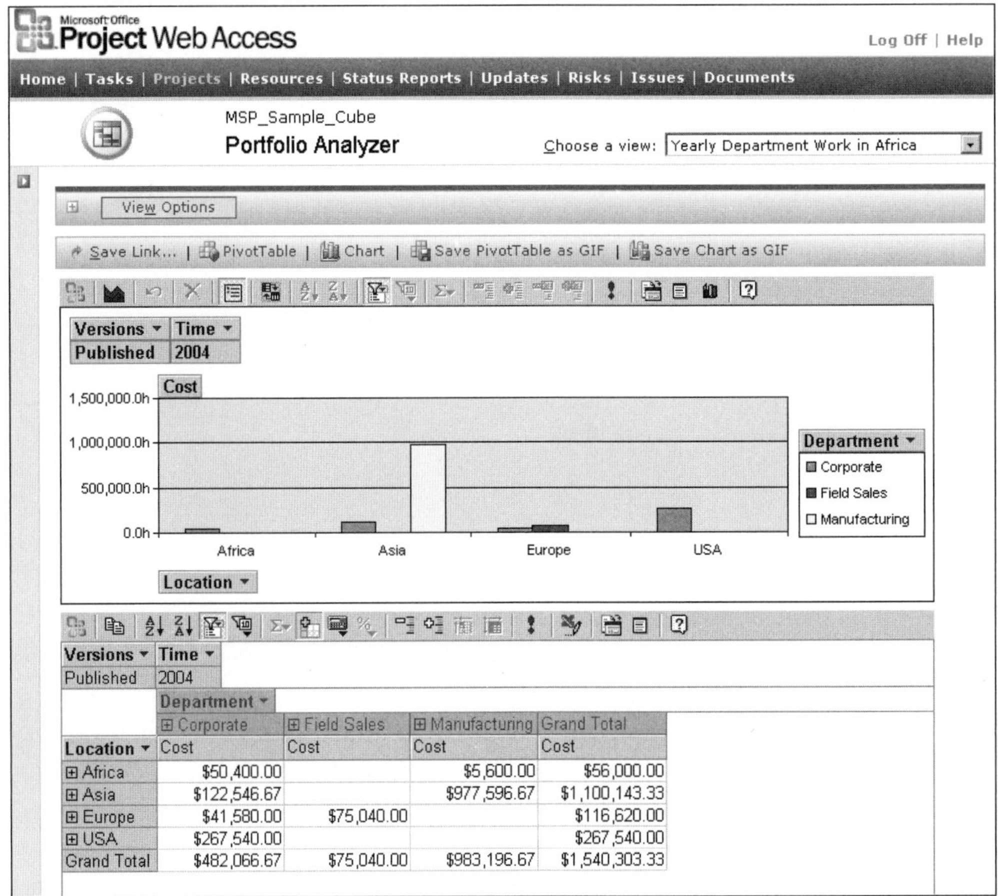

Versions	Time			
Published	2004			
	Department			
	⊞ Corporate	⊞ Field Sales	⊞ Manufacturing	Grand Total
Location	Cost	Cost	Cost	Cost
⊞ Africa	$50,400.00		$5,600.00	$56,000.00
⊞ Asia	$122,546.67		$977,596.67	$1,100,143.33
⊞ Europe	$41,580.00	$75,040.00		$116,620.00
⊞ USA	$267,540.00			$267,540.00
Grand Total	$482,066.67	$75,040.00	$983,196.67	$1,540,303.33

Figure 15-12: Set Quarters field to show FY 2004 project costs only

To complete your custom Portfolio Analyzer view, you must convert the PivotChart display from a standard bar chart to an exploded 3D pie chart. Click the Chart Type button on the PivotChart toolbar shown in Figure 15-13.

Figure 15-13: PivotChart toolbar

When you click the Chart Type button, the system opens the Commands and Options dialog box and displays the Type page, as shown in Figure 15-14. Select the desired chart type and sub-type, which in this case is the exploded pie chart. Notice that the PivotChart reformats immediately when you make the change.

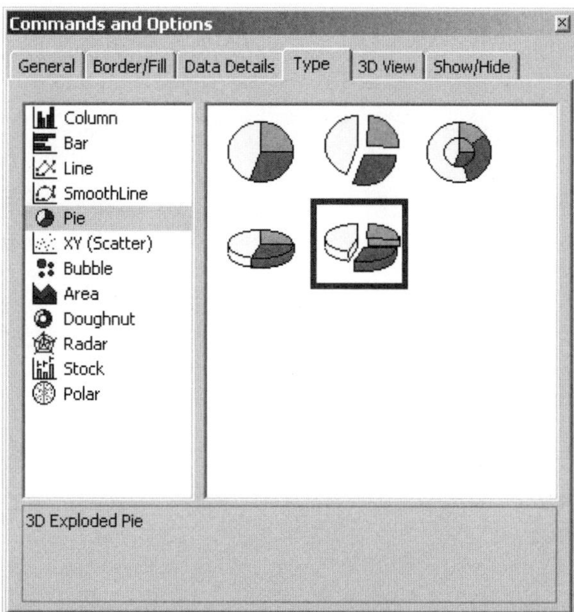

Figure 15-14: Change the chart type in the Commands and Options dialog

After you select the new chart type for the PivotChart, close the Commands and Options dialog box. Figure 15-15 shows your completed custom Portfolio Analyzer view.

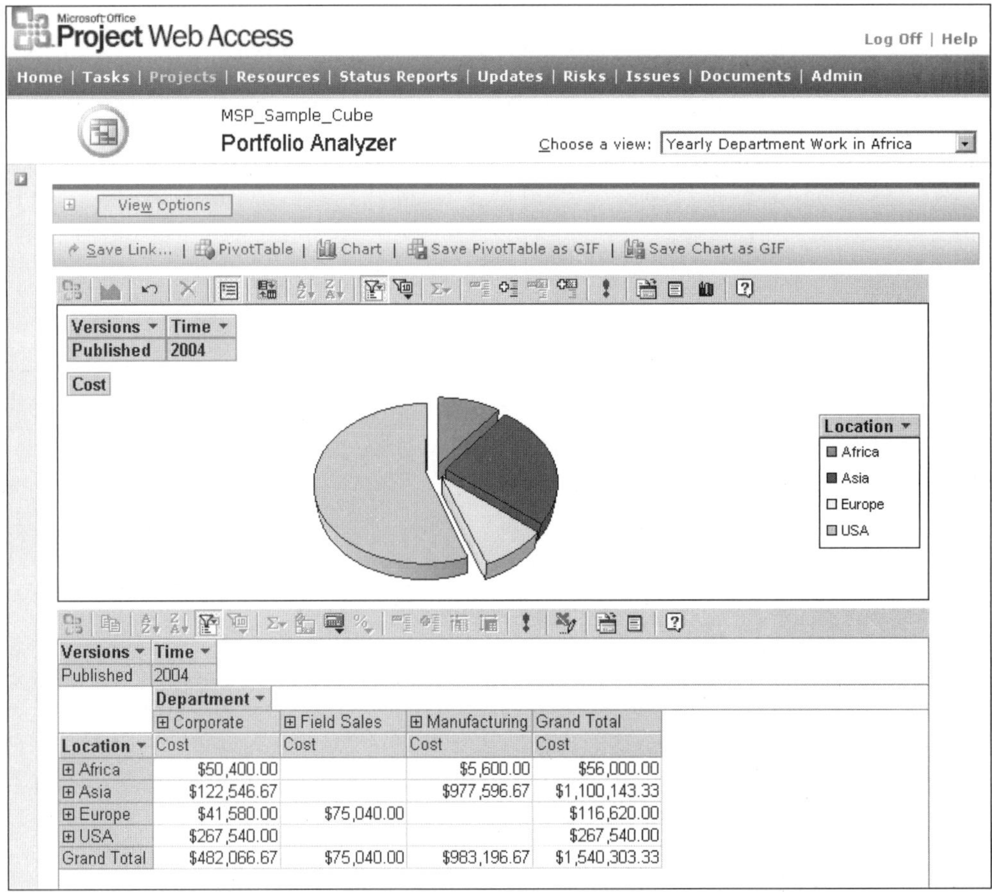

Versions	Time			
Published	2004			
	Department			
	⊞ Corporate	⊞ Field Sales	⊞ Manufacturing	Grand Total
Location	Cost	Cost	Cost	Cost
⊞ Africa	$50,400.00		$5,600.00	$56,000.00
⊞ Asia	$122,546.67		$977,596.67	$1,100,143.33
⊞ Europe	$41,580.00	$75,040.00		$116,620.00
⊞ USA	$267,540.00			$267,540.00
Grand Total	$482,066.67	$75,040.00	$983,196.67	$1,540,303.33

Figure 15-15: Custom Portfolio Analyzer view

To save this customized Portfolio Analyzer view as a personal view, click the Save Link button on the Portfolio Analyzer toolbar and give your view a name. Once you save the link, your new personal view is visible in the Saved Links section of the Actions pane.

If you create a custom Portfolio Analyzer view that would be useful to others in your organization, ask your Project Server administrator to create an enterprise Portfolio Analyzer view based on your specifications. You cannot share a personal view saved as a link.

Additional Portfolio Analyzer Options

Like the Project Center, the Portfolio Analyzer page contains a toolbar at the top of the page. Figure 15-16 shows the Portfolio Analyzer toolbar.

Figure 15-16: Portfolio Analyzer toolbar

The Portfolio Analyzer toolbar offers you the following actions:

- Click the Save Link button to save the current view as a customized Portfolio Analyzer view.
- Click the PivotTable button to display only the PivotTable.
- Click the Chart button to display only the PivotChart.
- Click the PivotTable and Chart button to display both the PivotTable and the PivotChart. This option is available when only the Chart or the PivotTable is displayed, but not both.
- Click the Save PivotTable as GIF button to save the PivotTable area as an image file in the GIF format.
- Click the Save Chart as GIF button to save the PivotTable area as an image file in the GIF format.

If you elect to save your PivotTable or PivotChart as a GIF file, the system displays the dialog box shown in Figure 15-17. Give your GIF image file a name and click the OK button.

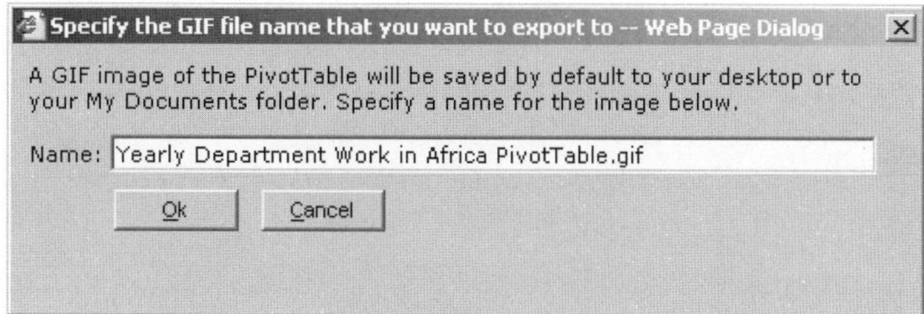

Figure 15-17: Confirmation to save the PivotTable as a GIF image file

Before the system saves your GIF image file to your Desktop folder, it displays the warning dialog shown in Figure 15-18. Click the Yes button to confirm the save or click the No button to cancel the action.

Figure 15-18: Save GIF image file to the My Documents folder

The PivotTable and PivotChart each have their own unique toolbar. Figures 15-19 and 15-20 show the PivotChart and PivotTable toolbars.

Figure 15-19: PivotChart toolbar

Figure 15-20: PivotTable Toolbar

The PivotChart toolbar offers a variety of helpful options, such as changing the Chart Type, showing or hiding the Legend, and running the Chart Wizard to format the Chart. The PivotTable toolbar offers additional helpful options, such as applying sorting and filtering to the PivotTable data, adding subtotals and totals to the data, creating custom formulas, and exporting the data to Excel.

The Commands and Options button is available on either toolbar. Click this button to open the respective Commands and Options dialog box. Use this dialog to apply additional formatting or to change the layout of either the Chart or the Pivot Table. Figures 15-21 and 15-22 show the Commands and Options dialog boxes for both the PivotChart and the PivotTable areas of the Portfolio Analyzer.

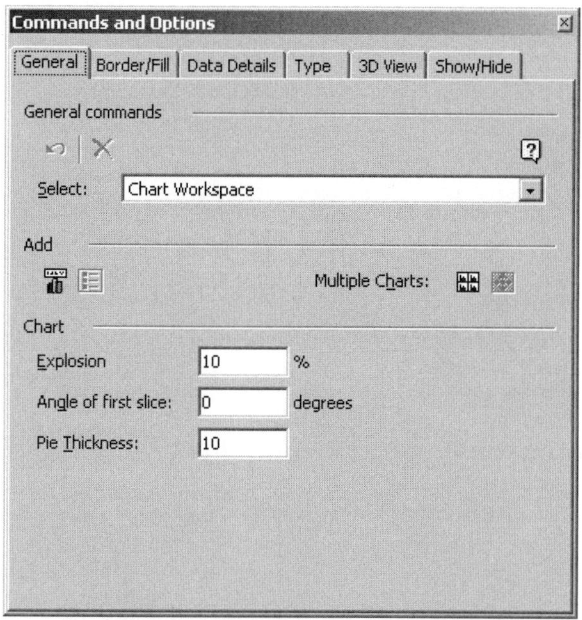

Figure 15-21: PivotChart Commands and Options dialog box

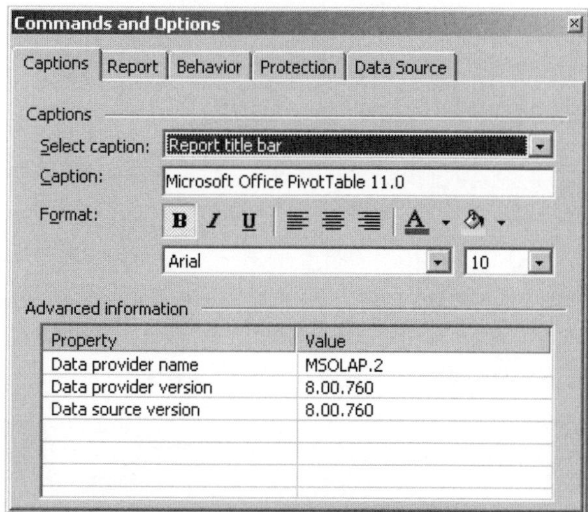

Figure 15-22: PivotTable Commands and Options Dialog Box

Tips for Using the Portfolio Analyzer

Problem: When I drag a field to a drop area, the system does not display the field's real name. Instead, it displays a generic name, such as Level02, as shown in Figure 15-23.

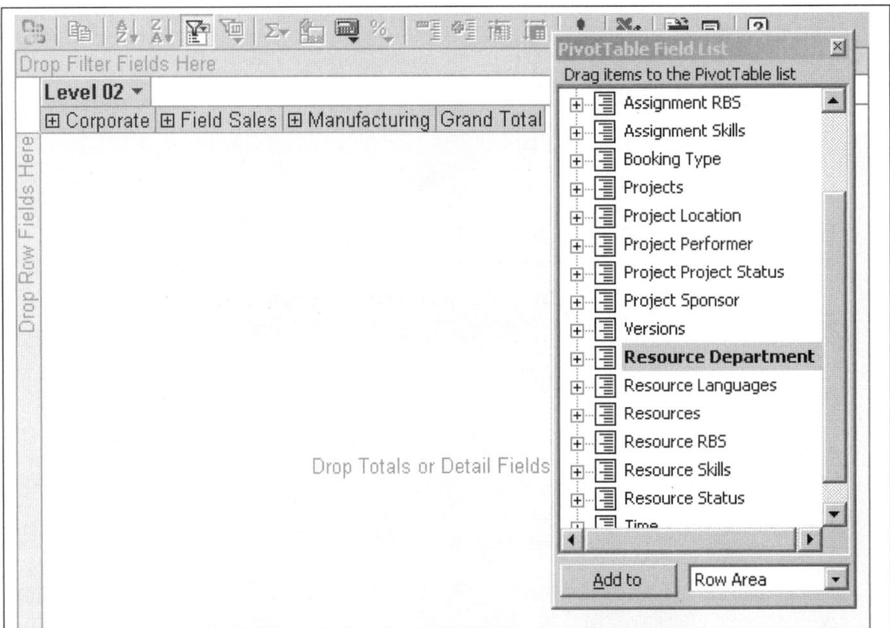

Figure 15-23: Field name displays as Level02 instead of Department

Solution: Right-click the Level02 field name and select the Commands and Options selection from the shortcut menu. Select the Captions tab as shown in Figure 15-24. Change the Caption value to your desired name for the field and then close the Commands and Options dialog.

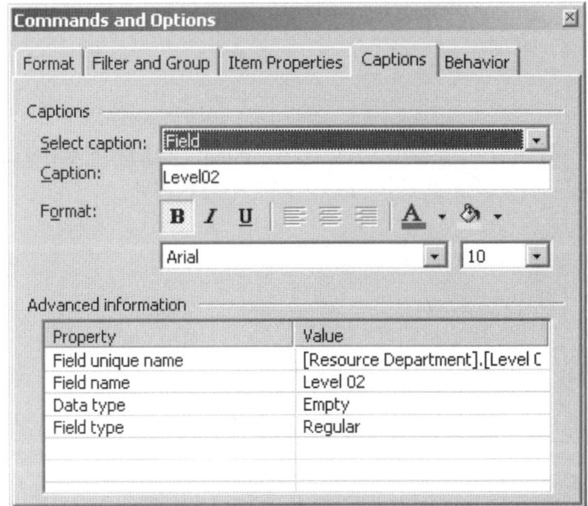

Figure 15-24: Commands and Options dialog, Captions page

Problem: The formatting of a field name is not correct for the type of data displayed in the field. For example, in Figure 15-25 the system has left aligned the text of the Work and Actual Work field names, while the data in each field is right justified naturally.

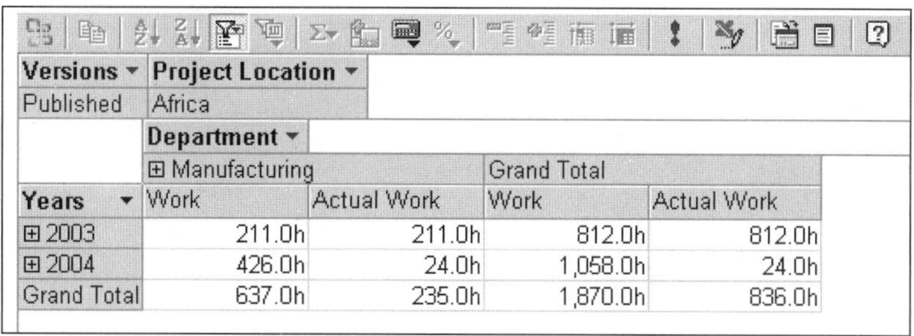

Versions	Project Location			
Published	Africa			
	Department			
	⊞ Manufacturing		Grand Total	
Years	Work	Actual Work	Work	Actual Work
⊞ 2003	211.0h	211.0h	812.0h	812.0h
⊞ 2004	426.0h	24.0h	1,058.0h	24.0h
Grand Total	637.0h	235.0h	1,870.0h	836.0h

Figure 15-25: Left aligned formatting of Work and Actual Work field names

Solution: Right-click the Work or Actual Work field name and select the Commands and Options selection from the shortcut menu. Select the Captions tab shown in Figure 15-26. Click the Align Right button in the Format section and then close the Commands and Options dialog.

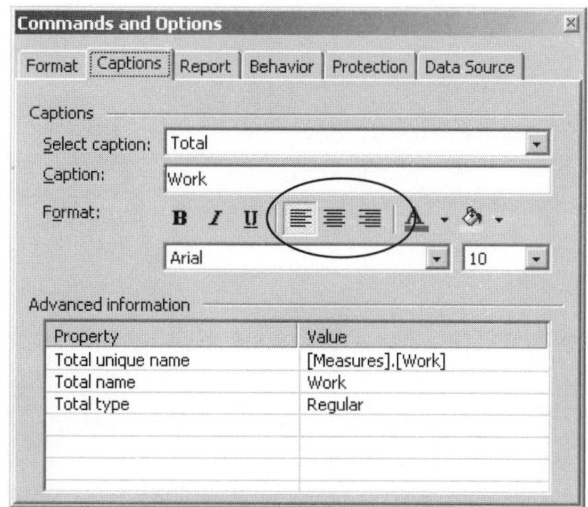

Figure 15-26: Commands and Options dialog, Format page

Problem: I created a new Portfolio Analyzer view, but the Legend does not display on the right side of the PivotChart.

Solution: By default, the Legend does not display in the PivotChart when you create a new Portfolio Analyzer view. To display the Legend, click the Show/Hide Legend button on the PivotChart toolbar shown in Figure 15-27.

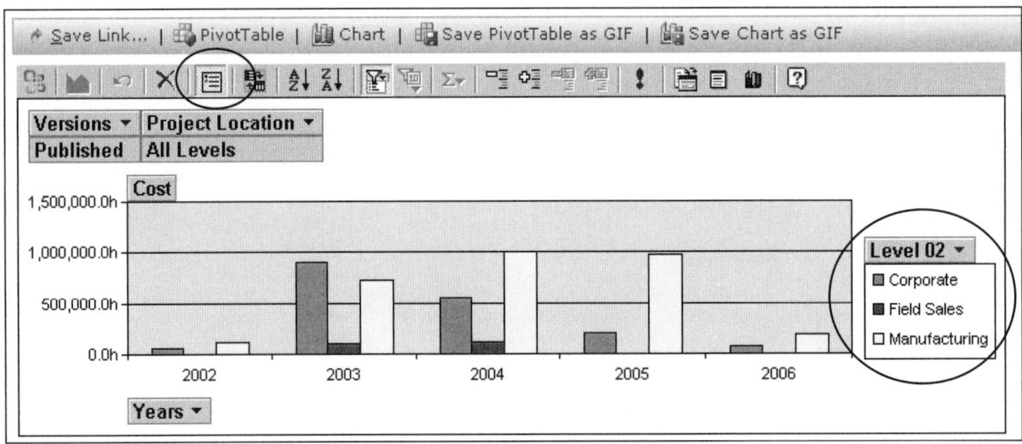

Figure 15-27: PivotChart with Legend

Problem: How can I create a custom formula in the Data Fields drop area of the PivotTable?

Solution: To create a custom formula, click the Calculated Totals and Fields button on the PivotTable toolbar and select Create Calculated Total from the menu as shown in Figure 15-28.

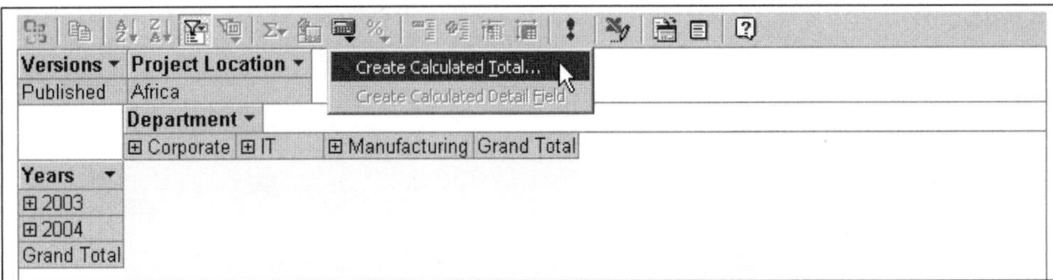

Figure 15-28: Create a Calculated Total

The system displays the Commands and Options dialog with the Calculation tab selected shown in Figure 15-29.

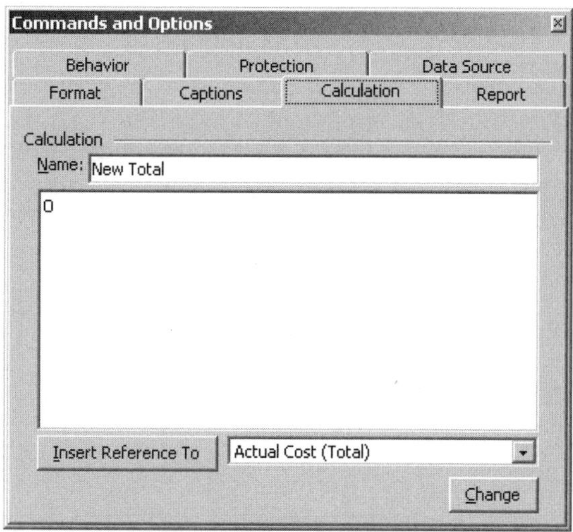

Figure 15-29: Commands and Options dialog, Calculation page

To create the custom calculation, complete the following steps:

1. Give the calculation a meaningful name, such as Remaining Availability
2. Click the field list to the right of the Insert Reference To button and select a field, such as the Availability (Total) field
3. Click the Insert Reference To button and the field is entered in the Calculation section
4. Select the text area of the Calculation section and enter any mathematical operators needed to perform a calculation, such as the minus sign to subtract a value from the Availability field
5. Continue adding fields and mathematical operators as needed to create the final formula
6. Click the Change button when you have completed the formula to display the results in the Data fields drop area

Notice in Figure 15-30 that I created a custom formula to calculate the Remaining Availability for resources in the system.

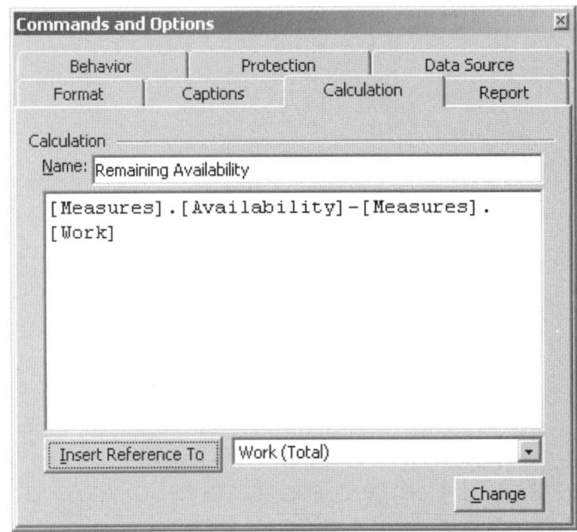

Figure 15-30: Commands and Options dialog, Calculation page with Remaining Availability formula

Figure 15-31 displays the Remaining Availability field in the PivotTable.

Versions	Project Location			
Published	Africa			
	Department			
	⊞ Corporate	⊞ IT	⊞ Manufacturing	Grand Total
Years	Remaining Availability	Remaining Availability	Remaining Availability	Remaining Availability
⊞ 2002	16896	54912	39072	240768
⊞ 2003	33398	107324	77045	473990
⊞ 2004	33536	107192	77126	475030
⊞ 2005	33280	108160	76960	474240
⊞ 2006	15744	51168	36408	224352
Grand Total	132854	428756	306611	1888380

Figure 15-31: Remaining Availability custom formula

When you create a custom formula, the system displays the values using the General number format. To apply a different number format, click the Format tab in the Commands and Options dialog and select a format from the Number drop down list in the Text Format section of the dialog. For example, a better number format for the values shown previously in Figure 15-31 would be the Standard format, which displays commas in each number.

Using the Portfolio Modeler

The Portfolio Modeler provides a workspace to do "what if" analysis for making changes to staffing and timelines for plans. It features a resource optimization engine driven by parameters you define through its interface. You can use the Portfolio Modeler to build models and explore scenario-based scheduling alternatives by comparing them to each other.

To launch the Portfolio Modeler, click the Model Projects with Portfolio Modeler link on the Actions pane of the Project Center. The system displays the Model Projects with Portfolio Modeler page shown in Figure 15-32. In the figure, notice that I collapsed the Actions pane, which allows me to see the complete information about the two existing models in the grid. All of the functions you activate from this page are on the toolbar above the grid.

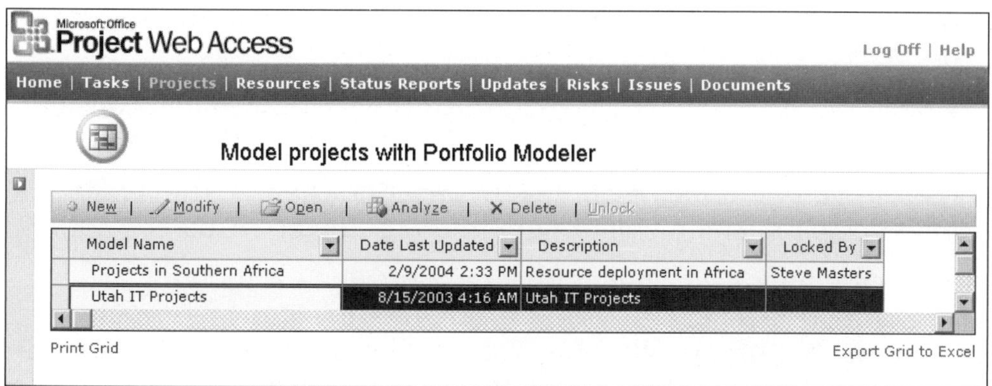

Figure 15-32: Model projects with Portfolio Modeler page

The functions of the buttons on the Portfolio Modeler toolbar are as follows:

- **New** launches a series of steps to create a new model
- **Modify** allows you to make changes to the existing model you select in the grid
- **Open** allows you to open an existing model
- **Analyze** compares resource demand and availability in the model's plans
- **Delete** permanently removes a model from the system
- **Unlock** resets a locked model, which is similar to checking in resources and projects

Warning: You cannot perform any of the functions on the Portfolio Modeler toolbar on a locked model. The only people who can unlock a model are the person who locked it and a Project Server administrator.

Creating a New Model

Click the New button and the system displays the Model projects with Portfolio Modeler page shown in Figure 15-33. Enter a name and description for your new model, select the projects you want to include in your model, and then select the resources you want to consider in your new model. You have three choices for selecting resources:

- Use the resources that already have assignments in the selected projects
- Select an RBS level at or below which the system should consider resources
- Choose your specific resources by selecting them in the Available resource pane and moving them to the Selected resources pane

I want to create a model to help me determine when A.datum's manufacturing projects in Malaysia are likely to finish, given the fact that there are a number of overallocations in these projects. I want the model to locate and substitute available resources for overallocated resources in an attempt to optimize the schedule of each Malaysia manufacturing project.

Notice in Figure 15-33 that I selected three Malaysia manufacturing projects and selected resources at or below the Malaysia RBS level. Selecting an RBS level allows the system to select other resources in the Enterprise Resource Pool and potentially to ignore the current assignments in the three projects.

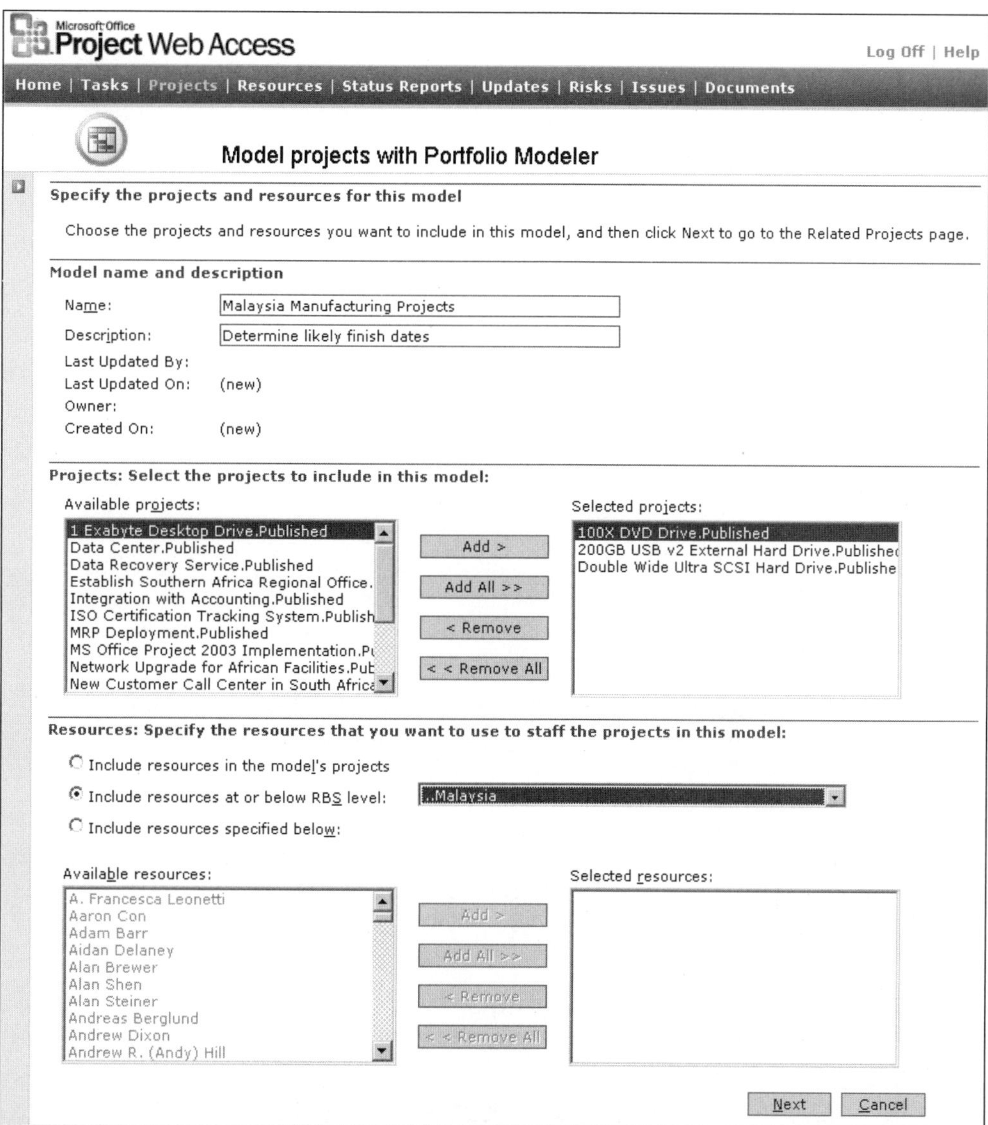

Figure 15-33: Create a new model projects and resources page

Click the Next button and the system displays the related projects page. The system identifies other projects in the system with direct and indirect relationships to the selected projects, and displays them in the related projects page as shown in Figure 15-34. As with the Resource Substitution Wizard, a project has a direct relationship when it shares resources with one of the selected plans. A project has an indirect relationship when it shares resources with a project that shares resources with one of the selected model projects. In the figure, notice that I did not select any related projects for my new model.

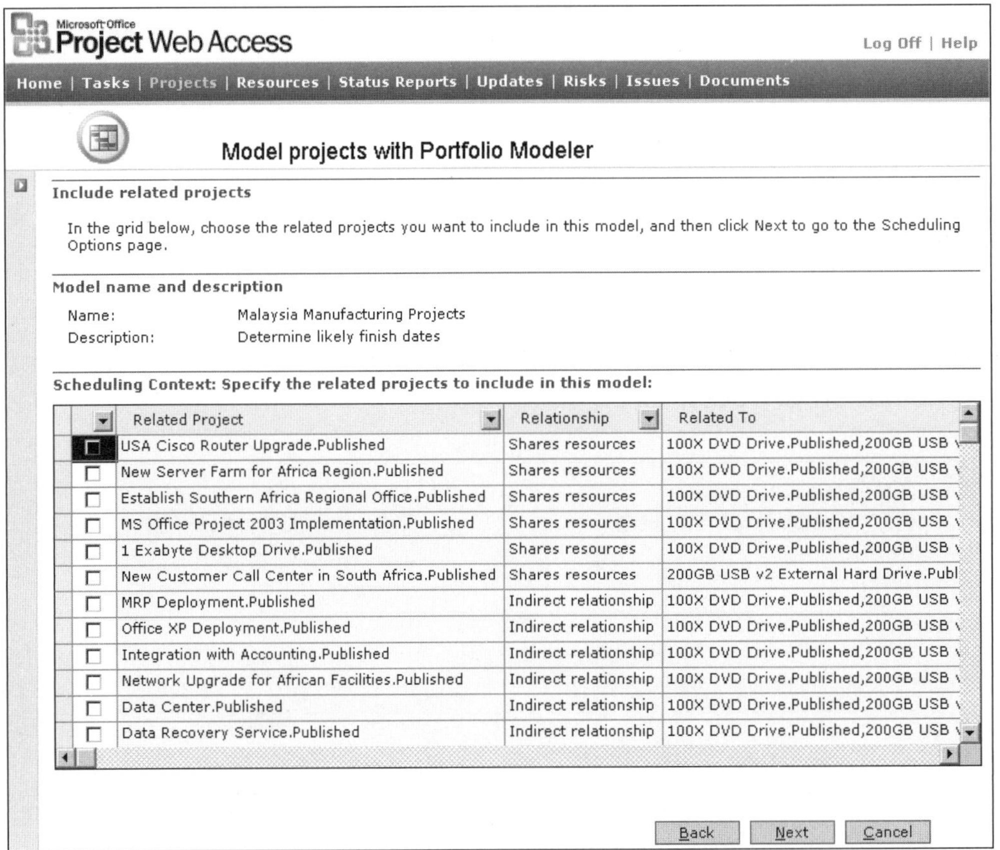

Figure 15-34: Select related projects to include in your new Portfolio Model

Click the Next button and the system displays the scheduling options page, shown in Figure 15-35. For each project in the model, you can set a Priority number, select Scheduling Options, and set a Start no earlier than date. Setting a Priority number for each project allows the system to determine which project receives preference when resolving scheduling conflicts for resources.

The Scheduling Options allow you to select the scheduling behavior for each included project. Notice the Schedule Options pick list shown in Figure 15-35. These options are:

- **Keep dates and assignments** instructs the Portfolio Modeler not to change dates and assignments in the selected project. The system will not optimize dates or reassign resources to assignments.
- **Use current assignments** keeps the current assignments in the plan as set, but allows the Portfolio Modeler to change dates and attempt to resolve over allocated resource assignments.

- **Reassign resources in project** instructs the Portfolio Modeler that it may reassign resources for the selected project only. The modeler substitutes resources based on capacity and skill if the system is able to optimize the schedule in so doing.
- **Reassign resources in model's pool** allows the Portfolio Modeler to use resources included in the virtual resource pool formed by the combination of resources in the model's projects and any additional resources you included based on the combination of this selection and the steps you took in specifying resources for the model.

Setting a Start no earlier than date allows you to set a threshold date before which the modeler does not attempt to reschedule the project. You can use any combination of dates here.

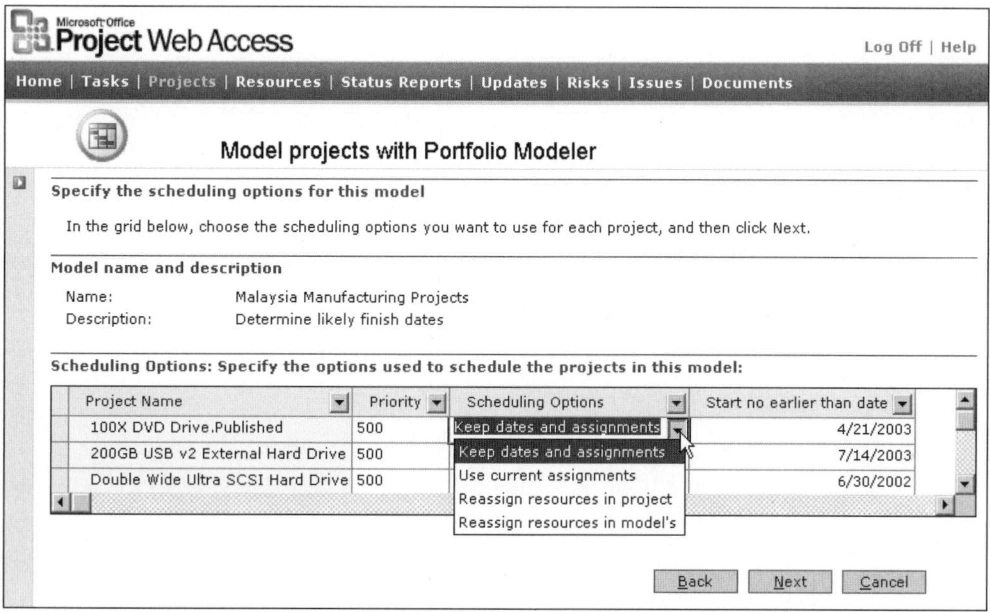

Figure 15-35: Set scheduling options, priorities and start date thresholds

For comparison purposes, I select the Keep dates and assignments option for each project in my model. Doing so allows me to see the "big picture" on the projects I select for the model. Click the Next button and the system redisplays the new model in the Model projects with Portfolio Modeler page.

Opening a Model

To open your Portfolio Model, select the model in the grid and click the Open button. Figure 15-36 displays the model I created. The model consists of three sections:

- The Model name and description section gives general information about the model.
- The Project Scheduling section shows each project in the model, along with a Gantt bar representing the resource utilization in the project.
- The Resource Assignments for Selected Project displays resource utilization information for each resource in the selected project.

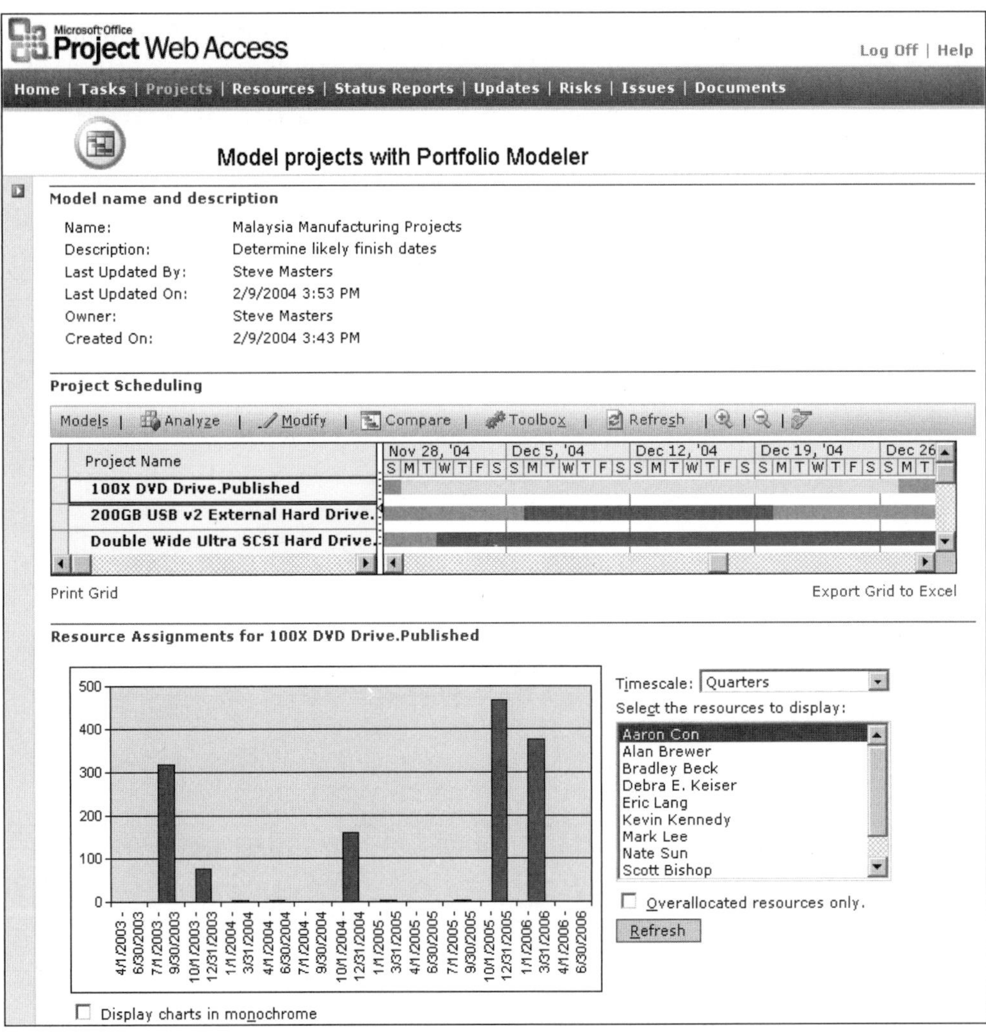

Figure 15-36: An open model

In Figure 15-36, I dragged the divider bar in the grid to the left to give myself a better view of the Gantt bar for each project. The bar colors display green, yellow, or red. In the figure, the 100X DVD Drive project shows a yellow bar portion in December 2004, while the other two projects show red bars during the same period. The meaning of the green, yellow, and red bars is as follows:

- **Green** indicates that there are no resources over allocations occurring during the time period spanned
- **Yellow** indicates that resources are over allocated, but there are no overallocations more than 10% of demand over availability
- **Red** indicates that there are resources over allocated at a rate of 10% or greater of demand over availability

In this case, the results are clear: all three projects are suffering from overallocations that will affect the finish date of each project. To further study resource allocation for a selected project in the model, examine the Resource Assignments of Selected Project section. This section of the page allows you to look at resource loading in the project to help you pinpoint the trouble spots.

Use the Timescale pick list to set the timescale on the chart. By default, the Timescale value is set to Auto, which means that the system selects the earliest project start date and latest project finish date, and then selects the best date formatting for the data. Select one or more names from the Select the resources to display list to graph an individual resource or a group of resources. Select the Overallocated resources only option to view only overallocated resources. Click the Refresh button to redisplay the graph based on any selection changes that you make.

I took the following actions to create the stacked bar chart shown in Figure 15-37:

- Selected the 200GB USB v2 External Hard Drive project in the Project Scheduling section
- Set the Timescale option to Auto
- Selected the Overallocated resources only option
- Selected all of the resources listed in the Select the resources to display list
- Clicked the Refresh button
- Hovered the mouse pointer over one of the stacked bar sections to display a screentip containing information about the overallocated resource

Notice that the screentip for the stacked bar section reveals that the project manager has severely overallocated Scott Bishop with a 292% allocation during the last quarter of 2005.

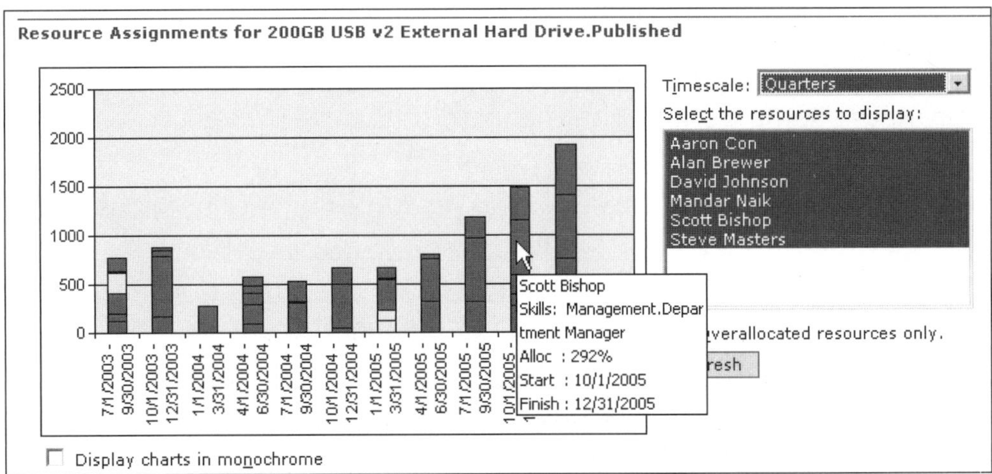

Figure 15-37: Resource Assignments for Selected Project section of the model

Modifying your Model

Whether you select modify from the Model projects with Portfolio Modeler home page or select it from the tool bar in the single model display shown in the previous two figures, the system takes you through same series of screens you worked through when you created your model. In other words, refer back to the Creating a New Model section of this module to review the steps for modifying a model.

Select a project from the Project Scheduling section, shown previously in Figure 15-36, and then click the Toolbox button on the toolbar to open the Portfolio Model Property Toolbox shown in Figure 15-38. Although you cannot change the name of the model using this dialog, you can change almost every parameter in the model. For each project in the model, I changed the parameters to allow the modeler to make reassignments of resources using all the resources in the model.

To change the parameters of each project in the model without closing the Portfolio Model Property Toolbox dialog, make changes to the first project and click the Apply button, then select the next project from the grid. This dialog is a bit unusual, in that it allows you to select objects outside of the dialog.

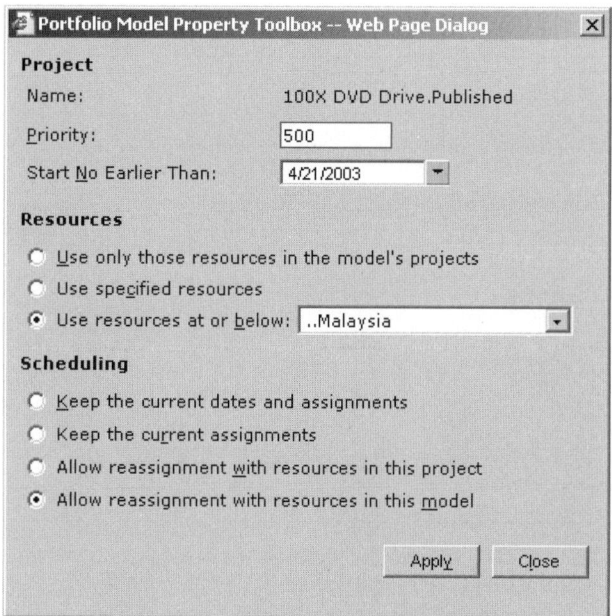

Figure 15-38: Portfolio Model Property Toolbox dialog box

After applying my changes, the modeler was able to resolve resources overallocations across all three projects, as shown in Figure 15-39. Allowing the system to substitute available resources for overallocated resources certainly solved the overallocation problem, but what impact has this action had on the finish dates of the three projects in the model?

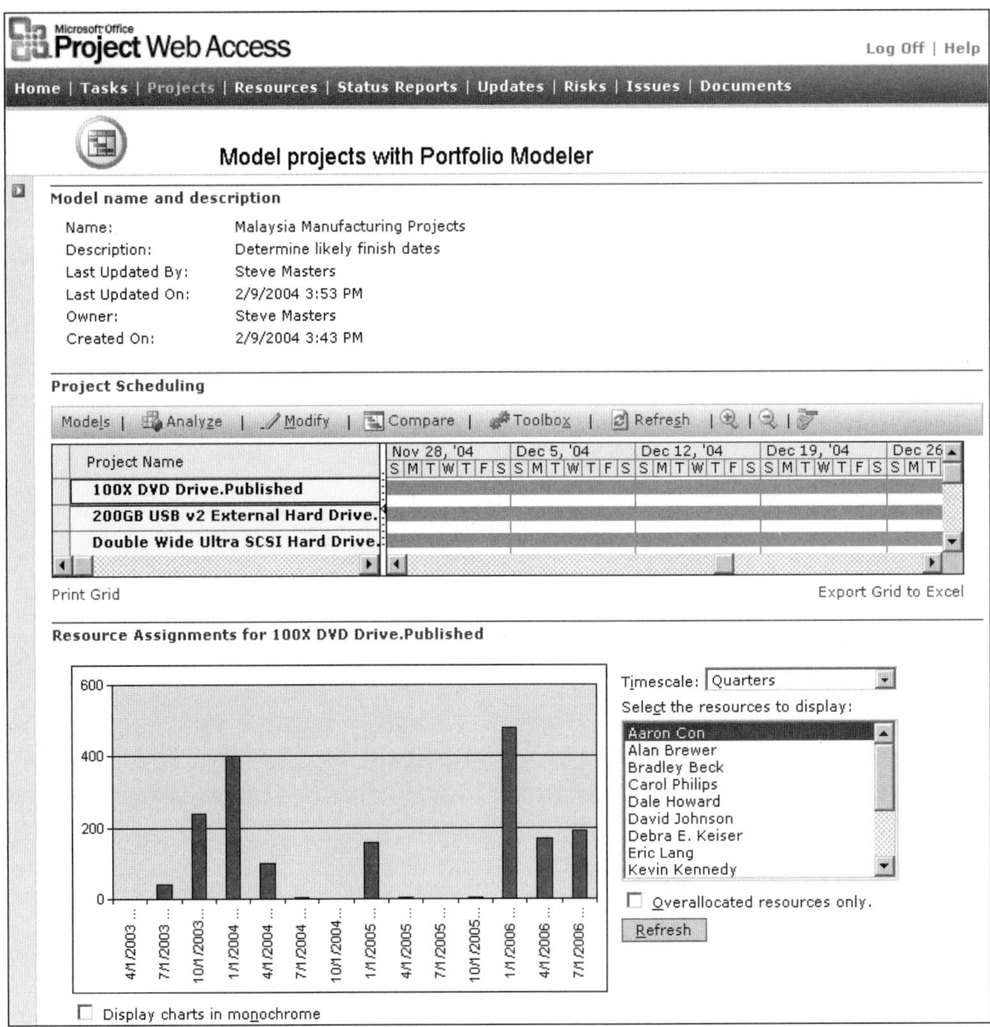

Figure 15-39: Portfolio Model after making changes in the Property Toolbox

Analyze Your Model

Clicking the Analyze button on the toolbar displays another version of the Model project with Portfolio Modeler page shown in Figure 15-40. The Model Name and Description section displays vital statistics for the model. The Summary Statistics section displays data for the shortest possible schedule and the revised schedule that the system is proposing in the model. For both scenarios, the following information displays:

- Start Date
- Finish Date
- Resource Utilization
- Total work
- Resource Overhead

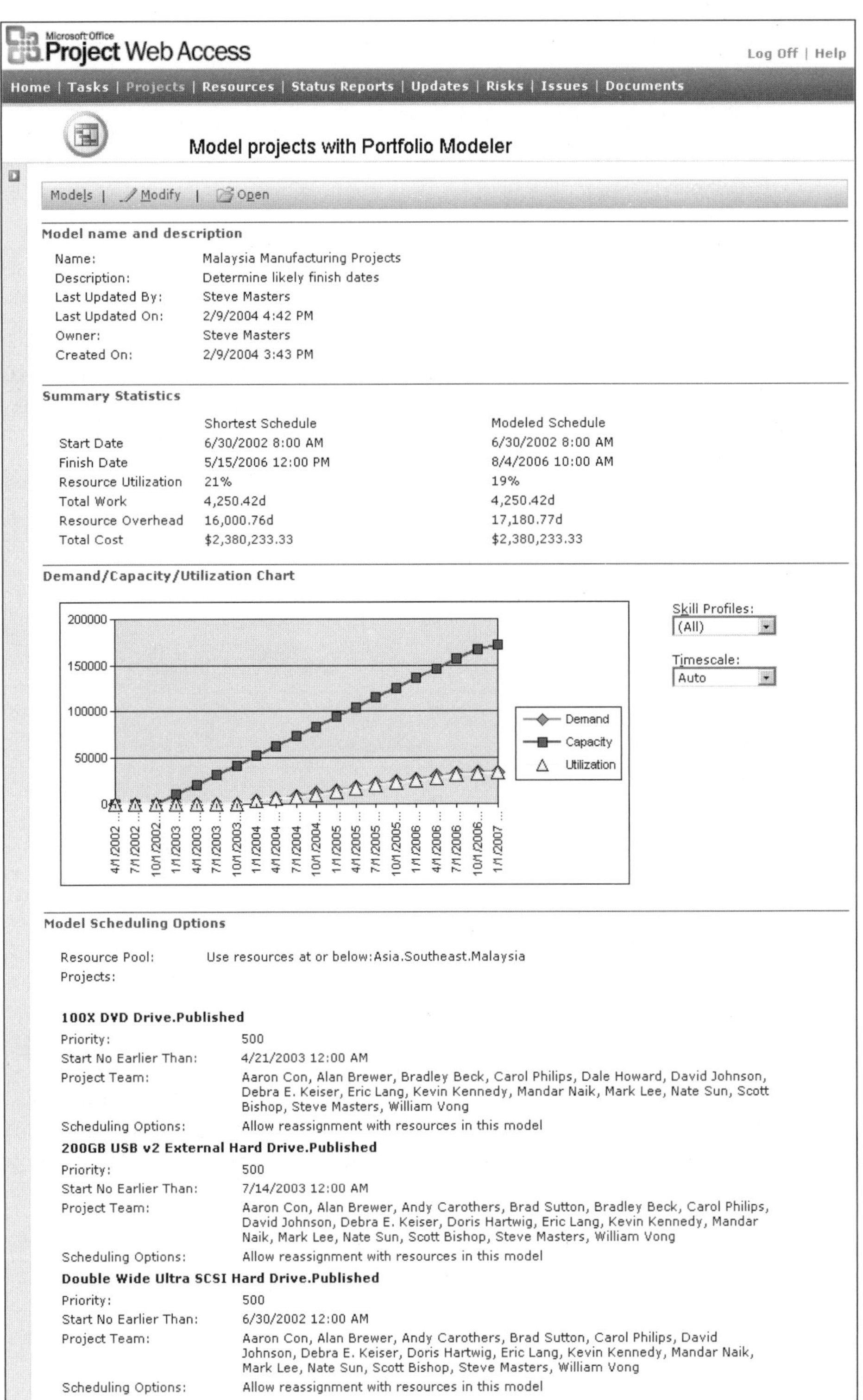

Figure 15-40: Analyze Model results

Resource utilization refers to the percentage of resource demand versus the available capacity. Resource overhead refers to spare capacity in the model. In other words, resource overhead is the total availability of all resources less the workload prescribed in the projects contained in the model. In the example, the modeled schedule finishes more than a month later than the shortest possible scenario. A manager, given these alternatives, might base a decision to go with the modeled schedule in order to preserve greater resource availability for other work.

Notice in the figure that the shortest schedule for the three projects is from 6/6/02 to 5/15/06. The modeled schedule will not finish until 8/4/06. This is the result of resolving resource overallocations in the selected projects and is probably the most realistic schedule for the three projects. This information has met my objective for creating the model, which was to determine the most likely finish date for the three Malaysia manufacturing projects.

The Demand/Capacity/Utilization Chart section displays a chart that maps demand, capacity, and utilization for the projects in the model. You can filter the display by selecting values from the Skill Profiles pick list, or by changing the Timescale of the display to days, weeks, months, quarters, or years. The Timescale selection defaults to Auto.

The Model Scheduling Options section enumerates the teams on each project based on the selected scheduling options.

Comparing Models

I created two different versions of my Malaysia Manufacturing model. One model reassigns resources in the model's pool, which allows the system to substitute available resources for overallocated resources. The other model uses the current resource assignments, but the system may delay tasks to level resource overallocations in the model's projects. Now I want to compare the results of these two models to determine which model gives me the earliest finish dates for the projects in the model.

To compare models, open one of the models to compare and then click the Compare button on the Portfolio Modeler toolbar. The system displays the page shown in Figure 15-41. Select the models that you want to compare and then click the OK button. I selected both of my Malaysia Manufacturing models.

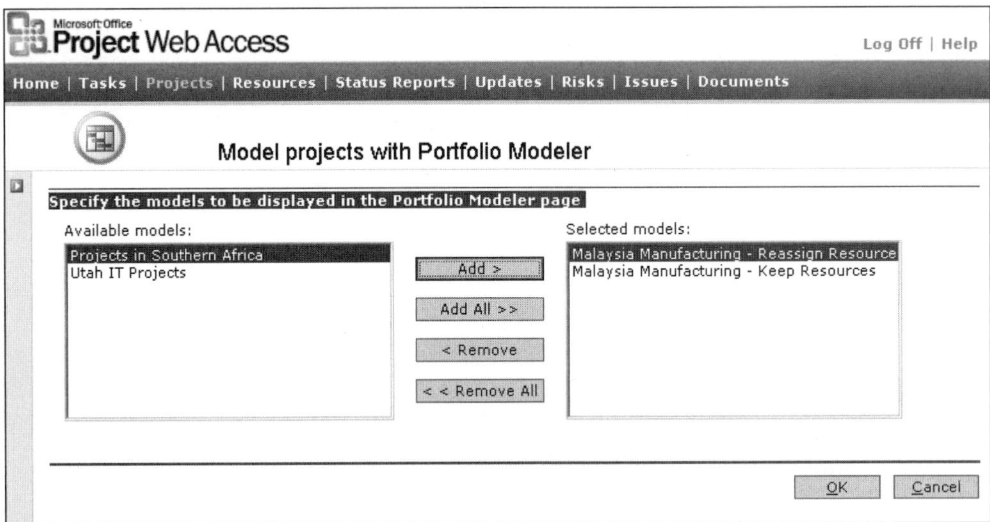

Figure 15-41: Select models to compare

The system displays the Portfolio Modeler page with the combined details of your selected models. Scrolling further down the page reveals the Resource Assignments section, which now responds to all versions of the schedules in the grid, as shown in Figure 15-42. Use the compare models page the same way you used it for single model by selecting a project in the grid and then selecting one or more resources in the Resource Assignments section.

Notice in the figure that I scrolled the Gantt Chart to reveal the finish dates of each project in the two models. The model that reassigns resources from the model's pool shows a significantly earlier finish date for each project than the model that keeps the resource assignments. In fact, the difference in finish dates ranges from as little as six months to as much as a year. This difference is significant enough to cause me to run the Resource Substitution Wizard on each of the three projects in the models to accomplish the earlier finish date on each project.

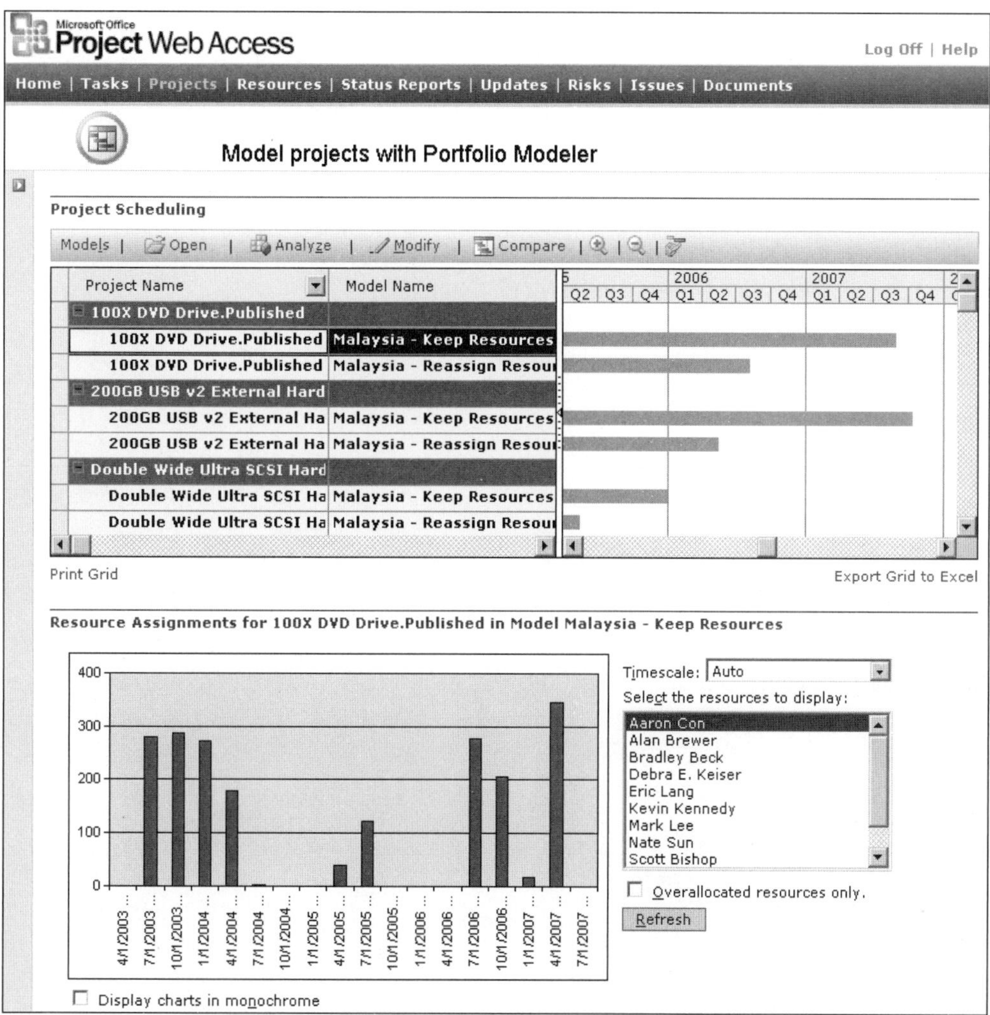

Figure 15-42: Compare two portfolio models

The Portfolio Modeler can answer high-level what-if questions, but it never quite reveals all its secrets. For example, I cannot take the results of the model and then push a button to get the projects updated with the results of the model. Unfortunately, you cannot use the output from the Portfolio Modeler outside of the Portfolio Modeler's interface.